ENCOUNTERS
Chinese Language and Culture

Student Book 1

▶ *Annotated Instructor's Edition*

ENCOUNTERS
Chinese Language and Culture

Student Book 1
▶ *Annotated Instructor's Edition*

汉
语
和
中
国
文
化

▶ **Cynthia Y. Ning**
University of Hawai'i at Mānoa

▶ **John S. Montanaro**
Yale University

Instructor's Annotations by **Amy Shen**
Middlebury-Monterey Language Academy

Audio Program Created by **Julian K. Wheatley**

Yale UNIVERSITY PRESS
New Haven and London

CIPG

Published with assistance from the Office of the President, Yale University.

Director of Digital Publishing: David Schiffman

Project Director: Mary Jane Peluso
Editorial Assistant: Elise Panza
Project Manager: Karen Hohner
Copy Editor: Jamie Greene
Managing Editor: Jenya Weinreb
Designer and Compositor: Wanda España/Wee Design Group
Illustrator: Huifeng Lü
Cover Designer: Sonia Shannon
Art Managers: Karen Hohner with assistance from Linda Rodolico
Production Controller: Maureen Noonan
Marketing Managers: Sarah Clark and Niamh Cunningham

Printed in the United States of America.

ISBN: 978-0-300-16162-5 (student edition)
ISBN: 978-0-300-16166-3 (annotated instructor's edition)
Library of Congress Control Number: 2009934896

A catalogue record for this book is available from the British Library.

This paper meets the requirements of ANSI/NISO Z39.48-1992 (Permanence of Paper).

10 9 8 7 6 5 4 3 2 1

We dedicate *Encounters* to the memory of John DeFrancis, who began his seven-decade career as the first Ph.D. student in Chinese Studies at Yale University and who then published numerous books and articles on the subject of China and the Chinese language. He was a gentle man who lived a full, good life and gave so much to so many.

Contents

Unit One: "We're all one family" 17

四海一家 *Sìhǎiyìjiā*
Introducing yourself by nationality and background

Unit Three: "Don't leave before I arrive" 69
不見不散 *Bújiànbúsàn*
Making an appointment

Unit Seven: "Meeting our needs" 163

各有所求 *Gèyǒusuǒqiú*
Discussing personal needs

Unit Nine: "You get what you pay for"

一分價錢 一分貨 *Yì fēn jiàqian yì fēn huò*
Shopping and bargaining

Preface

Welcome to **Encounters: Chinese Language and Culture**! The publication of this book brings a long-held dream to reality: it inaugurates a groundbreaking language teaching program and sets a new standard in the field of language teaching.

Acutely attentive to the needs of today's students and teachers, the program encourages learning through approaches that are practical, communicative, culturally rich, and delightfully engaging.

Encounters is designed for English-speaking individuals ready to embark on the adventure of learning Mandarin Chinese. Lively and immediate, the program immerses the learner in Chinese language and culture right from the start. **Encounters** employs a range of techniques to encourage rapid and confident student progress. Those who are learning the Chinese language—as well as their teachers—will find a new level of inspiration at each stage of their **Encounters** experience.

A fully integrated array of learning materials focuses on communication and authentic language used in real-life contexts. Central among these materials is a dramatic video series, filmed entirely on location throughout China. The **Encounters** textbook features abundant exercises and learning activities linked to the video episodes and other media.

Informed by the latest language learning research and enriched by the creativity of a remarkable team of language and media experts who participated in its development, **Encounters** represents a new generation of language programs. It masterfully guides learners along a well-prepared path toward intercultural communication and understanding, a path that also leads to fuller participation in the modern global community.

We hope that the **Encounters** program will assist you on an enjoyable and successful learning journey. We wish you well as you encounter the fascinating language, people, and culture of China!

—Cynthia Y. Ning, **University of Hawai'i at Mānoa**
—John S. Montanaro, **Yale University**

Academic Committee

YALE UNIVERSITY PRESS

Richard C. Levin
理查德雷文
President, Yale University
耶鲁大学校长

Linda K. Lorimer
罗琳达
Secretary and Vice President,
　Yale University
耶鲁大学副校长兼校务卿

Dorothy Robinson
多乐茜 罗宾逊
Vice President and General
　Counsel, Yale University
耶鲁大学副校长兼法律总顾问

John Donatich
约翰 多纳蒂奇
Director, Yale University Press
耶鲁大学出版社社长

Mary Jane Peluso
玛丽珍 珀卢索
Project Director
项目主任
Publisher of World Languages,
　Yale University Press
耶鲁大学出版社世界语言部
　出版人

Cynthia Y. Ning
任友梅
Author
语言教学部分撰稿人
Associate Director,
　University of Hawai'i
　Center for Chinese Studies
夏威夷大学中国研究中心
　副主任
U.S. Director, Confucius Institute
　at the University of Hawai'i
孔子学院 院长
Executive Director,
　Chinese Language Teachers
　Association, 2000–2009
中文教师学会 执行主任

John S. Montanaro
孟德儒
Author
语言教学部分撰稿人
Senior Lector in Chinese,
　Yale University
耶鲁大学 资深中文讲师

David Murray
大卫 莫瑞
Executive Producer and
　Creative Director
总制片、总导演

CHINA INTERNATIONAL PUBLISHING GROUP

Cai Mingzhao
蔡名照
President Emeritus, China
　International Publishing Group
中国国际出版集团 前任总裁

Zhou Mingwei
周明伟
President, China International
　Publishing Group
中国国际出版集团 总裁

Huang Youyi
黄友义
Vice President and Editor-in-
　Chief, China International
　Publishing Group
中国国际出版集团 副总裁、
　总编辑

Wang Gangyi
王刚毅
Deputy Editor-in-Chief, China
　International Publishing Group
中国国际出版集团 副总编辑

Xu Lin
许琳
Director-General of Hanban
　(Confucius Institute
　Headquarters)
国家汉办/孔子学院总部 总
　干事长

Wang Junxiao
王君校
Senior Project Officer
学术顾问
President, Sinolingua
华语教学出版社 社长

Han Hui
韩晖
Project Director
项目主任
Editor-in-Chief, Sinolingua
华语教学出版社 总编辑

Guo Hui
郭辉
Assistant Project Director
项目主任助理
Associate Editor-in-Chief,
　Sinolingua
华语教学出版社 总编辑助理

Zhou Kuijie
周奎杰
Culture Consultant
文化顾问
Former Editor-in-Chief,
　New World Press
原新世界出版社总编辑

Zhao Rongguo
赵荣国
Producer
制片

Liu Jiefeng
刘杰峰
Producer
制片

Lu Jianming
陆俭明
Professor, Peking University
北京大学中文系 教授

Li Xiaoqi
李晓琪
President, International College
　for Chinese, Peking University
北京大学对外汉语教育学院
　院长

Wu Zhongwei
吴中伟
Vice President, School of
　International Cultural
　Exchanges, Fudan University
复旦大学国际文化交流学院
　副院长

Liu Songhao
刘颂浩
Associate Professor,
　International College for
　Chinese Language Studies,
　Peking University
北京大学对外汉语教育学院
　副教授

Ma Jianfei
马箭飞
Deputy Chief Executive,
　Confucius Institute
　Headquarters/Hanban
孔子学院总部 副总干事

Wu Yongyi
吴勇毅
Vice President, Professor,
　East China Normal University
华东师范大学对外汉语学院
　副院长、教授

Sun Dejin
孙德金
Professor, Beijing Language
　and Culture University
北京语言大学 教授

Acknowledgments

Encounters was initiated in the fall of 2006 by President Richard C. Levin of Yale University and Mr. Cai Mingzhao, then President of China International Publishing Group. A number of people have been and continue to be involved in this extraordinary program. We thank everyone who has touched *Encounters* in some way.

Cyndy Ning dedicates her work to her husband, Allan Ngai Lim Yee, who died suddenly in 2009, and to her daughter, Robyn Ning Yee. John Montanaro thanks his wife, Patricia, his daughter, Pamela, and his son, John Scott, as well as his "fabulous five" grandchildren, Andrew, Jacob, Alyssa, Madison, and Meghan.

The authors and the publisher thank Sheree Carter-Galvan, Pamela Chambers, Rosita Chang, Annelise Finegan, Katherine Gilbert, Chunman Gissing, Nora Guo, Eric Gustafson, Hazel Hasegawa, Hugo Krispyn, Frederick Lau, Helen Lee, Rongzhen Li, Yuhong Li, Fan Liu, Alexis Mills, Pauline Ning, Robert Ning, Sam Ning, Noreen O'Connor-Abel, Amy Shen, Jialin Sun, David Topolewski, Stephen Tschudi, Daniel Tschudi, Qinghong Wang, Yingjing Wang, Julian Wheatley, Kristine Wogstad, Myrtle Wong, Kuang-tien Yao, Robyn Yee, Martin Yu, Meiping Zhu, and Chuanlu Zhu.

We also deeply appreciate the work of all our reviewers at various stages and of different components of the *Encounters* project:

Gloria Bien, Colgate University
Peter Bonanno, Suffield Academy
Lixin Cai, Concordia University
Bei (Ben) Chen, University of North Texas
Chiu-Hung Chen, University of Miami
Leeann Chen, Embry-Riddle Aeronautical University
Xiaoqiang Cheng, Indiana University South Bend
De Chao (Ralph) Chiao, Columbus Alternative High School
Ruby Shu Costea, Montgomery College
Erica Dieselman, Hingham High School
Amy Dooling, Connecticut College
Wen-Hua Du, University of Wisconsin–Milwaukee
Scott Galer, Brigham Young University–Idaho
Bernard Geoxavier, Belmont Hill School
Sharon Guan, DePaul University
Jeffrey J. Hayden, Kalamazoo College
Jing Ping He, Marvin Ridge High School, Union County Public School
Wei Hong, Purdue University
Chi-Chiang Huang, Hobart and William Smith Colleges
Hsu Chu-Ju Huang, Millburn High School

Jen-Syan Hwang, Central High School (St. Paul)
Yanmei Jia, Perry County Central High School
Li Jin, DePaul University
Haishan Lai, University of Richmond
Qiang Li, University of Iowa
Weijie Li, Kapiolani Community College
Wendan Li, University of North Carolina at Chapel Hill
Yu Li, Emory University
Huey Hannah Lin, West Virginia University
Annie W. Liu, North Central College
Jack Liu, California State University
Lin Liu, Snowden International School
Shuyu Liu, Laney College
Michelle Low, University of Northern Colorado
Christopher Lupke, Washington State University
Lixia Ma, Phillips Academy
Duosi Meng, University of Illinois at Chicago
Liuxi Meng, Kennesaw State University
Lili Pan, Lexington High School
Ying Peng, Loyola University
Terry Qian, Loyola Marymount University
Adam Ross, Lakeside School

Cynthia Shen, University of Florida
LanLan Sheng, Newton South High School
Miao-Fen Tseng, University of Virginia
Tracy Tsou, Concord-Carlisle High School
Jing Wang, Indiana University–Purdue University Indianapolis (IUPUI)
Xiaojun Wang, Western Michigan University
Helen Wu, University of Toronto Scarborough
Yongan Wu, University of North Florida
Janet Xing, Western Washington University
Wen Xing, Trinity University
Weirong Yan, Missouri State University
Yinong Yang, Buckingham Browne & Nichols
Xiaohua Yu, Piedmont High School
Fangyuan Yuan, University of Pennsylvania/U.S. Naval Academy
Jing Zhai, Marquette University
Weidong Zhang, Winona State University
Yan Zhang, University of Wyoming
Zheng-sheng Zhang, San Diego State University
LanHui Zhang-Ryder, Northern Illinois University
Yongping Zhu, University of Wisconsin, Madison

Introduction

Overview

The comprehensive *Encounters* program:
- Employs a functional, task-based approach.
- Presents authentic language and culture through engaging dramatic video episodes.
- Focuses on communication in the spoken language.
- Includes reading material in both traditional and simplified characters.
- Links cultural video interviews to language functions.
- Presents clearly focused grammar instruction and practice.
- Adheres to ACTFL Proficiency Guidelines.
- Assists teachers with a fully annotated instructor's edition, materials to excite students' interest, and a wide selection of useful tools in various media.

Program Components

The *Encounters* program comprises:
- A beautifully produced *video series*, filmed entirely on location in China and featuring a dramatic story line and segments devoted to Chinese culture and history.
- A full-color *student textbook*, completely integrated with the video series and other *Encounters* components. The introductory unit presents the basics of Mandarin Chinese: the four tones, pronunciation, pinyin spelling, numbers, radicals, and traditional and simplified characters.
- An *annotated instructor's edition* of the textbook, packed with teaching tips, extra classroom activities, and suggestions for using the program in the classroom.
- A *character writing workbook* showing each character's evolution, etymology, and usage. Stroke diagrams guide students in forming the characters; strategies for remembering characters are also provided.
- An *audio program* to assist students with listening comprehension, pronunciation, vocabulary, and model conversations.
- A *website* that offers students and teachers streaming video and audio content, and other resources for speaking, reading, and writing Chinese.

▶ The Dramatic Story Line

A hip artist, an adventurous Australian traveler, a thoughtful Chinese scholar, a worried American father, a young teacher from the United States, and another teacher from China: these are just some of the international characters whose stories unfold in the *Encounters* video series.

This compelling story transports viewers to the real cities, villages, homes, schools, markets, streets, and cultural sites of this vast nation. In these various places, the nine main characters find that their lives intersect in unexpected ways. They make discoveries about themselves and others, they converse with strangers and friends, and along the way they provide viewers with remarkable insights into the language and culture of China.

▶ The Cast of Characters

APRIL, 24, of Chinese origin. She is quiet but resilient and strong. Born in the United States to a Chinese immigrant family, she grew up in San Diego. April accompanies her husband, Alejandro, to China.

ALEJANDRO, 29, Mexican American, married to April. He is passionate and has a very big personality. A photographer assigned to document the changes happening in contemporary China, he believes in the value of his work.

LYNN, 25, an American from Los Angeles. She leaves her home and, through a series of detours, eventually travels to Yangshuo to teach English. She tries hard to fit in and be accepted by the community, clearing away misunderstandings along the way.

TANG YUAN, 24, Chinese, a folk artist in Yangshuo. He loves art and has achieved some local success. He is kind, warm-hearted, and very respectful of his parents, but he can also behave rebelliously.

CHEN FENG, 27, Chinese, a businessman in Beijing, originally from a small village in southern China. He is idealistic, confident, and extremely ambitious. Though he is a bit of a workaholic, he also enjoys taking risks. At the beginning of his career, he works hard and expects the same from everyone else (although he is the hardest on himself). He and Li Wen are a couple.

 **LI WEN**, 27, Chinese, teaches English in Yangshuo. She is gentle and very understanding. She and Chen Feng have been together for some time; however, because of the distance between them, things haven't always been easy. After serious discussions, they decide that Li Wen should quit her job in Yangshuo and move to Beijing because it's best for their relationship.

 **MAO ZHIPENG** (also known as Xiao Mao), 28, Chinese, a college friend of Chen Feng's and a partner in the firm that Chen Feng directs. He is keenly observant of the business market, and his personality balances Chen Feng's risk-taking nature. He is from Beijing, and as such, he can't shake some of the common attitudes associated with people from the capital city—namely, a sense of privilege and entitlement. Lured by high-paying employment and the related prestige at a bigger company, he struggles between loyalty to a friend and the tug of reality.

 **PROF. YANG**, 58, Chinese, professor at Chen Feng's university. He loves Tai Chi and Chinese chess and is very skilled at calligraphy. He is tender and caring, often acts as a father figure to Chen Feng, and gives advice by drawing metaphors from life. He is a good friend and a great teacher.

 **MICK**, Australian, a traveling cyclist. He is funny, adventurous, and gregarious, but not much is known about his age, profession, or background. He has been all over the world, but he is troubled from time to time by his aimless wanderings.

In addition to the dramatic narrative that propels the action in each *Encounters* episode, cultural segments explore and illuminate aspects of life in China. Real people from various walks of life discuss their perspectives on such topics as Chinese perceptions of foreign visitors, courteous bargaining in street markets, major Chinese festivals, and different forms of appropriate greetings.

Because *Encounters* is a fully integrated program, the material presented in each episode is linked to corresponding chapters and activities in the textbook, to audio activities, and to an array of online offerings, including practice exercises and related cultural information.

▌A Unit Tour

The **Encounters** textbook presents a carefully structured and cumulative approach to learning Mandarin Chinese. Students progress from listening and speaking activities to the more challenging skills of reading and writing Chinese characters. The emphasis is on communicative skills, as the primary goal of the **Encounters** program is to foster proficiency in everyday Chinese.

Each unit offers an inviting combination of in-class, individual, pair, and group activities. Humor, music, and a lighthearted attitude encourage learners to approach the study of Chinese with enthusiasm and confidence. "FYI" boxes provide dozens of study and learning tips, and appealing illustrations keep interest levels high. By weaving cultural information throughout the text—rather than relegating it only to end-of-chapter notes—**Encounters** reinforces the notion that language is inseparable from culture.

Colorful icons illustrate, at a glance, the variety of learning opportunities and activities available in each chapter.

watch episode

watch video

listen

unit rap

Unit titles are presented in English, pinyin, and Chinese characters. Traditional characters are used to evoke decorative calligraphy, which is often presented only in the traditional form, even in China.

The introductory page for each textbook unit features a photograph from the corresponding video episode. Skills taught and practiced in the unit are related to the events that students observe in the episode.

A list of skills to be covered in the unit clarifies learning goals and helps students stay organized.

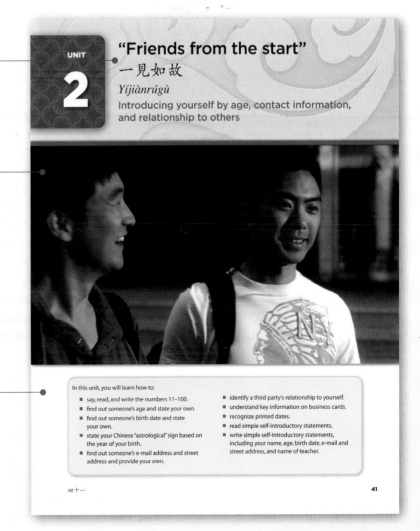

UNIT

2

"Friends from the start"

一見如故

Yíjiànrúgù

Introducing yourself by age, contact information, and relationship to others

In this unit, you will learn how to:

■ say, read, and write the numbers 11–100.
■ find out someone's age and state your own.
■ find out someone's birth date and state your own.
■ state your Chinese "astrological" sign based on the year of your birth.
■ find out someone's e-mail address and street address and provide your own.

■ identify a third party's relationship to yourself.
■ understand key information on business cards.
■ recognize printed dates.
■ read simple self-introductory statements.
■ write simple self-introductory statements, including your name, age, birth date, e-mail and street address, and name of teacher.

四十一

Each unit contains several interesting and enlightening "Encounters," presenting material that covers common real-life situations.

Various listening and learning activities are enriched by their connections to the ongoing video and by their insights into Chinese culture.

FYI boxes, liberally scattered throughout the book, provide relevant cultural information that will both fascinate students and deepen their understanding of the Chinese language and the culture and people of China.

Attractive illustrations, intriguing cultural commentary, and exercises that are directly tied to events in the video combine to spark student interest and encourage learning.

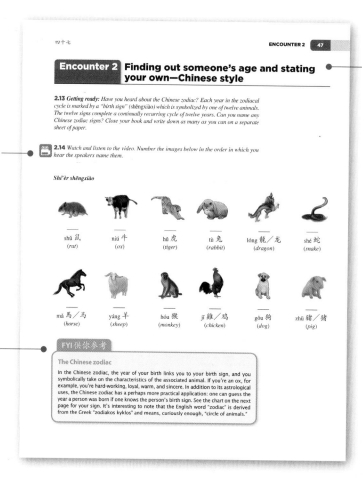

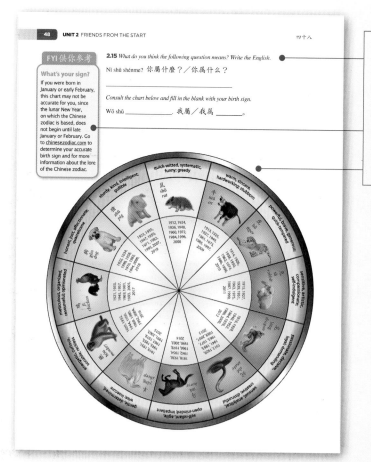

Suggestions for practice conversations appear throughout each unit. Students build confidence and practical conversational skills through these entertaining oral exercises.

2.16 *Mingling: Walk around the room and find out your classmates' signs. Consult the chart and, using their answers, try to figure out whether they are the same age as, older than, or younger than you.*

2.17 *Homework: Outside of class, determine the birth signs of three people. Draw a picture or bring a photograph of each person, and note approximately how old each one is (for example, "in her 40s"). Use this information to report your findings to the class.*

Encounter 3   Finding out someone's birth date and stating your own

▶ Months of the year

2.18 *If January is yīyuè or 一月, write the names of the remaining eleven months in either pinyin or characters (or both) in the blanks below.*

February   _____

March   _____

April   _____

May   _____

June   _____

July   _____

August   _____

September   _____

October   _____

November   _____

December   _____

2.19 *Pair work: With a partner, take turns saying each month of the year. After you go through the sequence once, repeat so you each have an opportunity to say every month. Repeat this process until you are both comfortable with the sequence. Finally, test each other on the Chinese names of the months by dictating random months for your partner to translate.*

2.26 *Watch and listen to the video segment. Then fill in the blanks below.*

a. What are the two numbers you hear in this exchange? _____ and _____

b. What do you think *nián* 年 means? _____

c. What do you think the following means? Write the English.

Nǐ shì něi nián shēng de? 你是哪年生的？ _____

d. Fill in the blanks with your own year of birth.

Wǒ shì _____ nián shēng de.   我是_____年生的。

Grammar Bits 语法点滴

The *shì . . . de* construction

When an event has already happened and the interest is in the specifics (when, why, where, how, etc.) of the event, Chinese uses the *shì . . . de* construction to zero in on the specifics.

The pattern is: Subject + *shì* + specific information + verb + *de*.

Examples:

Nǐ **shì** něi nián shēng **de**? Wǒ **shì** yī-jiǔ-bā-jiǔ nián shēng **de**.
(In which year were you born? I was born in 1989.
⇒ *It was <u>in 1989</u> that I was born.)*

Nǐ **shì** jǐ yuè jǐ hào shēng **de**? Wǒ **shì** bāyuè shíbā hào shēng **de**.
(On which day were you born? I was born on September 18.
⇒ *It was <u>on September 18</u> that I was born.)*

We will learn more about the *shì . . . de* construction in future Encounters. Notice that, in Chinese, verbs do not change form; they don't conjugate to match number, gender, tense, or anything else. Verbs are constant and invariable. You will learn to indicate tense and other grammatical points primarily by adding words. Here's an example: A Chinese might answer the question "How are you feeling?" by saying *Wǒ jīntiān hěn hǎo, zuótiān bù hǎo.* Try to figure out the meaning and, in the process, learn a bit about tense in Chinese.

Numerous Grammar Bits boxes shed light on grammar issues as they arise. These short lessons, highlighted in separate boxes, provide students with a manageable amount of information and an important review tool.

With a strong emphasis on practicality, lessons deal with up-to-date issues and communication in today's world. This Encounter, constructed around the topic of e-mail, asks students to listen, speak, and write about e-mail. An FYI box enriches the lesson with a discussion of translation, transliteration, and how English and Chinese terms sometimes intermingle in our high-tech, interconnected world.

Encounter 4   Finding out someone's e-mail and street address and stating your own

▶ Asking for someone's e-mail address

2.29 *Watch and listen to the video segment. Can you figure out what each of the following means? Fill in the blanks below in English.*

e-mail dìzhǐ: _____   diànyóu dìzhǐ: _____

diànzǐ yóuxiāng: _____

FYI 供你参考

Translation vs. transliteration

Foreign terms, products, and names are rendered into Chinese in at least two different ways. "Hot dog" combines the Chinese words for "hot" and "dog," yielding *règǒu* 熱狗／热狗. This is *translation*. In the second process, *transliteration*, "McDonald's" becomes *Màidāngláo* 麥當勞／麦当劳, which simply combines Chinese sounds similar to the sounds of the original foreign name. Transliteration is often done with little or no meaning intended in the new Chinese word. Syllables with bad connotations are, of course, avoided. Sometimes words are both translated and transliterated. For example, "e-mail" becomes *yīmèir* 伊妹兒／伊妹儿 when transliterated, and *diànzǐ yóujiàn* 電子郵件／电子邮件 (electronic mail) when translated. The latter term is now commonly abbreviated as *diànyóu* 電郵／电邮. Sometimes, the English term "e-mail" is used without translation or transliteration. If you do separate Internet searches, you'll get the most hits for "e-mail 地址," followed by "電郵地址／电邮地址," and the fewest hits for "伊妹兒地址／伊妹儿地址." This indicates that the English term "e-mail" is far more commonly used by the Chinese than either the translated term *diànyóu* or the transliterated term *yīmèir*. In this age of high-tech, rapid Westernization, and the spread of English all over the world, certain terms are more commonly used in their original English form than in the Chinese equivalent term. "E-mail" is the best example.

2.30 *Fill in your own e-mail address in the blanks below.*

Q: Nǐ de diànyóu dìzhǐ shì shénme?
你的電郵地址是甚麼？／你的电邮地址是什么？

A: Wǒ de diànyóu dìzhǐ shì _____
我的電郵地址是 _____。
我的电邮地址是 _____。

2.31 *Mingling: Using your class roster, find out the e-mail addresses of 5–10 classmates. Helpful questions to determine if what you've written is correct include Zhè yàng duì ma? (Is this correct?) or Zhè yàng duì bu duì? (Is this correct or not?)*

A rap written specifically for each unit sets key expressions and vocabulary in a fun musical setting. Go to the *Encounters* website at www.EncountersChinese.com.

♫ Unit Rap

Go to the **Encounters** *website at* www.EncountersChinese.com *and listen to the song to review key expressions from Unit 2. Listen again and sing along!*

Encounter 6   Reading and writing

▶ Reading familiar sentences in Chinese characters

2.43 *Pair work: Read the following dialogues (written in traditional characters) aloud with a partner, using the English as a guide. Note: In Chinese texts, numbers are almost always written in Arabic numerals, both for convenience and space-saving. However, be sure to "pronounce" them in Chinese. It's good practice. Exception: Read the e-mail address as you would normally.*

FYI 供你参考

Listing things in Chinese fashion

The ancient Chinese (about 4,000 years ago) began a system with ten "Celestial Stems" (天干 *tiāngān*) and 12 "Earthly Branches" (地支 *dìzhī*) to enumerate dates in cycles of 60 years. The 天干地支 system continues to this day. "Celestial Stems" consist of the following characters:

甲 *jiǎ*, 乙 *yǐ*, 丙 *bǐng*, 丁 *dīng*, 戊 *wù*, 己 *jǐ*, 庚 *gēng*, 辛 *xīn*, 壬 *rén*, 癸 *guǐ*

These characters are commonly used as a numbering system in modern China, Japan, Korea, and Vietnam, much as Roman numerals (I, II, III) or letters of the alphabet (A, B, C) are used in the West. 甲 and 乙 represent "A" and "B" in this unit's dialogues.

① 甲：你幾歲了？ *(How old are you?)*
乙：我八歲了。 *(I'm eight.)*
甲：他呢？ *(How about him?)*
乙：他兩歲，很小。 *(He's two; he's little.)*

② 甲：你多大了？ *(How old are you?)*
乙：我二十八了。 *(I'm 28.)*

③ 甲：您多大歲數了？ *(How old are you?)*
乙：我七十五了。 *(I'm 75.)*

As a first step to "intensive reading," dialogues based on familiar content are set out in both traditional and simplified characters. Decoding these dialogues helps students gain basic literacy skills in Chinese.

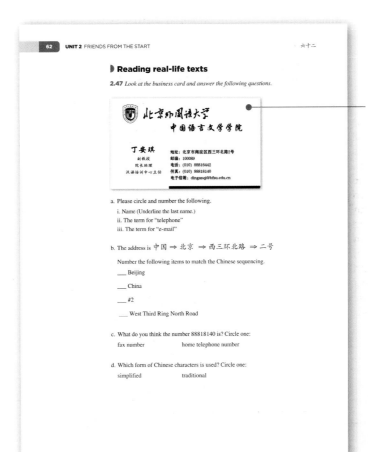

By incorporating materials found in real life—business cards and newspapers, for example—lessons provide practical information enabling students to perform everyday tasks in Chinese.

Each unit includes a list of Chinese characters for writing mastery.

Cultural Bits boxes, which connect to the cultural segments of the video, provide a jumping-off point for explorations of Chinese society. Thought-provoking questions encourage students to investigate how Chinese culture is different from or similar to their own.

A complete Recap section appears at the conclusion of every unit. These pages include a summary of grammar topics, a vocabulary list, and a checklist of tasks that students are expected to have mastered in the unit. The Recap encourages students to review their progress, identify gaps in their learning, and congratulate themselves on their accomplishments.

We invite you to explore this exciting new language program and encourage you to visit *www.EncountersChinese.com*.

"You'll pick it up fast"

一學就會

Yì xué jiù huì

Introduction to Chinese

In this Introduction, you will:

- practice the four tones of Mandarin Chinese as you learn the numbers 1–10.
- learn about tonal shifts (sandhi) and the special case of *yī* (the number one).
- become familiar with the pronunciation of Chinese and the pinyin system of spelling Chinese syllables.
- practice linking pinyin spelling with the sounds of Chinese by working with two poems from the Tang dynasty.
- learn about numbers and radicals.
- learn about traditional and simplified characters.

For additional materials to support this unit, go to the *Encounters* website at *www.EncountersChinese.com*.

1

Invite students to flip through the textbook to preview the stills from the film before watching the video. The introductory episode sets the tone for the rest of the film and introduces the major characters. Relax and enjoy!

You have already met some of the characters in *Encounters* in the Introduction on pages xxi-xxii. Watch the Introductory Episode of the dramatic series to find out more about who these characters are and where they live. You will get to know them well as you continue through units 1–10.

Now, let's learn about the Chinese language.

Encounter 1 Tones and numbers

0.1 • To reinforce students' ability to recognize the four tones, have them work with the arm motions presented in exercise 0.6 on page 3.

Repeatedly say "help" and hold arms straight out to the side.

Repeatedly say "what?" and lift arms upwards at a 45-degree angle.

Repeatedly say "'kay" and bend both elbows so the arms form a V.

Repeatedly say "fine!" and drop arms downwards at a 45-degree angle.

0.1 *Watch the animation about the four tones on the video.*

0.2 *Listen to these numbers and circle the ones you hear.*

0 = líng	1 = yī	2 = èr	3 = sān	4 = sì	5 = wǔ
6 = liù	7 = qī	8 = bā	9 = jiǔ	10 = shí	

The numbers 1, 3, 7, and 8 are pronounced in the FIRST of the four full tones of Mandarin, as in the "Help!" of the animation. This is the high, level tone, as when you are not sure and say "Ummm" in a high pitch. Can you hum the first tone?

0.2 This exercise introduces the **first** tone ("high level"). Say the numbers 1, 3, 7, and 8 or have students listen to the pronunciation examples on the *Encounters* website (online).

0.3 *Listen to these numbers and circle the ones you hear.*

0 = líng	1 = yī	2 = èr	3 = sān	4 = sì	5 = wǔ
6 = liù	7 = qī	8 = bā	9 = jiǔ	10 = shí	

The numbers 0 and 10 are pronounced in the SECOND of the four full tones of Mandarin, as in the "What?" of the animation. This is the rising tone, like the rising pitch of an English question, such as "Yes?" Can you hum the second tone?

0.3 This exercise introduces the **second** tone ("rising"). Say the numbers 0 and 10 or have students listen to the examples online.

0.4 This exercise introduces the **third** tone ("dipping"). Say the numbers 5 and 9 or have students listen to the examples online.

0.4 *Listen to these numbers and circle the ones you hear.*

0 = líng	1 = yī	2 = èr	3 = sān	4 = sì	5 = wǔ
6 = liù	7 = qī	8 = bā	9 = jiǔ	10 = shí	

The numbers 5 and 9 are pronounced in the THIRD of the four full tones of Mandarin, as in the "'kay" of the animation. This is the dipping tone, like the first syllable of "uh-huh." Can you hum the third tone?

0.5 This exercise introduces the **fourth** tone ("falling"). Say the numbers 2, 4, and 6 or have students listen to the examples online.

0.5 *Listen to these numbers and circle the ones you hear.*

0 = líng	1 = yī	2 = èr	3 = sān	4 = sì	5 = wǔ
6 = liù	7 = qī	8 = bā	9 = jiǔ	10 = shí	

The numbers 2, 4, and 6 are pronounced in the FOURTH of the four full tones of Mandarin, as in "Fine!" of the animation. This is the falling tone, like the emphatic pitch on "Yes!" Can you hum the fourth tone?

0.6 *Listen to these numbers and make the appropriate arm motions based on the tone.*

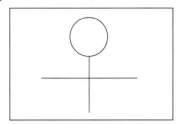

First tone:
Arms straight out to the side, level

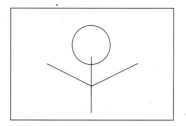

Second tone:
Arms raised at 45° angle

Third tone:
Arms crooked at elbows in a "V"

Fourth tone:
Arms lowered at 45° angle

0.7 *Draw the appropriate tone marks (for example: ā, á, ǎ, or à) over each of the boldfaced letters. Note that the tone mark is always placed above a vowel, never above a consonant.*

l**i**ng	**y**i	**e**r	s**a**n	s**i**	w**u**	l**i**u	q**i**	b**a**	j**i**u	sh**i**
sh**i**	j**i**u	b**a**	q**i**	l**i**u	w**u**	s**i**	s**a**n	**e**r	**y**i	l**i**ng
w**u**	q**i**	j**i**u	s**a**n	**y**i	b**a**	l**i**u	s**i**	**e**r	l**i**ng	sh**i**
s**a**n	q**i**	l**i**ng	s**i**	**y**i	w**u**	sh**i**	l**i**u	**e**r	b**a**	j**i**u

FYI 供你参考

The neutral tone

Besides the four full tones, there's yet another—the neutral tone—so called because it is said lightly, without stress, and is much shorter in length than any of the four full tones. It has no tone mark. Some words that have only a grammatical function routinely have a neutral tone, as do many suffixes. In some (though not all) two-syllable words, the second syllable has a neutral tone. Even though a neutral tone is unstressed, it is not completely without pitch; this it takes from the preceding full-tone syllable. Here are eight of the numbers followed by the measure word *ge*—the numbers "one" and "two" have been excluded. More about these numbers and *ge* will follow in this and later units; for the moment, just note that *ge* is pronounced in the neutral tone.

sān ge	sì ge	wǔ ge	liù ge
qī ge	bā ge	jiǔ ge	shí ge

FYI 供你参考

Tonal shifts (sandhi) on *yī* (the number one)

In connected speech, tones are rarely given their full value. Tones in juxtaposition can influence each other and change their value. This is called sandhi. A few words regularly change their tone in certain environments. An example is *yī* (the number one).

• It stays first tone when it stands alone, as during counting.
• It becomes second tone when followed by a fourth tone: *yī + bàn* ⇒ *yíbàn* (half).
• It becomes fourth tone when followed by a first, second, or third tone: *yī + tiān* ⇒ *yìtiān* (a day); *yī + nián* ⇒ *yìnián* (a year); *yī + miǎo* ⇒ *yìmiǎo* (a second).
• In the middle of a phrase, *yī* is usually neutral: *xiǎngyixiǎng* (think a moment). As we go on, we will see examples of this and other tonal shifts.

▶ More on numbers

 0.8 *Write the telephone numbers below as you hear them.*

a. Buckingham Palace, London: _____

b. Opera House, Sydney: _____

c. Louvre Museum, Paris: _____

d. "Bird's Nest" Stadium, Beijing: _____

e. Taj Mahal, Agra: _____

f. White House, Washington, D.C.: _____

0.9 *Write your own telephone number, including area code, in pinyin with tone marks.*

__ __ __ – __ __ __ – __ __ __ __

FYI 供你参考

Pinyin

Pinyin is a system of spelling out the sounds of Mandarin Chinese using the letters of the English alphabet, along with the umlauted *ü*. It is an aid to accurate pronunciation used by Chinese and foreigners alike. Developed in China in the 1950s, pinyin is now used all over the world, including Taiwan. Although not developed specifically for speakers of English, it is a fairly easy system to learn. Always keep in mind, however, that the sounds of the language must be mastered through the ear, not the eye.

0.10 *Pair work: Watch and listen to the video segment. Practice "finger-counting" yourself. Then work with a partner. One person calls out a number randomly from 1 through 10, and the other makes the corresponding hand signal. Then reverse: One person makes a hand signal and the other person calls out the corresponding number.*

Encounter 2 | Chinese syllables

All Chinese syllables are composed of three parts.

The initial consonant: There are 21 initial consonants in Chinese (plus *y* and *w*). They are called initials because, unlike consonants in English, they appear only at the beginning of a syllable. Note that syllables in pinyin can begin with one or two consonants, but each letter or consonant combination represents only one sound.

The final vowel: Each syllable ends with a vowel, or with a final *n* or *ng*. Note that two vowels can be combined to form one sound (diphthong).

The tone: As you have already learned, there are four full tones in Mandarin, plus a neutral tone.

> ### FYI 供你参考
>
> **About Chinese sounds**
>
> Chinese has the ability to express meaning with as much vividness and clarity as any other language, but it does so with a fairly limited stock of approximately 400 unique sounds or, more precisely, syllables. When you studied English, one of your first tasks was to learn the alphabet. This knowledge helped form the basis of a useful supply of sounds and words. In studying Chinese, you will need to learn the syllables of Chinese. The foundation of all Chinese words is its set of single-syllable sounds, the 400 or so monosyllables. Thus Chinese is often thought of as a monosyllabic language, in part because each Chinese character is a single syllable. However, Chinese words are most commonly constructed with two syllables. In fact, more than 80 percent of Chinese words are composed of at least two syllables. Three- and four-syllable words exist but are far less common.

The following charts present the vowels and consonants of Chinese. Note that all the sounds in the charts are one syllable, not two. Remember: Derive the sounds from what you hear, not from what you see. Keep in mind that the pinyin alphabet is only a memory aid, a device to help learners recall the actual sound. Chinese children use pinyin in their textbooks more or less as you are going to do. Listen carefully to the sounds of Chinese syllables and refer to these charts often, especially in the beginning weeks of study. Acquiring decent pronunciation is one of your most important tasks.

▶ The initial consonants + *y* and *w*

0.11 *Look at the chart on page 6. Listen to the initial consonants, in boldface, which are combined with a final vowel (not in boldface) in order to make them pronounceable. Pronounce the hint as you would in English. The first hint* (awe) *provides a guide to the pronunciation of the Chinese final vowel* o. *Note that all the sounds in this chart are pronounced in the first tone, just the way Chinese children practice them in school. In fact, Chinese children often commit the chart to memory.*

0.11 Perform the following activity to introduce initial consonants.

1. Make copies of the initial consonants (*b-, p-, m-, f-,* etc.) and final vowel combinations (*-ai, -ao, -an, -ang,* etc.) from page 6 on two different colors of cardstock paper. Make enough copies to distribute one "set" per student. Cut each of the individual consonants and vowels into squares, and store the squares in small plastic bags.

2. Distribute the sets, and have students randomly spread out the squares on their desks.

3. Pronounce an initial consonant, and have students identify the corresponding square. Keep repeating the initial until the correct square is identified. Point to the correct square and repeat until all students have correctly identified it.

4. Proceed in this manner until all initials have been introduced.

(Hint: Begin with the easiest initials—*b, p, m, f, d, t, n, l, g, k,* and *h*. Have students follow the chart and arrange these squares on their desks.)

5. Collect the bags again after the activity and keep them for next time; you won't have to make them again.

The Initial Consonants				Hint
bo	po	mo	fo	(awe) > bwaw > pwaw > mwaw > fwaw
de	te	ne	le	(uh) > duh > tuh > nuh > luh
ge	ke	he		(uh) > guh > kuh > huh
ji	qi	xi		(ee) > jee > chee > syee
zi	ci	si		(zz) > dz > tsz > sz
zhi	chi	shi	ri	(rr) > jr > chr > shr > rrr

There are two additional letters—*y* and *w*—used in pinyin when none of the above consonants begin a word.

w (pronounced /w/ as in English "**win**" and "**war**"). Chinese example: *wei* (way), *wu* (woo)

y (pronounced /y/ as in English "**yes**" and "**you**"). Chinese examples: *ying* (rhymes with "sing"), *you* (rhymes with "low")

The final vowels + *n* and *ng*

0.12 Consider using the same activity from 0.11 to introduce and practice final vowels. Alternatively, you could skip a detailed exercise with final vowels until later in *Encounters* when students have had more interaction with *pinyin*.

0.12 *Listen to the final vowels, in boldface below, which are here combined with selected initial consonants. Note that the final vowels can be either a single vowel or a combination of vowels, sometimes with* n *or* ng.

	+ a	+ e	+ i	+ o	+ u	+ n	+ ng
a (ba)			bai	bao		ban	bang
e (ne)			nei			nen	neng
i (ji)	jia	jie			jiu	jin	jing
i + a (jia)			jiao		jian	jiang	
							jiong
o					dou		dong
u (zhu)	zhua		zhui	zhuo		zhun	
u + a (zhua)			zhuai			zhuan	zhuang
ü (jü)		jüe				jün	
		lüe					
							jüan

Encounter 3 Poems from the Tang dynasty (618–907 CE)

In normal speech, speakers of Chinese (as of any other language) tend to run words together and slur their pronunciation (often because others can understand them anyway, and they wish to save time and effort). In common conversations, a beginning learner usually cannot tell which tones specific words have. In Tang poetry, however, tones are highly valued. When reciting poetry, native speakers tend to enunciate each syllable; tones and rhymes serve to accentuate the beauty of the lyricism. The following exercises introduce you to two of the best known of the Tang poems for the foreign learner: *Jìng yè sī* 靜夜思 "Thoughts on a Quiet Night," by poet *Lǐ Bái* (also pronounced *Lǐ Bó*) 李白 (701–762 CE), and *Dēng Guànquèlóu* 登鸛雀樓 "Climbing Stork Tower," by *Wáng Zhīhuàn* 王之渙 (668–742 CE). By working through these poems, you will begin to get a sense for the sounds of Chinese and how pinyin represents these sounds. If you feel up to it, go ahead and memorize one or both of the poems. When you recite a poem, you will delight many a native speaker of Chinese!

▶ "Thoughts on a Quiet Night"

 0.13 *Watch and listen to Chinese school children reciting "Thoughts on a Quiet Night." As you listen, write the correct tone marks over each of the syllables below.*

(Line 1) Chuang qian ming yue guang.
(Line 2) Yi shi di shang shuang.
(Line 3) Ju tou wang ming yue.
(Line 4) Di tou si gu xiang.

"Waiting for Guests by Lamplight," National Palace Museum, Taipei, Taiwan

Now complete the following note about Tang poetry.

This example is typical of one kind of Tang poem. It is made up of _____ lines,

including _____ characters in each line, for a total of _____ characters. Lines

_____, _____, and _____ rhyme, and each of the rhyming words in this poem

is in the _____ tone.

0.14 Key:

Ch q   m   y   g
Y   sh d   sh sh
J   t   w   m   y
D   t   s   g   x

 0.14 *Listen again.* <u>*Don't look at the previous exercise.*</u> *Write the initial consonant for each of the characters in the poem.*

(Line 1) ____uáng ____ián ____íng ____uè ____uāng.

(Line 2) ____í ____ì ____ì ____àng ____uāng.

(Line 3) ____ǔ ____óu ____àng ____íng ____uè.

(Line 4) ____ī ____óu ____ī ____ù ____iāng.

0.15 Key:

Chuáng qián míng yuè guāng.
Yí shì dì shàng shuāng.
Jǔ tóu wàng míng yuè.
Dī tóu sī gù xiāng.

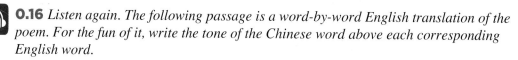 **0.15** *Listen again. We've flipped the next exercise upside down, so you're not tempted to peek. Write the appropriate letter in each of the blanks.*

(Line 4) Dī tó___ sī g___ù x___ā___.

(Line 3) Jǔ tó___ wà___ mí___ y___è.

(Line 2) Yí shì dì shà___ sh___ā___.

(Line 1) Ch___á___ q___á___ mí___ y___è g___ā___.

0.16 Key:

Béd frónt bríght mòon brílliant.
Suspéct bè gròund upòn fròst.
Líft héad gàze bríght mòon.
Lowēr héad thīnk ancèstral hōme.

 0.16 *Listen again. The following passage is a word-by-word English translation of the poem. For the fun of it, write the tone of the Chinese word above each corresponding English word.*

(Line 1) Bed front bright moon brilliant.

(Line 2) Suspect be ground upon frost.

(Line 3) Lift head gaze bright moon.

(Line 4) Lower head think ancestral home.

0.17 Key:

Chuáng qián míng yuè guāng.
Yí shì dì shàng shuāng.
Jǔ tóu wàng míng yuè.
Dī tóu sī gù xiāng.

0.17 *Listen again. The following passage is a translation into more natural (but not lyrical) English. Below each English line, write out a transcription in pinyin (complete with tones!) of that line.*

(Line 1) Before my bed, the moonlight is bright.

_____

(Line 2) I take it for frost on the ground.

_____

(Line 3) Lifting my head, I gaze at the bright moon.

_____

(Line 4) Lowering my head, I think of my old home.

_____

0.18 *Listen again. The following is the poem in traditional Chinese characters. Circle the word for "moon" as you come across it.*

床前明月光，
疑是地上霜。
舉頭望明月，
低頭思故鄉。

 0.19 *Listen for the last time. The following is the poem in simplified Chinese characters. Circle each character whose simplified form is different from the traditional.*

床前明月光，
疑是地上霜。
举头望明月，
低头思故乡。

0.20 *How many characters did you circle in the previous exercise? Answer: _____. What percentage of the characters used in this text have been simplified? Answer: _____ percent.*

This percentage roughly holds true for many texts you will encounter as you study Chinese (but not for very short ones, like signs). The issue of traditional vs. simplified characters (along with their history) will be further explored and explained in Unit 1.

▶ "Climbing Stork Tower"

0.21 *Now watch and listen to a recitation of the poem "Climbing Stork Tower" by the poet Wáng Zhīhuàn. As you listen, write the correct tone marks over each of the syllables below.*

(Line 1) Bai ri yi shan jin.

(Line 2) Huang He ru hai liu.

(Line 3) Yu qiong qian li mu,

(Line 4) Geng shang yi ceng lou.

Now complete the following note:

This poem, like the previous one, is made up of _____ lines, including _____ characters in each line, for a total of _____ characters. Lines _____ and _____ rhyme, and each of the rhyming words in this poem is in the _____ tone.

0.22 Key:

Whíte sùn lēan mountāin ènd.
Yéllow Ríver entèr seǎ flów.
Wìsh exháust thōusand mǐle gàze.
Mòre ascènd onē stóry flóor.

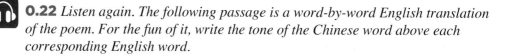

0.22 *Listen again. The following passage is a word-by-word English translation of the poem. For the fun of it, write the tone of the Chinese word above each corresponding English word.*

(Line 1) White sun lean mountain end.

(Line 2) Yellow River enter sea flow.

(Line 3) Wish exhaust thousand mile gaze.

(Line 4) More ascend one story floor.

0.23 Key:

Bái rì yī shān jìn.
Huáng Hé rù hǎi liú.
Yù qióng qiān lǐ mù.
Gèng shàng yī céng lóu.
(NOTE: Students will hear *yì*, but tell them to write *yī*.)

0.23 *Listen again. The following passage is a translation into more natural (but not lyrical) English. Below each line, write out a transcription in pinyin (complete with tones!) of that line.*

(Line 1) The white sun sets in the mountains.

_____

(Line 2) The Yellow River flows to the seas.

_____

(Line 3) To gaze another thousand miles.

_____

(Line 4) Climb up to yet another story.

_____

0.24–0.26 Have students work in pairs to complete the exercises. If possible, copy 0.25 and 0.26 onto a transparency. Project these exercises on the board, and invite volunteers to share the answers.

0.24 Key:
白日依山盡,
黃河入海流。
欲窮千里目,
更上一層樓。

0.25 Key:
白日依山尽,
黃河入海流。
欲穷千里目,
更上一层楼。

0.24 *Listen again. The following is the poem in traditional Chinese characters. Circle the words for "sun," "mountain," and "one" as you come across them.*

白日依山盡,
黃河入海流。
欲窮千里目,
更上一層樓。

0.25 *Listen for the last time. The following is the poem in simplified Chinese characters. Circle each character whose simplified form is different from the traditional.*

白日依山尽,
黄河入海流。
欲穷千里目,
更上一层楼。

0.26 *How many characters did you circle in the previous exercise? Answer: _____.
What percentage of the characters used in this text have been simplified? Answer:
_____ percent. Compare your answer here with the one you obtained for exercise 0.21.*

0.26 Key:
4; 20%

You are now ready to memorize one or more of the poems, if you'd like. Memorization
is an important part of the Chinese educational system, and is generally mandatory for
students in school.

Encounter 4   Introduction to Chinese characters

0.27 *The earliest records of Chinese characters on oracle bone inscriptions include
versions that are more pictographic than modern Chinese characters. Match these
"pictographic" characters with their English equivalents.*

person
soil, earth
mouth
moon
mountain
fire
tree
sun
rain
water

0.28 *Now, based on the matches you made in the previous exercise, can you figure
out what these modern characters mean?*

0.28 Key:
火 fire; 口 mouth; 木 wood; 人
person; 日 sun; 山 mountain; 土 soil,
earth; 水 water; 月 moon; 雨 rain

火 口 木 人 日 山 土 水 月 雨

0.29 *Label each character in the previous exercise with one of the following identifications.*

rén (*human, person*)   tǔ (*soil, earth*)   shuǐ (*water*)   yǔ (*rain*)   mù (*tree, wood*)

shān (*mountain*)   kǒu (*mouth*)   rì (*sun*)   huǒ (*fire*)   yuè (*moon*)

◗ Recognizing radicals

In addition to standing on their own, the ten characters above also serve as radicals, or "meaning components," of many other Chinese characters. Radicals can be thought of as building blocks that provide a broad link to the meaning of multicomponent characters. Notice how the first character below means "mountain range" and its radical component is, naturally, "mountain." Radicals can serve you well as memory aids; there are nearly 200 of them, but you should concentrate on learning the 50 most common ones.

0.30 *Circle the radicals you recognize in the characters below.*

嶺	旦	雲	吹	峰
mountain range	dawn, day	clouds	to blow	peak, summit
映	雪	吞	峽	晚
shine, reflect	snow	to swallow	canyon, gorge	evening, night
雷	喝	朔	地	址
thunder	to drink	new moon	earth, land	site, location
林	朧	墳	枯	松
forest	rising moon	grave, tomb	withered	pine tree

0.31 *Some radicals can be somewhat altered when combined with another character component. Match the full forms on the left with the combination form on the right.*

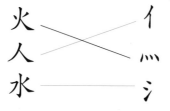

火   亻
人   灬
水 ———— 氵

0.32 *Circle the radicals in the following characters.*

燈   焦   熱   仙
lantern, light   scorch   hot   an immortal

濺   波   傭   你
splash, splatter   wave, ripple   a servant   you

0.33 *Try to identify the radicals in the following characters.*

楚   吻   坤   晶   位   侶
崩   岳   有   森   唱   棟
洋   炒   暗   海   塊   吃
露   煙   基   僑   需   崎
期   梧   溪   朗   煮   只

▶ Recognizing numbers

0.34 *Read the following characters aloud.*

O 0   一 1   二 2   三 3   四 4   五 5
六 6   七 7   八 8   九 9   十 10

0.34-0.36 • Have students work in pairs to complete the exercises.
• Invite volunteers to write the answers on the board.
• To reinforce recognition, write the characters on flashcards and drill them in random order.

0.34 You may wish to point out that "zero" in Chinese characters is technically "零"; however, these days the Arabic numeral "0" is almost always used instead.

0.35 *Write the Arabic numerals for each of the following telephone numbers.*

八O八・九五六・二六九二   _____

九一六・二二九・O三七O   _____

七一八・九六六・六一五五   _____

五一二・三O二・二四OO   _____

0.35 Key:
(808) 956-2692
(916) 229-0370
(718) 966-6155
(512) 302-2400

0.36 *The Chinese character* 元 *(yuán) is the primary denomination in Chinese currency, equivalent in usage (but not in value) to a "dollar" in U.S. currency. What is the cost indicated by the following price tags?*

十元 _____   六元 _____   九元 _____

0.36 Key:
10 yuán
6 yuán
9 yuán

❱ **Reading real-life texts**

0.37 *This is a sign for an establishment in Beijing called "The Vulcan Bar." Label each of the three large characters on the sign with one of the following: person, mountain, fire.*

What do you think a "mountain of fire" means? Write the English term: _____

0.38 *This is a sign for a famous spicy Sichuan dish. The character* 煮 *(zhǔ) means "boiled." Circle the radical for this character on the sign.*

What does the radical mean? _____

What is the main ingredient of this dish? _____

In what has this ingredient been boiled? _____

Suggest a good English name for this dish: _____

0.39 *This is a sign in a college cafeteria.* 區／区 *(qū) means "area."*

How much does each dish in this area cost? Write the English: _____

🎵 Unit Rap

Go to the **Encounters** *website at www.EncountersChinese.com and listen to the song to review the numbers introduced in this unit. Listen again and sing along!*

Encounter 5 Writing

▶ Learning to write characters

0.40 *For stroke order and other useful information about each of the following characters from this unit, go to the* **Character Writing Workbook.** *Practice writing them until you can reproduce them on demand.*

一, 二, 三, 四, 五, 六, 七, 八, 九, 十

火, 口, 木, 人, 山, 水

0.41 *Write your telephone number (including area code) in Chinese characters.*

___ ___ ___ – ___ ___ ___ ___ – ___ ___ ___ ___

Cultural Bits 文化点滴

What is culture?

View the video segment "What is culture?" and then discuss the following questions with your classmates.

- Give a few examples of ways in which cultural understanding is crucial for certain bits of language, such as the expression *Chi le ma*?
- What is the difference between "large C" culture and "small c" culture? Give some examples of each.
- What images do you associate with Chinese culture?
- What are the four major inventions that China is known for?
- What are some elements that can contribute to culture shock, and how can they be avoided?

Cultural Bits

Since culture is an open-ended topic, we have not provided "answer keys" to these questions. Rather, you might encourage students to develop their own "answer keys," perhaps in the form of an online blog, based on what they learn from the cultural video, input from you and others, and their own experience.

Recap

▶ Vocabulary

Numbers

líng zero   **sān** three   **liù** six   **jiǔ** nine

yī one   **sì** four   **qī** seven   **shí** ten

èr two   **wǔ** five   **bā** eight

▶ Checklist of "can do" statements

After completing this unit, you should be able to perform each of the following tasks:

Structure of Chinese

☐ Make an accurate statement in English describing Chinese tones.

☐ At least some of the time, identify the tone of a Chinese syllable by indicating a number (if done orally) or a tone mark (if written).

☐ At least some of the time, identify the initial sound of a Chinese syllable by selecting the corresponding pinyin letter(s).

☐ At least some of the time, identify the final sound of a Chinese syllable by selecting the corresponding pinyin letter(s).

Listening and speaking

☐ Recognize and say the numbers 1–10 in various orders.

Reading and writing

☐ Recognize and write the characters for the numbers 1–10.

☐ Recognize ten common characters that are also radicals and write six of them.

☐ Identify ten common radicals in characters.

☐ Recognize the Chinese character for *yuán*.

Checklist

• Have students work in pairs to go through the "can do" list in class.

• Give 20–30 minutes for students to do this activity.

• Tell students that putting check marks in the boxes is NOT the objective. The point is to check if they can really DO the things on the list. To make sure, students can demonstrate that they CAN by DOING IT for a partner! You may also wish to have student pairs demonstrate selected skills to the class.

• Circulate around the class and give assistance and encouragement as necessary.

"We're all one family"

四海一家

Sìhǎiyìjiā

A note on pinyin orthography Since writing Chinese in pinyin is a relatively modern convention, rules for details such as word spacing were officially standardized only recently. This textbook attempts to follow official orthography, but you may find that it differs from usage on signs and in other publications that use pinyin. Following official orthography, Chinese *chéngyǔ* 成語 / 成语 (idioms), which generally consist of four-character sayings, are written with no spaces between the pinyin representations of individual characters. The titles of Units 1–7 and 10 are *chéngyǔ* and are therefore written without spaces. The titles of the Introductory Unit and Units 8 and 9, although also four characters long, are not set idioms and are thus written with spaces.

Introducing yourself by nationality and background

In this unit, you will learn how to:

- greet someone.
- introduce yourself.
- say good-bye.
- understand formal and informal speech.
- say where you come from.

- ask for and give telephone numbers.
- express your thanks.
- apologize to someone.
- ask for repetition and clarification.
- understand traditional versus simplified characters.

Encounter 1   Greeting people and introducing yourself

▶ Greeting people

1.1 *View Episode 1 of the dramatic series. Don't worry if you don't fully understand everything that is being said; just listen and enjoy!*

1.2 *What might you say in English when you greet someone? Make a list below.*

_____

_____

1.3 *Watch and listen to the video segment. Then check the greetings you hear.*

☐ Nǐ hǎo!
☐ Hǎo ma?
☐ Nín hǎo!
☐ Xiǎo Wáng!
☐ Zěnmeyàng?
☐ Hǎo, hǎo.
☐ Hěn hǎo.

Compare your answers with those of your classmates and teacher.

1.4 *Watch and listen to the video segment. Can you understand the meanings of the individual expressions below? Match the appropriate terms.*

a. Nǐ hǎo!   1. *Hello.* (formal; polite)

b. Nín hǎo!   2. *Hello.* (informal)

c. Hǎo ma?   3. *How about you?*

d. Hǎo.   4. *Fine.*

e. Nǐ ne?   5. *How are you? / Are you well?* (informal)

f. Wǒ yě hěn hǎo.   6. *I'm fine too.*

Compare your answers with those of your classmates and teacher.

FYI 供你参考

Greetings in Chinese

In Chinese culture, as in Western cultures, there are generally two types of word-based greetings—those that are exchanged with little or no further conversation, such as "Hi!" and "Hello!" (*Nǐ hǎo!* in Chinese), and those that follow a question-and-answer pattern, such as "How are you?" and "How have you been?" (*Nǐ hǎo ma?* in Chinese). Both are considered friendly and informal. As a beginning student of Chinese, you can safely use *Nǐ hǎo* as a common, informal greeting regardless of either the time of day or person addressed. As you will learn in this unit, the response to *Nǐ hǎo* is usually a *Nǐ hǎo* in return.

However, in Chinese culture (as in all cultures), context determines which greeting you will use and when. When you greet a person of a higher status, such as your teacher, you should use the more formal and polite *Nín hǎo* or *Nín hǎo ma?* *Nín* is roughly equivalent to the French "vous" or the Spanish "usted." It is also a good idea to use the polite form when greeting someone at a formal business or social occasion or someone who is significantly senior to you. Remember: when in doubt, use *nín*. It shows courtesy and respect—two highly valued characteristics in Chinese culture—and it presents you as a cultured and sophisticated individual.

In addition to *Nín (Nǐ) hǎo!* or *Nín (Nǐ) hǎo ma?*, another conventional greeting is simply to say the person's last name, followed by a respectful title, such as "Mr.," "Ms.," or "Professor." For example, *Yáng Xiānsheng* (Mr. Yang); *Zhāng Nǚshì* (Ms. Zhang); and *Lǐ Lǎoshī* (Professor Li, literally: Teacher Li). You can also combine last name, title, and a respectful greeting, such as in this formula: *Zhāng Lǎoshī, nín hǎo!* (with a slight nod of the head).

1.5 *Mingling: Turn to a nearby classmate and greet him or her in Chinese. Then repeat the exchange with a different classmate. If you know your classmate's name (Chinese or English), say it before the greeting. If you are interacting with your teacher, remember to use the polite form and/or a respectful title (e.g.,* Lǐ Lǎoshī, nín hǎo*).*

FYI 供你参考

Other common greetings

Here are some other common ways to greet friends:

Zǎo! *(early morning, until around 9:00 or 10:00 A.M.)*

Zǎoshang hǎo! *(similar to* zǎo *with the same time restrictions, but much more formal)*

Keep in mind that *nǐ hǎo* can be used at any time of day. If you already know the person you are greeting, you don't actually need to say anything. You could just smile, nod, and say the person's name or name and title.

Greetings in Chinese

• Research indicates that a valuable method of successful student learning is peer teaching. Therefore, we invite students using *Encounters* to teach many of the program's FYI and Grammar Bits components to their classmates.

• Assign students one or more clearly defined tasks before they attempt to read and teach the FYI and Grammar Bits sections. This provides a focus so students can absorb information more effectively.

• Divide the class into three groups, and assign each group one paragraph. Groups should read the paragraph and prepare a short lecture or presentation for the class. Provide assistance as necessary.

1.5 • Begin this activity by having the class brainstorm and list the greetings they already know in Chinese.

• Have students suggest answers "popcorn" style, and invite a volunteer to write the class's suggestions on the board.

• If necessary, remind students to review exercise 1.4 for possible answers.

• Consider having a confident pair demonstrate the conversation before the entire class mingles. Circulate around the classroom and provide prompts and assistance as necessary.

More common greetings

• Have students read this FYI with partners to learn some common ways that Chinese people greet one another. Students should then practice these greetings with their partners. While they are practicing, circulate around the classroom and provide assistance as necessary.

• To conclude the activity, invite volunteer pairs to demonstrate the greetings for the class.

1.6 • Have students read the instructions before you play the video; have them work in pairs to assist each other.

▶ Introducing yourself

 1.6 *Watch and listen to the video segment. What do you think they are saying to each other? Fill in the blanks in English.*

Lynn: Nǐ hǎo! Wǒ jiào Lynn.
          Hello. _____ Lynn.

Lǐ Wén: Nǐ hǎo! Wǒ jiào Lǐ Wén.
          Hello. _____ Li Wen.

Chén Fēng: Nín hǎo, Zhōu Lǎoshī.
            Wǒ jiào Chén Fēng.
            Hello, Professor Zhou.
            _____ Chen Feng.

Máo Zhìpéng: Wǒ jiào Máo
              Zhìpéng.

              _____
              Mao Zhipeng.

• Replay and pause the video as needed, but make sure students have time to discuss answers. Invite volunteers to write the answers on the board.

1.6 Key: My name is *(for all four blanks)*

1.7 Have students work in pairs to assist each other. To conclude this exercise, have students walk around the classroom, greet their classmates, and introduce themselves.

1.7 *Write your name in Chinese (pinyin with tones) or English to complete the sentence below. Use your first name or your full name, as you prefer. Practice saying the two sentences below quickly and smoothly, five to ten times.*

Nǐ hǎo! Wǒ jiào _____.

Introductions

Check comprehension of this FYI by stimulating a brief class discussion. Ask, "In the United States, when we introduce ourselves, which part of our name do we often give before the other? Do people do the same thing in China? Why or why not? Which way do you prefer?"

FYI 供你参考

Introductions

Have you noticed that Chinese people tend to introduce themselves using full names, whereas Westerners often do so with just first names? Take a moment to consider what this might indicate about Chinese and Western values related to one's identity. How do you generally like to introduce yourself?

In Chinese culture, it is more important to identify the group you belong to first—for example, your family, your workplace—before moving on to other details when introducing yourself. In Chinese, the last name comes first and is generally included as part of the introduction.

1.8 Key:

a. gāoxìng
b. nín
c. Hěn gāoxìng rènshi nǐ.
d. Nice meeting you!

 1.8 *Watch and listen to the video segment. Fill in the blanks with pinyin.*

a.
Lynn: Nǐ hǎo. Wǒ jiào Lynn. Hěn gāoxìng
          rènshi nǐ.

Lǐ Wén: Nǐ hǎo. Wǒ jiào Lǐ Wén. Rènshi nǐ
          wǒ yě hěn _____.

b.
Nín hǎo, Zhōu Lǎoshī. Wǒ jiào Chén Fēng.
Hěn gāoxìng rènshi _____.

c.

Zhào Yǒnggāng: Hěn gāoxìng rènshi nǐmen.

Alejandro: _____

_____.

d. What do you think is the meaning of *Hěn gāoxìng rènshi nǐ*? Write the English below:

_____

1.9 *Mingling: Turn to two or three classmates and say your name in Chinese, using the sentences you have just practiced. Use your English name if you do not have a Chinese name. Listen carefully to their responses and take notes.*

▶ Grammar: Personal pronouns

1.10 *As a class, name these famous people. Then complete each blank below with an appropriate English name. Note that* tā *means "he/she" and* míngzi *means "name."*

Tā jiào shénme? OR Tā jiào shénme míngzi?

      a.   b.   c.   d.

a. Tā jiào _____.
b. Tā jiào _____.

c. Tā jiào _____.
d. Tā jiào _____.

1.11 Key:
a. 2
b. 3
c. 1
d. 6
e. 4
f. 5

1.11 *Match the Chinese personal pronouns on the left with the appropriate English on the right. The suffix* -men *forms plural pronouns when it is added to singular pronouns.*

a. wǒ	1. *he/she*
b. nǐ	2. *I*
c. tā	3. *you* (singular)
d. wǒmen	4. *you* (plural)
e. nǐmen	5. *they*
f. tāmen	6. *we*

Encounter 2 Leave-taking and more introductions

▶ Saying good-bye

1.12 This is a simple video clip, and the answers are rather straightforward. Move through this exercise quickly.

1.12 Key: Good-bye, Lynn!; Li Wen, good-bye!

 1.12 *Watch and listen to the video segment. What do you think they are saying to each other? Fill in the blanks in English.*

Lǐ Wén: Zàijiàn, Lynn!

_____

Lynn: Lǐ Wén, zàijiàn!

_____

1.13 Have students perform this exercise with multiple classmates until they are comfortable saying good-bye in Chinese and can do so quickly and fluently.

Saying good-bye

Assign students one or more clearly defined teaching tasks before they begin reading this FYI. Divide the class into three groups, and distribute the following assignments to each group.

1. What is a polite way to say good-bye to someone if you know his or her name or title? Prepare a brief lecture/presentation in English to teach your classmates. Make sure to include an informative demonstration.

2. This FYI introduces four additional ways to say good-bye. Prepare a brief lecture/demonstration to teach these phrases to your classmates. Make sure to include an informative demonstration.

3. How do you say good-bye to a teacher? Prepare a brief lecture/demonstration to teach your classmates. Make sure to include an informative demonstration.

1.13 *Mingling: Say good-bye to your classmates, using their English or Chinese names.*

FYI 供你参考

Saying good-bye

Most cultures and languages have several ways to say good-bye. The most common way in Chinese is *zàijiàn* (*again + see = see you again/soon*).

Try to develop the habit of saying good-bye to your friends by saying their name (and title, if you know it) before *zàijiàn*; it's more polite and authentic. For example: *Mǎlì* (Mary), *zàijiàn*. OR *Yáng Lǎoshī, zàijiàn*. Do remember to say good-bye; don't just walk out of class when it ends without saying good-bye to your teacher.

Just as with greetings, there are also many conventional ways to say good-bye in Chinese culture. Try some of the following examples in an appropriate context. Pay particular attention to how English has influenced Chinese in one of the examples below.

> *Míngtiān jiàn* (*tomorrow + see*): See you tomorrow.
> *Yìhuǐr jiàn* (*little while + see*): See you in a little while/in a few moments.
> *Báibái*: sound loan from English "bye-bye" that is often added to another form; thus, *Zàijiàn, báibái!*

When saying good-bye to your teacher, remember that it's best to use his or her last name plus the term for "teacher" (*lǎoshī*); thus, *Wáng Lǎoshī, zàijiàn!*

◗ Grammar: The verbs *shì, jiào, xìng*

1.14 *Watch and listen to the video segment. Then fill in the blanks below.*

a. Chén Fēng, zhèi wèi _____ Yáng Jiàoshòu.
    Chen Feng, this is Professor Yang.

b. Wǒ _____ Mèng, _____ Mèng Dérú.
    My last name is Meng; my name is Meng Deru.

c. _____ Zhāng, _____ Zhāng Fúxīng.
    My last name is Zhang; my name is Zhang Fuxing.

1.15 *Match the Chinese on the left with the appropriate English on the right.*

a. shì   1. *be called, have the first name X*
b. jiào   2. *have the last name X*
c. xìng   3. *be*

1.16 *Complete the following self-introduction by a man named Manuel García. He is saying, "My last name is García; my name is Manuel García."*

Wǒ _____
García, _____
        Manuel García.

1.17 *Write the same self-introduction for yourself in pinyin, using your English or Chinese name. Try to write the pinyin with tone marks.*

_____

Repeat this self-introduction aloud until you are comfortable with the words and can say the sentences quickly and accurately.

1.18 *Mingling: With a partner, practice saying hello, introducing yourself, and saying good-bye. After you both have had an opportunity to share, move to a new partner and repeat the process. Continue to circulate around the room to interact with new partners.*

Grammar Bits 语法点滴

Stative verbs

In Chinese, words that describe the subject—that say how it is or is not—are called "stative verbs" (some people call them "adjectives").

> hǎo *(be good, fine, OK)*
>
> gāoxìng *(be happy, delighted, glad)*

Stative verbs (SV) can be preceded by adverbs, such as *hěn* (a light sense of "very"). It is a good idea to always precede a stative verb used by itself with *hěn* (except in greetings).

> Wǒ hěn hǎo. *(I'm fine)*
>
> Wǒ hěn gāoxìng. (I'm happy.)

Equative verbs

Chinese also has "equative verbs" that are like an "equal" sign (thus: subject = noun). You already know three:

jiào *(be called/named)*	**xìng** *(be surnamed, have the last name X)*
Wǒ jiào Mike.	Wǒ xìng Wáng.
Tā jiào Mark, Mark Phelps.	Lǎoshī xìng Chén.
Nǐ jiào shénme míngzi?	

Jiào may introduce either the full name (surname + given name) or just the given name, but NEVER just the surname; that's the function of *xìng*.

> **shì** *(be)*
>
> Wǒ shì lǎoshī.
>
> Tā shì Gāo Lǎoshī.

Note that although there is a tone mark on the linking verb *shì*, it is usually not stressed in connected speech: *shì* is pronounced in a neutral tone.

Also note that Chinese verbs do not change form to match the subject. In English, the verb "to be" must be conjugated to form "I **am**," "you **are**," "he/she **is**," etc.; in Chinese, the verb *shì* remains *shì*, regardless of the subject.

Remember that *shì* is NOT used to link subjects or pronouns with stative verbs (adjectives). The English "I am well/fine/OK" does NOT become ~~Wǒ shì hǎo~~ in Chinese, but instead becomes *Wǒ hěn hǎo*.

▶ Grammar: Negation

 1.19 *Watch and listen to the video segment, and then answer the following questions.*

a. How much did the bicyclist think the bottle of water cost? _____ kuài (¥)

b. How much was it really? _____ kuài (¥)

c. Based on what you hear, what does *bù* mean? *bù* = _____

1.20 *Watch and listen to the video again. Write the missing tones on the following sentences.*

a. Bù dong, bù dong. *(I don't understand.)*

b. Bú shi shui, shi shui. *(It's not "sleep"; it's "water.")*

c. Yí kuai wu, bú shi wu kuai. *(It's ¥1.5, not ¥5.)*

1.21 *Indicate with a* ∧ *where* bù *belongs in each of the following sentences. Note: Grammatically,* bù *should precede the verb.*

a. Wǒ shì Mary Smith.

b. Wǒ jiào Mary.

c. Wǒ xìng Smith.

d. Wǒ shì Měiguórén. *(I am American.)*

e. Wǒ shì Zhōngguórén. *(I am Chinese.)*

1.22 *Write a complete sentence in pinyin about one thing you are NOT.*

_____

FYI 供你参考

More on tone sandhi: The negative adverb *bù*

Tone sandhi, you'll remember, occurs when certain words change tones in certain environments. *Yī* (number one) is an example that you learned about in the introductory unit. *Bù* is another. Before the fourth tone, *bù* changes to the second tone: *bú*.

> Bú xìng Zhōu. *([I'm] not surnamed Zhou.)*
> Bú shì wǒ. *(It's not me.)*

Recognizing when these words change tones will become automatic with practice.

Practice: How would you pronounce *bù* if you added it to each of these words?

gāo *(tall)*	máng *(busy)*	hǎo *(good)*	lèi *(tired)*
jiāo *(teach)*	xué *(learn)*	xiě *(write)*	bèi *(memorize)*

▶ Formal and informal speech

1.23 *Watch and listen to the video segment. Match the Chinese sentences with their correct English equivalents. Note:* Qǐngwèn *means "May I ask . . ." and always precedes the inquiry.*

a. Tā xìng shénme?
b. Wǒ xìng Fàn.
c. Qǐngwèn, nín guìxìng?

1. *My last name is Fan.*
2. *May I ask your (honorable) last name?*
3. *What's his last name?*

1.24 *Based on what you have learned so far, fill in the following blanks with the correct pinyin.*

a. you (formal): _____

b. you (informal): _____

c. Hello (informal): __*Nǐ hǎo*__.

d. Hello (formal): _____.

e. What's your last name (formal): __*Nín guìxìng*__?

f. What's his last name (informal): _____?

FYI 供你参考

Levels of formality

Although *Nǐ xìng shénme?* is grammatically correct and often used in casual conversation, many Chinese would consider it too informal and abrupt if used when first meeting someone. When directly addressing someone older or of a higher social status than yourself (for example, your teacher or a client), it is more culturally appropriate to use *Nín guìxìng?* The response will generally then include *Miǎn guì*, meaning "Please dispense with the word *honorable*." Therefore, *Miǎn guìxìng Fàn* means "My last name is Fan, please dispense with the word *honorable*." The expression *Tā xìng shénme?* is always accepted when referring to a third party.

1.25 *Mingling: Circulate around the room, greeting classmates and asking their last names. Use informal speech with your classmates and formal speech with your teacher.*

Encounter 3 Talking about where you come from

1.26 *Watch and listen to the video segment. Then read the following fragments and circle the choice that correctly completes each sentence.*

a. Lynn is _____.
    • Chinese   • American
b. Lynn is from _____.
    • Los Angeles   • New York
c. Li Wen is from _____.
    • Guilin   • Shanghai

1.27 *Match the corresponding Chinese and English below.*

a. *I am American.*   1. Wǒ shì Shànghǎirén.
b. *I'm from Shanghai.*   2. Nǐ shì nǎli rén?
c. *Where are you from?*   3. Wǒ shì Měiguórén.

1.28 *Based on the exchange you watched in the video segment above, answer the following questions.*

a. What do you think *Měiguó nǎr* means? _____

b. What is the meaning of *nǎr* by itself? _____

1.29 *Read the exchange below and write the corresponding English equivalents where they are missing.*

A: Wǒ shì Měiguórén. *(I am an American.)*
    Wǒ jiā zài Měiguó. *(My home is in America.)*
B: Měiguó nǎr? (_____)
A: Wǒ jiā zài Niǔyuē *(New York)*; wǒ shì Niǔyuērén.
    (_____)

1.30 *Complete the following conversation with your own information. If you are not Chinese or American, you can visit a website like www.zhongguolu.com/phrasebook/countries.html to learn the name of your country in pinyin. Write that name in the first blank below. This is how you would say, "I am a person from _____." On the second blank, write the name of your state, province, or city in English. This is how you would say, "My home is in _____."*

A: Nǐ shì nǎr de rén?
B: Wǒ shì _____ rén. *(name of country)*
A: Nǐ jiā zài nǎr?
B: Wǒ jiā zài _____. *(name of state, province, or city)*

Practice the above conversation with a partner until you are comfortable and can pronounce the sentences smoothly and accurately.

1.31 Review the language items
students need to perform this
task. Have the class brainstorm an
appropriate list, and invite volunteer
scribes to take notes on the board.
If students have difficulty thinking
of the terms and phrases, remind
them to use previous exercises
for guidance. If necessary, have
a confident pair demonstrate the
conversation for the class.

Grammar Bits

If students have questions about the
ma question particle, direct them to
read this Grammar Bits section on
their own.

1.31 *Mingling: Turn to a partner and have the following guided dialogue. First, greet
your partner by name, and then:*

A: Ask where he/she is from.

B: Respond with the name of a country.

A: Ask where in this country he/she is from.

B: Respond with the name of a state/province/city in Chinese or English.

Reverse roles and practice the dialogue again.

Grammar Bits 语法点滴

The particle *ma*

There are many ways to form questions in Chinese. One of the simplest is to add
the question particle *ma* at the end of a statement. You don't need to change the
word order, but your intonation should rise slightly at the end, as in English.

Tā shì Měiguórén.   ⟶   Tā shì Měiguórén ma?

▶ Recognizing tones

1.32 Key:

Dàjiā hǎo.
Nǐ hǎo.

Wǒ jiào Máo Zhìpéng.
Wǒ jiā zài Běijīng.
Wǒ shì Běijīngrén.

Tā jiào Chén Fēng.
Tā bú zài zhèlǐ.
Tā zài Běijīng.

Zhāng Xiàozhǎng, nín hǎo.
Nǐ hǎo, Lǐ Wén.
Zhāng Xiàozhǎng, nín máng ma?
Bù máng, bù máng. Yǒu shì ma?

1.32 *Watch and listen to the video segment. Mark the correct tone (for example: ā, á, ǎ,
or à) over each of the boldfaced letters.*

Dajia **ha**o. *(Hi, everybody.)*
Ni hao. *(Hi.)*

Wo jiao Mao Zhi**pe**ng. *(My name is Mao Zhipeng.)*
Wo jia zai Beijing. *(I live in Beijing.)*
Wo shi Beijingren. *(I am a Beijinger.)*

Ta jiao Chen Feng. *(His name is Chen Feng.)*
Ta b**u** zai zheli. *(He's not here.)*
Ta zai Beijing. *(He's in Beijing.)*

Zhang Xiaozhang, **ni**n hao. *(Hi, Principal Zhang.)*
Ni hao, Li Wen. *(Hi, Li Wen.)*
Zhang Xiaozhang, nin **ma**ng ma? *(Principal Zhang, are you busy?)*
Bu mang, b**u** mang. **Yo**u shi ma? *(Not busy, not busy. What's up?)*

❯ Grammar: Question words *nǎr, shénme, shéi*

1.33 *Review the second exchange from the previous activity and write the appropriate English equivalent in the blank below.*

Q: Tā shì shéi?

A: Tā shì Máo Zhìpéng. Tā shì Běijīngrén.

shéi = _____

1.34 *Match the appropriate Chinese and English question words.*

a. nǎr   1. *who*

b. shénme   2. *where*

c. shéi   3. *what*

Encounter 4   Asking for and giving phone numbers

1.35 *Watch and listen to the video segment. Then fill in the blanks below.*

a. What's your telephone number? Fill in the blank: *Nǐ de diànhuà hàomǎ shì* _____?

b. Write the pinyin for the term that means "telephone **number**": *diànhuà* _____

c. Write the pinyin for the word that marks possession: _____
   (Hint: nǐ de diànhuà hàomǎ = *your telephone number*)

d. Write the pinyin for "My telephone number is":

   _____

e. Write the pinyin for the term that indicates "and yours?": _____
   (Hint: Listen to what Lynn says after she tells Li Wen her telephone number.)

f. Write the English meaning of *shǒujī*: _____

1.36 *Complete the following sentences about yourself. Use the statements below for Mary Smith as a guide.*

I am Mary Smith. I am American. My home is in Boston. My home phone (or cell phone) number is 617-635-4500.

Wǒ jiào _____.

Wǒ shì _____.
   (*Write the pinyin of your country + rén.*)

Wǒ jiā zài _____.
   (*Write the name of your state or city in English.*)

Wǒ de _____ shì _____.
   (*Write your home or cell phone number.*)

1.37 *Watch and listen to the video segment. What is each person asking? Fill in each blank with the corresponding word or phrase from the box.*

cell phone number / where someone lives / nationality

name / home phone number

a. Nǐ jiào shénme míngzi?

_____

b. Nǐ shì nǎli rén?

_____

c. Nǐ jiā zhù nǎr?

_____

d. Nǐ jiālǐ de diànhuà hàomǎ shì duōshao?

_____

e. Nǐ de shǒujī hàomǎ shì duōshao?

_____

1.38 *Mingling: Turn to a classmate and ask the questions above. Note his or her responses below.*

Name: _____ Home phone number: _____

Nationality: _____ Cell phone number: _____

Hometown: _____

Grammar Bits 语法点滴

Review of question words

Question words are, obviously, words that ask for information or denote interrogative sentences. If you use a question word, then your sentence does not need the particle *ma*. Carefully note the position of Chinese question words. How is it different from English? The examples below illustrate various uses of *shénme*, *shéi*, *nǎr*, *něi*, and *duōshao*. In all of these examples, the answer to the question replaces the question word. Can you provide an answer to each question about the fictitious people below?

Tā jiào shénme? *(What is her name?)*
Tā jiào Wáng shénme? *(He is called Wang what?)* [Answer with Wang's FULL name.]
Tā xìng shénme? *(What is her [sur]name?)*
Tā shì shéi? *(Who is he/she?)*
Shéi shì Wáng Lǎoshī? *(Who is Professor Wang?)* [You would point him out.]
Nǐ zài nǎr? *(Where are you?)*
Zhāng Lǎoshī shì nǎr de rén? *(Where is Professor Zhang from?)*
Nǐ shì něi guó rén? *(What's your nationality?)*
Tā de diànhuà hàomǎ shì duōshao? *(What is his/her telephone number?)*

Encounter 5 Expressing thanks, apologizing, and asking for clarification

▶ Thanking and apologizing

1.39 *Watch and listen to the video segment. Then match each Chinese expression with the appropriate English equivalent.*

a. Qǐng.
b. Xièxie.
c. Duìbuqǐ.
d. Búyòng xiè.
e. Méi guānxi. ——————
f. Bú kèqi. ——————

1. *You're welcome.*
2. *I'm sorry.*
3. *Please go ahead.*
4. *Thank you.*
5. *That's all right. / No problem.*
6. *No need to be so polite. (You're welcome.)*

1.40 *Mingling:* *Turn to a partner and practice saying "thank you" (followed by "you're welcome") and "I'm sorry" (followed by "that's all right"). Continue until you both feel confident with the exchanges.*

1.41 *Pair work:* *Complete the "red/white" activity with a partner, following these directions.*

a. Hold a red chip in one hand and a white chip in the other. Do not let your partner know which chip is in each hand.
b. Invite your partner (say *Qǐng . . .*) to choose one of your hands. Reveal the selected chip and share it with your partner.
c. If your partner selects the red chip, he or she should say *Xièxie*, since you have shared something good (red is a lucky color in Chinese culture). You should respond with *Búyòngxiè*.
d. If your partner selects the white chip, you should say *Duìbuqǐ* since you have shared something sad (white is linked to mourning in Chinese culture). He or she should respond with *Méi guānxi*.
e. Reverse roles, and then continue with a different partner.

1.41 The goal of this activity is to train students to recognize actual situations in which they will use the vocabulary they are learning.

• Prepare a set of red and white poker chips or other red and white items (e.g., small slips of paper, beads, marbles), and bring them to class. There should be enough objects for each student to have one of each color.

• Be sure to model this activity carefully before asking the students to perform it independently. Demonstrate the activity with several students, explaining the process and offering help and support, as necessary.

• When you are confident that students can do the activity in pairs, distribute the chips and provide any necessary assistance as they do the activity.

• This is a good opportunity to reinforce and extend the symbolic meanings of red and white in Chinese culture. Red is generally joyful and used for births, weddings, and New Year celebrations. White is worn at funerals and to mourn the passing of someone close.

• Challenge students to suggest reasons for why these colors might have these meanings.

▶ Asking for clarification

1.42 *Watch and listen to the video segment. The following sentences are useful to keep in mind if you have trouble understanding what someone says. Read them carefully and then match the corresponding English and Chinese phrases.*

a. *Sorry. I don't understand.*
b. *Please say it again.*
c. *Please speak slower.*
d. *I understand now. Thank you.*

1. Qǐng shuō màn yìdiǎnr.
2. Qǐng zài shuō yíbiàn.
3. Wǒ dǒng le, xièxie.
4. Duìbuqǐ, wǒ bù dǒng.

1.43 *Fill in the blanks using the correct pinyin equivalents.*

a. understand: _____   d. slow: _____

b. speak or say: _____   e. slower: _____

c. say it again: _____

1.44 *Write answers to the following questions in pinyin.*

What would you say if . . .

a. someone spoke to you in Chinese
   using words you don't yet know?

_____

b. someone mumbled or did not
   speak clearly?

_____

c. someone spoke too quickly for you
   to understand?

_____

d. you finally understand what someone has been trying to tell you?

_____

▶ Putting it all together

1.45 *Mingling: Circulate around the room, interview six people, and complete the chart below. Remember to ask for clarification, if necessary, and use polite language if you interview your teacher. Begin each exchange with a greeting and finish by saying good-bye. Remember to also express thanks and apologies, when necessary, at the appropriate time.*

Name	Nationality	Hometown	Home phone #	Cell phone #

1.46 *Conversation: If possible, have a conversation with a native Chinese speaker. Provide the following information about yourself: name, nationality, telephone number. Ask for the same information from the other person. Remember to greet, thank, apologize, ask for clarification as necessary, and say good-bye. Share and discuss this dialogue with your teacher and classmates.*

🎵 Unit Rap

Go to the **Encounters** *website at* www.EncountersChinese.com *and listen to the song to review key expressions from Unit 1. Listen again and sing along!*

Encounter 6　Reading and writing

▶ Recognizing traditional vs. simplified characters

1.47 *Read the following terms aloud.*

我 (*I, me*)　　　　　　　　你 (*you*)　　　　　　　　　他 (*he*)

我們 (*we*)　　　　　　　　你們 (*you [plural]*)　　　　他們 (*they*)

你好! (*Hello!*)　　　　　　你好嗎? (*How are you?*)　　請 (*please, please go ahead*)

謝謝! (*Thank you!*)　　　　謝謝你! (*Thank you!*)　　　對不起 (*I'm sorry.*)

謝謝您! (*Thank you! [polite]*)　再見! (*Good-bye!*)

1.45 • This is a capstone listening-speaking activity for the unit. *Encounters* assesses students by their ability to perform real-life tasks in Chinese, not by how well they perform on a grammar test. Use this activity as a test to assess your students' mastery of the material introduced in Unit 1.

• Allocate at least 15 minutes for this activity. You can use this activity in several ways:

1. Mingle among and interact with your students to get a sense of how well they have mastered the spoken communication goals of this unit. (This is good for smaller classes.)

2. Pair students at random, and have them interact appropriately. Rate each student individually.

3. Initiate conversations with students on a one-on-one basis, and rate them individually.

1.46 If possible, ask a native Chinese speaker to attend class for this exercise. If this is not possible, arrange for students to independently interview native speakers, either in person or on the phone. If the interviews are performed outside of class, remind students to bring their notes to class to share.

1.47 • Have students work in pairs to complete this activity. Tell them to use the English as a bridge to determine the sound for these characters.

• Avoid reading these words aloud to students before they complete the activity.

• This activity is designed for students to figure out the answers themselves. Therefore, resist the temptation to give students the answers when they are stuck or ask you directly for help. With confidence and time, students should be able to make the connections between Chinese characters and English meanings. Though the process might be frustrating and slow, the rewards of self-discovery and independent learning are worthwhile.

• If student are demonstrating difficulty making the appropriate connections, allow them to review earlier exercises in this unit for guidance.

FYI 供你参考

Development of simplified characters

The characters in the previous activity are written in a form usually called "traditional" characters. Their forms are identical to the forms that have been used in China for centuries. In 1956, and again in 1964, the government of the People's Republic of China (PRC) published lists of "simplified" characters. Some of the traditionally used characters were simplified by reducing the number of total strokes needed to write them. For example, the character 見, traditionally written with seven strokes, was simplified to 见, written with four strokes. Only about a quarter to one-third of all characters in use were simplified; the rest were not. The hope was that if the characters were easier to write, they would be easier to learn. Taiwan, Hong Kong, and many overseas Chinese communities, however, continue to use only the traditional forms. The research community is divided on whether simplified or traditional characters are easier to learn, but in all Chinese-speaking communities, whether they use simplified or traditional forms, in the past decades the literacy rate has gone from one of the lowest in the world to one of the highest—currently just over 90 percent.

A "divided language" situation currently exists for the written Chinese language, unfortunately complicating your learning efforts. Will there be a unification of China's written language in the future? Stay tuned!

Development of simplified characters

Before students read this FYI, divide the class into equal groups, and assign each group a different question to answer. Groups should prepare short presentations to teach their topics to the class. Examples include:

• How many systems are used to write Chinese today? What are they?

• Who simplified the Chinese writing system? When and why did it happen? Did it help Chinese people learn to read and write?

• What percent of the characters were simplified?

• Today, who uses the simplified system, and who uses the traditional system?

1.48 Key:

a. 6
b. 9
c. 8
d. 7
e. 11
f. 1
g. 10
h. 2
i. 4
j. 5
k. 3
l. 13
m. 21
n. 16
o. 12
p. 22
q. 14
r. 20
s. 15
t. 17
u. 19
v. 18

1.48 *In each group, match the traditional characters in the left column with their simplified equivalents in the right column. Keep in mind that only about a quarter to one-third of all characters have been simplified.*

a. 我	1. 你好吗	l. 再見	12. 叫
b. 你	2. 你请	m. 是	13. 再见
c. 他	3. 谢谢您	n. 姓	14. 么
d. 他們	4. 谢谢	o. 叫	15. 字
e. 你好	5. 谢谢你	p. 甚	16. 姓
f. 你好嗎	6. 我	q. 麼	17. 对
g. 請	7. 他们	r. 名	18. 起
h. 你請	8. 他	s. 字	19. 不
i. 謝謝	9. 你	t. 對	20. 名
j. 謝謝你	10. 请	u. 不	21. 是
k. 謝謝您	11. 你好	v. 起	22. 什

▶ Recognizing radicals

1.49 *Review the radicals in the introductory unit, pages 11–14. Look for any occurrences of those radicals in both lists above. Try to link the meaning of the radical with the meaning of the character. Keep in mind that when radicals are part of multicomponent characters, their forms often change. Notice how some radicals have been simplified and are now written with fewer strokes. Share your conclusions with your classmates.*

1.49 Discussing how radicals relate to these characters will help students see the logic behind the Chinese writing system. It will also help students' memorization and make reading and writing tasks less daunting.

▶ Reading real-life texts

1.50 *This sign is on the campus of the university that Chen Feng, Li Wen, and Xiao Mao once attended. It says, "[Making our environment] green, beautiful, and clean / depends on you, on me, and on him (others)." Circle and label the terms "me," "you," "him."*

1.50–1.53 If possible, copy this page to a transparency, so you can project it on the board and invite volunteers to circle the appropriate characters in the real-life text.

1.50 Key: me–我；you–你；him–他

1.51 *On the same campus is this plaque.* 的 *is a particle that marks possession. Circle the term for "we." "We" + de = "our."*

1.51 Key: we–我们

1.52 Note that the character 后 (last character on line 2 of the sign) should properly be 候. Both are pronounced *hòu*, but 后 means "behind," while 候 means "to wait." Native speakers often take shortcuts (后 is much easier to write than 候), and they sometimes make mistakes.

1.52 Key: please–请 ; thank you–谢谢

1.52 *This handwritten sign on the desk of a receptionist says, "I'll be right back. Please wait just a bit! Thank you!" Circle the terms "please" and "thank you." Note that the second* xiè *in* xièxie *is here represented with a mark meaning "ditto, repeat the previous character."*

1.53 Key: Answers will vary.

1.53 *This is a handwritten note that someone has passed to you in class. If you wanted to be friendly and polite, what would you write back? For now, write in English.*

你好！我叫王小明。請問，
你姓甚麼？叫甚麼名字？
謝謝你告訴我。

_____

_____

_____

▶ Learning to write characters

1.54 *For stroke order and other useful information about each of the following characters from this unit, go to the* Character Writing Workbook. *Choose traditional or simplified characters and practice writing them until you can reproduce them on demand.*

我，你，他，們／们，好，嗎／吗，是，姓，叫，甚／什，
麼／么，名，字，請／请，謝／谢，再，見／见，對／对，
不，起

▶ Writing a note

1.55 *Write a brief note to a classmate, telling him or her your name and asking for your classmate's name. Use characters as much as possible; substitute with pinyin or English as necessary. Use courtesy terms (for example, "thank you") whenever possible.*

Cultural Bits 文化点滴

Introductions, greetings, and good-byes

View the video segment "Introductions, greetings, and good-byes" and then discuss the following questions with your classmates.

- What role do introductions by friends play in getting to know people in Chinese society?
- What elements determine your status in regard to someone else? List some.
- What are some greetings other than *Nǐ hǎo* that Chinese often use with each other?
- What are some ways you can take leave of a person?
- What is the significance of the leave-taking statement *Wǒ bú sòng le, a?*

1.55 • Encourage students to complete this exercise independently, but allow them to work in pairs if necessary. Suggest to students that they write their notes in pinyin first, then "translate" their writing into characters. When they finish writing, students should proofread their partners' writing before turning in their drafts to the teacher.

• If time allows, and students permit, randomly deliver the class mail. Students should then read these notes and write appropriate responses.

Recap

▶ Grammar

Stative verbs

Stative verbs, which describe the subject, can be preceded by adverbs such as *hěn* or negated with *bù*. Do not use *shì* with stative verbs.

hǎo (*be good, be fine, be OK*)
    Wǒ hěn hǎo. (NOT: ~~Wǒ shì hǎo.~~)
    Tāmen bù hǎo.

gāoxìng (*be happy, be delighted, be glad*)
    hěn gāoxìng
    bù gāoxìng
    Tā bù gāoxìng.

Equative verbs

Equative verbs link the subject with a noun that states what it is.

jiào (*be called*)
    Wǒ jiào Alejandro.

xìng (*have the surname*)
    Wǒ xìng Lǐ, jiào Lǐ Wén.

shì (*be*)
    Wǒ shì Zhōngguórén, bú shì Měiguórén.

Question words

Question words ask for information or denote interrogative sentences. The particle *ma* is not needed when a question word is used.

shéi (*who?*)
    Tā shì shéi? Tā jiào Lǐ Wén.

shénme (*what?*)
    Nǐ jiào shénme? Wǒ jiào Wáng Lì.

nǎr (*where?*)
    Nǐ jiā zài nǎr? Wǒ jiā zài Běijīng.

duōshao (*what number?*)
    Nǐ diànhuà duōshao hào?

Plurals

The suffix *-men* is added to the pronouns *wǒ*, *nǐ*, and *tā* to create the plural forms *wǒmen*, *nǐmen*, and *tāmen*.

Particles *ma* and *ne*

The particle *ma* is used at the end of a statement to form a question.
    Tā shì Měiguórén. ⇒ Tā shì Měiguórén ma?

The particle *ne* after X means "And what about X?"
    Wǒ hěn hǎo. Nǐ ne?
    Lǐ Wén shì Guìlínrén. Chén Xiàozhǎng ne?

Adverbs

Adverbs should precede verbs in a sentence.

The word *hěn* means "very," but when it precedes a stative verb, it often has little meaning.
    Wǒ hěn hǎo.

The word *yě* means "also." It can precede a verb or another adverb.
    Wǒ yě shì Měiguórén.
    Wǒ yě bú xìng Yáng.
    Wǒ yě hǎo.
    Wǒ yě hěn hǎo.

Possessive marker *de*

The word *de*, used after an appropriate noun or pronoun, marks possession.
    Nǐ de diànhuà hàomǎ shì duōshao?
    Jiālǐ de diànhuà hàomǎ shì duōshao?

Negation with *bù*

The word *bù* is used immediately before a verb or adverb to create a negative statement. It cannot be used to modify nouns.
    Wǒ bú shì Shànghǎirén.
    (NOT: ~~Wǒ bù Shànghǎirén.~~)

▶ Vocabulary

Beginning in Unit 2, vocabulary lists will include Chinese characters as well as English and pinyin. For now, concentrate on learning the sounds and meanings of the words.

Numbers

líng zero
yī one
èr two
sān three
sì four
wǔ five
liù six
qī seven
bā eight
jiǔ nine
shí ten

Pronouns

nǐ you
nǐmen you (plural)
nín you (formal)
tā he, she, it
tāmen they, them
wǒ I, me
wǒmen we, us

Place names

Běijīng Beijing
Déguó Germany
Guìlín Guilin
Jiāzhōu California
Luòshānjī Los Angeles
Měiguó United States
Niǔyuē New York
Shànghǎi Shanghai
Sūzhōu Suzhou
Zhōngguó China

Nouns/noun phrases

Déguórén German (person)
diànhuà hàomǎ telephone number
jiā home
jiālǐ de diànhuà hàomǎ home telephone number
Měiguórén American (person)

míngzi full name, first name
Niǔyuērén New Yorker
shǒujī hàomǎ cell phone number
Zhōngguórén Chinese (person)

Titles

lǎoshī teacher
xiàozhǎng principal

Stative verbs

duì be right
gāo be tall
gāoxìng be happy
hǎo be good
lèi be tired
máng be busy

Equative verbs

jiào be called, have the first name X
shì be
xìng be surnamed, have the last name X

Adverbs

hěn very
yě also, too

Question particles/ words/phrases

duōshao what (number)
ma (question particle)
nǎr where
ne and what about X?
shéi who
shénme what
zěnmeyàng How's it going?

Greetings

hài Hi!
hǎo ma How are you?

nǐ hǎo Hello, good day.
nǐ zǎo Good morning to you.
nín hǎo Hello. (formal)
zǎo Good morning.
zǎoshang hǎo Good morning.

Good-byes

báibái bye-bye
míngtiān jiàn See you tomorrow.
yìhuǐr jiàn See you in a little while.
zàijiàn Good-bye.

Thanks and response

búyòng xiè You're welcome.
xièxie Thank you.

Apology and response

duìbuqǐ I'm sorry.
méi guānxi That's all right. / No problem.

Invitation/request

qǐng Please go ahead of me.
qǐngwèn May I ask . . .

Idiomatic or combinational usages

guìxìng surnamed
nǐ shì nǎr de rén / nǎli rén Where are you from?
nǐ shì něi guó rén What country are you from?
nín guìxìng What's your name? (formal)
qǐng shuō màn yìdiǎnr Please speak a little slower.
qǐng zài shuō yìbiàn Please say it again.
wǒ bù dǒng I don't understand.
wǒ dǒng le I understand.
wǒ jiā zài Běijīng My home is in Beijing.

❱ Checklist of "can do" statements

After completing this unit, you should be able to perform each of the following tasks:

Listening and speaking

- ☐ Greet a friend by name.
- ☐ Greet your teacher by name and title.
- ☐ Say good-bye to your friend.
- ☐ Say good-bye to your teacher.
- ☐ Greet a new friend and provide your name.
- ☐ Ask the name of a new friend.
- ☐ Say where you are from.
- ☐ Ask a new friend where he or she is from.
- ☐ Give someone your telephone number.
- ☐ Ask for your friend's telephone number.
- ☐ Thank a friend.
- ☐ Thank your teacher.
- ☐ Respond to a thank-you from a friend.
- ☐ Apologize to someone.
- ☐ Respond to someone's apology.
- ☐ Say you do not understand.
- ☐ Ask someone to repeat a statement.

Reading and writing

- ☐ Recognize and write some common characters related to introductions.
- ☐ Read and write common phrases related to introductions.
- ☐ Read and write common courtesy phrases.

Understanding culture

- ☐ Name three cities in China.
- ☐ Name three Chinese surnames.
- ☐ Make an accurate statement in English describing Chinese tones.
- ☐ Make an accurate statement in English regarding the use of formal and informal terms for "you" in Chinese.
- ☐ Make an accurate statement about greeting formulas, both Chinese and Western.

Checklist

• Have students work in pairs to go through this checklist and demonstrate selected skills to the class. Reserve 20–30 minutes for students to complete this activity.

• Tell students that putting check marks in each box is NOT the point. The point is to check if they can really do the things on the list.

"Friends from the start"
一見如故
Yíjiànrúgù
Introducing yourself by age, contact information, and relationship to others

In this unit, you will learn how to:

- say, read, and write the numbers 11–100.
- find out someone's age and state your own.
- find out someone's birth date and state your own.
- state your Chinese "astrological" sign based on the year of your birth.
- find out someone's e-mail address and street address and provide your own.

- identify a third party's relationship to yourself.
- understand key information on business cards.
- recognize printed dates.
- read simple self-introductory statements.
- write simple self-introductory statements, including your name, age, birth date, e-mail and street address, and name of teacher.

Encounter 1 Finding out someone's age and stating your own

2.1 Exercise 2.1 is designed to teach students the numbers 11–100 by providing clues that enable them to recognize patterns and figure out the numbers on their own. Let your students learn by doing, even if it takes time and struggle.

2.1 *Getting ready:* *You already know how to read and say the numbers one through ten; learning numbers through 100 is the next step. Fill in the blanks below with pinyin and Chinese characters. Pronounce each number. Note that yìbǎi (100) involves tone sandhi. Remember the rule?*

0 = líng 〇

1 = yī 一

2 = èr 二

3 = sān 三

4 = sì 四

5 = wǔ 五

6 = liù 六

7 = qī 七

8 = bā 八

9 = jiǔ 九

10 = shí 十

11 = shíyī 十一

12 = shí'èr 十二

13 = shísān 十三

14 = shísì 十四

15 = shíwǔ 十五

16 = shíliù 十六

17 = shíqī 十七

18 = shíbā 十八

19 = shíjiǔ 十九

20 = èrshí 二十

21 = èrshíyī 二十一

22 = èrshí'èr 二十二

23 = èrshísān 二十三

24 = èrshísì 二十四

25 = èrshíwǔ 二十五

26 = èrshíliù 二十六

27 = èrshíqī 二十七

28 = èrshíbā 二十八

29 = èrshíjiǔ 二十九

30 = sānshí 三十

31 = sānshíyī 三十一

42 = sìshí'èr 四十二

53 = wǔshísān 五十三

64 = liùshísì 六十四

75 = qīshíwǔ 七十五

86 = bāshíliù 八十六

97 = jiǔshíqī 九十七

98 = jiǔshíbā 九十八

99 = jiǔshíjiǔ 九十九

100 = yìbǎi 一百

2.1 (continued)

• Warm-up: Review numbers 0–10 by asking students to count aloud forward, backward, by even numbers, and by odd numbers.

• Have students work in pairs or small groups to complete this exercise and then compare their answers with multiple classmates.

• When students have questions, encourage them to first ask their classmates to see if anyone knows the answer.

• Circulate around the classroom to monitor progress and assist as necessary.

2.2 *With a partner or small group, take turns saying the numbers 1–100 forward, backward, by odd numbers, by even numbers, by fives, and by tens.*

yī, sān, wǔ, qī ...

2.2 • Mingle around the classroom to observe how fluently students can say these numbers.

• Give students enough time to do this exercise. Knowing the numbers and fluently saying them are different skills. After 2.1, students will *know* the numbers. 2.2 is designed for students to practice *saying* the numbers.

• When you feel students are ready, challenge them to complete the following activity.

1. Students secretly write down five random numbers on a piece of scratch paper.
2. Students take turns reading their numbers aloud to a partner who writes down what he or she hears.
3. Students then verify answers with each other after the dictation.

2.3 加 (jiā) *means "add" or "plus";* 减／減 (jiǎn) *means "minus" or "subtract";* 等於／等于 (děngyú) *means "equals, be equal to." What do you think the following statements mean?*

一加一等於二／一加一等于二

二減一等於一／二减一等于一

Make as many of these "math statements" as you can in one minute.

2.4 *Complete the following statements using Arabic numerals.*

三十一加十等於／三十一加十等于 _____

十九加七十八等於／十九加七十八等于 _____

五十四加四十等於／五十四加四十等于 _____

九十減二等於／九十减二等于 _____

六十七減十四等於／六十七减十四等于 _____

八十三減五十六等於／八十三减五十六等于 _____

2.5 *View Episode 2 of the dramatic series.*

2.6 *What would you say in English to ask someone's age and to state your own? Would you use different language with people of different ages? Make a list.*

_____

_____

_____

2.3 • Have students complete this exercise in pairs.
• Make sure that students understand the meaning of the two statements: "one plus one equals two" and "two minus one equals one."
• Circulate around the room, observing performance and providing assistance as necessary.

2.4 • Have students work in pairs to assist each other.
• When students ask you a question directly, make every attempt to pose the question back to the entire class. Remind students to use their partners as support.
• Have students compare their answers with multiple classmates, and then invite volunteers to share the answers on the board.

2.4 Key:
41
97
94
88
53
27

2.5 Play the video once, and ask students to relax and take in as much as they can.

2.6 • Possible answers: *How old are you? I am 19. He is turning 40 next year. I think she is in her 50s.* The goal of this activity is to encourage students to think about how we talk about age in real life.
• Invite students to answer "popcorn style." In other words, students volunteer answers spontaneously without raising their hands. This process should be quick and lively; students "pop" up their answers in rapid succession like popcorn popping.
• Have volunteers write answers on the board or on chart paper. Keep this list, and make sure to revisit it after completing this unit to check if students have learned enough Chinese to say everything on the list. The purpose of this activity is to help students connect what they're learning with real-life communication needs.

2.7–2.8 Have students read the instructions before you play the audio segment, and allow them to work in pairs to assist each other. Replay and pause the segment as needed, but make sure students have time to discuss answers. Invite volunteers to write the answers on the board.

2.7 *Watch and listen to the video segment. Then fill in the blanks below.*

2.7 Key:

a. How old are you?
b. 24

a. What do you think *Nǐ duō dà le* means? _____

b. Tang Yuan is _____ years old.

2.8 Key:

a. 5
b. 1
c. 2
d. 6
e. 4
f. 3

2.8 *Match the Chinese and English below.*

a. Nǐ duō dà le? Nǐ jǐ suì le?

你多大了？你幾歲了？／

你多大了？你几岁了？

1. *I'm eighteen years old.*

b. Wǒ shíbā suì le.

我十八歲了。／

我十八岁了。

2. *Oh, you're nineteen.*

c. Ò, nǐ shíjiǔ suì le.

噢，你十九歲了。／

噢，你十九岁了。

3. *I am, too.*

d. Nǐ ne?

你呢？

4. *I am eighteen years old, too.*

e. Wǒ yě shíbā suì le.

我也十八歲了。／

我也十八岁了。

5. *How old are you?*

f. Wǒ yě shì.

我也是。

6. *How about you?*

Grammar Bits 语法点滴

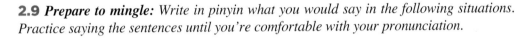

Sentences without verbs

Notice that when asking about or giving age, the number alone + *suì* suffices. No verb, such as *shì*, is required. In Chinese, when giving standard formulas such as age, price, or even one's place of origin (*Wǒ Běijīngrén*), no verb is required, although it is not wrong to include it.

However, in the negative, a verb is always required: *Wǒ bú shì qīshíwǔ suì, wǒ qīshíliù suì.*

2.9 *Prepare to mingle:* *Write in pinyin what you would say in the following situations. Practice saying the sentences until you're comfortable with your pronunciation.*

a. Ask a classmate his or her age.

_____

b. Confirm that you understand, once someone has told you his or her age (for example, "Oh, you're 19!").

_____

c. Respond when someone asks you your age.

_____

2.10 *Mingling:* *Move around the room, asking classmates their ages and stating your own in reply.*

FYI 供你参考

Calculating age

Chinese do not calculate age as people in many other cultures do. They actually count the time in the womb, so when you're born, you're already one. And when Chinese New Year comes around (late January to mid-February)—it doesn't matter in what month you're born in your birth year—you're two! Perhaps for this reason, when Chinese ask others their age, they often include the word *jīnnián* (this year). *Nǐ jīnnián duō dà le?* (How old are you this [calendar] year? / How old are you [currently]?)

When a Chinese asks someone older than 60 his or her age, different language is used to indicate respect: *Nín (jīnnián) duō dà suìshu le? Wǒ qīshíwǔ le.*

Nín jīnnián duō dà suìshu le?

Wǒ qīshíwǔ (le).

2.11 • Have students read
the instructions before you
play the video.

• Have students work in pairs to
assist each other.

• Replay and pause the video as
needed, but make sure students have
time to discuss answers.

• Invite volunteers to write the
answers on the board.

2.11 Key: b

2.12 • This exercise is designed for
students to use appropriate language
in different situations.

• Prepare the following items before
class:

1. masking tape

2. pictures of people clipped
from magazines, catalogs,
newspapers, etc. (Additional
pictures can be found on the
Internet.)

• Have the class brainstorm and list
appropriate questions and statements
about age that they already know in
Chinese.

• Have students suggest answers
"popcorn" style, and invite a
volunteer to write the suggestions on
the board.

• If necessary, remind students to
review exercises 2.8 and 2.11 and
the FYI box on page 45 for possible
suggestions.

• Consider having a confident pair
demonstrate the conversation before
the entire class mingles.

• Circulate around the classroom
and provide assistance as necessary.

Grammar Bits

If students have questions about the
meaning and usage of the particle
le, direct them to read this Grammar
Bits section on their own.

2.11 *Watch and listen to the video segment. What is the appropriate way to ask this person his age, from what you gathered in the segment? Check one.*

☐ a. Nǐ duō dà le?

你多大了？

☐ b. Nín duō dà suìshu le?

您多大歲數了？／您多大岁数了？

☐ c. Nǐ jǐ suì le?

你幾歲了？／你几岁了？

2.12 *Mingling: Your teacher will hand you an image of a person. Tape this image to your chest; you now "are" this person. Move around the classroom and ask each of your classmates his or her age. Remember to be appropriately deferential to seniors.*

Grammar Bits 语法点滴

Changing things up with *le*

You may have noticed the use of the particle *le* in some of the sentences in this Encounter. (*Nǐ jīnnián duō dà le?*) Using *le* indicates a newly arising situation, or a change in the current state of affairs. Change is easily seen with respect to age, since our age is constantly changing over time. Therefore, a literal translation of *Nǐ jīnnián duō dà le?* might be "How old have you **gotten to be**?" or "How old are you **now**?" After the response to such a question is given, a Chinese person will often use *le* to confirm the response, as a form of endearment for a child or respect for an elder, but leave it off for someone close in age. Thus: *Ò, nǐ jiǔ suì le!* (Wow, you're 9 already; [you grew so fast!]) or *Nín jiǔshí le!* (You're 90! [Congratulations!]), but *Ò, nǐ èrshí suì* (Oh, you're 20).

Another example of a change in the current state of affairs was practiced in Unit 1. After the teacher explains a point and asks if you understand, you can reply with *Wǒ dǒng le* (I understand *now* [I didn't before]). We will discover that *le* has many uses, and you'll learn more about them in future lessons.

Encounter 2 Finding out someone's age and stating your own—Chinese style

2.13 *Getting ready: Have you heard about the Chinese zodiac? Each year in the zodiacal cycle is marked by a "birth sign" (shēngxiào) which is symbolized by one of twelve animals. The twelve signs complete a continually recurring cycle of twelve years. Can you name any Chinese zodiac signs? Close your book and write down as many as you can on a separate sheet of paper.*

 2.14 *Watch and listen to the video. Number the images below in the order in which you hear the speakers name them.*

2.13 Have students work in pairs or small groups to brainstorm a list.

Shí'èr shēngxiào

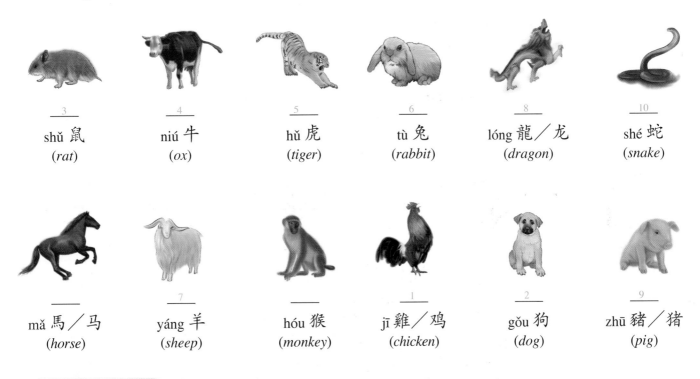

3	4	5	6	8	10
shǔ 鼠 (rat)	niú 牛 (ox)	hǔ 虎 (tiger)	tù 兔 (rabbit)	lóng 龍／龙 (dragon)	shé 蛇 (snake)

	7		1	2	9
mǎ 馬／马 (horse)	yáng 羊 (sheep)	hóu 猴 (monkey)	jī 雞／鸡 (chicken)	gǒu 狗 (dog)	zhū 豬／猪 (pig)

FYI 供你参考

The Chinese zodiac

In the Chinese zodiac, the year of your birth links you to your birth sign, and you symbolically take on the characteristics of the associated animal. If you're an ox, for example, you're hard-working, loyal, warm, and sincere. In addition to its astrological uses, the Chinese zodiac has a perhaps more practical application: one can guess the year a person was born if one knows the person's birth sign. See the chart on the next page for your sign. It's interesting to note that the English word "zodiac" is derived from the Greek "zodiakos kyklos" and means, curiously enough, "circle of animals."

The Chinese zodiac

The Chinese zodiac is likely common knowledge to many Americans. If students are interested, they can read this FYI for fun on their own.

FYI 供你参考

What's your sign?

If you were born in January or early February, this chart may not be accurate for you, since the lunar New Year, on which the Chinese zodiac is based, does not begin until late January or February. Go to chinesezodiac.com to determine your accurate birth sign and for more information about the lore of the Chinese zodiac.

2.15 *What do you think the following question means? Write the English.*

Nǐ shǔ shénme? 你屬什麼？／你属什么？

_____

Consult the chart below and fill in the blank with your birth sign.

Wǒ shǔ _____. 我屬／我属 _____。

2.15 • Make sure students understand that the question here means "What's your sign?"

• Remind students to use exercise 2.14 and the FYI notes on pages 47 and 48 to help determine their birth signs.

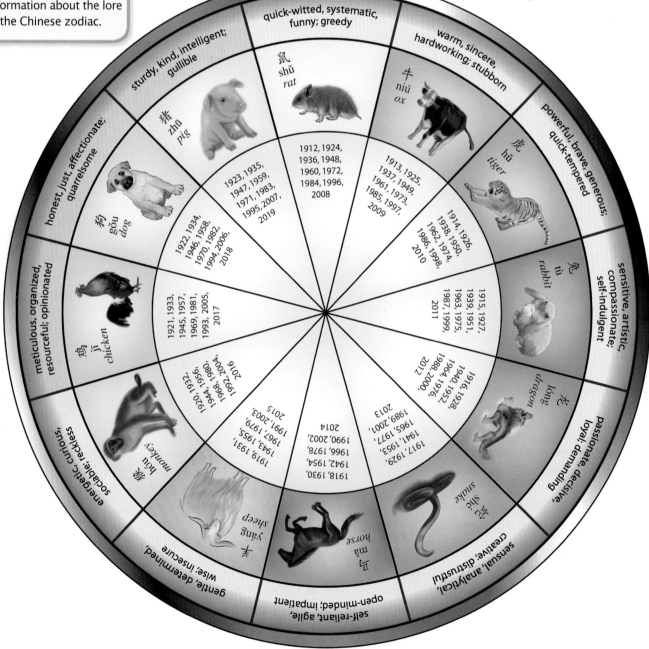

2.16 *Mingling: Walk around the room and find out your classmates' signs. Consult the chart and, using their answers, try to figure out whether they are the same age as, older than, or younger than you.*

2.17 *Homework: Outside of class, determine the birth signs of three people. Draw a picture or bring a photograph of each person, and note approximately how old each one is (for example, "in her 40s"). Use this information to report your findings to the class.*

Encounter 3   Finding out someone's birth date and stating your own

▶ Months of the year

2.18 *If January is yīyuè or 一月, write the names of the remaining eleven months in either pinyin or characters (or both) in the blanks below.*

February   _____

March   _____

April   _____

May   _____

June   _____

July   _____

August   _____

September   _____

October   _____

November   _____

December   _____

2.19 *Pair work: With a partner, take turns saying each month of the year. After you go through the sequence once, repeat so you each have an opportunity to say every month. Repeat this process until you are both comfortable with the sequence. Finally, test each other on the Chinese names of the months by dictating random months for your partner to translate.*

2.16 • Write the following sentences on the board and introduce them to students:

1. Wǒmen yǒu . . . ge rén bǐ wǒ dà. (*We have . . . people older than I.*)
2. Wǒmen yǒu . . . ge rén bǐ wǒ xiǎo. (*We have . . . people younger than I.*)
3. Wǒmen yǒu . . . ge rén gēn wǒ yíyàng dà. (*We have . . . people who are the same age as I.*)

• Determining the information to complete these sentences accurately is the goal for the interviews students will conduct in class. Tell students to take notes if they find it helpful.

• During the activity, mingle with your students to monitor progress and assist as necessary.

• Finally, have students use the sentence frames to share their survey results with a partner or the entire class.

2.18 Key:

èryuè 二月
sānyuè 三月
sìyuè 四月
wǔyuè 五月
liùyuè 六月
qīyuè 七月
bāyuè 八月
jiǔyuè 九月
shíyuè 十月
shíyīyuè 十一月
shí'èryuè 十二月

2.19 • Make sure students read the instructions and understand the task that is expected of them.

• During the activity, circulate around the room to observe performance and provide assistance if necessary.

2.20 This exercise allows students to infer the pattern for saying dates in Chinese, based on the example in the direction line. Do not explicitly teach the construction; this would take away an important learning opportunity from students.

❱ Days of the month

2.20 *If January 1 is* yīyuè yīhào *or* 一月一號／一月一号, *write the following dates in either pinyin or characters (or both) in the blanks below.*

January
19

yīyuè shíjiǔhào
一月十九 號／号

February
14

èryuè shísìhào
二月十四 號／号

March
17

sānyuè shíqīhào
三月十七 號／号

April
1

sìyuè yīhào
四月一 號／号

May
1

wǔyuè yīhào
五月一 號／号

June
21

liùyuè èrshíyīhào
六月二十一 號／号

July
4

qīyuè sìhào
七月四 號／号

August
26

bāyuè èrshíliùhào
八月二十六 號／号

September
28

jiǔyuè èrshíbāhào
九月二十八 號／号

October
31

shíyuè sānshíyīhào
十月三十一 號／号

November
4

shíyīyuè sìhào
十一月四 號／号

December
25

shí'èryuè èrshíwǔhào
十二月二十五 號／号

2.21 *Pair work: With a partner, take turns saying a date in Chinese. Respond to your partner by saying the date in English.*

2.22 Key:
Táng Yuǎn: sìyuè shíbāhào
Lynn: qīyuè sānshíhào

2.22 *Watch and listen to the video segment. Write each person's birth date in either pinyin or characters (or both) below.*

Táng Yuǎn: _____   Lynn: _____

FYI 供你参考

The Chinese calendar

For at least 4,000 years, China followed what is called a lunisolar calendar, with months determined by the phases of the moon (there are 30 days a month, from new moon on the first of the lunar month to full moon on the fifteenth and back) and "leap months" added to synchronize with the movement of the sun. On October 10, 1929, China adopted the Western (solar) calendar for official business, but informally still noted the passage of time through the traditional calendar. Chinese New Year is generally the second new moon (on very rare occasions, the third new moon) after the winter solstice; it usually falls between January 21 and February 20 in any given year and is celebrated for a full month.

The Chinese calendar
Have students read this FYI in class, then check comprehension by asking the following questions: *Traditionally, what calendar was used in China? How does it work? What calendar is used for official business in China today? Why does the Chinese New Year often fall at the end of January or beginning of February on the Western calendar?*

 2.23 *Watch and listen to the video for exercise 2.22 again. How do you ask about the specific day of someone's birthday? Fill in the blanks.*

Nǐ de shēngrì shì ____yuè ____hào?

你的生日是幾月幾號？／你的生日是几月几号？

Fill in the blanks below with the appropriate numbers to indicate your birthday.

Wǒ de shēngrì shì ____yuè ____hào.

我的生日是 __月 __ 號／号。

2.24 *Now write the English meanings of the items below.*

shēngrì 生日 _____

jǐ 幾／几 _____

2.25 *Mingling: Walk around and find out your classmates' birthdays. Then arrange yourselves in a line, organized chronologically by birthday (the student with the earliest birthday should stand at the front of the line). Once everyone has found his or her appropriate place in line, you each state your birthday, beginning with the first student in line.*

FYI 供你参考

Talking about dates

When talking about dates, the word *hào* 號 / 号 is most commonly used, as in *bāyuè wǔ hào*. *Bāyuè wǔ rì* is also used in speech, although it is more formal and less common. *Rì* 日 means "sun" and, by extension, "day." So, *shēng* + *rì* (birth + day) ⇒ "birthday."

2.23 Key:
a. Nǐ de shēngrì shì jǐ yuè jǐ hào?
b. Answers for students' own birthdays will vary.

2.24 Key:
birthday
how many (a question word to elicit numbers)

2.25 • Check to make sure students know the question and answer needed to complete this task. Tell them to refer to exercise 2.23 if they need help. Invite volunteers to write the question and answer on board.

• Demonstrate the correct exchange with two or three students.

• As students mingle and practice asking about birthdays, circulate around the classroom to participate. Observe performance and provide assistance if necessary.

2.26 *Watch and listen to the video segment. Then fill in the blanks below.*

a. What are the two numbers you hear in this exchange? _____ and _____

b. What do you think *nián* 年 means? _____

c. What do you think the following means? Write the English.

Nǐ shì něi nián shēng de? 你是哪年生的？ _____

d. Fill in the blanks with your own year of birth.

Wǒ shì _____ nián shēng de. 我是_____年生的。

Grammar Bits 语法点滴

The *shì . . . de* construction

When an event has already happened and the interest is in the specifics (when, why, where, how, etc.) of the event, Chinese uses the *shì . . . de* construction to zero in on the specifics.

The pattern is: Subject + ***shì*** + specific information + verb + ***de***.

Examples:

Nǐ **shì** něi nián shēng **de**? Wǒ **shì** <u>yī-jiǔ-bā-jiǔ nián</u> shēng **de**.
(In which year were you born? I was born in 1989.
⇒ *It was <u>in 1989</u> that I was born.)*

Nǐ **shì** jǐ yuè jǐ hào shēng **de**? Wǒ **shì** <u>bāyuè shíbā hào</u> shēng **de**.
(On which day were you born? I was born on August 18.
⇒ *It was <u>on August 18</u> that I was born.)*

We will learn more about the *shì . . . de* construction in future Encounters. Notice that, in Chinese, verbs do not change form; they don't conjugate to match number, gender, tense, or anything else. Verbs are constant and invariable. You will learn to indicate tense and other grammatical points primarily by adding words. Here's an example: A Chinese might answer the question "How are you feeling?" by saying *Wǒ jīntiān hěn hǎo, zuótiān bù hǎo.* Try to figure out the meaning and, in the process, learn a bit about tense in Chinese.

2.27 *Listen and write down the birth dates as you hear them.*

Elizabeth I
Year: _1533_
Month: _September_
Day: _7_

Napoleon Bonaparte
Year: _1769_
Month: _August_
Day: _15_

Ludwig van Beethoven
Year: _1770_
Month: _December_
Day: _16_

Abraham Lincoln
Year: _1809_
Month: _February_
Day: _12_

Florence Nightingale
Year: _1820_
Month: _May_
Day: _12_

Sun Yat-Sen
Year: _1866_
Month: _November_
Day: _12_

Mahatma Gandhi
Year: _1869_
Month: October
Day: _2_

Jackie Chan
Year: _1954_
Month: _April_
Day: _7_

Amy Tan
Year: _1952_
Month: _February_
Day: _19_

Barack Obama
Year: _1961_
Month: _August_
Day: _4_

Zhang Ziyi
Year: _1979_
Month: _February_
Day: _9_

Rihanna
Year: _1988_
Month: _February_
Day: _20_

2.28 *Mingling: Walk around, find out your classmates' dates of birth (including year), and write them on a copy of your roster. Remember, express a year by saying it "telephone style," digit by digit, just as you would say your telephone number (diànhuà hàomǎ). 1987 = yī-jiǔ-bā-qī nián.*

Nǐ shì něi nián shēng de? Shēngrì shì jǐ yuè jǐ hào?

Wǒ shì _____ nián shēng de. Shēngrì shì ____ yuè ____ hào.

Encounter 4 Finding out someone's e-mail and street address and stating your own

▶ Asking for someone's e-mail address

2.29 *Watch and listen to the video segment. Can you figure out what each of the following means? Fill in the blanks below in English.*

e-mail dìzhǐ: _____   diànyóu dìzhǐ: _____

diànzi yóuxiāng: _____

FYI 供你參考

Translation vs. transliteration

Foreign terms, products, and names are rendered into Chinese in at least two different ways. "Hot dog" combines the Chinese words for "hot" and "dog," yielding *règǒu* 熱狗／热狗. This is <u>translation</u>. In the second process, <u>transliteration</u>, "McDonald's" becomes *Màidāngláo* 麥當勞／麦当劳, which simply combines Chinese sounds similar to the sounds of the original foreign name. Transliteration is often done with little or no meaning intended in the new Chinese word. Syllables with bad connotations are, of course, avoided. Sometimes words are both translated and transliterated. For example, "e-mail" becomes *yīmèir* 伊妹兒／依妹儿 when transliterated, and *diànzǐ yóujiàn* 電子郵件／电子邮件 (electronic mail) when translated. The latter term is now commonly abbreviated as *diànyóu* 電郵／电邮. Sometimes, the English term "e-mail" is used without translation or transliteration. If you do separate Internet searches, you'll get the most hits for "e-mail 地址," followed by "電郵地址／电邮地址," and the fewest hits for "伊妹兒地址／伊妹儿地址." This indicates that the English term "e-mail" is far more commonly used by the Chinese than either the translated term *diànyóu* or the transliterated term *yīmèir*. In this age of high-tech, rapid Westernization, and the spread of English all over the world, certain terms are more commonly used in their original English form than in the Chinese equivalent term. "E-mail" is the best example.

2.30 *Fill in your own e-mail address in the blanks below.*

Q: Nǐ de diànyóu dìzhǐ shì shénme?
    你的電郵地址是甚麼？／你的电邮地址是什么？

A: Wǒ de diànyóu dìzhǐ shì _____.
    我的電郵地址是 _____。
    我的电邮地址是 _____。

2.31 *Mingling: Using your class roster, find out the e-mail addresses of 5–10 classmates. Helpful questions to determine if what you've written is correct include* Zhè yàng duì ma? *(Is this correct?) or* Zhè yàng duì bu duì? *(Is this correct or not?)*

Grammar Bits 语法点滴

Take your pick: *ma* vs. *bu*

You have already learned that questions may be formed by simply adding the query particle *ma* to a statement. Another way of asking questions is to use *bu* to provide verbal alternatives—positive and negative choices—and "invite" the other person to pick one and thus answer the question. The following are different ways to ask "Is this right?":

Zhè yàng duì ma? 這樣對嗎？／这样对吗？ *(Is this right?)* OR
Zhè yàng duì bu duì? 這樣對不對？／这样对不对？ *(Is this right or not?)*

These two question forms are interchangeable. Note that the negative adverb *bu* is not stressed in this case. To answer the question, simply reply with *Duì* OR *Bú duì*.

▶ Asking for a street address

 2.32 *Watch and listen to the video segment. How do you ask where someone lives? Write the pinyin below.*

_____

FYI 供你参考

Chinese addresses

Chinese addresses, like Chinese names, move from large to small units. To write to the President of the United States, for example, the address would appear as follows, according to Chinese custom:

USA	美國／美国
Washington, D.C.	華盛頓／华盛顿
Pennsylvania Avenue, #1600	賓夕法尼亞大道1600號／宾夕法尼亚大道1600 号
To: President So-and-so	某某總統收／某某总统收

2.33 *Match the corresponding terms below.*

a. *M street*

b. *(single) house number 123*

c. *apartment building number 123*

d. *apartment number 123*

1. 123 shì 室

2. 123 hào lóu 號樓／号楼

3. 123 hào 號／号

4. M jiē 街

2.34 *Watch and listen to the video segment from exercise 2.32 again. Match the columns and then number the items by the order in which Chen Feng says them.*

_____ a. Hebei Province   1. Tángshān shì

_____ b. Heping Avenue   2. Héběi shěng

_____ c. #100   3. yì bǎi hào

_____ d. Tangshan City   4. Hépíng dàjiē

2.35 *Fill in the blanks with your own address.*

Q: Nǐ jiā zhù nǎr?

你家住哪兒？／你家住哪儿？

A: (for a single-family house)

Wǒ jiā zhù _____ jiē, _____ hào.

我家住_____街，_____號／号 。

(for a multiple-unit building)

Wǒ jiā zhù _____ jiē, _____ hào lóu, _____ shì.

我家住_____街，_____號樓／号楼，_____室。

2.36 *Pair work: Exchange addresses with one or more classmates, using the question and answer formula above.*

Encounter 5 Identifying a third party's relationship to yourself

2.37 *Watch and listen to the video segment. What does* tóngxué *mean?*

☐ teacher   ☐ classmate

2.38 *Watch and listen to the video segment. Then complete each of the following sentences.*

a. The woman in pink is introducing Miss Wang, who is her . . .   ☐ good friend.   ☐ colleague.

b. Twice, the woman in the hat introduces Rongzhen, who is her . . .   ☐ good friend.   ☐ colleague.

c. Chen Feng introduces Wang Li, who is his . . .   ☐ good friend.   ☐ colleague.

2.39 *Watch and listen to the video segment. Then match the corresponding items below.*

a. *relative*   1. línjū 鄰居   A. 亲戚

b. *neighbor*   2. qīnqi 親戚   B. 邻居

 2.40 *Watch and listen to the video segment. Then match the corresponding items below.*

a. *professor* ——— 1. jiàoshòu 教授   A. 学生

b. *teacher*   2. tóngxué 同學   B. 教授

c. *student*   3. lǎoshī 老師   C. 老师

d. *classmate*   4. xuéshēng 學生   D. 同学

Grammar Bits 语法点滴

"This," "that," and some other things

Zhè (this) and *nà* (that) are called "specifiers" (SP) in Chinese. Both are used as subjects in expressions. For example: *Zhè kāfēi hěn hǎo* (This is great coffee). When followed by a measure word, *zhè* and *nà* usually appear as *zhèi* and *nèi*. For example: *Zhèi ge xuéshēng* (This [measure word] student). Measures (also called classifiers) are used to indicate or count people and things. Specific nouns usually require specific measures. For example, *wèi* is used as a polite measure to show respect for persons. Measures are always used when a noun is accompanied by a number; for example: *Nèi sān wèi lǎoshī* (Those three teachers). As you learn more nouns, you will also learn their appropriate measure words.

 2.41 *Watch and listen to the video. What do you think* Zhèi wèi shì nǐ de shénme rén *means? Write the English.*

_____

Note: The above question in its full form, as seen here, may be considered too blunt and direct. It is often shortened to simply Zhèi wèi shì . . . ? *(And this is . . . ?).*

2.42 *Mingling: Draw a simple sketch of three people you know. Walk among your classmates, sharing your pictures and looking at theirs. Ask your classmates to identify the people in their pictures, and respond to their questions in return. Use the dialogue below.*

Q: Zhèi wèi shì (nǐ de shénme rén)?

這位是（你的甚麼人）？／这位是（你的什么人）？

A: Zhèi wèi shì wǒ de _____. Tā jiào _____.

這／这位是我的 _____。他叫 _____。

qīnqi 親戚／亲戚; péngyou 朋友; tóngxué 同學／同学; tóngshì 同事;

lǎoshī 老師／老师; xuéshēng 學生／学生; línjū 鄰居／邻居

🎵 **Unit Rap**

Go to the **Encounters** website at www.EncountersChinese.com *and listen to the song to review key expressions from Unit 2. Listen again and sing along!*

Encounter 6 Reading and writing

▶ Reading familiar sentences in Chinese characters

2.43 • Have students work in pairs to complete this activity. Avoid reading this dialogue aloud for your students or having them repeat after you. Tell them to use the English as a bridge to determine the sound for these characters.

• Students will likely see unfamiliar characters and ask you what they are. Encourage students to figure it out on their own, even if it takes some struggle. Tell them to use characters they already know and the English translations as hints to "guess" at the meaning and sound of the unknown characters.

• Keep in mind that reading fluency is not the goal of this activity. Tell students not to get discouraged if they have trouble reading quickly and accurately.

• Have students complete this exercise multiple times before they move on to 2.44 and 2.45.

2.43 *Pair work: Read the following dialogues (written in traditional characters) aloud with a partner, using the English as a guide. Note: In Chinese texts, numbers are almost always written in Arabic numerals, both for convenience and space-saving. However, be sure to "pronounce" them in Chinese. It's good practice. Exception: Read the e-mail address as you would normally.*

FYI 供你参考

Listing things in Chinese fashion

The ancient Chinese (about 4,000 years ago) began a system with ten "Celestial Stems" (天干 *tiāngān*) and 12 "Earthly Branches" (地支 *dìzhī*) to enumerate dates in cycles of 60 years. The 天干地支 system continues to this day. "Celestial Stems" consist of the following characters:

甲 *jiǎ*, 乙 *yǐ*, 丙 *bǐng*, 丁 *dīng*, 戊 *wù*, 己 *jǐ*, 庚 *gēng*, 辛 *xīn*, 壬 *rén*, 癸 *guǐ*

These characters are commonly used as a numbering system in modern China, Japan, Korea, and Vietnam, much as Roman numerals (I, II, III) or letters of the alphabet (A, B, C) are used in the West. 甲 and 乙 represent "A" and "B" in this unit's dialogues.

1 甲：你幾歲了？ (*How old are you?*)
乙：我八歲了。 (*I'm eight.*)
甲：他呢？ (*How about him?*)
乙：他兩歲，很小。 (*He's two; he's little.*)

2 甲：你多大了？ (*How old are you?*)
乙：我二十八了。 (*I'm 28.*)

3 甲：您多大歲數了？ (*How old are you?*)
乙：我七十五了。 (*I'm 75.*)

4 甲：你屬甚麼？ *(What's your sign?)*

乙：我屬＿＿＿。 *(I'm a ＿＿＿.)*

> 鼠 *(rat)*; 牛 *(ox)*; 虎 *(tiger)*; 兔 *(rabbit)*; 龍 *(dragon)*; 蛇 *(snake)*;
> 馬 *(horse)*; 羊 *(sheep)*; 猴 *(monkey)*; 雞 *(chicken)*; 狗 *(dog)*; 豬 *(pig)*

5 甲：你是哪年生的？你的生日是幾月幾號？
(Which year were you born in? When is your birthday?)

乙：我是１９７８年生的，我的生日是一月一號。
(I was born in 1978; my birthday is January 1.)

6 甲：你的 e-mail 地址是甚麼？ *(What is your e-mail address?)*

乙：我的 e-mail 地址是 123abc@EncountersChinese.com.
(My e-mail address is 123abc@EncountersChinese.com.)

7 甲：你家住哪兒？ *(Where do you live?)*

乙：我家住南京路１２３號。 *(I live at 123 Nanjing Road.)*

8 甲：這位是你的甚麼人？ *(What is this person's relationship to you?)*

乙：那是我的＿＿＿。 *(That's my ＿＿＿.)*

> 親戚 *(relative)*; 朋友 *(friend)*; 同學 *(classmate)*; 同事 *(colleague)*;
> 老師 *(teacher)*; 學生 *(student)*; 鄰居 *(neighbor)*

2.44 Pair work: *Read the dialogues aloud with a partner, this time without any English.*

1 甲：你幾歲了？
乙：我八歲了。
甲：他呢？
乙：他兩歲，很小。

2 甲：你多大了？
乙：我二十八了。

2.44-2.45

• Have students read these dialogues multiple times, focusing on reading fluency.

• Encourage students to *not* refer to exercise 2.43 for help. Instead, ask them to rely on their partners to help them read new characters. Tell them to practice being each other's teacher.

• After students practice reading the dialogues a few times, play the audio and have them check their pronunciation.

3 甲：您多大歲數了？

乙：我七十五了。

4 甲：你屬甚麼？

乙：我屬＿＿＿。

> 鼠，牛，虎，兔，龍，蛇，馬，羊，猴，雞，狗，豬

5 甲：你是哪年生的？你的生日是幾月幾號？

乙：我是１９７８年生的，我的生日是一月一號。

6 甲：你的 e-mail 地址是甚麼？

乙：我的 e-mail 地址是 123abc@EncountersChinese.com.

7 甲：你家住哪兒？

乙：我家住南京路１２３號。

8 甲：這位是你的甚麼人？

乙：那是我的＿＿＿。

> 親戚，朋友，同學，同事，老師，學生，鄰居

2.45 Pair work: *Read the dialogues aloud one more time, this time with simplified characters.*

1 甲：你几岁了？

乙：我八岁了。

甲：他呢？

乙：他两岁，很小。

2 甲：你多大了？

乙：我二十八了。

3 甲：您多大岁数了？

乙：我七十五了。

4 甲：你属什么？
乙：我属_____。

鼠，牛，虎，兔，龙，蛇，马，羊，猴，鸡，狗，猪

5 甲：你是哪年生的？你的生日是几月几号？
乙：我是１９７８年生的，我的生日是一月一号。

6 甲：你的 e-mail 地址是什么？
乙：我的 e-mail 地址是 123abc@EncountersChinese.com.

7 甲：你家住哪儿？
乙：我家住南京路１２３号。

8 甲：这位是你的什么人？
乙：那是我的_____。

亲戚，朋友，同学，同事，老师，学生，邻居

2.46 *Match the corresponding simplified characters, traditional characters, and English.*

a. 学生　　　1. 屬馬　　　A. *what day (of the month)*
b. 亲戚　　　2. 哪兒　　　B. *how old (of age)*
c. 什么　　　3. 鄰居　　　C. *classmate*
d. 几岁　　　4. 同學　　　D. *relative*
e. 同学　　　5. 學生　　　E. *age*
f. 老师　　　6. 歲數　　　F. *neighbor*
g. 岁数　　　7. 甚麼　　　G. *what*
h. 属马　　　8. 幾號　　　H. *where*
i. 邻居　　　9. 親戚　　　I. *teacher*
j. 哪儿　　　10. 老師　　　J. *student*
k. 几号　　　11. 幾歲　　　K. *be born in the Year of the Horse*

2.46 • Have students complete this exercise in pairs, if necessary.
• Encourage students to use previous exercises in this unit to find answers.
• Have students compare their answers with multiple classmates.
• Invite volunteers to share answers on the board.

2.46 Key:
a. 5. J
b. 9. D
c. 7. G
d. 11. B
e. 4. C
f. 10. I
g. 6. E
h. 1. K
i. 3. F
j. 2. H
k. 8. A

▶ Reading real-life texts

2.47–2.50 If possible, copy
this page to a transparency so you
can project it on the board. Invite
volunteers to circle the appropriate
characters in the real-life texts.

2.47 Key:

a. i. 工安琪
    ii. 电话
    iii. 电子信箱
b. 2, 1, 4, 3
c. fax number
d. simplified

2.47 *Look at the business card and answer the following questions.*

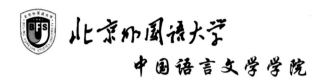

北京外国语大学
中国语言文学学院

丁安琪

副教授
院长助理
汉语培训中心主任

地址：北京市海淀区西三环北路2号
邮编：100089
电话：(010) 88816442
传真：(010) 88818140
电子信箱：dinganqi@bfsu.edu.cn

a. Please circle and number the following.

   i. Name (Underline the last name.)

   ii. The term for "telephone"

   iii. The term for "e-mail"

b. The address is 中国 ⇒ 北京 ⇒ 西三环北路 ⇒ 二号

   Number the following items to match the Chinese sequencing.

   ___ Beijing

   ___ China

   ___ #2

   ___ West Third Ring North Road

c. What do you think the number 88818140 is? Circle one:

   fax number   home telephone number

d. Which form of Chinese characters is used? Circle one:

   simplified   traditional

2.48 *Look at the business card and answer the following questions.*

台灣華語文教學學會
Association of Teaching Chinese as a Second Language

理事長 | 信世昌 博士
國立台灣師範大學華語文教學研究所 教授

網站 | http://www.atcsl.org
電話 | 02-2341-9812 分機10   電子信箱 | hsins@ntnu.edu.tw
傳真 | 02-2341-9746   地址 | 台北市和平東路一段162號 師大華研所

a. Please circle and number the following.

   i. Name (Underline the last name.)

   ii. The term for "telephone"

   iii. The term for "fax"

   iv. The term for "e-mail address"

   v. The term for "street address"

b. The address is 台北市 ⇒ 和平東路 ⇒ 一段 ⇒ 162 號

   Number the following items to match the Chinese sequencing.

   ___ Heping (Peace) Road East

   ___ #162

   ___ Section 1

   ___ Taipei City

c. Which form of Chinese characters is used? Circle one:

   simplified   traditional

2.49 *Look at the newspaper banner and answer the following questions.*

2.49 Key:

a. i. September 25, 2009
   ii. 中華民國九十八年/2009年9月25日
b. 日
c. 月
d. August 7 (八月七日)
e. traditional

a. Please circle and number the following:

   i. Date in English

   ii. Date in Chinese

b. Can you find and label the character for "sun"? Here, it means "day," as in "daily newspaper."

c. Can you find and label the character for "moon"? It's in an ad for moon cakes—a traditional Chinese dessert for the mid-Autumn Festival.

d. Can you find the lunar calendar date? It's different from the Western calendar date.

   Write the date in English: _____

e. Which form of Chinese characters is used? Circle one:

   simplified   traditional

2.50 Key:

a. i. 2009 年 9 月 25 日
   ii. 星期五
b. Friday
c. i. 麦迪臣街148A华榕大厦一楼
   ii. 福州市湖东路168号宏利大厦（公寓楼）27层
d. simplified

2.50 *Look at the newspaper banner and answer the following questions.*

a. Please circle and number the following:

   i. Date in Chinese

   ii. Day of the week

b. What is the day of the week? Write in English: _____

c. There is an ad for an insurance company. Please circle and number the following:

   i. The address in New York

   ii. The address in China

d. Which form of Chinese characters is used? Circle one:

   simplified   traditional

▶ Learning to write characters

2.51 *For stroke order and other useful information about each of the following characters from this unit, go to the* **Character Writing Text**. *Choose traditional or simplified characters and practice writing them until you can reproduce them on demand.*

您，多，大，小，幾／几，歲／岁，了，的，地，址
年，月，日，號／号，生，那，哪，兒／儿，這／这，位

▶ Writing a note

2.52 *Write a brief self-introduction in your choice of traditional or simplified Chinese characters. Include information about your name, age, birth date, e-mail address, street address, and the name of your teacher.*

2.52 • Encourage students to complete this exercise independently, but allow them to work in pairs if necessary. Suggest that they write their notes in pinyin first, then "translate" their writing into characters. When they finish writing, students should proofread their partners' writing before handing in their drafts to the teacher.

• If time allows, and students permit, randomly deliver the class mail. Students should then read these notes and write appropriate responses.

Cultural Bits 文化点滴

Self-introduction

View the video segment "Self-introduction" and then discuss the following questions with your classmates.

- What might you want to tell a new informal Chinese acquaintance about yourself upon meeting him or her for the first time?
- What are the benefits of being "overly polite"?
- What is the role of the "social title"?
- Why do Chinese people ask each other *Nǐ shǔ shénme?* How many of the twelve animals can you name? Do you know yours?

Recap

▶ Grammar

Sentence-ending particle *le*

Use *le* at the end of a sentence to show that a change of state has occurred.

> Wǒ yǐqián bù dǒng, xiànzài dǒng le. *(I didn't understand before, [but] now I do.)*

Specifiers

Use specifiers with appropriate numbers and nouns to specify a particular thing.

> Zhè kāfēi hěn hǎo. *(This [kind of] coffee is very good.)*
> zhèi wèi lǎoshī *(this teacher)*
> nèi wèi lǎoshī *(that teacher)*
> nèi sān wèi lǎoshī *(those three teachers)*

Formulating questions

Add *ma* to the end of a statement to ask a "yes/no" question. A *ma* question is usually answered by repeating the verb either affirmatively or negatively.

> Tā hǎo ma? Tā hěn hǎo. Tā bù hǎo. *(How is he/she? He/She is well. He/She is not well.)*

Add *ne* to inquire about a topic already mentioned. This has the general meaning of asking "And what about X?"

> Wǒ jiào Chén Lǐrén. Qǐng wèn, nín ne? *(My name is Chen Liren. And yours?)*

Use unstressed *bu* to pose positive and negative alternatives and to have the listener choose between them.

> Tā hǎo bu hǎo? Bù hǎo. *(Is he/she well? [He/She is] not well.)*

The *shì . . . de* construction

Use the *shì . . . de* construction to zero in on an aspect of a past event.

> Wǒ shì yī-jiǔ-líng-líng nián shēng de. *(I was born in 1900.)*
> Wǒ shì zuótiān lái de, bú shì jīntiān lái de. *(It was yesterday that I came, not today.)*

Time words

Words expressing specific moments in time precede the verb and usually follow the subject of a sentence.

> Wǒ zuótiān bù hǎo. Jīntiān hǎo le. *(I wasn't well yesterday. Today I'm better.)*

▶ Vocabulary

Chinese zodiac

gǒu 狗 dog
hóu 猴 monkey
hǔ 虎 tiger
jī 雞／鸡 chicken/rooster
lóng 龍／龙 dragon
mǎ 馬／马 horse
niú 牛 ox
shé 蛇 snake
shǔ 鼠 rat/mouse
tù 兔 rabbit
yáng 羊 sheep/ram
zhū 豬／猪 pig/boar

Nouns

diànyóu 電郵／电邮 e-mail
dìzhǐ 地址 address, location
hào 號／号 number in a series
hàomǎ 號碼／号码 number (as in: telephone number, room number, etc.)
jiā 家 home
jiē 街 street
lóu 樓／楼 (storied) building
shēngrì 生日 birthday
shì 室 room (as in: apartment unit)
shí'èr shēngxiào 十二生肖 twelve animals of the Chinese zodiac
suìshu 歲數／岁数 age, years of age

Common verbs

děngyú 等於／等于 be equal to
duì 對／对 be correct, be right
jiā 加 add
jiǎn 減／减 subtract
shēng 生 give birth to, bear
shǔ 屬／属 belong (to one of the 12 zodiac signs)
zhù 住 live, reside, stay

Measure word

wèi 位 [used for people of rank or status]

People

jiàoshòu 教授 professor
lǎoshī 老師／老师 teacher
línjū 鄰居／邻居 neighbor
péngyou 朋友 friend
qīnqi 親戚／亲戚 relative
tóngshì 同事 colleague, fellow worker
tóngxué 同學／同学 classmate
xuéshēng 學生／学生 student

Pronouns

nà 那 that
nèi 那 that
zhè 這／这 this
zhèi 這／这 this

Question words and associated vocabulary

dà 大 old (in age)
duō 多 how, to what extent
jǐ 幾／几 how many
něi 哪 which
suì 歲／岁 year (of age)
yàng 樣／样 kind, type, shape

Time words

jīnnián 今年 this year
nián 年 year (of time)
yuè 月 month
    Yīyuè 一月 January
    Èryuè 二月 February
    Sānyuè 三月 March
    Sìyuè 四月 April
    Wǔyuè 五月 May
    Liùyuè 六月 June
    Qīyuè 七月 July
    Bāyuè 八月 August
    Jiǔyuè 九月 September
    Shíyuè 十月 October
    Shíyīyuè 十一月 November
    Shí'èryuè 十二月 December

Numbers (11–100)

shíyī 十一 11
shí'èr 十二 12
. . .
èrshí 二十 20
èrshíyī 二十一 21
. . .
yìbǎi 一百 100

❱ Checklist of "can do" statements

After completing this unit, you should be able to perform each of the following tasks:

Listening and speaking

- ☐ Understand and say numbers from 1 to 100.
- ☐ Understand statements from others about age.
- ☐ In a culturally appropriate manner, ask a variety of persons about their age.
- ☐ Ask others about their birth sign and provide your own.
- ☐ Ask others about their birth date and provide your own.
- ☐ Understand when others say their birth year and state your own.
- ☐ Find out someone's e-mail address and provide your own.
- ☐ Find out someone's street address and provide your own.
- ☐ Specify someone's relationship to you and ask others about their relationship to a third party.

Reading and writing

- ☐ Write a brief description of yourself, providing your full name, age, birth date, e-mail address, street address, and the name of your teacher.
- ☐ Recognize printed dates.
- ☐ Understand key information on a name card.

Understanding culture

- ☐ Name four common Chinese surnames, one for each of the four tones.
- ☐ Make an accurate statement about differences in the way Westerners and Chinese count birthdays.
- ☐ Say under which "animal sign" you were born and state which personal characteristics are related to your sign.

Checklist

Have students work in pairs to go through this checklist and demonstrate selected skills to the class. Reserve 20–30 minutes for students to complete this activity. Tell students that putting check marks in each box is NOT the point. The point is to check if they can really do the things on the list.

"Don't leave before I arrive"

不見不散

Bújiànbúsàn

Making an appointment

In this unit, you will learn how to:

- ask for and say the time of day and days of the week.
- express relative time, using divisions of the day.
- find out someone's availability in terms of date and time, and state your own.
- decide on a meeting time.
- read dates and times on calendars and schedules.

- read simple written or printed messages regarding availability and appointments.
- write a simple question asking about someone's availability.
- write a simple statement confirming an appointment.

For additional materials to support this unit, go to the **Encounters** website at **www.EncountersChinese.com**.

Encounter 1 Telling time

3.1 *View Episode 3 of the dramatic series.*

3.2 *Getting ready:* *How would you ask for the time in English? If someone asked you the time, how would you say it was 2:20?*

_____

3.3 *Watch and listen to the video segment. What do you think* Xiànzài jǐ diǎn zhōng *means? Write the English below.*

_____

3.4 *How would you say what time it is? Fill in the blanks below with pinyin and characters.*

five o'clock	= _____ diǎn zhōng	_____ 點鐘／点钟
six o'clock	= _____ diǎn zhōng	_____ 點鐘／点钟
seven o'clock	= _____ diǎn zhōng	_____ 點鐘／点钟
eight o'clock	= _____ _____ _____	_____ 點鐘／点钟
nine o'clock	= _____ _____ _____	_____ 點鐘／点钟
ten o'clock	= _____ _____ _____	_____ 點鐘／点钟

FYI 供你参考

Two words for "two"

Chinese has two words for "two." You've already learned *èr*, which is used when counting, for example. However, when stating the time "on the hour," one says *liǎng diǎn (zhōng)* for "two o'clock," not *èr diǎn zhōng*. Clock time is said with a combination of numbers and measure words. You already know the numbers. Measure words, as noted in Unit 1, are used with numbers and nouns to count everything from time to teaspoons. Most nouns have their own particular measure word. Whenever two of anything are counted or numbered with a measure word (two books, two people, etc.), *liǎng* is used to express "two."

> *liǎng diǎn zhōng* (two o'clock)
> *liǎng běn shū* (two books)
> *liǎng ge rén* (two people)

 3.5 *Listen to the audio segment. Using a classroom clock (a clock face with moveable hands) or your fingers, indicate the time that each person is saying.*

3.6 Pair work: *With a partner, take turns asking for and telling the time, using your clock as a visual aid.*

Xiànzài jǐ diǎn zhōng?

Wǔ diǎn zhōng.

 3.7 *Watch and listen to the video segment. What is an alternate way of saying* Xiànzài jǐ diǎn zhōng? 現在幾點鐘？／现在几点钟？ *Fill in the blank below.*

Jǐ diǎn _____? 幾點了？／几点了？

3.8 *Match the corresponding times below.*

5:27	a. Wǔ diǎn shíwǔ fēn	1. 五點四十五分／五点四十五分
5:15	b. Wǔ diǎn sìshíwǔ fēn	2. 五點三十分／五点三十分
5:45	c. Wǔ diǎn sānshí fēn	3. 五點十五分／五点十五分
5:30	d. Wǔ diǎn èrshíqī fēn	4. 五點二十七分／五点二十七分

What does fēn 分 *mean? Write the English equivalent:* _____

3.9 *Listen to the audio segment. Using a classroom clock, indicate the time each person is saying.*

3.10 *Match the times with the pinyin terms in columns two and three, and the corresponding characters in column four.*

3:45	a. liù diǎn sānshí	1. yì diǎn yí kè	A. 兩點半／两点半
5:15	b. liǎng diǎn sānshí	2. liǎng diǎn bàn	B. 七點三刻／七点三刻
1:15	c. wǔ diǎn shíwǔ	3. sān diǎn sān kè	C. 六點半／六点半
6:30	d. yì diǎn shíwǔ	4. wǔ diǎn yí kè	D. 三點三刻／三点三刻
7:45	e. qī diǎn sìshíwǔ	5. liù diǎn bàn	E. 一點一刻／一点一刻
2:30	f. sān diǎn sìshíwǔ	6. qī diǎn sān kè	F. 五點一刻／五点一刻

What does bàn 半 *mean, in this context?* Circle one: half past   quarter past

What does yí kè 一刻 *mean?* Circle one: half past   quarter past

3.11 *Pair work:* Work with a partner. Using the classroom clock as a visual aid, take turns asking for and telling the time. Practice saying the time in alternate ways, when possible.

FYI 供你參考

Time measure words

The following measure words are relevant to telling time:

diǎn: counts hours—*liǎng diǎn (zhōng)* (two o'clock)
fēn: counts minutes—*yì fēn (zhōng)* (one minute); *liǎng diǎn èrshí fēn* (two twenty, twenty after two)
miǎo: counts seconds—*yì miǎo (zhōng)* (one second)

The questions *Xiànzài jǐ diǎn zhōng?* and *Jǐ diǎn le?* literally mean "What time is it on the hour?" However, note that the expected answer to both is an exact time, including the hour and minute. Therefore, *Xiànzài jǐ diǎn zhōng?* can be answered with *Wǔ diǎn shí fēn.*

3.12 *Watch and listen to the video segment. Fill in the following blanks with the correct equivalent of each time.*

10:53 = shí diǎn wǔshísān fēn = chà _____ fēn shíyī diǎn

10:55 = shí diǎn wǔshíwǔ fēn = chà _____ fēn shíyī diǎn

10:58 = shí diǎn wǔshíbā fēn = chà _____ fēn shíyī diǎn

11:03 = shíyī diǎn líng sān fēn = shíyī diǎn guò _____ fēn

11:08 = shíyī diǎn líng bā fēn = shíyī diǎn guò _____ fēn

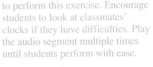

Alternate ways of telling time

You may have noticed that there are many ways of saying the same time. In English, 5:05 can be "five past five," "five oh five," or "five minutes past five o'clock." Similarly, in Chinese, there are alternate ways of saying the times between ten minutes before and ten minutes after the hour. In the previous exercise, you saw that *shí diǎn wǔshísān fēn* and *chà qī fēn shíyī diǎn* are both equally acceptable ways of saying 10:53. Furthermore, it would also be acceptable to say *shíyī diǎn chà qī fēn.*

For up to ten minutes after the hour, you can use the terms *líng* (zero) and *guò* (past) interchangeably, as you also saw in the previous exercise.

Finally, you may also have noted that when the words *zhōng* (o'clock) or *fēn* (minute) appear in the final position, they may be omitted. Thus:

yì diǎn zhōng = yì diǎn

liǎng diǎn èrshí fēn = liǎng diǎn èrshí

3.13 *Listen to the audio segment. Using a classroom clock, indicate the time each person is saying.*

3.14 *Pair work: Work with a partner. Using the classroom clock as a visual aid, take turns asking for and saying any time between ten minutes before and ten minutes after the hour. Use* chà *(either before or after the hour) and* guò *or* líng.

3.15 *Group work: Work in a group. Pick any time (at random) within a 12-hour period. Ask your classmates about the times they have chosen and then line up in chronological order, beginning with 1:00. If more than one person picks exactly the same time, they should stand together and act as one person. Once the line has been formed, report your time (as the old "time callers" did in past centuries) loudly and clearly:* Xiànzài ___ diǎn ___ fēn! *If anyone is out of place, work as a group to correct the error, and then begin reporting again from the beginning. Continue until everyone has reported his or her time in order with no errors.*

3.12 Have students watch the video and then fill the blanks and compare answers with classmates. Ask the class to guess the meaning for *chà* (to lack) and *guò* (to pass) in context. Ask the class when one can use *chà* and *guò* to tell time. (Key: Refer students to the FYI: Alternate ways of telling time.)

3.12 Key:

qī
wǔ
liǎng
sān
bā

3.13 Have students sit in a circle to perform this exercise. Encourage students to look at classmates' clocks if they have difficulties. Play the audio segment multiple times until students perform with ease.

3.13 Key:

11:57 – shí'èr diǎn chà sān fēn
12:05 – shí'èr diǎn guò wǔ fēn
12:01 – shí'èr diǎn líng yī fēn
12:58 – yì diǎn chà liǎng fēn
1:05 – yì diǎn guò wǔ fēn
1:58 – liǎng diǎn chà liǎng fēn
2:06 – liǎng diǎn guò liù fēn
3:07 – sān diǎn guò qī fēn
3:56 – sì diǎn chà sì fēn
4:01 – sì diǎn guò yī fēn
7:08 – qī diǎn guò bā fēn
8:55 – jiǔ diǎn chà wǔ fēn
9:58 – shí diǎn chà liǎng fēn
10:05 – shí diǎn guò wǔ fēn

3.14 Before starting, ask students to confirm two ways to say "1:56" using *chà: Chà sì fēn liǎng diǎn. / Liǎng diǎn chà sì fēn.*

3.15 • Have students read the instructions to understand the task they are about to perform as a class.

• Before starting, you may want to emphasize that each person will choose one time that is HIS OR HER time and then ask other people, *Jǐ diǎn le?* or the equivalent. Indicate clearly that everyone should line up from "earliest" on one side to "latest" on the other.

• If you find it necessary, invite 3–4 volunteers to do a demonstration with you.

• During the activity, participate as a member, observe student interactions, and assist as necessary.

FYI 供你参考

Lining up units of time

Units of time in a series are expressed in the same way as many elements of Chinese grammar: largest to smallest. This is opposite of typical English conventions. Example:

Xiǎo wáwa chūshēng zài èr-líng-líng-jiǔ nián, shíyīyuè shísān hào, shí'èr diǎn èrshí fēn.
(The baby was born at 12:20 P.M., on November 13, 2009.)

▶ Reading practice

3.16 *Pair work: With a partner, take turns reading the following questions and answers aloud, with the help of the English. Then change roles.*

甲: 現在幾點鐘？／現在几点钟？ *(What time is it?)*
乙: 兩點鐘。／两点钟。 *(Two o'clock.)*

甲: 現在幾點了？／现在几点了？ *(What time is it now?)*
乙: 兩點半。／两点半。 *(Half past two.)*

甲: 現在幾點了？／现在几点了？ *(What time is it now?)*
乙: 兩點三刻。／两点三刻。 *(Two forty-five.)*

甲: 現在幾點鐘？／现在几点钟？ *(What time is it?)*
乙: 三點差十分。／三点差十分。 *(Ten to three.)*

甲: 幾點了？／几点了？ *(What time is it now?)*
乙: 三點過十分。／三点过十分。 *(Ten past three.)*

甲: 現在幾點了？／现在几点了？ *(What time is it now?)*
乙: 你去買個錶不行嗎？？？／你去买个表不行吗？？？
    Nǐ qù mǎi ge biǎo bù xíng ma??? (Can't you go buy a watch???)

3.16 Avoid reading this dialogue aloud for your students or having them repeat after you, as this exercise is designed for students to use the English translation as a bridge to infer the meaning and pronunciation of the characters.

Encounter 2　Divisions of the day and relative time

 3.17 *Watch and listen to the video segment. Look at the following timeline. Can you tell what the conversation was about? Circle three terms you heard.*

3.17 Key:
Words circled: *shàngwǔ, xiàwǔ, wǎnshang*

zhōngwǔ　　　　　　　　　　　　　　　　　　　　　bànyè

| shàngwǔ | | | | | | | | | | | xiàwǔ | | | | | | | | | | | |
|1|2|3|4|5|6|7|8|9|10|11|12|1|2|3|4|5|6|7|8|9|10|11|12|

← yèlǐ →　　　　　← zǎoshang →　　　　　　← wǎnshang →

3.18 *Match the pinyin with the corresponding English.*

a. Nǐ nàr xiànzài jǐ diǎn zhōng?

b. Qī diǎn zhōng.

c. Shì shàngwǔ háishi xiàwǔ?

d. Xiàwǔ.

e. Wǒmen zhèr shì wǎnshang qī diǎn zhōng.

1. *A.M. or P.M.?*

2. *P.M.*

3. *What time is it there now?*

4. *It's seven in the evening here.*

5. *Seven o'clock.*

3.18 Before students complete this activity, ask them to read the questions and sentences and decide who might be having this conversation. (Hint: The two people are probably not in the same city!) After students finish matching, have them perform the dialogue with partners.

3.18 Key:
a. 3
b. 5
c. 1
d. 2
e. 4

Grammar Bits 语法点滴

Stating alternatives with *háishi*

You've already learned that one way to ask a question in Chinese is to pose affirmative and negative alternatives with *bu*: *Nǐ hǎo bu hǎo?* Another way is to mark the alternatives more explicitly with *háishi* in the pattern *Shì X háishi Y?* (Is it X or Y?) X and Y can be simple nouns or other expressions. Examples:

Shì shàngwǔ háishi xiàwǔ? (Is [that] A.M. or P.M.?)
Nǐ dà háishi tā dà? (Are you older or is he/she older?)

3.19 *Match the pinyin with the corresponding English.*

a. zǎoshang	1. *before noon,* A.M.
b. shàngwǔ	2. *afternoon,* P.M.
c. zhōngwǔ	3. *morning*
d. xiàwǔ	4. *at night, in the middle of the night*
e. wǎnshang	5. *midnight*
f. bànyè	6. *noon*

3.20 Mingling: *Fill in the blanks below with a time of your choice.*

Q: Nǐ nàr xiànzài jǐ diǎn zhōng?

A: Wǒmen zhèr shì _____ _____.
                        (DIVISION)   (HOUR)

Now walk around the room asking and answering the above question. Line up according to the answers, from earliest to latest.

3.21 *Look at the timeline below. Match the characters with the corresponding pinyin.*

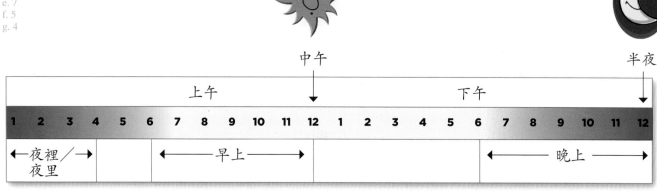

a. zǎoshang	1. 上午
b. shàngwǔ	2. 下午
c. zhōngwǔ	3. 早上
d. xiàwǔ	4. 夜裡／夜里
e. wǎnshang	5. 半夜
f. bànyè	6. 中午
g. yèlǐ	7. 晚上

▶ **Reading practice**

3.22 *Pair work:* *With a partner, take turns reading the following questions and answers aloud, using the English as a guide. Then change roles.*

甲: 你那兒現在幾點鐘？／你那儿现在几点钟？
   (What time is it there now?)

乙: 七點鐘。／七点钟。 *(Seven o'clock.)*

甲: 是上午還是下午？／是上午还是下午？ *(A.M. or P.M.?)*

乙: 下午。我們這兒是晚上七點鐘。／下午。我们这儿是晚上
   七点钟。 *(P.M. It's seven in the evening here.)*

3.22 Avoid reading this dialogue aloud for your students or having them repeat after you. Remind students to use the English translation as a bridge to the meaning and pronunciation of these characters.

Encounter 3 **Days of the week**

3.23 *Watch and listen to the video segment. Match the corresponding pinyin, English, and characters below.*

a. Xīngqīyī ———————	1. Monday	A. 星期一
b. Xīngqī'èr	2. Thursday	B. 星期三
c. Xīngqīsān	3. Saturday	C. 星期五
d. Xīngqīsì	4. Tuesday	D. 星期天
e. Xīngqīwǔ	5. Friday	E. 星期二
f. Xīngqīliù	6. Sunday	F. 星期六
g. Xīngqītiān	7. Wednesday	G. 星期四

3.23 Key:
a. 1. A
b. 4. E
c. 7. B
d. 2. G
e. 5. C
f. 3. F
g. 6. D

Grammar Bits 语法点滴

Suggesting with *ba*

The sentence-ending particle *ba* accompanies suggestions, assumptions, or suppositions (and sometimes reluctant agreement).

Hǎo, wǒmen zǒu ba! *(OK, let's go.)*

Nǐ shì Zhāng Lǎoshī ba? *(You're Professor Zhang, right?)*

Wǔ diǎn le ba? *(It's five o'clock now, right?)*

Xiànzài jiù zǒu? Hǎo ba. *(We're leaving now, already? Oo-kay.)*

Grammar Bits
Have students read this note in pairs for understanding. Check comprehension by asking the class to teach you the meaning, form, and use of *ba*. If you find it necessary, you can ask students to write a skit in pairs, making sure to include at least three out of the four functions of *ba* mentioned.

3.24 Photocopy or create a one-page calendar for students to use in this activity. An Internet search will lead you to several websites where you can create simple weekly and monthly calendars.

3.24 *Pair work: Work with a partner. Using a calendar, take turns asking and answering questions. Follow the model below.*

甲: 五月八號是星期幾？／五月八号是星期几？

乙: 五月八號是星期_____。／五月八号是星期_____。

Repeat the exchange five or six times each, until you both feel comfortable with the material.

3.25 • Before this activity, provide sufficient time for students to look up their birthdays in a calendar.

• If necessary, invite a confident pair to do a demonstration, and then have the class mingle.

3.25 *Mingling: Look at a calendar and see what day of the week your birthday is this year. Then walk around the class asking and answering the following question.*

你的生日是星期幾？／你的生日是星期几？

3.26 Key:

blanks: 六、天
circle: 星期天

3.26 週／周 Zhōu *is a formal term meaning "week" and* 末 mò *means "end." Knowing this, can you fill in the blanks below with the correct characters?*

週末／周末 zhōumò = 星期_____ 和 hé *(and)* 星期_____

3.27 You may want to review this information by asking the class: What are the three possible ways to say "Monday"? What are the three possible ways to say "Sunday"? Can one say *zhōu tiān*?

Recall that 日 *means "sun." What do you think* 週日／周日 *means? Circle one of the following:* 星期一　星期天

3.27 *As you know, "week" in Chinese is* 星期 xīngqī. *A term that is interchangeable with* 星期 *is* 禮拜／礼拜 lǐbài. *A third, more formal (written) term for "week" is* 週／周, *as you learned in the previous exercise.* 天 *and* 日 *are interchangeable when used with* 星期 *and* 禮拜／礼拜, *but you can only use* 日 *with* 週／周. *Keeping all this in mind, please match the terms below.*

a. 星期一	1. 禮拜三／礼拜三	A. 週二／周二
b. 星期二	2. 禮拜五／礼拜五	B. 週四／周四
c. 星期三	3. 禮拜二／礼拜二	C. 週六／周六
d. 星期四	4. 禮拜天（日）／礼拜天（日）	D. 週三／周三
e. 星期五	5. 禮拜一／礼拜一	E. 週日／周日
f. 星期六	6. 禮拜六／礼拜六	F. 週一／周一
g. 星期天（日）	7. 禮拜四／礼拜四	G. 週五／周五

FYI 供你參考

The workweek in China

Until the mid-1990s, the usual workweek in China was six days, from Monday through Saturday, with Sunday off. Today, the five-day workweek with the weekend off is most common. When Chinese say the days of the week, they start with *Xīngqīyī* (Monday) and end with *Xīngqītiān* (Sunday), in contrast to American patterns of expression.

3.27 Key:

a. 5. F.
b. 3. A.
c. 1. D.
d. 7. B.
e. 2. G.
f. 6. C.
g. 4. E.

Encounter 4   More time words

3.28 *Watch and listen to the video segment. Then place the following time expressions along the timeline below.*

xiànzài	gāngcái	yìhuǐr

xiànzài
_____

just a while ago   right now   in a little while

3.28 Point out to students that the English words are in order; they only need to rearrange the order of the pinyin words.

3.28 Key:

just a while ago: *gāngcái*
right now: *xiànzài*
in a little while: *yìhuǐr*

3.29 *In pinyin, complete the transcription of the conversation you just heard.*

3.29 Key:

琳: Yìhuǐr, yìhuǐr.
唐母: *Come*
琳: Hǎo de. Yìhuǐr, yìhuǐr.
唐: *watermelon*
唐: gāngcái, Xiànzài

唐母：來啊，來啊！／来啊，来啊！

      Táng Mǔ: Lái a! Lái a!

      (Tang Yuan's mother: Come! Come!)

琳：好的。一會兒，一會兒。／一会儿，一会儿。

      Lín: Hǎo de. _____, _____.

      (Lynn: OK. In a bit, in a bit.)

唐母：琳老師！休息休息吧！吃西瓜了！／琳老师！休息休息吧！吃西瓜了！

      Táng Mǔ: Lín lǎoshī! Xiūxi xiūxi ba! Chī xīguā le!

      (Tang Yuan's mother: Teacher Lynn! Take a break! We're having watermelon!)

琳：我寫完博客就下去，啊。／我写完博客就下去，啊。

      Lín: Wǒ xiěwán bókè jiù xiàqu, a.

      (Lynn: I'll come down as soon as I finish writing my blog, OK?)

唐母：你快來啊！／你快来啊！

      Táng Mǔ: Nǐ kuài lái a!

      (Tang Yuan's mother: _____ quickly!)

琳：好的。一會兒，一會兒。／一会儿，一会儿。

      Lín: _____. _____, _____.

      (Lynn: OK. In a bit, in a bit.)

…

唐：琳，快吃西瓜。

      Táng: Lín, kuài chī xīguā.

      (Tang: Lynn, here, have some _____.)

(The plate is empty. Lynn is perplexed.)

唐：哦，對不起。剛才有西瓜。現在沒了。都被我吃了。／哦，对不起。刚才有西瓜。现在没了。都被我吃了。

      Táng: O, duìbuqǐ. _____ yǒu xīguā. _____ méi le. Dōu bèi wǒ chī le.

      (Tang: Oh, sorry. There was watermelon just now. Now there isn't any more. I ate it all.)

唐母：吃吧。我给你留着呢。

Táng Mǔ: Chī ba. Wǒ gěi nǐ liú zhe ne.

(Tang Yuan's mother: Have some. I saved some for you.)

唐：吃啊。

Táng: Chī a.

(Tang: Eat up.)

 3.30 *Watch and listen to the video segment. Practice saying each phrase as you make the corresponding gesture.*

3.31 *Pair work:* *With a partner, take turns saying the correct phrase in response to your partner's gesture.*

3.32 Have students read the instructions to understand their task. Invite 3–4 volunteers to demonstrate the interaction with you before the whole class mingles.

3.32 *Mingling:* *Take a blank card or a small piece of paper. Look at the time on the classroom clock and pick a time between right now (say, 9:06) and ten minutes from now (say, 9:16). Let's suppose you pick 9:11. Write this time on your card (large enough so others can read it easily). Now walk around the classroom, showing others your card and looking at the cards others hold. If both the classroom clock and a classmate's card have the same time—for example, 9:07—say,* <u>Xiànzài</u> *jiǔ diǎn líng (guò) qī fēn. If a classmate's card has an earlier time—for example, 9:06—say,* <u>Gāngcái</u> *jiǔ diǎn líng (guò) liù fēn. Your classmate would then say for your card (which has a later time),* <u>Yìhuǐr</u> *jiǔ diǎn shíyī fēn. Check each other and continue until you feel comfortable using all of the expressions.*

3.33 Key:
a. 2
b. 1

 3.33 *Watch and listen to the video segment. Match the corresponding Chinese and English expressions below.*

a. zǎo yìdiǎnr   1. *a little later*

b. wǎn yìdiǎnr   2. *a little earlier*

3.34 Demonstrate the interaction with a volunteer. Tell the class that you are thinking of a "secret time" and they are supposed to guess what that time is. Follow the instructions, giving hints such as *Zǎo yìdiǎnr* or *Wǎn yìdiǎnr* and finally confirming the correct time with *Duì le!* Then reverse roles with the class. Allow the class to come up with and agree on a time in secret. (You may need to leave the room.) Ask them to use the same language to give you hints and confirm your guesses.

3.34 *Pair work:* *Play the "guess the time" game with a partner. Student A writes a time on a piece of paper, and Student B tries to guess that time. If Student B guesses correctly, Student A says* Duì le! *Otherwise Student A responds by saying* Zǎo yìdiǎnr *or* Wǎn yìdiǎnr. *Continue until Student B guesses the time correctly, and then reverse roles. Play as necessary until you are comfortable with the terms in use.*

3.35 Key:
a. 1. B
b. 2. A

3.35 一點兒／一点儿 *are the characters for* yìdiǎnr, *meaning "a little." Here are two new characters:* 早 *and* 晚. *You can tell that they both have to do with the time of day, since the "sun" radical,* 日 rì, *appears in each. In one, the sun is higher than in the other. Can you guess what each means? Match the corresponding characters, English, and pinyin below.*

a. 早   1. *early*   A. wǎn

b. 晚   2. *late*   B. zǎo

3.36 *Watch and listen to the video segment. Then fill in the blanks below with time expressions in pinyin, to express the day relative to the circled date (that is, yesterday, two days from now, etc.).*

12 月						
週一	週二	週三	週四	週五	週六	週日
1	2	3	④	5	6	7

sān tiān yǐqián _____ _____ jīntiān _____ _____ _____

3.37 *Match the corresponding items below.*

a. three days ago	1. qiántiān	A. 三天以後/三天以后
b. the day before yesterday	2. sān tiān yǐqián	B. 後天/后天
c. yesterday	3. hòutiān	C. 明天
d. today	4. zuótiān	D. 今天
e. tomorrow	5. sān tiān yǐhòu	E. 昨天
f. the day after tomorrow	6. míngtiān	F. 前天
g. three days from now	7. jīntiān	G. 三天以前

3.38 *Pair work: Work with a partner. On index cards, write today's day (say it's Tuesday), plus three days before (Saturday, Sunday, and Monday) and three days after (Wednesday, Thursday, and Friday). Lay the cards in order on your desk, and drill the terms by taking turns pointing at a card and having your partner say what it represents (for example, Sunday would be* qiántiān *and Wednesday would be* míngtiān*). Continue until you are both comfortable with the terms.*

3.39 *Watch and listen to the video segment. Then fill in the blanks below with pinyin.*

October

Su	Mo	Tu	We	Th	Fr	Sa
		1	2	3	4	5
6	7	8	9	10	11	12
13	14	15	16	17	18	19
20	21	22	23	24	25	26
27	28	29	30			

_____

_____

zhèi ge xīngqī

_____

_____

3.36 This can be a challenging listening activity for students. Make sure you leave enough time to play the video multiple times, if needed. If students appear stuck, it may be helpful to play the video in conjunction with exercise 3.37 so that they can start associating the written forms with the audio input. Some students may prefer to do exercise 3.37 first, before completing 3.36.

3.36 Key:

qiántiān, zuótiān, míngtiān, hòutiān, sān tiān yǐhòu

3.37 Key:

a. 2. G
b. 1. F
c. 4. E
d. 7. D
e. 6. C
f. 3. B
g. 5. A

Useful phrases

Zhè shì něi tiān? *(What day is this?)*

Bú duì! *(Incorrect!)*

Duì le! *(Correct!)*

3.38 • Have enough index cards ready to distribute to students (three per student).

• Introduce, review, and practice using the useful phrases from this activity.

• If necessary, demonstrate the appropriate interaction with the class. Go through the activity once, and then reverse roles.

3.39 Key:

liǎng ge xīngqī yǐqián
shàng ge xīngqī
xià ge xīngqī
liǎng ge xīngqī yǐhòu

3.40 *Match the corresponding items below.*

a. two weeks ago	1. 兩個星期以後	A. 这个星期
b. last week	2. 這個星期	B. 两个星期以前
c. this week	3. 上個星期	C. 上个星期
d. next week	4. 兩個星期以前	D. 下个星期
e. two weeks from now	5. 下個星期	E. 两个星期以后

3.41 *Pair work: Work with a partner. On index cards, write today's date (say it's 10/15), plus the dates a week ago (10/8), two weeks ago (10/1, China's National Day), a week from now (10/22), and two weeks from now (10/29). Lay the cards in order on your desk, and drill the terms by taking turns pointing to a card and having your partner say what week it represents (for example, 10/15 would be* zhèi ge xīngqī *and 10/29 would be* liǎng ge xīngqī yǐhòu *or* xià xià ge xīngqī*). Continue until you are both comfortable with the terms.*

3.42 *Mingling: Your teacher will hand you a slip. Look at the slip and circulate among your classmates, asking and answering questions according to the following pattern.*

Q: Nǐ de shì shénme shíhòu? *(When is yours?)*

A: Wǒ de shì _____. *(Mine is _____.)*

Based on the answers, line up from earliest to latest.

FYI 供你参考

Chinese concepts of time

It may help to realize that Chinese people "face" and "look up to" the past, and they "go backward and downward" into the future. Consider the following terms:

yǐqián
in front of me
(the past)

shàng ge yuè
the month above
(last month)

qiántiān
the day in front
(day before yesterday)

xiànzài
(now)

hòutiān
the day behind
(day after tomorrow)

xià ge yuè
the month below
(next month)

yǐhòu
behind me
(the future)

This is tricky for speakers of English, who typically go forward into the future. However, with practice, you too can learn to turn yourself around for Chinese.

Encounter 5   Making an appointment

3.43 *Watch and listen to the video segment. When did they finally decide to meet? Write the day and time in English or pinyin:* _____

3.44 *Match the corresponding pinyin and English below.*

a. Wǒmen shénme shíhòu jiàn?
我們甚麼時候見？／我们什么时候见？

1. *Let's meet at XX, OK?*

b. XX xíng ma?
XX 行嗎？／XX 行吗？

2. *When shall we meet?*

c. XX kěyǐ ma? _____
XX 可以嗎？／XX 可以吗？

3. *Would XX be OK?*

d. Nǐ XX yǒu kòng ma?
你 XX 有空嗎？／你 XX 有空吗？

4. *Are you busy XX?*

e. Nǐ XX yǒushì ma?
你 XX 有事嗎？／你 XX 有事吗？

5. *Would XX work?*

f. Duìbuqǐ, wǒ XX yǒushì.
對不起，我 XX 有事。／对不起，我 XX 有事。

6. *Wait a minute.*

g. Wǒmen XX jiàn, xíng ma?
我們 XX 見，行嗎？／我们 XX 见，行吗？

7. *Are you free XX?*

h. Děng yì děng.
等一等。

8. *Sorry, I'm busy XX.*

3.45 Have a volunteer demonstrate making an appointment with you (and vice versa) before asking the class to mingle. Circulate around the classroom and offer assistance as necessary.

3.45 *Mingling: Walk around the room and arrange meeting times during the coming week with at least three of your classmates. Use your real appointment calendars, if possible. Write the names of the people you are meeting and the times you are meeting them.*

Meet _____ at _____

Meet _____ at _____

Meet _____ at _____

FYI 供你参考

Beijing time

Typically, things start earlier in China. While "nine to five" prevails in the United States, many employees in China are on the job as early as 7:30 or 8:00. The early-to-work habit is offset by the pleasant tradition of a two-hour midday break, observed in the workplace and in schools by workers and students sleeping at their desks. In urban areas, this "siesta" habit is on the decline, though, as China integrates into the global marketplace.

Note that there are no time zones in China, unlike other large countries, including the United States. Time across China is set to the time in Beijing. 6:00 A.M. in Beijing is 6:00 A.M. in the Gobi Desert in China's far west. Whereas the sun may have risen in Beijing, it might still be pitch black in the Gobi Desert. In winter in *Xīnjiāng*, China's westernmost province, the sun does not rise until about 10:00 in the morning, official time. However, many people in *Xīnjiāng* follow their own unofficial time, usually about two hours behind Beijing time.

Beijing time

Check comprehension with the following questions:

1. Do Chinese people go to work from 9–5, like many people in the United States do?

2. China is as "wide" as the United States—both countries span roughly the same distance, east to west. How many time zones does China have?

3. How might people in California feel if they had to conduct their lives according to a "standard time" that was based in Washington, D.C.? How do people in Western China solve this problem?

♫ Unit Rap

Go to the **Encounters** *website at www.EncountersChinese.com and listen to the song to review key expressions from Unit 3. Listen again and sing along!*

Encounter 6 Reading and writing

▶ Reading familiar sentences in Chinese characters

3.46 • Avoid reading this dialogue aloud for your students or having them repeat after you. Tell them to use the English and familiar characters as bridges to determine the meaning and pronunciation of unknown characters.

• Keep in mind that reading fluency is not the goal of this activity. Tell students to not get discouraged if they have trouble reading quickly and accurately.

• Have students complete this exercise multiple times before they move on to 3.47 and 3.48.

3.46 *Pair work: Read the following dialogues (written in traditional characters) aloud with a partner, using the English as a guide.*

1 甲：現在幾點鐘？ *(What time is it now?)*

乙：上午九點半。 *(Nine-thirty in the morning.)*

2 甲：我們明天八點三刻見，對不對？ *(We're meeting tomorrow at 8:45, right?)*

乙：不是八點四十分嗎？ *(Isn't it 8:40?)*

甲：噢，對，八點四十分。 *(Oh, right. 8:40.)*

3 甲：現在幾點了？ *(What time is it?)*

乙：四點過五分！甚麼事？ *(Five past four! What's going on?)*

甲：四點鐘？夜裡四點鐘？ *(Four? Four o'clock at night?)*

乙：對！怎麼了？ *(Yes. What's up?)*

甲：對不起，對不起。沒事！沒事！ *(Sorry, sorry. Nothing! Nothing!)*

4 甲：我們兩點見，對不對？ *(See you at two, right?)*

乙：對，對，對，下午兩點。我差點兒忘 (wàng) 了。
(Right, right, right, two o'clock in the afternoon. I almost forgot.)

5 甲：七月五號是不是星期天？ *(Is July 5th a Sunday?)*

乙：不，是星期六。 *(No, it's a Saturday.)*

甲：星期六。好。我們中午見，對不對？ *(Saturday. OK. We're meeting at noon, right?)*

乙：對。中午十二點鐘見。 *(Right. See you at twelve noon.)*

6 甲：十月九號是週末嗎？ *(Is October 9th a weekend?)*

乙：不，是禮拜一。 *(No, it's a Monday.)*

7 甲：今天星期幾？ *(What day of the week is it today?)*

乙：昨天星期六，今天星期天。 *(Yesterday was Saturday; today is Sunday.)*

8 甲：我們明天是早上六點見嗎？ *(Are we meeting at six tomorrow morning?)*

乙：不，是晚上六點。 *(No, six tomorrow evening.)*

甲：早一點兒，行嗎？ *(Can we make it earlier?)*

乙：四點半可以嗎？ *(Would four-thirty work?)*

甲：可以。明天見。 *(It would. See you tomorrow.)*

9 甲：你一會兒有沒有空？ *(Will you have some time in a little while?)*

乙：對不起，我剛才有空。一會兒有一點兒事。 *(Sorry, I was free just now. I have something to do in a little while.)*

Note: In English, any time past midnight tends to be called "morning," so the more idiomatic translation here would be "Four o'clock in the morning?" However, in Chinese, the hours between midnight and about 5 A.M. (when roosters start crowing and sunrise nears) can be referred to as either "night" or "morning."

甲：那現在有空嗎？ (In that case, are you free now?)

乙：有，有，有…… (I am, I am, I am . . .)

10 甲：你的生日是幾月幾號？ (When is your birthday?)

乙：是下個月的三十一號。 (The 31st of next month.)

3.47–3.48

- Have students read these dialogues multiple times, focusing on reading fluency.

- Encourage students *not* to refer to exercise 3.46 for help. Instead, ask them to rely on the dialogue context and their partners to help them read new characters.

- After students practice reading the dialogues a few times, play the audio and have them check their pronunciation.

3.47 Pair work: *Read the dialogues aloud with a partner, this time without any English.*

1 甲：現在幾點鐘？

乙：上午九點半。

2 甲：我們明天八點三刻見，對不對？

乙：不是八點四十分嗎？

甲：噢，對，八點四十分。

3 甲：現在幾點了？

乙：四點過五分！甚麼事？

甲：四點鐘？夜裡四點鐘？

乙：對！怎麼了？

甲：對不起，對不起。沒事！沒事！

4 甲：我們兩點見，對不對？

乙：對，對，對，下午兩點。 我差點兒忘 (wàng) 了。

5 甲：七月五號是不是星期天？

乙：不，是星期六。

甲：星期六。好。我們中午見，對不對？

乙：對。中午十二點鐘見。

6 甲：十月九號是週末嗎？

乙：不，是禮拜一。

7 甲：今天星期幾？

乙：昨天星期六，今天星期天。

8 甲：我們明天是早上六點見嗎？

乙：不，是晚上六點。

甲：早一點兒，行嗎？
乙：四點半可以嗎？
甲：可以。明天見。

9 甲：你一會兒有沒有空？
乙：對不起，我剛才有空。一會兒有一點兒事。
甲：那現在有空嗎？
乙：有，有，有……

10 甲：你的生日是幾月幾號？
乙：是下個月的三十一號。

3.48 *Pair work: Read the dialogues aloud one more time, this time in simplified characters.*

1 甲：现在几点钟？
乙：上午九点半。

2 甲：我们明天八点三刻见，对不对？
乙：不是八点四十分吗？
甲：噢，对，八点四十分。

3 甲：现在几点了？
乙：四点过五分！什么事？
甲：四点钟？夜里四点钟？
乙：对！怎么了？
甲：对不起，对不起。没事！没事！

4 甲：我们两点见，对不对？
乙：对，对，对，下午两点。我差点儿忘 (wàng) 了。

5 甲：七月五号是不是星期天？
乙：不，是星期六。
甲：星期六。好。我们中午见，对不对？
乙：对。中午十二点钟见。

6 甲：十月九号是周末吗？
乙：不，是礼拜一。

7 甲：今天星期几？
乙：昨天星期六，今天星期天。

8 甲：我们明天是早上六点见吗？
乙：不，是晚上六点。
甲：早一点儿，行吗？
乙：四点半可以吗？
甲：可以。明天见。

9 甲：你一会儿有没有空？
乙：对不起，我刚才有空。一会儿有一点儿事。
甲：那现在有空吗？
乙：有,有,有……

10 甲：你的生日是几月几号？
乙：是下个月的三十一号。

3.49 • Have students complete this exercise in pairs, if necessary.

• Encourage students to refer to previous exercises in this unit to find answers.

• Have students compare their answers with multiple classmates.

• Invite volunteers to share the answers on the board.

3.49 Key:

a. 13. C
b. 7. E
c. 10. I
d. 2. B
e. 17. G
f. 9. K
g. 1. A
h. 11. D
i. 3. J
j. 6. L
k. 4. F
l. 8. P
m. 12. R
n. 15. S
o. 5. M
p. 18. Q
q. 16. N
r. 14. O
s. 19. H

3.49 *Match the corresponding simplified characters, traditional characters, and English.*

a. 现在	1. 甚麼	A. *what*
b. 几点钟	2. 對不對	B. *is that right*
c. 我们	3. 見	C. *now*
d. 对不对	4. 禮拜	D. *two o'clock*
e. 吗	5. 對不起	E. *what time (which hour)*
f. 过	6. 週末	F. *week*
g. 什么	7. 幾點鐘	G. *(particle marking a question)*
h. 两点	8. 星期幾	H. *next month*
i. 见	9. 過	I. *we, us*
j. 周末	10. 我們	J. *meet*
k. 礼拜	11. 兩點	K. *past, over (the hour)*
l. 星期几	12. 早一點兒	L. *weekend*
m. 早一点儿	13. 現在	M. *sorry*
n. 一会儿	14. 幾月幾號	N. *something to attend to*
o. 对不起	15. 一會兒	O. *what date*
p. 刚才	16. 一點兒事	P. *which day of the week*
q. 一点儿事	17. 嗎	Q. *just now*
r. 几月几号	18. 剛才	R. *a little earlier*
s. 下个月	19. 下個月	S. *in a while*

❯ Reading real-life texts

3.50 *The following is a bulletin board posting by a couple looking for childcare services. Fill in the English, based on the Chinese text.*

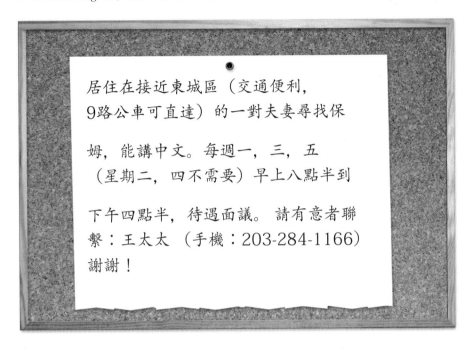

居住在接近東城區（交通便利，
9路公車可直達）的一對夫妻尋找保

姆，能講中文。每週一，三，五
（星期二，四不需要）早上八點半到

下午四點半，待遇面議。 請有意者聯
繫：王太太（手機：203-284-1166）
謝謝！

3.50–3.52 If possible, copy these real-life texts to a transparency so you can project them on the board. Invite volunteers to circle the appropriate characters. Point out that one does not need to understand every character to complete the given tasks. Students should look for characters they know and try to extrapolate needed information from those.

3.50 Key:
Monday, Wednesday, Friday
Tuesday, Thursday
8:30 A.M. – 4:30 P.M.
Cell phone: 203-284-1166

A couple living near the eastern downtown district (convenient to public transportation, direct access via Route 9) seeks a childcare provider who speaks Chinese. Needed every _____ (not needed _____) from _____ to _____. Salary to be determined after interview. Interested parties please contact Mrs. Wang (_____: _____). Thank you!

3.51 You may need to prepare younger learners by teaching them how military time works before having them do this activity.

3.51 Key:
a. June 2
b. 9:00
c. 13:00/1:00 P.M.
d. 21:30/9:30 P.M.

3.51 *The following is a competition-day schedule for a sports team. The items listed include a wake-up call, breakfast, practice, lunch, a preparation meeting, travel, the match, and dinner. Answer the questions below.*

a. What date is posted on the schedule? Write the correct month and day in English.

_____

b. Fill in the appropriate times in the blanks below.

Breakfast (*zǎocān* 早餐) _____ A.M.

Lunch (*wǔcān* 午餐) _____ P.M.

Dinner (*wǎncān* 晚餐) _____ P.M.

3.52 *These two handwritten notes both arrange meeting times. Fill in the blanks below.*

Note 1:

小明. 五月十七号星期天.
下午四点半在图书馆门口
见. 好吗?

唐润

Xiao Ming: Let's meet at the entrance to the library on _____,
(DAY OF THE WEEK)

_____, at _____, OK? Tang Run.
(DATE)　　　　　(TIME)

Note 2:

我明天早上八
點一刻在車站
等你, 行嗎?

I'll wait for you _____ at _____ at the bus stop, all right?
(DAY)　　　　　　　(TIME)

▶ Learning to write characters

3.53 *For stroke order and other useful information about each of the following characters from this unit, go to the* Character Writing Workbook. *Choose traditional or simplified characters and practice writing them until you can reproduce them on demand.*

現／现，在，點／点，分，半，上，下，午，早，晚，今，
天，星，期，時／时，候，有，事，等

▶ Writing a note

3.54 *Write a note to a friend named* 王今*, telling her when you will meet up with her. If you need to write a term for which you don't know the characters, use pinyin.*

Cultural Bits 文化点滴

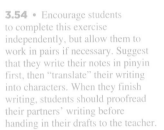

Time and timeliness

View the video segment "Time and timeliness" and then discuss the following questions with your classmates.

- How punctual would it seem the Chinese tend to be?
- What should you keep in mind regarding punctuality when you have an appointment with someone in China?
- What is the role of the cell phone in making and keeping appointments?
- What do *chàbuduō*, *còuhuo*, and *mǎshàngdào* imply in terms of punctuality?

3.54 • Encourage students to complete this exercise independently, but allow them to work in pairs if necessary. Suggest that they write their notes in pinyin first, then "translate" their writing into characters. When they finish writing, students should proofread their partners' writing before handing in their drafts to the teacher.

• If time allows, and students permit, randomly deliver the class mail. Students should then read these notes and write appropriate responses.

• A sample note: 王今：我们后天下午四点半见；行吗？

Recap

▶ Grammar

Sentence-ending particle *le*

As you learned in an earlier unit, *le* is used at the end of a sentence to show that a change of state has occurred. This is called Change-of-State (COS) *le*.

Xiànzài jǐ diǎn le? (*What time is it getting to be? [We had better get on with our plans.]*)
Liǎng diǎn le! (*It's 2:00! [already—gosh it's so late!]*)
Wǒ yǐqián bù dǒng, xiànzài wǒ dǒng le. (*I didn't understand before, [but] now I do.*)

Measure words (MW) and the always handy *ge*

Several new measure words were introduced in this unit, mostly relating to time on the clock.

diǎn (MW for hours) sān diǎn zhōng (*3:00*)
kè (MW for quarter hours) sān diǎn yí kè (*3:15/ quarter past three*)
fēn (MW for minutes) qī diǎn wǔ fēn (*7:05*)

An additional measure word, *ge*, is an all-purpose measure and can replace most other measures. Keep in mind that you should learn the appropriate measure word with the related noun, but *ge* can be used with almost all nouns in a "language emergency."

yī ge xīngqī *(one week)*
sān ge yuè *(three months)*
sì ge shǒujī *(four cell phones)*

Specifying "here" and "there"

In order to specify a particular thing in Chinese, specifiers are used with appropriate measure words, numbers, and nouns.

Zhè shì wǒ de. *(This is mine.)*
nèi sān wèi lǎoshī *(those three teachers)*

To specify "here" and "there," similar words are used: *zhèr* and *nàr*.

Nǐ zài nàr, wǒ zài zhèr. *(You're there and I'm here.)*
Zhèr bù xíng, nàr hǎo. *(This [place] will not do; it's better there.)*

Be careful to distinguish: zhè   zhèi   zhèr
nà   nèi   nàr

Forming questions

There are several ways to form questions, and their use is often dictated by context and meaning.

Add the query particle *ma* to the end of a sentence.

Tā hǎo ma? *(How is he/she?)*

Add the particle *ne* to the end of a sentence to indicate a follow-up question.

Wǒ xìng Lǐ. Tā ne? *(My last name is Li. And his/hers?)*

Use a question word.

Shéi xìng Zhōu? *(Who is surnamed Zhou?)*

Provide alternatives with an untoned *bu* between the same verb.

Xīngqīyī hǎo bu hǎo? *(Is Monday all right?)*

Provide alternatives with *háishi*.

Nǐ gāo háishi wǒ gāo? *(Are you tall[er] or am I tall[er]?)*

Add *zěnmeyàng* to the end of a remark.

Xīngqītiān zěnmeyàng? *(What about Sunday?)*

Adding tone to whole sentences

Sentence-ending particles often add tone or emotion to an entire question or statement.

Add the particle *ba* to create a tone of suggestion.

Zǒu ba! *(Shall we go? / Let's be off, OK?)*

Add the particle *a* to suggest a certain heartiness, especially in greetings.

Hǎo a! *(Hi!)*
Zǎo a! *(Morning!)*

Forming tenses in Chinese

All verbs in Chinese are static and unchanging. The various tenses and their complications are expressed by adding words, not by changing the verb.

Wǒ zuótiān bù hǎo, jīntiān hǎo le, míngtiān bù zhīdào. *(I wasn't well yesterday, [but] I'm better today; I don't know about tomorrow.)*

Sān nián yǐqián wǒ zài Zhōngguó, míngnián wǒ hái yào qù. *(Three years ago I was in China; next year I'm going again.)*

▶ Vocabulary

Days of the week

Xīngqīyī 星期一 Monday

Xīngqī'èr 星期二 Tuesday

Xīngqīsān 星期三 Wednesday

Xīngqīsì 星期四 Thursday

Xīngqīwǔ 星期五 Friday

Xīngqīliù 星期六 Saturday

Xīngqītiān 星期天 Sunday

zhōurì 週日／周日 Sunday

zhōumò 週末／周末 weekend

Particles

ba 吧 [particle of suggestion]

nà 那 then, in that case

Pronouns

nàr 那兒／那儿 there

zhèr 這兒／这儿 here

Telling time (on the clock)

bàn 半 half an hour

chà 差 lack ("before the hour")

diǎn zhōng 點鐘／点钟 o'clock

fēn 分 minute (clock time)

guò 過／过 exceed ("past the hour")

kè 刻 quarter of an hour

líng 零 zero

shíhou 時候／时候 time; time on the clock

Time words

bànyè 半夜 midnight

gāngcái 剛才／刚才 just a moment ago

hòutiān 後天／后天 the day after tomorrow

jīntiān 今天 today

míngtiān 明天 tomorrow

qiántiān 前天 the day before yesterday

shàng ge yuè 上個月／上个月 last month

shàngwǔ 上午 morning, A.M.

tiān 天 day

wǎn 晚 late

wǎnshang 晚上 evening (from 6 P.M. until midnight)

xià ge yuè 下個月／下个月 next month

xiànzài 現在／现在 now; at present

xiàwǔ 下午 afternoon, P.M.

yǐhòu 以後／以后 after

yìhuǐr 一會兒／一会儿 (in a) little while

yǐqián 以前 before

zǎo 早 early; Good morning.

yèli 夜裡／夜里 at night, during the night, nighttime

zǎoshang 早上 morning (until 9–10 A.M.)

zhōngwǔ 中午 noon, midday

zuótiān 昨天 yesterday

Verbs

děi 得 must; need to

děng 等 wait; wait for; await

jiàn 見／见 meet up with (someone)

kěyǐ 可以 can, may

lái 來／来 come

méiyǒu 沒有 not have; be without

xíng 行 pass muster; be OK

yǒu 有 have

yǒukòng 有空 be free, have free time

yǒushì 有事 be busy; have something to do; be occupied

zǒu 走 leave; depart

Other words and expressions

háishi 還是／还是 or; rather

jǐ 幾／几 how many

kòng 空 free time

liǎng 兩／两 two (used with measures)

shàng 上 last (in a series)

tài 太 too; excessively

xià 下 next (in a series)

xīguā 西瓜 watermelon

yìdiǎnr 一點兒／一点儿 a bit; a little; some

❱ Checklist of "can do" statements

After completing this unit, you should be able to perform each of the following tasks.

Listening and speaking

☐ Understand and formulate questions about specific clock times.

☐ Understand statements and ask questions about divisions of the day.

☐ Ask and answer questions about days of the week and calendar dates.

☐ Arrange a mutually agreeable meeting time in a culturally appropriate manner.

☐ Provide your availability in terms of time of day, day of the week, calendar date, and in times relative to the present or the future.

☐ Understand when others give their availability relative to date and time.

☐ Negotiate and confirm a meeting time.

Reading and writing

☐ Read and understand simple notes about meeting times and dates.

☐ Write a simple statement about others' availability.

☐ Write a simple note confirming an appointment.

☐ Understand the layout of a handwritten or e-mail message.

Understanding culture

☐ Explain the concept of notating time "backward and downward" in Chinese.

☐ Explain what Beijing Standard Time means to the Chinese mainland.

Checklist

• Have students work in pairs to go through this checklist and demonstrate selected skills to the class. Reserve 20–30 minutes for students to complete this activity. Tell students that putting check marks in each box is NOT the point. The point is to check if they can really do the things on the list.

• You may want to lead the class in revisiting the list of expressions that students made for exercise 3.2; have they learned enough Chinese to say everything on the list, to satisfy real-life communication needs?

"If only we had met sooner"

相見恨晚

Xiāngjiànhènwǎn

Talking about your nationality and background

In this unit, you will learn how to:

- ask and answer questions about nationality.
- ask and answer questions about place of birth and places lived.
- ask and answer questions about travel experiences.
- ask and answer questions about language(s) spoken.

- recognize the names of 10–15 countries on postcards and in telephone directories.
- read simple self-introductory statements about nationality, place of birth, places lived, and language(s) spoken.
- write simple self-introductory statements including nationality, place of birth, places lived, and language(s) spoken.

Encounter 1 Expressing nationality

4.1 • Before watching Episode 4, ask students what they remember from previous episodes. Encourage them to respond in Chinese and English.

• Play the video clip twice, if necessary.

• Allow time for students to discuss the video among themselves. Understanding the plot is crucial for students to complete the unit's exercises.

4.2 • Possible answers: *What country are you from? Where are you from? I am American. I am from Nigeria.* The goal here is to encourage thinking about how people talk about countries and nationalities in real life.

• Invite students to offer answers "popcorn style."

• Have volunteers write answers on the board or on chart paper. Keep this list, and make sure to revisit it after completing this unit to check if students have learned enough Chinese to say everything on the list. The purpose of this activity is to help students connect what they're learning with real-life communication needs.

4.3 Key:
Nǐ shì něi guó rén?

4.4–4.5

• These exercises are designed to teach students the Chinese names for countries. There is no need to teach the words explicitly beforehand.

• Encourage students to read the pinyin words aloud to themselves or to their partners. In many cases, the sound of the words is a strong clue to meaning.

4.4 Key: Éguó, Zhōngguó, Rìběn

a. 3
b. 4
c. 5
d. 11
e. 12
f. 10
g. 6
h. 7
i. 2
j. 9
k. 8
l. 1·

4.1 *View Episode 4 of the dramatic series.*

4.2 *Getting ready:* How would you ask someone about his or her nationality in English? If someone asked you about your nationality, what would you say?

_____

4.3 *Watch and listen to the video segment. Write the pinyin transcription for the question "What nationality are you?"*

_____

4.4 *Match the corresponding pinyin and English for each of the following country names. Note: They are all examples of transliteration—using Chinese syllables that sound nearly the same as the pronunciation of the foreign term—except for three. Can you identify the three?*

_____   _____   _____

a. Měiguó   1. *Germany (Deutschland)*

b. Mòxīgē   2. *Thailand*

c. Yīngguó   3. *America*

d. Fǎguó   4. *Mexico*

e. Xībānyá   5. *England*

f. Yìdàlì   6. *Russia*

g. Éguó   7. *India (Hindu)*

h. Yìndù   8. *Japan*

i. Tàiguó   9. *China*

j. Zhōngguó   10. *Italy*

k. Rìběn   11. *France*

l. Déguó   12. *Spain (España)*

4.5 *Match the corresponding items below.*

a. Zhōngguórén 中國人   1. *English*   A. 泰国人

b. Měiguórén 美國人   2. *German*   B. 日本人

c. Rìběnrén 日本人   3. *Spanish*   C. 德国人

d. Hánguórén 韓國人   4. *Japanese*   D. 中国人

e. Fǎguórén 法國人   5. *Chinese*   E. 英国人

f. Déguórén 德國人   6. *Indian*   F. 西班牙人

g. Yīngguórén 英國人   7. *Thai*   G. 法国人

h. Yìndùrén 印度人   8. *Russian*   H. 美国人

i. Xībānyárén 西班牙人   9. *Korean*   I. 印度人

j. Yìdàlìrén 意大利人   10. *Italian*   J. 俄国人

k. Tàiguórén 泰國人   11. *American*   K. 韩国人

l. Éguórén 俄國人   12. *French*   L. 意大利人

4.6 *Write in pinyin what you would say if someone asked about your nationality. Ask your teacher if you don't know how to write the pinyin of your nationality.*

_____

4.6 Write *Qǐngwèn . . . zěnme shuō?* ("Excuse me, how do you say . . . ?") on the board for students to use as a prompt to ask you about any words they do not know. Sample answer: *Wǒ shì Měiguórén.*

4.7 *Mingling: If your class is very diverse, walk around and ask where your classmates are from, taking notes on their responses. If your class is homogeneous, choose a country (not your own) where you might like to be a citizen. Then walk around the class and find out where everyone is "from."*

4.7 • Before releasing students to mingle, make sure they know how to ask and answer questions about nationality. Review exercises 4.4 and 4.5 if needed. Invite a confident pair to do a demonstration if you find it necessary.

• During the activity, mingle with your students to observe their performance. Do not interrupt students' dialogues to correct pronunciation unless the mistakes change the intended meaning. Instead, make a mental note and review correct pronunciation with the entire class after the activity.

• Recap the activity by asking the class, for example, *Wǒmen yǒu jǐ ge tóngxué shì Měiguórén? Wǒmen yǒu jǐ ge tóngxué shì Yìdàlìrén?* ("How many of us are Americans? How many of us are Italians?")

Qǐngwèn, nǐ shì něiguó rén?

Wǒ shì . . .

▶ Reading practice

4.8 • Have students read these characters aloud multiple times to themselves and to a partner.
• Discourage students from writing the pinyin forms next to the characters. Instead, tell students to flip back to previous pages to look up the pinyin when they forget a character.

4.8 *Read the following country names aloud.*

中國／中国   美國／美国   日本

英國／英国   印度   西班牙

韓國／韩国   法國／法国   德國／德国

意大利   泰國／泰国   俄國／俄国

Encounter 2 Talking about your birthplace and where you have lived

4.9 • Possible questions and answers: *Where were you born? Did you grow up in China? Are you from California originally? No, I'm from Vermont, and moved here five years ago.*
• Invite students to offer answers "popcorn style."

4.9 *Getting ready: How would you ask people in English where they were born and where they have lived? If someone asked you the same questions, what would you say?*

_____

_____

4.10 • Before playing the video, ask students to read through the dialogue to see if they can predict some of the answers from context.
• Have students compare answers with multiple classmates, and have volunteers share their answers on the board.

4.10 Key:
a.
A. born
B. Guilin; Beijing
A. was born in Beijing; home; Shanghai
b.
A. the United States
B. born; home; Where

4.10 *Watch and listen to the video segment. Complete the English transcription of each dialogue.*

a.

A: Where were you _____?

B: I was born in _____, but I grew up in _____. How about you?

A: I _____, and my _____ is in Beijing, but I've also lived in _____.

b.

A: Where in _____ do you come from?

B: I was _____ in Washington and I've lived in many places. Now my _____ is in Honolulu. And you? _____ have you lived?

A: I have only lived here.

4.11 *Match the pinyin with the corresponding English below.*

a. Wǒ shēngzai Běijīng.   1. *My home is in Beijing.*

b. Wǒ shì zài Běijīng zhǎngdà de.   2. *I was born in Beijing.*

c. Wǒ jiā zài Běijīng.   3. *I've lived in Beijing before.*

d. Wǒ zhùzai Běijīng.   4. *I grew up in Beijing.*

e. Wǒ yǐqián zài Běijīng zhùguo.   5. *I live in Beijing.*

4.11 Key:
a. 2
b. 4
c. 1
d. 5
e. 3

4.12 • If students have a hard time, tell them that corresponding questions and answers most likely share a similar sentence pattern or key words. With this in mind, they should find answers for *b*, *c*, and *d* rather quickly.
• For *a*, you might need to tell them that *chūshēng = shēng.*
• For *e*, ask students to recall the meaning of *Zhōngguó.*

4.12 *Match the questions with the appropriate answers below.*

a. Nǐ shì zài nǎr chūshēng de?   1. *Wǒ yǐqián zài Běijīng zhùguo.*

b. Nǐ shì zài nǎr zhǎngdà de?   2. *Wǒ shì Běijīngrén.*

c. Nǐ jiā zài nǎr?   3. *Wǒ shēngzai Běijīng.*

d. Nǐ zài nǎr zhùguo?   4. *Wǒ shì zài Běijīng zhǎngdà de.*

e. Nǐ shì Zhōngguó nǎli rén?   5. *Wǒ jiā zài Běijīng.*

4.12 Key:
a. 3
b. 4
c. 5
d. 1
e. 2

4.13 *Match the pinyin with the corresponding characters.*

a. Nǐ shì zài nǎr chūshēng de?   1. 你在哪兒住過？／你在哪儿住过？

b. Wǒ shēngzai Fǎguó.   2. 我是北京人。

c. Nǐ shì zài nǎr zhǎngdà de?   3. 你是在哪兒出生的？／你是在哪儿出生的？

d. Wǒ shì zài Éguó zhǎngdà de.   4. 你是在哪兒長大的？／你是在哪儿长大的？

e. Nǐ jiā zài nǎr?   5. 我是在俄國長大的。／我是在俄国长大的。

f. Wǒ jiā zài Měiguó.   6. 我以前在日本住過。／我以前在日本住过。

g. Nǐ zài nǎr zhùguo?   7. 你是中國哪裡人？／你是中国哪里人？

h. Wǒ yǐqián zài Rìběn zhùguo.   8. 我生在法國。／我生在法国。

i. Nǐ shì Zhōngguó nǎli rén?   9. 你家在哪兒？／你家在哪儿？

j. Wǒ shì Běijīngrén.   10. 我家在美國。／我家在美国。

4.13 Tell students not to get stuck on unfamiliar characters. They should rather use the pinyin and familiar characters as bridges to figure out answers.

4.13 Key:
a. 3
b. 8
c. 4
d. 5
e. 9
f. 10
g. 1
h. 6
i. 7
j. 2

FYI 供你参考

So, where are you from?

In major cities of the Western world, people often ask where someone was born and grew up, or where a person has lived. These facts may have nothing to do with ethnicity or citizenship; an ethnically Chinese person with U.S. citizenship may have been born and raised in India, and subsequently lived all over Europe, for example. In China, these questions and the language you have learned so far in this unit are less commonly used. Instead, Chinese people often ask each other *Nǐ de lǎo jiā zài nǎr?* 你的老家在哪兒？／你的老家在哪儿？which literally means, "Where is your old home?" The response is usually where someone was born and raised. Foreigners are often confused by this question and need the specificity of the language introduced thus far. For example, how could you identify your "old home" when you were born in one place, raised for a while in another place, and then moved every two years throughout your childhood?

Another typical Chinese question about origins is *Nǐ de zǔjí zài nǎr?* 你的祖籍在哪兒？／你的祖籍在哪儿？or "Where is your ancestral home?" The response to this question is usually where someone's father's family lived for many generations. A Chinese person currently living in Beijing or Shanghai may have an ancestral home in the Shandong or Hunan countryside, for example.

4.14 *How would you describe your background—where you were born, where you grew up, where you have lived, and where you live now? Write the following statements in pinyin, using the English as a guide. If you don't know how to say the name of a town in Chinese, just write it in English, or ask your teacher.*

I was born in . . . _____

I grew up in . . . _____

I've lived in . . . _____

Right now, I live in . . . _____

4.15 Mingling: *Ask several classmates where they were born, where they grew up, where they have lived, and where they live now. Tell the same about yourself. Take some notes about your classmates below.*

Name: _____

Background: _____

Name: _____

Background: _____

Name: _____

Background: _____

4.16 *Fill in the following paragraph with details about yourself. Complete the sentences with either pinyin or English.*

4.16 Tell students to use exercise 4.13 to figure out the meaning of unfamiliar characters.

我生在＿＿＿＿＿＿＿＿＿＿，是在＿＿＿＿＿＿＿＿＿＿＿長大的。我住過

＿＿＿＿＿＿＿＿＿＿。現在我家在＿＿＿＿＿＿＿＿＿＿＿。

Grammar Bits 语法点滴

Sharing experiences: Verb + *guo*

When you want to say that you have or haven't had an experience, use the verbal suffix *guo* (tonally neutral) in conjunction with the appropriate verb. Chinese verbs with the *guo* suffix typically mirror English expressions in the present perfect, such as "Have you ever . . . ?" The reference is always to past actions, never present or future. Therefore, verb + *guo* constructions imply a finished and complete action; it is no longer being performed. To form the negative expression, use *méi* or *méiyǒu* in conjunction with *guo*.

Nǐ qùguo Zhōngguó ma?	*(Have you ever been to China?)*
Qùguo. Qùnián qùguo.	*(Yes, I have. I went last year.)*
Méi(yǒu) qùguo, kěshì hěn xiǎng qù.	*(No, I haven't, but I'd really like to go.)*

4.17 • Possible answers: *Have you been to China? What places have you been to? I've never been to China. I haven't been anywhere outside the United States.*

• Have volunteers add answers to the list they began in exercise 4.2. Keep this list and revisit it after completing the unit to see if students have learned enough Chinese to say everything on the list.

Encounter 3 Talking about travel experiences

4.17 *Getting ready: How would you ask people in English where they have traveled or would like to travel? If someone asked you the same question, what would you say?*

_____

4.18–4.19

• Play the video multiple times and feel free to pause the video and give hints, if necessary. Allow time for students to discuss and compare answers with one another.

• If students are stuck on exercise 4.18, have them move on and complete exercise 4.19 before returning to 4.18.

4.18 *Watch and listen to the video segment. Number the English translations below in the order in which the Chinese sentences occur in the dialogue.*

_____3_____ I haven't been anywhere outside of China. How about you?

_____6_____ I don't want to go anywhere.

_____2_____ Suzhou, Beijing, Shanghai, Guangzhou.

_____1_____ What places have you been to?

_____4_____ I've gone to many places.

_____7_____ I like staying at home. I don't like traveling.

_____5_____ Europe, South America, Asia, Africa.

Grammar Bits • After students have read this Grammar Bits in pairs, have them write and perform a skit with at least three exchanges (i.e., each person must speak at least three times), using *dōu* at least four times.
• While students write their skits, circulate in the room to assist, observe, and check students' comprehension of the usage of *dōu*. Pay special attention to the word order in students' *dōu* sentences.
• Have pairs exchange and proofread each others' scripts before they memorize and perform them.

4.19 *Now complete the pinyin transcription of the dialogue.*

Lynn: Nǐ dōu dàoguo _____ dìfang?

Tang: Sūzhōu, Běijīng, Shànghǎi, Guǎngzhōu. Búguò, wǒ méiyou chūguo guó. Chúle _____ de zhèi xiē dìfāng, wǒ nǎr dōu _____ qùguo. Nǐ ne?

Lynn: Wǒ qùguo hěn _____ dìfang: Ōuzhōu, Nán Měizhōu, _____, _____, dōu qùguo. Kěshì, háiyǒu hěn duō dìfang méi qùguo.

Tang: Wǒ nǎr dōu bù _____ qù. Wǒ xǐhuan dāizai jiālǐ, _____ xǐhuan lǚxíng.

4.19 Key:
Lynn: shénme
Tang: Zhōngguó; méi
Lynn: duō; Yàzhōu; Fēizhōu
Tang: xiǎng, bù

Grammar Bits 语法点滴

The "flexible" adverb *dōu*

The adverb *dōu* operates in several language environments. First, it can mean "all."

> Wǒmen dōu hǎo. *(We are all well.)*
> Wǒmen dōu bù hǎo. *(All of us are not well. = None of us is well.)*

Second, *dōu* supports "all inclusive/exclusive" statements with the help of question words.

shéi + dōu ⇒ "everyone"
shéi + dōu + bù ⇒ "no one"
> Q: Shéi qù? *(Who is going?)*
> A: Shéi dōu qù. *(Everyone is going.)*
> B: Shéi dōu bú qù. *(No one is going.)*

nǎr + dōu ⇒ "everywhere"
nǎr + dōu + bù ⇒ "nowhere"
> Q: Nǐ xiǎng qù nǎr? *(Where do you want to go?)*
> A: Wǒ nǎr dōu xiǎng qù. *(I'd like to go everywhere.)*
> B: Wǒ nǎr dōu bù xiǎng qù. *(I don't want to go anywhere.)*

shénme + dōu ⇒ "everything"
shénme + dōu + bù ⇒ "nothing"
> Q: Nǐ yào shénme? *(What do you want?)*
> A: Wǒ shénme dōu yào. *(I want everything.)*
> B: Wǒ shénme dōu bú yào. *(I don't want anything.)*

Third, *dōu* acts to "totalize" when requesting and providing particulars or lists.

> Nǐ dōu qùguo nǎr? *(Where all have you been to?)*
> Zhōngguó, Rìběn, Hánguó, wǒ dōu qùguo. *(China, Japan, Korea—I've been to them all.)*

Always remember that, in Chinese grammar, word position is of greatest importance.

Nǐ dōu qùguo shénme dìfang?

Wǒ nǎr dōu méi qùguo.

4.20 *Circle the correct English translation of each term below.*

a. 都 dōu   *(all) (everywhere)*

b. 到過／到过 dàoguo   *(talked to) (been to)*

c. 甚麼地方／什么地方 shénme dìfang   *(this place) (what place)*

d. 哪兒都没去過／哪儿都没去过 nǎr dōu méi qùguo   *(haven't been anywhere)*
   (have been everywhere)

e. 去過／去过 qùguo   *(gone to) (lived at)*

f. 歐洲／欧洲 Ōuzhōu   *(Australia) (Europe)*

g. 南美洲 Nán Měizhōu   *(North America) (South America)*

h. 非洲 Fēizhōu   *(Europe) (Africa)*

i. 哪兒都不想去／哪儿都不想去 nǎr dōu bù xiǎng qù   *(have not been anywhere)*
   (don't want to go anywhere)

j. 喜歡／喜欢 xǐhuan   *(like to) (want to)*

k. 呆在家裡／呆在家里 dāizai jiālǐ   *(live in a place) (stay at home)*

l. 旅行 lǚxíng   *(travel) (stay put)*

4.21 *Match the corresponding English and pinyin below.*

a. *What are all the places you have been to?*   1. Nǐ xiǎng qù { shénme dìfang? / nǎr? }

b. *Where would you like to go?*   2. Nǐ dōu qùguo { shénme dìfang? / nǎr? }

4.22 *Answer each question below by filling in the blank with either pinyin or English.*

你都去過甚麼地方？／你都去过什么地方？ Nǐ dōu qùguo shénme dìfang?

我去過／我去过 _____

你想去甚麼地方？／你想去什么地方？ Nǐ xiǎng qù shénme dìfang?

我很想去 _____

4.23 *Mingling: Speak to two or more of your classmates. Find out where they've traveled and where they would like to travel.*

4.20 • Have students work in pairs to complete this exercise.
• Before starting the exercise, make sure to give students time to read the Grammar Bits in class for understanding.
• There is no need to teach grammar explicitly, as exercise 4.20 creates a context for students to apply their knowledge. Students will understand the grammar by using it.
• Remind students they can use exercises 4.18, 4.19, and Grammar Bits if they need help.

4.20 Key:
a. dōu – all
b. dàoguo – been to
c. shénme dìfang – what place
d. nǎr dōu méi qùguo – haven't been anywhere
e. qùguo – gone to
f. Ōuzhōu – Europe
g. Nán Měizhōu – South America
h. Fēizhōu – Africa
i. nǎr dōu bù xiǎng qù – don't want to go anywhere
j. xǐhuan – like to
k. dāizai jiālǐ – stay at home
l. lǚxíng – travel

4.21 Key:
a. 2
b. 1

4.22 • Students may ask you how to say some English place names in Chinese. Be ready to act as a live dictionary to supply new words. For states and big cities, provide pinyin equivalents. For others, ask students to write the names in English.
• On the board, write . . . *zěnme shuō?* ("How to you say . . . ?") as a prompt for students to elicit words from you.

4.23 • Mingle with your students, and assist when necessary.
• Do not interrupt students to correct pronunciation, unless the errors severely alter students' intended meaning.
• If you notice that students are having a hard time producing the appropriate language, provide necessary guidance as they practice the interview one more time with the same partner.

Encounter 4 Talking about languages spoken

4.24 • Possible answers: *Do you speak Swahili? What's your native tongue? How many languages do you speak? I took French for two years, but can't really speak it. I am fluent in Hindi. She is bilingual. My first language is German.*

• Have volunteers add answers to the list they began in exercise 4.2. Keep this list and revisit it after completing the unit to see if students have learned enough Chinese to say everything on the list.

4.25 Key:
Zhōng

4.26 Key:
a. 1. B
b. 3. A
c. 2. C

4.24 Getting ready: *How would you ask someone in English if he or she speaks a certain language? If someone asked you the same question, what would you say?*

_____

_____

4.25 *Watch and listen to the video segment. Fill in the blank below.*

Nǐ huì shuō _____ wén ma?   *(Do you speak Chinese?)*

4.26 *Match the corresponding items below.*

a. 會説 huì shuō

b. 會説一點兒 huì shuō yìdiǎnr

c. 不會説 bú huì shuō

1. *can speak*

2. *can't speak*

3. *can speak a little*

A. 会说一点儿

B. 会说

C. 不会说

Deflecting a compliment

Give students the following task before they read this section: Read this FYI with a partner, and then prepare a short skit in which one person asks the other if he or she can speak Chinese. The first person should respond modestly, and the second should then compliment this person on how well he or she speaks Chinese.

FYI 供你参考

Deflecting a compliment

Modesty is a cardinal virtue in Chinese culture. If someone asks if you can speak a language, you might downplay your ability, as the people in the video do. Even if you were fluent, you might only say *Huì shuō yìdiǎnr* 會説一點兒／会说一点儿 or *Huì shuō* 會説／会说. Other people might compliment you, however: *Nǐ shuō de hěn hǎo!* 你説得很好!／你说得很好! (You speak very well!). The proper response to such a compliment, traditionally, is to deny it by saying something like *Bù, bù, shuō de bù hǎo* 不，不，説得不好／不，不，说得不好. A common denial is *Nǎli, nǎli* 哪裡，哪裡／哪里，哪里, which literally means "Where, where" but by extension means "How could you say that? I'm not good at all." Another popular expression is *Guòjiǎng, guòjiǎng* 過奬,過奬／过奖,过奖, which means "You flatter me." In modern, urban China, however, you'll also find some Chinese being OK with your simply accepting the compliment, as Westerners do, by saying *Xièxie* 謝謝／谢谢.

4.27 • To prepare students for this activity, review the FYI note on this page for understanding. Have volunteers write all possible polite responses on the board.

• Encourage students to use body language in their dialogues. Use the video as a model.

4.27 Pair work: *Compliment your partner on his or her Chinese by saying* Nǐ Zhōngwén shuō de hěn hǎo! *Your partner should respond to your compliment with a polite response. Practice a few times, each time with a different response. Then switch roles.*

4.28 *Watch and listen to the video segment. Match the corresponding pinyin and English.*

a. Zhōngwén / Zhōngguóhuà

b. Yīngwén / Yīngyǔ

c. Rìwén / Rìyǔ / Rìběnhuà

d. Hánwén / Hányǔ / Hánguóhuà

e. Fǎwén / Fǎyǔ / Fǎguóhuà

f. Déwén / Déyǔ / Déguóhuà

g. Xībānyáwén / Xībānyáyǔ / Xībānyáhuà

h. Éwén / Éyǔ / Éguóhuà

i. Yìndùwén / Yìndùyǔ / Yìndùhuà

1. *English*

2. *Chinese*

3. *Russian*

4. *Hindi*

5. *Korean*

6. *German*

7. *French*

8. *Japanese*

9. *Spanish*

4.29 *Watch and listen to the video segment. Write, in English, the language that each of the following people speaks.*

a. _____

b. _____

c. _____

d. _____

e. _____

f. _____

g. _____

h. _____

FYI 供你参考

Chinese languages and dialects

The language situation in China is both simple and complex, as it is in most countries as large as China. It is complex because there are many spoken languages (sometimes called "dialects") in the country, but it is also simple because nearly all Chinese people speak the national language—*Pǔtōnghuà* 普通話／普通话 (common language). It is the language taught in Chinese schools, heard in the media (on the radio, on television, and in the movies), and taught in *Encounters*. More good news is that the form of Mandarin Chinese spoken in Taiwan (called *Guóyǔ* 國語／国语, meaning "national language") and in Chinese communities throughout Southeast Asia (called *Huáyǔ* 華語／华语, meaning "Sino language") is virtually the same as *Pǔtōnghuà*. A person from Taiwan speaking the standard language has little or no difficulty speaking with someone from Mainland China. The written language, except for the differences between simplified and traditional characters, does not differ at all.

Some Chinese "dialects" include:

• *Guǎngdōnghuà* 廣東話／广东话—spoken in the southern province of Guangdong and Hong Kong; called "Cantonese" in the United States
• *Shànghǎihuà* 上海話／上海话—spoken in Shanghai and nearby communities
• *Mǐnnányǔ* 閩南語／闽南语—spoken in southern Fujian province on the coast of China opposite Taiwan; called *Táiwānhuà* 台灣話／台湾话 in Taiwan

4.30 *What languages do you speak? Fill in the blanks below with as many languages as you see fit. Write in pinyin.*

Q: Nǐ huì shuō shénme huà?

A: Wǒ huì shuō _____.

Wǒ yě huì shuō yìdiǎnr _____, kěshì shuō de bù hǎo.

4.31 *Mingling: Make a list of all the languages you speak. (For the purposes of this exercise, if you know even one word of that language, count it.) Walk around the room and speak to at least three people. Find out which languages they speak and tell them which languages you speak.*

Nǐ huì shuō shénme huà?

Wǒ huì shuō . . .

▶ Putting it all together

4.32 *Prepare to mingle: Make a list of six questions you know how to ask in pinyin. For each question, write how you would answer if it were asked of you.*

_____

_____

_____

_____

_____

4.32 • Divide the class into 3–4 small groups. Tell students that their task as a class is to brainstorm and

> **Some ideas:**
> name
> age
> birth sign
> phone number
> address
> nationality
> places lived
> places traveled
> languages spoken

come up with questions to elicit the information listed in the box. They should also think of possible ways to answer these questions. Assign each group 2–3 categories, and have group members negotiate among themselves to divide up the list.

• Remind students to refer back to previous units in their textbook for guidance.

• Write all nine categories on the board. Invite volunteers from each group to fill the board with the questions and answers they identified.

4.33 *Mingling: Mingle with your classmates. Take turns asking and answering questions. Speak to each classmate for a minute or two and then take your leave and move on. Continue until your teacher tells you time is up.*

4.33 • To create an interesting context for this activity, tell students that the class is about to have a party. Point out that the situation described in the instructions is a common occurrence at parties. To make the party feel more real, play quiet music in the background.

• Join the party and mingle with your students! Provide guidance when necessary.

• Use this "party" as an opportunity to assess students' speaking and listening skills for the unit.

♫ Unit Rap

Go to the **Encounters** *website at* www.EncountersChinese.com *and listen to the song to review key expressions from Unit 4. Listen again and sing along!*

Encounter 5 Reading and writing

▶ Reading familiar sentences in Chinese characters

4.34 *Pair work: Read the following dialogues (written in traditional characters) aloud with a partner, using the English as a guide.*

1 甲：你是哪國人？ *(What's your nationality?)*
乙：我是英國人。你呢？ *(I'm English. And you?)*
甲：我是德國人。 *(I'm German.)*

2 甲：你是日本人嗎？ *(Are you Japanese?)*
乙：不，我是韓國人。你呢？ *(No, I'm Korean. And you?)*
甲：我是泰國人。 *(I'm Thai.)*

4.34 • Avoid reading these dialogues aloud for your students or having them repeat after you. Tell them to use the English and familiar characters as bridges to determine the meaning and pronunciation of unknown characters.

• Keep in mind that reading fluency is not the goal of this activity; students are merely gaining practice in matching unfamiliar characters with meaning. Tell students to not get discouraged if they have trouble reading quickly and accurately.

• Have students complete this exercise multiple times before they move on to 4.35 and 4.36.

3 甲：你是西班牙人，對不對？ *(You're Spanish, right?)*

乙：不，我是印度人。 *(No, I'm Indian.)*

4 甲：你是哪國人？ *(What's your nationality?)*

乙：我是美國人，可是我是在法國出生的。 *(I'm American, but I was born in France.)*

甲：你家在哪兒？ *(Where is your home?)*

乙：在中國！我家在北京。 *(In China! My home is in Beijing.)*

5 甲：你在哪裡住過？ *(Where have you lived?)*

乙：我住過很多地方。中國，歐洲，日本——都住過。 *(I've lived many places. China, Europe, Japan—I've lived in them all.)*

甲：你去過非洲嗎？ *(Have you been to Africa?)*

乙：沒有。可是很想去。你呢？你住過甚麼地方？ *(No, but I'd really like to go. And you? Where have you lived?)*

甲：我在美國出生，美國長大的，我一直住在美國。可是我明年會去非洲。 *(I was born in the United States, [I] grew up in the United States, I've lived in the United States throughout [yìzhí]. But next year I'll go to Africa.)*

6 甲：那個人叫Alex。我想他是法國人。 *(That person's name is Alex. I think he's French.)*

乙：不對，不對。他是英國人，可是他會說法語。 *(No, no. He's English, but he can speak French.)*

7 甲：你會說日語嗎？ *(Can you speak Japanese?)*

乙：不會。我只會說中文。 *(No. I can only speak Chinese.)*

8 甲：你去過歐洲嗎？ *(Have you been to Europe?)*

乙：去過。我去過德國和法國。今年我會去俄國。 *(I have. I've been to Germany and France. This year I'm going to Russia.)*

甲：你會說俄語嗎？ *(Can you speak Russian?)*

乙：只會說一點兒。 *(I can only speak a little.)*

9 甲：老師，您去過美國嗎？ *(Teacher, have you been to the United States?)*

乙：沒有。我只去過亞洲很多國家。日本，泰國…… *(No. I've only been to many countries in Asia. Japan, Thailand . . .)*

甲：您想去美國旅行嗎？ *(Would you like to go traveling in the United States?)*

乙：想，也想去歐洲旅行。 *(Yes, I'd also like to travel in Europe.)*

10 甲：你喜歡旅行嗎？ *(Do you like to travel?)*

乙：不喜歡。我哪兒都不想去。我只想呆在家裡。 *(No. I don't want to go anywhere. I just want to stay home.)*

4.35 *Pair work: Read the dialogues aloud with a partner, this time without any English.*

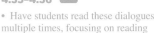

4.35–4.36

- Have students read these dialogues multiple times, focusing on reading fluency.
- Encourage students *not* to refer to exercise 4.34 for help. Instead, ask them to rely on the dialogue context and their partners to help them read new characters.
- After students practice reading the dialogues a few times, play the audio and have them check their pronunciation.

1 甲：你是哪國人？

乙：我是英國人。你呢？

甲：我是德國人。

2 甲：你是日本人嗎？

乙：不，我是韓國人。你呢？

甲：我是泰國人。

3 甲：你是西班牙人，對不對？

乙：不，我是印度人。

4 甲：你是哪國人？

乙：我是美國人，可是我是在法國出生的。

甲：你家在哪兒？

乙：在中國！我家在北京。

5 甲：你在哪裡住過？

乙：我住過很多地方。中國，歐洲，日本都住過。

甲：你去過非洲嗎？

乙：沒有。可是我很想去。你呢？你住過甚麼地方？

甲：我在美國出生，美國長大的，我一直住在美國。可是我明年會去非洲。

6 甲：那個人名字叫Alex。我想他是法國人。

乙：不對，不對。他是英國人，可是他會說法語。

7 甲：你會說日語嗎？

乙：不會。我只會說中文。

8 甲：你去過歐洲嗎？

乙：去過。我去過德國和法國。今年我會去俄國。

甲：你會說俄語嗎？

乙：只會說一點兒。

9 甲：老師，您去過美國嗎？

乙：沒有。我只去過亞洲很多國家。日本，泰國……

甲：您想去美國嗎？

乙：想，也想去歐洲旅行。

10 甲：你喜歡旅行嗎？

乙：不喜歡。我哪兒都不想去。我只想呆在家裡。

4.36 *Pair work: Read the dialogues aloud one more time, this time in simplified characters.*

1 甲：你是哪国人？

乙：我是英国人。你呢？

甲：我是德国人。

2 甲：你是日本人吗？

乙：不，我是韩国人。你呢？

甲：我是泰国人。

3 甲：你是西班牙人，对不对？

乙：不，我是印度人。

4 甲：你是哪国人？

乙：我是美国人，可是我是在法国出生的。

甲：你家在哪儿？

乙：在中国！我家在北京。

5 甲：你在哪里住过？

乙：我住过很多地方。中国，欧洲，日本都住过。

甲：你去过非洲吗？

乙：没有。可是我很想去。你呢？你住过什么地方？

甲：我在美国出生，美国长大的，我一直住在美国。可是我明年会去非洲。

6 甲：那个人叫Alex。我想他是法国人。

乙：不对，不对。他是英国人，可是他会说法语。

7 甲：你会说日语吗？

乙：不会。我只会说中文。

8 甲：你去过欧洲吗？

乙：去过。我去过德国和法国。今年我会去俄国。

甲：你会说俄语吗？

乙：只会说一点儿。

9 甲：老师，您去过美国吗？

乙：没有。我只去过亚洲很多国家。日本，泰国……

甲：您想去美国吗？

乙：想，也想去欧洲旅行。

10 甲：你喜欢旅行吗？

乙：不喜欢。我哪儿都不想去。我只想呆在家里。

4.37 *Match the corresponding simplified characters, traditional characters, and English.*

a. 哪国	1. 去過	A. *Korea*
b. 韩国	2. 哪裡	B. *be able to speak*
c. 泰国来的	3. 韓國	C. *which country*
d. 哪里	4. 哪國	D. *come from Thailand*
e. 住过	5. 泰國來的	E. *have been to*
f. 欧洲	6. 住過	F. *where*
g. 去过	7. 甚麼地方	G. *have lived in*
h. 呆在家里	8. 會说	H. *Europe*
i. 什么地方	9. 歐洲	I. *grow up*
j. 会说	10. 長大	J. *what places*
k. 长大	11. 俄國	K. *have never been to*
l. 俄国	12. 哪兒都不想去	L. *French person*
m. 没去过	13. 法國人	M. *Russia*
n. 法国人	14. 喜歡	N. *don't want to go anywhere*
o. 喜欢	15. 呆在家裡	O. *remain at home*
p. 哪儿都不想去	16. 没去過	P. *like*

▶ Reading real-life texts

4.38–4.41
• If possible, copy these exercises onto a transparency for the convenience of comparing and sharing answers in class.
• Have students work in pairs or small groups to assist each other.

4.38 *Look at the sign in the window of a restaurant. Circle the characters for "India."*

4.38 Key:
India: 印度

4.39 Key:
Korea: 韓國

4.39 *Look at the sign in the window of a restaurant. Circle the characters for "Korea."*

4.40 Key:
a. Spain: 34
    France: 33
    Japan: 81
    Germany: 49
b. Russia: 7
    USA: 1
    Thailand: 66
    Italy: 39
    Britain: 44

Students have not learned the characters for Argentina (54), Australia (61); Canada (1), Mexico (52), Hong Kong (852), and Singapore (65). If students are curious, you may wish to teach these new countries once the exercise has been completed.

4.40 *This is a table of long-distance direct-dial country codes to use when you are making a call out of China.*

国际直拨电话国家代码一览表		
阿根廷 54	美国 1	西班牙 34
澳大利亚 61	墨西哥 52	新加坡 65
俄国 7	日本 81	意大利 39
法国 33	泰国 66	德国 49
加拿大 1	香港 852	英国 44

a. Write the telephone codes for the following countries:

Spain _____   France _____   Japan _____   Germany _____

b. Write the telephone codes for five more countries:

Country   Code

_____   _____

_____   _____

_____   _____

_____   _____

_____   _____

4.41 *The following is a postcard mailed to Taiwan. What does it say? Fill in the blanks below.*

Lili:

_____?

_____ is lots of fun.

_____ quickly!

Rongrong

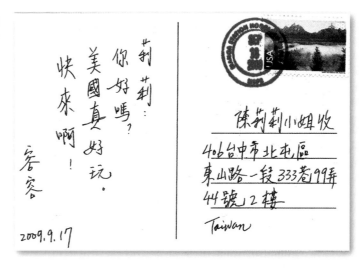

4.41 You may want to ask students to determine whether the note is written with simplified or traditional characters before they read it for meaning.

4.41 Key:
Lili:
<u>How are you?</u>
<u>America</u> is lots of fun.
<u>Come</u> quickly!
Rongrong

Learning to write characters

4.42 *For stroke order and other useful information about each of the following characters from this unit, go to the* Character Writing Workbook. *Choose either traditional or simplified characters and practice writing them until you can reproduce them on demand.*

國／国，中，英，美，出，會／会，説／说，話／话，
文，得，去，過／过，家，都，没，喜，歡／欢

Writing a note

4.43 *Write a few sentences to a new friend, telling him or her your nationality, where you have lived in the past, and what language(s) you speak.*

4.43 • Encourage students to complete this exercise independently, but allow them to work in pairs if necessary. Suggest that they write their notes in pinyin first, then "translate" their writing into characters. When they finish writing, students should proofread their partners' writing before handing in their drafts.

• If time allows, and students permit, randomly deliver the class mail. Students should then read these notes and write appropriate responses.

• A sample note:
你好，我是美国人。我在加州出生。我去过中国和欧洲。我会说法语和一点儿中文。

Cultural Bits 文化点滴

Social interaction

View the video segment "Social interaction" and then discuss the following questions with your classmates.

• What is the function of the name card in establishing new relationships?

• Why might people ask where you're from? or where your parents came from?

• What is *zǔjí*?

• What do *guānxi* and *gǎnqíng* mean? What is the significance of *guānxi* and *gǎnqíng*?

Recap

▶ Grammar

The *shì . . . de* construction: Review

This pattern zeroes in on specific aspects of past actions, such as when, where, how, what, etc.

Nǐ shì zài nǎr chūshēng de? *(Where were you born?)*

Wǒ shì zài Běijīng chūshēng de. *(I was born in Beijing.)*

Verb + *guo*

Use an appropriate verb + *guo* to express having had an experience in the past.

Nǐ qùguo shénme dìfang? *(Where have you been?)*

Wǒ qùguo Měiguó hé Rìběn, méi qùguo Zhōngguó. *(I've been to the United States and Japan [but I] haven't been to China.)*

dōu + verb

Dōu, when used before a verb, means "all."

Nǐ dōu dàoguo shénme dìfang? *(What [all] places have you been to?)*

Ōuzhōu, Yàzhōu, Běi Měizhōu—dōu qùguo. *(Europe, Asia, North America—[I've] been to all [of them].)*

dōu + question word

Dōu, when used in conjunction with a question word, is "all inclusive" in an affirmative statement and "all exclusive" in a negative statement.

Wǒ nǎr dōu xiǎng qù. *(I'd like to go anywhere and everywhere.)*

Wǒ nǎr dōu méi qùguo. *(I haven't been anywhere.)*

Wǒ nǎr dōu bù xiǎng qù. *(I don't want to go anywhere.)*

▶ Vocabulary

Continents

Běi Měizhōu 北美洲 North America
Fēizhōu 非洲 Africa
Nán Měizhōu 南美洲 South America
Ōuzhōu 歐洲／欧洲 Europe
Yàzhōu 亞洲／亚洲 Asia

Country names and nationalities

[Asia]

Hánguó / Hánguórén 韓國／韓國人 ‖ 韩国／韩国人 Korea / Korean
Rìběn / Rìběnrén 日本／日本人 Japan / Japanese
Tàiguó / Tàiguórén 泰國／泰國人 ‖ 泰国／泰国人 Thailand / Thai
Yìndù / Yìndùrén 印度／印度人 India / Indian
Zhōngguó / Zhōngguórén 中國／中國人 ‖ 中国／中国人 China / Chinese

[North America]

Měiguó / Měiguórén 美國／美國人 ‖ 美国／美国人 America / American

[Europe]

Déguó / Déguórén 德國／德國人 ‖ 德国／德国人 Germany / German
Éguó / Éguórén 俄國／俄國人 ‖ 俄国／俄国人 Russia / Russian
Fǎguó / Fǎguórén 法國／法國人 ‖ 法国／法国人 France / French
Xībānyá / Xībānyárén 西班牙／西班牙人 Spain / Spanish
Yìdàlì / Yìdàlìrén 意大利／意大利人 Italy / Italian
Yīngguó / Yīngguórén 英國／英國人 ‖ 英国／英国人 England / English

Languages

Déwén / Déyǔ / Déguóhuà 德文／德語／德國話 || 德文／德语／德国话 German

Éwén / Éyǔ / Éguóhuà 俄文／俄語／俄國話 || 俄文／俄语／俄国话 Russian

Fǎwén / Fǎyǔ / Fǎguóhuà 法文／法語／法國話 || 法文／法语／法国话 French

Hánwén / Hányǔ / Hánguóhuà 韓文／韓語／韓國話 || 韓文／韩语／韩国话 Korean

Rìwén / Rìyǔ / Rìběnhuà 日文／日語／日本話 || 日文／日语／日本话 Japanese

Xībānyáwén / Xībānyáyǔ / Xībānyáhuà 西班牙文／西班牙語／西班牙話 || 西班牙文／西班牙语／西班牙话 Spanish

Yìndùwén / Yìndùyǔ / Yìndùhuà 印度文／印度語／印度話 || 印度文／印度语／印度话 Hindi

Yīngwén / Yīngyǔ 英文／英語 || 英文／英语 English

Zhōngwén / Zhōngguóhuà 中文／中國話 || 中文／中国话 Chinese

Verbs

chūshēng 出生 be born
dāizai 呆在 stay (at)
dàoguo 到過／到过 been to
lái 來／来 come
lǚxíng 旅行 travel
qù 去 go
qùguo 去過／去过 gone to

shēngzai 生在 be born in
shuō 説／说 speak, say
xǐhuan 喜歡／喜欢 like, prefer
zhǎngdà 長大／长大 grow up
zhù 住 reside, live
zhùzai 住在 reside (at), live (at)

Auxiliary (helping) verbs

huì 會／会 can, be able to; be likely/sure to, will
xiǎng 想 want to; would like to; feel like

Adverbs

dōu 都 all
hái 還／还 still
háiyǒu 還有／还有 in addition there is
zhǐ 只 only

Other words and expressions

cóng 從／从 from
dìfang 地方 place
hé 和 and (connects nouns only, not clauses)
huà 話／话 words, speech; language
kěshì 可是 but, yet, however
míngnián 明年 next year
nǎli, nǎli 哪裡, 哪裡／哪里, 哪里 (polite rejection of a compliment)
yǐqián 以前 in the past, some time ago, formerly
yìzhí 一直 all along (in time or place)
zài 在 in, on, at

❭ Checklist of "can do" statements

After completing this unit, you should be able to perform each of the following tasks.

Listening and speaking
(Starred items are for review.)

☐ Ask questions about nationality.

☐ Understand when others tell their nationality.

☐ Ask others where their home is and provide information about your own home.

☐ Understand statements and ask questions about place of birth.

☐ Ask and answer questions about where you grew up.

☐ Pose questions to others about their travel experiences.

☐ Respond to questions about your own travel experiences.

☐ Ask and answer questions about places lived.

☐ Respond to and ask questions about languages spoken.

☐ *Tell others when your birthday is.

Reading and writing

☐ Recognize the names of 10–15 countries of the world.

☐ Read simple self-introductory statements about nationality, place of birth, places you have lived, and languages you can speak.

☐ Write simple self-introductory statements about your nationality, places you have lived, and languages you can speak.

Understanding culture

☐ Say what the standard national language of China is called and name two Chinese dialects.

☐ Give an example to explain how modesty is reflected in Chinese expressions.

Checklist

• Have students work in pairs to go through this checklist and demonstrate selected skills to the class. Reserve 20–30 minutes for students to complete this activity. Tell students that putting check marks in each box is NOT the point. The point is to check if they can really do the things on the list.

• Finally, lead the class to revisit the list they made for exercises 4.2, 4.17 and 4.24.

"Family and friends"

親朋好友

Qīnpénghǎoyǒu

Talking about family and friends

In this unit, you will learn how to:

- respond to and make introductory statements about family members.

- ask and answer questions about birth order.

- describe the physical appearance of family members.

- read photo captions and simple statements describing family members.

- write simple statements about members of your family.

Encounter 1   Talking about nuclear family members

As a homework assignment
before starting Unit 5, ask
students to flip through the
unit to preview the content.

5.1 • Before watching Episode 5, ask
students what they remember from
previous episodes. Encourage them to
respond in Chinese and English.

• Play the video clip twice, if
necessary.

• Allow time for students to
discuss the video among
themselves. Understanding
the plot is crucial for students
to complete the unit's exercises.

5.2 • Possible answers: *How
many siblings do you have? I am
the middle child. My parents are
divorced. I have a sister.* The goal
here is to encourage thinking about
how people talk about family in real
life.

• Invite students to offer answers
"popcorn style."

• Have volunteers write answers on
the board or on chart paper. Keep
this list, and make sure to revisit it
after completing this unit to check
if students have learned enough
Chinese to say everything on the list.
The purpose of this activity is to help
students connect what they're learning
with real-life communication needs.

5.3–5.4

• Tell students that exercises 5.3
and 5.4 are based on the same video
segment. If students have completed
5.3, they can move on to 5.4 without
being asked to do so.

• Feel free to play the video multiple
times, if necessary. Make sure to
provide time for students to check
answers with one another. Invite
volunteers to share the answers on
the board.

5.3 Key:
Nǐ jiālǐ dōu yǒu shénme rén?

5.4 Key:
a. 2
b. 4
c. 1
d. 5
e. 3
f. 8
g. 6
h. 7
i. 10
j. 9

5.1 *View Episode 5 of the dramatic series.*

5.2 Getting ready: *How would you ask someone about his or her family members? If someone asked you about yours, what would you say?*

_____

_____

5.3 *Watch and listen to the video segment. How do you ask, "Who are the members of your family?" Fill in the blanks with pinyin.*

Nǐ _____ dōu yǒu shénme _____?

5.4 *Match the corresponding pinyin and English below.*

a. fùmǔ		1.	*mother (mom)*
b. bàba		2.	*parents*
c. māma		3.	*older brother*
d. jiějie		4.	*father (dad)*
e. gēge		5.	*older sister*
f. mèimei		6.	*younger brother*
g. dìdi		7.	*sisters*
h. jiěmèi		8.	*younger sister*
i. xiōngdì		9.	*siblings*
j. xiōngdìjiěmèi		10.	*brothers*

5.5 *Produce an approximate description of your family with check marks or numbers on the lines below. (You may also create an imaginary family, if you'd like.)*

Wǒ jiālǐ yǒu _____ ge rén: _____ bàba, _____ māma, _____ ge gēge, _____ ge jiějie, _____ ge dìdi, _____ ge mèimei, hái yǒu wǒ.

5.5 Students might ask you how to
say new words such as "stepmother"
and "stepfather." Follow their
intrinsic motivation to learn, and
direct the class to skip ahead to
exercise 5.8 to learn these words.

5.6 Pair work: *Ask your partner about his or her family members and tell about yours. Take notes below.*

_____

_____

_____

_____

_____

Nǐ jiālǐ dōu yǒu shénme rén?

Wǒ jiālǐ yǒu . . .

5.6 • Direct students' attention to the model dialogue in the speech balloons.

• Have a confident pair do a demonstration before releasing students to conduct the dialogues in pairs.

• Tell students to take notes in English, since the focus of this exercise is on speaking, not writing.

Grammar Bits

• Remember, there is often no need for you to teach grammar explicitly. The exercises and activities in this book are designed for students to comprehend the grammar in context. However, it never hurts to devote time to discussing the Grammar Bits in class.

• Before students read the Grammar Bits, divide the class into three small groups. Give each group a different task:

1. Read the Grammar Bits to understand how *yǒu* and *méiyǒu* work. Prepare a PowerPoint presentation to teach the class. Make sure to include several examples.

2. Read the Grammar Bits to understand how *de* works. Prepare a PowerPoint presentation to teach the class. Make sure to include several examples.

3. Read the Grammar Bits to understand how *ge* works. Prepare a PowerPoint presentation to teach the class. Make sure to include several examples.

Grammar Bits 语法点滴

To have (*yǒu*) and to have not (*méiyǒu*)

All Chinese verbs can become negative with the addition of *bù* (for example, *bù xǐhuan*), with the exception of *yǒu* (have). Never say ~~*bù yǒu*~~; always say *méiyǒu* (not have, be without). When *méiyǒu* is used in connected speech, *-you* is often unstressed: *Wǒ méiyou xiōngdìjiěmèi* (I don't have any siblings).

To *de* or not to *de*

You have already learned how to form the possessive in Chinese: *wǒ de shǒujī* (my cell phone); *Zhāng Lǎoshī de diànhuà hàomǎ* (Professor Zhang's telephone number). However, constructions without *de* are common when one talks of personal relationships: *Wǒ tóngxué xìng Lǐ* (My classmate is surnamed Li); *Tā gēge shì wǒ de péngyou* (Her older brother is my friend). Recall that, in other constructions, when the noun directly relates to oneself and to no one else, *de* can also be omitted: *Wǒ míngzi jiào Lynn* (My name is Lynn).

The most versatile measure word: *ge*

Recall that measure words are used with nouns in combination with specifiers (*zhèi, zhè, nèi, nà*) and numbers (*zhèi sān ge rén*). You have already learned that the measure word *ge* is used with common objects (*yí ge shǒujī*) and certain time words (*yí ge zhōngtóu, yí ge zǎoshang, yí ge wǎnshang, yí ge xīngqī, yí ge yuè* [but NOT with *yì tiān* or *yì nián*, as *tiān* and *nián* are themselves measure words]). In this unit, you'll see that it is also used with people: *liǎng ge dìdi, sān ge péngyou, wǔ ge tóngxué*. However, many nouns have their own particular measure word that relates to a specific class of nouns. In some respects, this is similar to English, as in three <u>loaves</u> of bread; six <u>slices</u> of pizza; two <u>skeins</u> of yarn; a <u>flock</u> of ducks. Chinese has many measure words, as you will see in later units. While you should learn the measure word that relates to each particular noun, you will find that *ge* is used with more nouns than any other measure word—therefore, when in doubt, use *ge*. However, don't use *ge* indiscriminately; use the proper measure word whenever you can. A "loaf of yarn" sounds as strange in Chinese as it does in English.

▌ **Reading practice**

5.7 • Allow time for students to practice reading these words aloud with a partner until their speech is relatively fluent.

• Ask students not to label these words with pinyin, because this defeats the purpose of the exercise. Encourage them to use the English translation as a bridge to determine the pronunciation and meaning of these new characters.

• Remind students to use exercise 5.4 if they need help.

5.7 *Read the following family terms aloud, using the English as a guide.*

媽媽／妈妈 *mother (mom)*   弟弟 *younger brother*

爸爸 *father (dad)*   妹妹 *younger sister*

父母 *parents*   姐妹 *sisters*

哥哥 *older brother*   兄弟 *brothers*

姐姐 *older sister*   兄弟姐妹 *siblings*

Encounter 2 **Talking about immediate family members**

5.8 Key:
a. 6
b. 3
c. 2
d. 5
e. 4
f. 1

5.8 *Look at the following words.*

shēng 生 *give birth*

jì 繼／继 *continue, follow after*

yǎng 養／养 *raise*

Based on what you know, can you figure out the meanings of the terms below? Match each Chinese word with the corresponding English equivalent.

a. shēngfù 生父   1. *foster/adoptive mother*

b. shēngmǔ 生母   2. *stepfather*

c. jìfù 繼父／继父   3. *birth mother*

d. jìmǔ 繼母／继母   4. *foster/adoptive father*

e. yǎngfù 養父／养父   5. *stepmother*

f. yǎngmǔ 養母／养母   6. *birth father*

5.9 You may want to combine this list with the list from exercise 5.4 and have students circle all relevant words from both lists. The increased number of options creates greater variety and will engage all students, regardless of individual family composition.

5.9 *Circle any terms in the previous activity that apply to your family.*

FYI 供你参考

Addressing family members—Chinese style

Chinese children call their father *bàba* and their mother *māma*, just as American children might call their parents "mommy" and "daddy." In a family with several children, both male and female, siblings address one another not by their given names but rather by birth order and relationship combinations. Younger children will call the oldest brother *dàgē* (eldest brother), the next oldest *èrgē* (second brother), and so on. Oldest sisters are called *dàjiě*, *èrjiě*, etc., while younger ones are called *èrmèi*, *sānmèi*, etc. In a home with two children, brothers will still address each other according to their relationship—the younger addressing the older as *gē* or *gēge* and the older addressing the younger as *dì* or *dìdi*. In a one-child family (more and more common because of China's one-child policy), parents often address children with *háizi* (child) or an endearing nickname, such as *máomáo* (little fuzzy [head]) or *bèibèi* (little precious).

5.10 *Now look at the following words.*

tóng 同 *same* (Recall that *tóngxué* means "classmate.")

yì 異／异 *different*

Can you figure out the meaning of the following sentence? Check the correct translation below.

Tā shì wǒ tóngmǔ-yìfù de mèimei.

她是我同母異父的妹妹。／她是我同母异父的妹妹。

☐ She is my half sister (we have the same father and different mothers).

☐ She is my half sister (we have the same mother and different fathers).

To simplify things, you can drop the first half of the hyphenated term; thus, a *tóngmǔ-yìfù de mèimei* can be simply a *yìfù de mèimei*.

5.11 *If you have any half siblings, write a complete sentence explaining the relationship. For example:* Wǒ yǒu yí ge yìmǔ de gēge, yí ge yìfù de dìdi.

_____

Stepbrothers and stepsisters are generally not acknowledged as siblings, but as "my stepmother's daughter," for example. If you have any stepsiblings, describe them here.

_____

5.12 *Now, can you rewrite the description of your family with greater accuracy? If you don't have any "step," "half," or adoptive relationships to report, copy your statement from exercise 5.5.*

_____

_____

_____

5.13 • Make sure students understand the format of the list before they begin taking notes.

• Tell students to take notes in English.

• Have a confident pair perform a demonstration for the class.

• Mingle around the classroom to observe and assist, if necessary.

5.13 *Mingling: Walk around the room and ask your classmates* Nǐ jiālǐ dōu yǒu shénme rén? 你家裡都有甚麼人？／你家里都有什么人？ *Write in English what you can understand of their responses.*

名字：_____ 　　　 家人：_____

名字：_____ 　　　 家人：_____

名字：_____ 　　　 家人：_____

名字：_____ 　　　 家人：_____

名字：_____ 　　　 家人：_____

Encounter 3   Talking about birth order

5.14 • Possible answers: *Are you the baby in the family? Are you the oldest child? I am the only child. I am in the middle.*

• Add student responses to the list begun in exercise 5.2.

5.14 *Getting ready: How would you ask someone about his or her birth order? If someone asked you about yours, what would you say?*

_____

 5.15 *Watch and listen to the video segment. What is the birth order of each person? Check the correct boxes and fill in the correct numbers, if necessary.*

a. ☐ only child   b. ☐ only child   c. ☐ only child   d. ☐ only child

   ☐ eldest   ☐ eldest   ☐ eldest   ☐ eldest

   ☐ #_____   ☐ #_____   ☐ #_____   ☐ #_____

   ☐ youngest   ☐ youngest   ☐ youngest   ☐ youngest

5.15 • If time allows, play the video as many times as necessary until students tell you that they are comfortable enough to move on.

• Make sure to leave time for students to discuss answers among themselves.

• Have students work in pairs to share and compare answers with each other.

5.15   Key:

a. only child
b. eldest
c. youngest
d. #4

5.16 *How would you ask someone about his or her birth order? Fill in the blanks in the two questions below, which can be used interchangeably.*

Nǐ shì lǎo_____? 你是老幾？／你是老几？

OR

Nǐ zài jiālǐ shì lǎo_____? 你在家裡是老幾？／你在家里是老几？

5.17 *Tell something about your birth order. Which of the following are you? Circle one.*

dúshēngzǐ 獨生子／独生子 *an only son*

dúshēngnǚ 獨生女／独生女 *an only daughter*

lǎodà 老大 *the eldest*

lǎoèr 老二 *the second child*

lǎosān 老三 *the third child*

lǎosì 老四 *the fourth child*

. . .

lǎoyāo 老么／老幺 *the youngest child* (In northern China, people also say *lǎoxiǎo* 老小 for the youngest child.)

To preface a statement about your birth order, you can say *Wǒ shì* _____ OR *Wǒ* _____.

5.18 *Pair work: Ask your partner about his or her birth order. If your partner is not an only child, ask about his or her siblings.*

Nǐ shì lǎojǐ?

Wǒ shì . . .

Encounter 4 Describing family members

5.19 *Getting ready: How would you describe your family?*

_____

5.20 *Watch and listen to the video segment. Write at least one fact about each speaker's family, in English or in pinyin.*

1. _____
2. _____
3. _____

5.21 *Pair work: Tell your partner again who is in your family, this time in Chinese. Give one or more facts about each person, such as name, age, birthday, birth sign, where he or she lives, what language he or she speaks, etc. Write some information about your partner's family members.*

_____
_____
_____

5.22 *Watch and listen to the video segment. Match the corresponding pinyin and English terms.*

a. gāo   1. *fat*

b. ǎi   2. *neither fat nor thin (average)*

c. bù gāo (yě) bù ǎi   3. *tall*

d. pàng   4. *neither tall nor short (average)*

e. shòu   5. *short*

f. bú pàng (yě) bú shòu   6. *thin*

5.23 *Complete the following chart about physical appearances. Write the name or relationship of family members on each line and then check the appropriate physical characteristics.*

5.23 Encourage students to review exercises 5.4 and 5.8 if they need words for family members.

family member	gāo	ǎi	bù gāo (yě) bù ǎi	pàng	shòu	bú pàng (yě) bú shòu
	☐	☐	☐	☐	☐	☐
	☐	☐	☐	☐	☐	☐
	☐	☐	☐	☐	☐	☐
	☐	☐	☐	☐	☐	☐
	☐	☐	☐	☐	☐	☐
	☐	☐	☐	☐	☐	☐

5.24 • To prepare students, direct their attention to the sentences listed in the speech bubble. Have students read these pinyin sentences for understanding, and tell them to raise their hands if they have questions.

5.24 *Using the chart from the previous exercise, make statements about the physical appearance of several people in your family. Follow the model to the right.*

_____

_____

_____

Wǒ māma hěn shòu. Wǒ bàba yě hěn shòu. Wǒ bú pàng bú shòu. Wǒ dìdi yòu ǎi yòu pàng.*

yòu X yòu Y = both X and Y

▶ Reading practice

5.25 *Read the following expressions aloud, using the English as a guide.*

我媽媽很瘦。／我妈妈很瘦。 *My mother is thin.*

我爸爸也很瘦。 *My father is also thin.*

我不胖不瘦。 *I'm neither fat nor thin.*

我弟弟又矮又胖。 *My little brother is short and fat.*

• Check students' readiness by asking the class, "My mom is tall, *zěnme shuō*?" (*Wǒ māma hěn gāo.*) Make sure they can correctly use *hěn*. Very often, students will say *Wǒ māma shì gāo.*

• If students want to know more adjectives/stative verbs, allow them to elicit new words from you by asking: "*Qǐngwèn . . . zěnme shuō?*" List these words in pinyin and English on the board.

5.25 • Ask students not to label these words with pinyin, because this defeats the purpose of the exercise. Encourage them to use the English translation as a bridge to determine the pronunciation and meaning of these characters.

• Remind students to refer to exercise 5.22 if they need help.

Understanding cultural differences

Understanding cultural differences

• Divide the class into small groups.

• Have each group read the FYI and then write and perform a skit in English to demonstrate the content. Encourage students to make their skits entertaining.

Although cultural differences may be diminishing with the growth of the global village, differences in habits and perspectives may still be noticeable between cultures. What might be considered pushy, intrusive, nosy, or downright rude in the United States may be no more than a demonstration of concern, caring, and intimacy by your Chinese friends. Examples include: "How old are you?" "How much are you earning these days?" "Do you have a boyfriend/girlfriend yet? Why not?" "You're getting fat! You should watch what you eat!" Conversely, conversation topics and behavior quite acceptable in the United States might strike Chinese as shockingly antisocial or disharmonious. Examples include: "No, I don't feel like going, so I'm not going to go." "None of your business! I don't want to talk about it." "Why do you put up with this rule? It's such a hassle!" While a certain amount of tension is likely to be inevitable, awareness of cultural differences can help create the sought-after sense of harmony.

Encounter 5   More family and personal relationships

5.26   Key:

a. W
b. W
c. H
d. H
e. H
f. H and W
g. W

 5.26 *Watch and listen to the video segment. Write* W *before the term that means "wife" and* H *before the term that means "husband."*

a. _____ qīzi 妻子

b. _____ lǎopó 老婆

c. _____ zhàngfu 丈夫

d. _____ lǎogōng 老公

e. _____ xiānsheng 先生

f. _____ àiren 爱人／愛人

g. _____ tàitai 太太

From *xiānsheng/tàitai* to *àiren* and back again

Have the class read the FYI and make a timeline to reflect how the usage of certain words changed over time. Have them create the timeline on the board or on a piece of poster paper.

From *xiānsheng/tàitai* to *àiren* and back again: Language reflecting culture

Language terms are in a constant state of flux in all societies, and they reflect political as well as cultural trends. The fact that Chinese society has always been particularly sensitive to age and status and proper forms of address makes matters even more complicated for the language student.

For decades, *xiānsheng* 先生 was used as a general term of address for "Mr." as well as "husband," while *tàitai* 太太 was used for "Mrs." as well as "wife." In the past, *xiǎojiě* 小姐 was the common term for "Miss." All three terms indicated individuals with a degree of social status.

After the birth of the People's Republic in 1949, however, *tóngzhì* 同志 "comrade" replaced *xiānsheng* 先生, *tàitai* 太太, and *xiǎojiě* 小姐, becoming the general term of address for all three. This reflected the newfound prestige of the proletariat as well as the social ideal of gender equality. In the same fashion, *àiren* 爱人／愛人 "beloved person" was used to mean both "husband" and "wife." Now it appears the pendulum has swung once again. Both *tóngzhì* 同志 and *àiren* 愛人／爱人 are now used less, and older titles are regaining their place, to some extent. Especially in Chinese communities outside of the PRC, it's still quite common to use *xiānsheng* 先生 and *tàitai* 太太 for "husband" and "wife," and *xiǎojiě* 小姐 for "Miss," regardless of social status. However, in the PRC *xiǎojiě* 小姐 is now sometimes used to indicate a bargirl or prostitute, and *tóngzhì* 同志 is now used to mean a gay man or a lesbian. Both terms should be used with extreme caution.

As for "husband" and "wife," the Chinese can be rather cagey about these potentially embarrassing terms, presumably because the spousal relationship implies sexual activity. The informal terms *lǎogōng* 老公 ("old man") and *lǎopó* 老婆 ("old lady") are commonly used; *zhàngfu* 丈夫 (spouse, male) and *qīzi* 妻子 (spouse, female) are used only in formal situations; and such terms as *wǒ de nèi wèi* 我的那位 (that fellow/gal of mine) or *háizi tā bà / mā* 孩子他爸／媽（妈）(the child's dad/mom) abound in casual conversation. Look for the scene in Episode 4 of the dramatic series, for example, in which Tang Yuan's mother addresses her husband as "*Tā bà!*" ([His] Dad!).

5.27 Mingling: *Draw a picture of your spouse (or an imaginary spouse, if you're not married). Walk around the class and introduce your "spouse" to your classmates by saying, "Zhè shì wǒ ___." Then add another piece of information about your "spouse."*

5.28 *Watch and listen to the video segment. Then write the English equivalent of each of the following terms.*

男朋友 nánpéngyou _____

女朋友 nǚpéngyou _____

5.29 *How do you ask if someone has a girlfriend or boyfriend? Write the pinyin (or appropriate characters) here.*

_____

_____

5.30 Pair work: *Ask your partner whether he or she has a* 男朋友 *or* 女朋友. *If so, try to find out more about that boyfriend or girlfriend. If not, make small talk with your partner until you run out of time. Take some notes about what your partner said.*

_____

_____

5.27 Have students conduct a "trial run" with their partners before they mingle with the whole class. If they have questions during the trial, allow them to ask questions.

5.28 Key:
boyfriend
girlfriend

5.29 Key:
Nǐ yǒu nánpéngyou ma? 你有男朋友吗？
Nǐ yǒu nǚpéngyou ma? 你有女朋友吗？

5.30 • As a class, brainstorm language items needed to ask about a person you have never met before. Possible items: *Tā zhǎng de zěnmeyàng?* ("What does he/she look like?"); *Gāo bu gāo?* ("Is he/she tall?"); *Jiào shénme míngzi?* ("What is his/her name?")

• Tell students that if their partners don't have a boyfriend or girlfriend to talk about, they should ask about other family members.

5.31 *Watch and listen to the video segment. How many children does each speaker have? Fill in the correct numbers in the blanks below.*

a. _____   b. _____   c. _____

5.32 *Match the corresponding items.*

a. háizi	1. *daughter*	A. 孩子
b. nǚháir	2. *girl*	B. 男孩兒／男孩儿
c. nánháir	3. *child(ren)*	C. 女孩兒／女孩儿
d. érzi	4. *boy*	D. 女兒／女儿
e. nǚ'ér	5. *son*	E. 兒子／儿子

Note: *Háizi* 孩子 and *háir* 孩兒／孩儿 are interchangeable for "child." *Háir* 孩兒／孩儿 tends to be used in northern China, and *háizi* 孩子 everywhere else.

5.33 *How do you ask if someone has any children? Write the pinyin (or appropriate characters) here.*

_____

5.34 Pair work: *Draw a portrait of your children (real or imaginary) on a piece of paper. Turn to your partner and find out how many children he or she has, as well as something about each child. Then turn to another classmate and tell him or her about your partner's children.*

Encounter 6 Extending the family

5.35 Getting ready: *What would you say if someone asked you about your extended family?*

_____

_____

 5.36 *Watch and listen to the video segment. Then match the corresponding items below.*

a. *uncle: father's older brother*

b. *aunt: father's older brother's wife*

c. *uncle: father's younger brother*

d. *aunt: father's sister*

e. *uncle: mother's brother*

f. *aunt: mother's sister*

g. *paternal grandfather*

h. *paternal grandmother*

i. *maternal grandfather*

j. *maternal grandmother*

k. *grandparents*

1. bóbo de qīzi = bómǔ 伯母

2. bàba de gēge = bóbo 伯伯

3. māma de xiōngdì = jiùjiu 舅舅

4. māma de jiěmèi = āyí 阿姨

5. fùmǔ de fùmǔ = zǔfùmǔ 祖父母

6. bàba de dìdi = shūshu 叔叔

7. bàba de bàba = yéye 爺爺／爷爷

8. bàba de jiěmèi = gūgu 姑姑

9. bàba de māma = nǎinai 奶奶

10. māma de māma = wàipó 外婆

    or lǎolao 姥姥

11. māma de bàba = wàigōng 外公

    or lǎoye 姥爺／姥爷

5.35 • For younger learners, you might need to check before having them do the exercise to make sure they know what "extended family" is. (Possible answers: grandparents, uncles, aunts, etc.)

• Have the class brainstorm and offer answers "popcorn style." Possible answers: *My extended family is very big; it includes more than 20 people. I have two uncles on my mom's side and one aunt on my dad's side. All my grandparents are still alive, and I visit them often.*

• Add student responses to the list begun in exercise 5.2.

5.36 Key:
a. 2
b. 1
c. 6
d. 8
e. 3
f. 4
g. 7
h. 9
i. 11
j. 10
k. 5

Chinese terms for family members

Divide the class into three groups. Give each group one of the following tasks to guide their reading:

1. Read the FYI and identify all the new words that appear in the first paragraph. List the words on the board in both English and pinyin. Prepare a short lecture to teach the class these words.

2. Read the FYI and focus on the discussion of cousins in the first paragraph to answer these questions: Which character is used to denote cousins on the father's side? Which character is used to denote cousins on the mother's side? What is the meaning and significance of these two characters? Prepare a short lecture to teach the class these characters.

3. Read the FYI and focus on the second paragraph to find out the meaning and cultural background for *gōnggong*, *pópo*, and *gōngpó*. Prepare a short lecture to teach the class these words.

FYI 供你参考

Chinese terms for family members

If you find that Chinese family terms are complicated, it's because they are! And the list in exercise 5.36 isn't even complete. For example, *shěnshen* 嬸嬸／婶婶 is the wife of 叔叔, *yízhàng* 姨丈 is the husband of 阿姨, *gūzhàng* 姑丈 is the husband of 姑姑, and *jiùmā* 舅媽 is the wife of 舅舅—not to mention their children! Names for cousins (and nieces and nephews) differ depending on whether they are on the father's or mother's side of the family. Cousins on the father's side are *tánggē* 堂哥, *tángjiě* 堂姐, *tángdì* 堂弟, and *tángmèi* 堂妹. The character 堂 means "hall," and these terms imply that all cousins by patrilineal descent (following the father) share the same ancestral hall (and the father's last name). Cousins on the mother's side are *biǎogē* 表哥, *biǎojiě* 表姐, *biǎodì* 表弟, and *biǎomèi* 表妹, with the character 表 implying a relationship "outside" the patrilineal clan. Note that there is also differentiation by age and gender. One generation down, a brother's son is a *zhízi* 侄子 and his daughter is a *zhínǚ* 侄女, while a sister's son is a *wàisheng* 外甥 and her daughter is a *wàishengnǚ* 外甥女. Two generations down, children of a son are the *sūnzi* 孫子／孙子 and *sūnnǚ* 孫女／孙女, while children of a daughter are the *wàisūn* 外孫／外孙 and *wàisūnnǚ* 外孫女／外孙女. Again, these terms reflect direct descent through the male line and relegate the female line of descent to an indirect, external status (the character 外 means "outside").

For the learner, it does not simplify matters that there are also regional distinctions to consider. One regional variance presented here is for maternal grandparents. Many Chinese people living overseas have the terms *gōnggong* 公公 and *pópo* 婆婆 lodged firmly in their vocabularies as general terms of address for grandparents or anyone of their grandparents' generation. These are the terms for maternal grandparents that are widely used in southern China (where many overseas Chinese have ancestral roots). In modern standard parlance, however, *gōngpó* 公婆 is what a wife would call her husband's parents.

5.37 • Have students work in pairs to assist each other, if necessary.

• Tell students to refer to exercise 5.36 and the preceding FYI if they need help.

• Provide a sample answer on the board. For example, *shūshu: Uncle Roberto.*

5.37 *Write the Chinese terms for any grandparents, aunts, and uncles you have, together with what you call them in English.*

_____

_____

5.38 • Prepare index cards to pass out to students.

• To save time, you might want to have students bring pictures to class or draw the pictures as homework.

• Have a confident pair do a demonstration for the class, or you can play the *B* role and have the class guess about a picture you hold up.

5.38 *Pair work: Take three index cards and draw a person on one side of each card. On the other side, write down your relationship to that person. Then work with a partner to perform the following dialogue multiple times. Switch roles between pictures.*

A: Tā shì nǐ de shénme rén? *(What is he/she to you?)*

B: Nǐ cāicai kàn. *(Take a guess.)*

A: Tā shì nǐ de _____. *(He/She is your _____.)*

B: Duì. / Bú duì. *(Right. / Wrong.)*

Continue guessing until student B answers Duì. *Repeat for the next picture.*

Grammar Bits 语法点滴

Repeating verbs for effect

Verbs can be said twice in a row for effect, in which case the two verbs together form one word, such as *cāicai* (take a guess). This makes the verb less forceful or imperative, and more tentative and polite, as suggested by such English formations as "give it a try, have a look, try [VERB + -ing] a bit." The verb *kàn* (see) is sometimes added to enhance the informal, polite flavor. Here are some examples.

> Nǐ cāicai kàn. *(Take a guess—and let's see what you come up with.)*
> Nǐ chīchi kàn ba. *(Here, have a taste. Try some.)*
> Nǐ shuōshuo kàn. *(Try telling me. Try saying it.)*
> Nǐ kànkan ba. *(Why don't you take a look and see?)*
> Nǐ wènwen Lǐ Lǎoshī ba. *(Try asking Professor Li.)*

Grammar Bits

• After reading, have students make two suggestions to their partners. They can simply use the suggestions written on the page, or they can create new ones.

• If appropriate, point out that pronunciation is very important when saying the verb *wènwen*. If they make a mistake and say *wénwen* instead, they will change the meaning of the suggestion from "try asking . . ." to "try smelling . . ."

5.39 *Socializing: Bring some family pictures to class. Introduce family members to your classmates in Chinese, and ask questions about people your classmates introduce to you.*

5.39 • Tell students to bring pictures to class for this activity.

• Have students talk to classmates whom they didn't talk to during exercise 5.38.

• Encourage students to talk to as many classmates as possible in the given time.

FYI 供你参考

How people address one another in the community

Respect for age and status is shown both within the Chinese home and in the wider community. People often treat each other as members of one big extended family, even when there's no real family relationship involved. All children are called *xiǎo mèimei* 小妹妹 or *xiǎo dìdi* 小弟弟. Children call adults *shūshu* 叔叔 or *āyí* 阿姨. Young or middle-aged adults may call each other *gē* 哥 or *jiě* 姐, and older adults may call each other *bóbo* 伯伯 or *bómǔ* 伯母. Adults and children call elderly people (about 70 years old or older) *yéye* 爺爺／爷爷 and *nǎinai* 奶奶. In youth slang, young men call each other *gēmenr* 哥們兒／哥们儿.

How people address one another in the community

Have the class read this FYI together and then make a class poster listing all the new words.

🎵 Unit Rap

Go to the **Encounters** *website at* www.EncountersChinese.com *and listen to the song to review key expressions from Unit 5. Listen again and sing along!*

Encounter 7   Reading and writing

▶ Reading familiar sentences in Chinese characters

5.40 • Avoid reading this dialogue aloud for your students or having them repeat after you. Tell them to use the English and familiar characters as bridges to determine the meaning and pronunciation for unknown characters.

• Keep in mind that reading fluency is not the goal of this activity. Tell students not to get discouraged if they have trouble reading quickly and accurately.

• Have students complete this exercise multiple times before they move on to 5.41 and 5.42.

5.40 *Pair work: Read the following dialogues (written in traditional characters) aloud with a partner, using the English as a guide.*

1 甲：你家裡都有甚麼人？ *(Who all are in your family?)*

乙：只有我和我父母。你呢？ *(Just [zhǐ yǒu] my parents and me. And you?)*

甲：我家有我媽媽，我繼父，我，三個姐姐，兩個妹妹，還有我繼父的弟弟，我們家人很多！
(For my family, there's my mother, my stepfather, me, three older sisters, two younger sisters, and my stepfather's younger brother. There are a lot of people in my family!)

2 甲：你有哥哥姐姐嗎？ *(Do you have [older] brothers or sisters?)*

乙：沒有。我沒有兄弟姐妹。你呢？ *(No, I don't have any siblings. What about you?)*

甲：我也是獨生子。 *(I'm an only child too.)*

3 甲：你們家有幾個人？ *(How many are there in your family?)*

乙：我們家有四個人。我媽媽，我，一個妹妹，一個弟弟。我沒有爸爸。 *(There are four in my family. My mother, me, a younger sister, and a younger brother. I don't have a father.)*

甲：你妹妹弟弟幾歲了？ *(How old are your little brother and sister?)*

乙：妹妹十歲了，弟弟才一歲。 *(My sister's 10, my brother's only [cái] 1.)*

4 甲：Lynn 的父親是她的生父還是養父啊？ *(Is Lynn's father her birth father or adoptive father?)*

乙：我想是她生父，不是嗎？ *(I think he's her birth father, right?)*

5 甲：你家人都在哪裡？ *(Where is everyone in your family?)*

乙：我父母在英國，我姐姐和他丈夫在印度，我弟弟在美國。可是我爺爺奶奶，外公外婆都在中國。 *(My parents are in England, my older sister and her husband are in India, and my younger brother is in the United States. But my [paternal and maternal] grandparents are all in China.)*

6 甲：你是老幾？ *(Which child are you in your family?)*

乙：我是老大。你呢？ *(I'm the eldest. What about you?)*

甲：我是老么。 *(I'm the youngest.)*

7 甲：你很高。你父母也都很高嗎？ *(You're tall. Are both your parents tall too?)*

乙：我母親高，我父親很矮。我母親又高又瘦；我父親又矮又胖。 *(My mother's tall, and my father's short. My mother is tall and skinny, and my father is short and fat.)*

8 甲： Alejandro 有老婆嗎？ *(Does Alejandro have a wife?)*

乙：有。他妻子叫 April。 *(Yes. His wife's name is April.)*

甲：你呢？你有太太嗎？ *(How about you? Do you have a wife?)*

乙：沒有。可是我有個女朋友。 *(No. But I have a girlfriend.)*

9 甲：你和你先生有孩子嗎？ *(Do you and your husband have children?)*

乙：沒有。你們呢？ *(No. How about you?)*

甲：我和我太太有兩個孩子。 *(My wife and I have two children.)*

乙：男孩兒還是女孩兒？ *(Boys or girls?)*

甲：我們有一個女兒，一個兒子。 *(We have a daughter and a son.)*

10 甲：爺爺，奶奶！你們來了！ *(Grandpa, Grandma! You're here!)*

乙：小毛。你又高了啊！ *(Xiao Mao. You've grown taller!)*

甲：爸，媽！爺爺，奶奶來了！ *(Dad, Mom! Grandpa and Grandma are here!)*

乙：你伯伯，伯母來了嗎？ *(Have your uncle and aunt [paternal] come yet?)*

甲：還沒呢。阿姨舅舅來了。 *(Not yet, but Auntie and Uncle [maternal] are here.)*

11 甲：叔叔阿姨，你們好！ *(Hello, Uncle and Auntie!)*

乙：小妹妹，你好！你媽呢？ *(Hi, little girl! Where's your mother?)*

甲：在我姥姥，姥爺家！ *(She's at my [maternal] grandma and grandpa's home!)*

5.41 *Pair work: Read the dialogues aloud with a partner, this time without any English.*

1 甲：你家裡都有甚麼人？

乙：只有我和我父母。你呢？

甲：我家有我媽媽，我繼父，我，三個姐姐，兩個妹妹，還有我繼父的弟弟，我們家人很多！

2 甲：你有哥哥姐姐嗎？

乙：沒有。我沒有兄弟姐妹。你呢？

甲：我也是獨生子。

5.41–5.42

- Have students read these dialogues multiple times, focusing on reading fluency.

- Encourage students *not* to refer to exercise 5.40 for help. Instead, ask them to rely on the dialogue context and their partners to help them read new characters.

- After students practice reading the dialogues a few times, play the audio and have them check their pronunciation.

3 甲：你們家有幾個人？

乙：我們家有四個人。我媽媽，我，一個妹妹，一個弟弟。我沒有爸爸。

甲：你妹妹弟弟幾歲了？

乙：妹妹十歲了，弟弟才一歲。

4 甲：Lynn 的父親是她的生父還是養父啊？

乙：我想是她生父，不是嗎？

5 甲：你家人都在哪裡？

乙：我父母在英國，我姐姐和他丈夫在印度，我弟弟在美國。可是我爺爺奶奶，外公外婆都在中國。

6 甲：你是老幾？

乙：我是老大。你呢？

甲：我是老么。

7 甲：你很高。你父母也都很高嗎？

乙：我母親高，我父親很矮。我母親又高又瘦；我父親又矮又胖。

8 甲：Alejandro 有老婆嗎？

乙：有。他妻子叫 April。

甲：你呢？你有太太嗎？

乙：沒有。可是我有個女朋友。

9 甲：你和你先生有孩子嗎？

乙：沒有。你們呢？

甲：我和我太太有兩個孩子。

乙：男孩兒還是女孩兒？

甲：我們有一個女兒，一個兒子。

10 甲：爺爺，奶奶！你們來了！

乙：小毛。你又高了啊！

甲：爸，媽！爺爺，奶奶來了！

乙：你伯伯，伯母來了嗎？

甲：還沒呢。阿姨舅舅來了。

11 甲：叔叔阿姨，你們好！

乙：小妹妹，你好！你媽呢？

甲：在我姥姥，姥爺家！

5.42 Pair work: *Now try it once again, this time in simplified characters.*

1 甲：你家里都有什么人？

乙：只有我和我父母。你呢？

甲：我家有我妈妈，我继父，我，三个姐姐，两个妹妹，
　　还有我继父的弟弟，我们家人很多！

2 甲：你有哥哥姐姐吗？

乙：没有。我没有兄弟姐妹。你呢？

甲：我也是独生子。

3 甲：你们家有几个人？

乙：我们家有四个人。我妈妈，我，一个妹妹，一个弟弟。
　　我没有爸爸。

甲：你妹妹弟弟几岁了？

乙：妹妹十岁了，弟弟才一岁。

4 甲：Lynn 的父亲是她的生父还是养父啊？

乙：我想是她生父，不是吗？

5 甲：你家人都在哪里？

乙：我父母在英国，我姐姐和他丈夫在印度，我弟弟在美
　　国。可是我爷爷奶奶，外公外婆都在中国。

6 甲：你是老几？

乙：我是老大。你呢？

甲：我是老幺。

7 甲：你很高。你父母都很高吗？

乙：我母亲高，我父亲很矮。我母亲又高又瘦；我父亲又矮又胖。

8 甲： Alejandro 有老婆吗？

乙：有。他妻子叫 April。

甲：你呢？你有太太吗？

乙：没有。可是我有个女朋友。

9 甲：你和你先生有孩子吗？

乙：没有。你们呢？

甲：我和我太太有两个孩子。

乙：男孩儿还是女孩儿？

甲：我们有一个儿子，一个女儿。

10 甲：爷爷，奶奶！你们来了！

乙：小毛。你又高了啊！

甲：爸，妈！爷爷，奶奶来了！

乙：你伯伯，伯母来了吗？

甲：还没呢。阿姨舅舅来了。

11 甲：叔叔阿姨，你们好！

乙：小妹妹，你好！你妈呢？

甲：在我姥姥，姥爷家！

5.43 *Match the corresponding simplified characters, traditional characters, and English.*

a. 妈妈	1. 繼父	A. *only child (girl)*
b. 继父	2. 獨生女	B. *"same father, different mother"*
c. 继母	3. 爺爺	C. *mother*
d. 同父异母	4. 同父異母	D. *adoptive father*
e. 同母异父	5. 同母異父	E. *paternal grandfather*
f. 独生女	6. 媽媽	F. *"same mother, different father"*
g. 养父	7. 養母	G. *stepfather*
h. 养母	8. 養父	H. *adoptive mother*
i. 爷爷	9. 繼母	I. *stepmother*

▶ Reading real-life texts

5.44 *This is a family photo taken when Allan Yu (余毅廉) was a boy. Read the descriptions of his family members, and then answer the following questions.*

5.44 • If possible, copy exercise 5.44 onto a transparency so that you can project the exercise on the board for students to share and compare answers.

• Encourage students to work in pairs to assist each other and to share and compare answers.

我的名字叫余毅廉。我今年十一岁。这是我的全家福。坐着的那两位是我妈妈和爸爸。我立站在我妈的右边，靠后。我小妹妹站在我前面。顺着时钟排的还有我嫂嫂，我侄子，大哥，二哥，弟弟，和小侄女。我父母，两个哥哥，嫂嫂，和我都生在中国。我弟弟，妹妹，侄子和侄女都是在美国出生的。我属虎。我是1950年，四月十八日生的。我大哥比我大十五岁，他属猪。他和我嫂嫂有两个孩子：一个男孩儿，一个女孩儿。我二哥属鼠，弟弟属马，妹妹属猴。我觉得我妈妈很漂亮，我爸爸脾气很好。

a. What is Allan's birth date? Write in English: _____

b. What is Allan's birth order? _____

c. When was this picture taken? _____

d. Check the choice that correctly completes the sentence:

Allan's eldest brother has _____.

☐ two sons   ☐ two daughters   ☐ a son and a daughter

e. What do you think the term 嫂嫂 (*sǎosao*) means? Check the correct answer.

☐ younger brother's wife   ☐ older brother's wife   ☐ sister's husband

f. What is each person's birth sign? Write in English.

Allan: _____

Allan's younger brother: _____

Allan's younger sister: _____

g. Can you figure out each person's age at the time the picture was taken, based on his or her birth sign? Consult the chart on page 48, if necessary.

Allan's second eldest brother: _____

Allan's younger brother: _____

Allan's younger sister: _____

h. On the photo, label persons born in China with "C." Label persons born in America with "A."

5.44 Key:

a. April 18, 1950

b. third

c. when Allan was 11 years old

d. a son and a daughter

e. older brother's wife

f. Allan: tiger; Allan's younger brother: horse; Allan's younger sister: monkey

g. Allan's second eldest brother: 13; Allan's younger brother: 7; Allan's younger sister: 5

h. parents should be labeled with C; (clockwise, starting with Allan) C, C, A, C, C, A, A, A

▶ Learning to write characters

5.45 *For stroke order and other useful information about each of the following characters from this unit, go to the* Character Writing Workbook. *Choose either traditional or simplified characters and practice writing them until you can reproduce them on demand.*

裡／里，個／个，和，爸，媽／妈，哥，姐，弟，妹，兄，
男，女，父，母，親／亲，才，兩／两

▶ Writing a note

5.46 • If your students find this task too difficult, tell them to write their paragraphs in pinyin first and then turn these paragraphs into characters.

• When students "translate" their pinyin paragraphs into characters, tell them to use the vocabulary list on page 139 for help.

• Have partners proofread each other's drafts one more time before handing them in.

• A sample note: 这是我妈妈。妈妈又高又漂亮。妈妈属马，有三个哥哥，一个弟弟。

5.46 *Write a detailed note to accompany a family photo (draw your family if no photo is available). Identify each person and add a detail or two about each.*

Cultural Bits 文化点滴

Changing families

View the video segment "Changing families" and then discuss the following questions with your classmates.

- What is the significance of the family in China?
- What does "paternal lineage" mean and imply?
- What are some implications of being female in China?
- Name some members of a family in which there are "four generations under one roof" (*sìshì-tóngtáng*).
- What have been some of the consequences of the "one-child" policy?

Recap

▶ Grammar

The unique negative: *méi*

Always use the special negative *méi* for *méiyǒu*.

Wǒ yǒu yí ge jiějie. Wǒ méiyǒu mèimei. (*I have an older sister. I don't have a younger sister.*)

Possessives without *de*

When the relationship is close, constructions without *de* are common with personal pronouns.

Wǒ tàitai xìng Lǐ. (*My wife is surnamed Li.*)

BUT

Tā de péngyou jiào Mǎkè. (*Her friend is named Mark.*)

The versatile measure word: *ge*

Use the measure word *ge* to talk about people, including family members and personal relationships.

liǎng ge rén (*two people*)

sì ge péngyou (*four friends*)

jǐ ge háizi? (*how many children?*)

Use of *dōu* in lists: Review

When lists of things are asked for or given, the adverb *dōu* is regularly used. Note its position in the following examples.

Nǐ jiālǐ dōu yǒu shénme rén? *(Who do you have in your family?)*

Zhōngguó, Měiguó, Fǎguó, Déguó, wǒ dōu qùguo. *(I've been to China, the United States, France, and Germany.)*

Repeating the verb to lessen effect

Verbs can be repeated and said as one word to lessen the force of the verb and make it more of a suggestion. *Kàn* (see) is often added for increased effect. The sentence-ending particle *ba* is also often seen in this pattern.

Nǐ cāicai kàn. *(Take a guess and see [what you come up with].)*

Nǐ kànkan ba. *(Why don't you take a look and see?)*

▶ Vocabulary

Immediate family members

bàba 爸爸 father (dad)
dìdi 弟弟 younger brother
fùmǔ 父母 parents
gēge 哥哥 older brother
jiějie 姐姐 older sister
jiěmèi 姐妹 sisters
māma 媽媽／妈妈 mother (mom)
mèimei 妹妹 younger sister
xiōngdì 兄弟 brothers
xiōngdìjiěmèi 兄弟姐妹 brothers and sisters

Extended family members

āyí 阿姨 aunt (mother's sister)
bóbo 伯伯 uncle (father's older brother)
bómǔ 伯母 aunt (wife of father's older brother)
gūgu 姑姑 aunt (father's sister)
jìfù 繼父／继父 stepfather
jìmǔ 繼母／继母 stepmother
jiùjiu 舅舅 uncle (mother's brother)
lǎolao / wàipó 姥姥／外婆 (maternal) grandmother
lǎoye / wàigōng 姥爺／外公 ‖ 姥爷／外公 (maternal) grandfather
nǎinai 奶奶 (paternal) grandmother

shēngfù 生父 birth father
shēngmǔ 生母 birth mother
shūshu 叔叔 uncle (father's younger brother)
(tóngfù-)yìmǔ de xiōngdìjiěmèi (同父-) 異母的兄弟姊妹／(同父-) 异母的兄弟姐妹 half sibling (same father)
(tóngmǔ-)yìfù de xiōngdìjiěmèi (同母-) 異父的兄弟姊妹／(同母-) 异父的兄弟姐妹 half sibling (same mother)
yǎngfù 養父／养父 foster / adoptive father
yǎngmǔ 養母／养母 foster / adoptive mother
yéye 爺爺／爷爷 (paternal) grandfather

Birth order

dúshēngzǐ 獨生子／独生子 only child (boy)
dúshēngnǚ 獨生女／独生女 only child (girl)
lǎodà 老大 oldest child
lǎoèr 老二 second child
lǎoyāo 老么／老幺 youngest child

Other family relationships

àiren 愛人／爱人 spouse
érzi 兒子／儿子 son
háizi 孩子 child(ren)

lǎogōng 老公 husband
lǎopó 老婆 wife
nánháir 男孩兒／男孩儿 boy
nǚ'ér 女兒／女儿 daughter
nǚháir 女孩兒／女孩儿 girl
qīzi 妻子 wife
tàitai 太太 wife
xiānsheng 先生 husband
zhàngfu 丈夫 husband

Descriptive words

ǎi 矮 short
bù gāo (yě) bù ǎi 不高(也)不矮 neither tall nor short
bú pàng (yě) bú shòu 不胖(也)不瘦 neither fat nor thin
gāo 高 tall
pàng 胖 fat
shòu 瘦 thin
yòu . . . yòu 又……又 both . . . and
yòu ǎi yòu pàng 又矮又胖 both short and fat
yòu gāo yòu shòu 又高又瘦 both tall and thin

Other words and expressions

cāicai kàn 猜猜看 guess
méiyǒu 没有 not have, be without
yǒu 有 have

▶ Checklist of "can do" statements

After completing this unit, you should be able to perform each of the following tasks.

Listening and speaking

☐ Give details about the composition of your immediate family.

☐ Ask a friend about the members of his or her family.

☐ Ask and answer questions about extended family members.

☐ Be able to describe, in simple terms, some of your family members.

Reading and writing

☐ Understand the relationship of family members listed in simple photo captions.

☐ Read simple self-introductory statements about a family and family members.

☐ Write a simple statement about your family composition, and provide an additional descriptive statement for each member.

Understanding culture

☐ Test your new knowledge about Chinese families with a Chinese friend or acquaintance. Find out how he or she refers to immediate family members.

☐ Make two or three accurate statements in English about how China's patrilineal family structure is manifested in the Chinese language.

Checklist

• Have students work in pairs to go through this checklist and demonstrate selected skills to the class. Reserve 20–30 minutes for students to complete this activity. Tell students that putting check marks in each box is NOT the point. The point is to check if they can really do the things on the list.

• Finally, lead the class to revisit the list they made for exercises 5.2, 5.14, and 5.35.

"Happy at home and work"

安居樂業

Ānjūlèyè

Discussing school, professions, and careers

In this unit, you will learn how to:

- ask and answer questions about school and grade level.

- ask and answer questions about future professions.

- ask and answer questions about the reasons behind a future career choice.

- talk about the professions of family members and friends.

- read and understand information on want ads and help wanted signs.

- read and understand simple self-introductory statements about professions.

- write simple self-introductory statements about professions for yourself, your family, and your friends.

Encounter 1 Talking about school and grade level

As a homework assignment before starting Unit 6, ask students to flip through the unit to preview the content.

6.1 • Before watching Episode 6, ask students what they remember from previous episodes. Encourage them to respond in Chinese and English.

• Play the video clip twice, if necessary.

• Allow time for students to discuss the video among themselves. Understanding the plot is crucial for students to complete the unit's exercises.

6.2 • Possible answers: *I am a freshmen at Yale, and I don't know what I want to major in yet. I am a high school senior, and I hate the SATs! I chose to major in architecture because I have been fascinated by Frank Lloyd Wright since I was a kid.* The goal here is to encourage thinking about how people really talk about school and studies.

• Invite students to offer answers "popcorn style."

• Have volunteers write answers on the board or on chart paper. Keep this list, and make sure to revisit it after completing this unit to check if students have learned enough Chinese to say everything on the list. The purpose of this activity is to help students connect what they're learning with real-life communication needs.

 6.1 *View Episode 6 of the dramatic series.*

6.2 *Getting ready:* If someone asks what you do and you're a student, what would you say? Write two to three details in English about your studies.

_____

_____

 6.3 *Watch and listen to the video segment. Then match the questions with the responses.*

a. Nǐ shì xuéshēng ma?

你是學生嗎？／你是学生吗？

b. Nǐ zài nǎr niànshū?

你在哪兒念書？／你在哪儿念书？

c. Nǐ niàn jǐ niánjí?

你念幾年級？／你念几年级？

1. Wǒ zài _____ dàxué dúshū.

我在_____大學讀書。／我在_____大学读书。

2. Wǒ shì xuéshēng.

我是學生。／我是学生。

3. Sān niánjí.

三年級。／三年级。

6.3 Key:
a. 2
b. 1
c. 3

6.3–6.4

• Exercises 6.3 and 6.4 are based on the same video segment. If students have completed 6.3, they can move on to 6.4.

• Feel free to play the video multiple times, if necessary. Provide time for students to check answers with one another. Invite volunteers to share the answers on the board.

6.4 *Write the pinyin for "Are you a student?"*

_____

• If you feel that students are stuck, have them continue to exercise 6.5 and then return to these two exercises.

6.4 Key:

Nǐ shì xuéshēng ma?

6.5 *Check the statement below that pertains to you.*

☐ Wǒ niàn yánjiūshēngyuàn. Wǒ shì yánjiūshēng. 我念研究生院。我是研究生。
   (I am in graduate school. I am a graduate student.)

☐ Wǒ niàn dàxué. Wǒ shì dàxuéshēng. 我念大學。我是大學生。／我念大学。我是大学生。
   (I am in college. I am a college student.)

☐ Wǒ niàn gāozhōng. Wǒ shì gāozhōngshēng. 我念高中。我是高中生。
   (I am in high school. I am a high school student.)

☐ Wǒ niàn chūzhōng. Wǒ shì chūzhōngshēng. 我念初中。我是初中生。
   (I am in middle school. I am a middle school student.)

☐ Wǒ niàn xiǎoxué. Wǒ shì xiǎoxuéshēng. 我念小學。我是小學生。／我念小学。我是小学生。
   (I am in elementary school. I am an elementary school student.)

☐ Wǒ bú shì xuéshēng. Wǒ yǒu gōngzuò. 我不是學生。我有工作。／我不是学生。我有工作。
   (I am not a student. I have a job.)

Grammar Bits 语法点滴

Flexing your verbal muscles: Verb-object combinations

Niànshū 念書／念书 and *dúshū* 讀書／读书 both mean "to study." Both are examples of Chinese verbs that express action on a generalized object—called verb-object (VO) combinations. So, "to study" is "study-books" or *niànshū*, "to speak" is "say-words" or *shuōhuà*, "to earn" is "earn-money" or *zhuànqián*. All verb-object combinations can:

- be split and made specific: *niàn wǒ de Zhōngwén shū* (study <u>my Chinese</u> book)
- be split and minimized: *zhuàn yìdiǎnr qián* (earn <u>a little</u> money)
- be split and maximized: *zhuàn hěn duō qián* (earn <u>lots of</u> money)
- shift their object: *niànshū* ⇒ *niàn dàxué* (study <u>in college</u>)

6.6 *Match the corresponding English, pinyin, and characters.*

a. *graduate school*	1. gāozhōng	A. 初中
b. *college*	2. xiǎoxué	B. 大學／大学
c. *high school*	3. dàxué	C. 高中
d. *middle school*	4. yánjiūshēngyuàn	D. 小學／小学
e. *elementary school*	5. chūzhōng	E. 研究生院

Note: In Taiwan, graduate school is called *yánjiùsuǒ* 研究所。

Based on these terms, can you guess the meaning of the following characters? Fill in the blanks, using English.

大 _____   中 _____   小 _____

FYI 供你参考

The Chinese educational system

Preschool*	*Tuō'érsuǒ*			
Kindergarten*	*Yòuzhìyuán* [Taiwan] / *Yòu'éryuán* [PRC]			
Grade 1	*Xiǎoxué*	*Chūxiǎo*	*Xiǎoxué yī niánjí*	
Grade 2			*Xiǎoxué èr niánjí*	
Grade 3			*Xiǎoxué sān niánjí*	
Grade 4		*Gāoxiǎo*	*Xiǎoxué sì niánjí*	
Grade 5			*Xiǎoxué wǔ niánjí*	
Grade 6			*Xiǎoxué liù niánjí*	
Grade 7	*Zhōngxué*	*Chūzhōng*	*Chūzhōng yī niánjí*	(*Chūyī*)
Grade 8			*Chūzhōng èr niánjí*	(*Chū'èr*)
Grade 9			*Chūzhōng sān niánjí*	(*Chūsān*)
Grade 10		*Gāozhōng*	*Gāozhōng yī niánjí*	(*Gāoyī*)
Grade 11			*Gāozhōng èr niánjí*	(*Gāo'èr*)
Grade 12			*Gāozhōng sān niánjí*	(*Gāosān*)
First-year college	*Dàxué*		*Dàxué yī niánjí*	(*Dàyī*)
Second-year college			*Dàxué èr niánjí*	(*Dà'èr*)
Third-year college			*Dàxué sān niánjí*	(*Dàsān*)
Fourth-year college			*Dàxué sì niánjí*	(*Dàsì*)
Graduate school	*Yánjiùsuǒ* [Taiwan] / *Yánjiūshēngyuàn* [PRC]			

*Preschool children are generally two years old. By age three, children enter kindergarten, where they remain for three years. Children in first grade are usually six years old.

The Chinese educational system

• Have students read this FYI in pairs and then raise their hands to ask any questions they might have.
• Check comprehension by stimulating a class discussion where students compare the American and Chinese educational systems.
• Point to the list of Chinese grade levels, and ask the class, "What do you think the word *niánjí* means? It's repeated so many times." (*grade level*) Tell students to remember this word; they will use it to complete exercise 6.7.

6.7 • Tell students to refer to the information given in the preceding FYI to help them complete this exercise.
• Ask students to guess what *niàn* means in context. (*to attend*)

6.7 Key:
a. What grade are you in?
b. Answers will vary based on students' real-life situations.
c. Answers will vary based on students' real-life situations.

6.7 *What do you think the following means? Write the English.*

a. Nǐ niàn jǐ niánjí? 你念幾年級？／你念几年级？ _____

If you are in school, answer by underlining one choice and filling in the blank below.

b. Wǒ niàn
yánjiūshēngyuàn
dàxué
gāozhōng
chūzhōng
xiǎoxué
_____ niánjí.

Do this again for the same statement in characters.

c. 我念
研究生院
大學／大学
高中
初中
小學／小学
_____ 年級。

6.8 *Pair work:* *Ask your partner whether he or she, or anyone in his or her family, is in school. If the answer is "yes," press for details. Answer any questions your partner asks, then switch roles.*

Nǐ shì xuéshēng ma?

Shì de. Wǒ . . .

6.9 *Mingling:* *Now ask others in your class for the same information, asking and answering appropriate questions.*

Encounter 2   Discussing career choices

6.10 *Getting ready:* *How would you ask a fellow student what he or she wants to be in the future? Write a question as well as your own response to it.*

_____

_____

6.11 *Watch and listen to the video segment. Then answer each question by checking the appropriate column.*

	an actor	a doctor	doesn't know
a. What does the man in the grey T-shirt want to be?	☐	☐	☐
b. What do his parents want him to be?	☐	☐	☐
c. What does the man in the orange T-shirt want to be?	☐	☐	☐

6.8–6.9

• Exercise 6.8 serves as a warm-up activity for exercise 6.9.

• The dialogue described in exercise 6.8 is a rather open-ended one. Tell students that there is not one fixed script that they should follow. Encourage students to focus on meaning and be creative.

• As a class, brainstorm possible questions that would drive this dialogue forward. Have volunteers list these questions on the board. If necessary, review vocabulary for family members.

• When students perform comfortably in pairs, continue to exercise 6.9.

6.10 • Possible answers: *What do you want to do when you grow up? A photographer for National Geographic! What is your dream job? A pro skydiver!*

• Have volunteers add items to the list the class started in exercise 6.2. Keep this list, and make sure to revisit it after completing this unit to check if students have learned enough Chinese to say everything on the list.

6.11 • Play the video multiple times, if necessary, allowing time for students to discuss answers among themselves.

• Invite volunteers to write answers on the board.

6.11 Key:

a. actor
b. doctor
c. doesn't know

6.12 *Listen to the audio. What do you think each person's profession is? Circle one.*

1. 醫生／医生

   a. yīshēng
     doctor

   b. yùndòngyuán
     athlete

   c. jiàoshòu
     professor

2. 護士／护士

   a. sījī
     driver

   b. hùshi
     nurse

   c. gēxīng
     singer

3. 秘書／秘书

   a. mìshū
     secretary

   b. nóngmín
     farmer

   c. gōngrén
     laborer

4. 律師／律师

   a. gōngrén
     laborer

   b. jǐngchá
     police officer

   c. lùshī
     lawyer

5. 建築師／建筑师

   a. jiànzhùshī
     architect

   b. jiùhuǒyuán
     firefighter

   c. fúwùyuán
     waiter, salesclerk

6. 工程師／工程师

   a. mìshū
     secretary

   b. gōngchéngshī
     engineer

   c. jūnrén
     soldier

7. 演員／演员

   a. yǎnyuán
     actor

   b. jīnglǐ
     manager

   c. jiànzhùshī
     architect

8. 歌星

   a. jiàoshòu
     professor

   b. fúwùyuán
     waiter, salesclerk

   c. gēxīng
     singer

9. 運動員／运动员

   a. jūnrén
     soldier

   b. gōngrén
     laborer

   c. yùndòngyuán
     athlete

10. 經理／经理

   a. jīnglǐ
     manager

   b. jiànzhùshī
     architect

   c. yīshēng
     doctor

11. 工人

   a. lùshī
     lawyer

   b. yīshēng
     doctor

   c. gōngrén
     laborer

12. 司機／司机

   a. kuàijìshī
     accountant

   b. sījī
     driver

   c. hùshi
     nurse

13. 服務員／服务员
a. gēxīng
singer
b. fúwùyuán
waiter, salesclerk
c. jiànzhùshī
architect

14. 警察
a. jǐngchá
police officer
b. gōngrén
laborer
c. sījī
driver

15. 軍人／军人
a. jūnrén
soldier
b. yǎnyuán
actor
c. gōngchéngshī
engineer

16. 救火員／救火员
a. yùndòngyuán
athlete
b. jiùhuǒyuán
firefighter
c. gōngrén
laborer

17. 農民／农民
a. nóngmín
farmer
b. yǎnyuán
actor
c. yīshēng
doctor

18. 教授
a. sījī
driver
b. jǐngchá
police officer
c. jiàoshòu
professor

19. 會計師／会计师
a. jiùhuǒyuán
firefighter
b. yīnyuèjiā
musician
c. kuàijìshī
accountant

20. 作家
a. zuòjiā
writer
b. gōngrén
laborer
c. gēxīng
singer

21. 音樂家／音乐家
a. yīnyuèjiā
musician
b. lǜshī
lawyer
c. hùshi
nurse

22. 藝術家／艺术家
a. gōngchéngshī
engineer
b. yùndòngyuán
athlete
c. yìshùjiā
artist

23. 老師／老师
a. gēxīng
singer
b. lǎoshī
teacher
c. jūnrén
soldier

6.12 • Feel free to play the audio multiple times, as necessary, and allow time for students to discuss answers among themselves.
• Invite volunteers to write answers on the board.
• After students have completed this exercise, have them observe the list of words. Ask them, "Do some of these words share endings? If so, what are these endings?" (师 shī, 员 yuán, 家 jiā) "Can you see a pattern for which professions have similar endings?" If students cannot identify a pattern, direct them to read the note on the bottom of this page.

6.12 Key:
1. a	8. c	16. b
2. b	9. c	17. a
3. a	10. a	18. c
4. c	11. c	19. c
5. a	12. b	20. a
6. b	13. b	21. a
7. a	14. a	22. c
	15. a	23. b

Note: Did you notice overlaps in the professional titles? For example, *shī* 師／师 in *lǜshī, jiànzhùshī, gōngchéngshī, kuàijìshī,* and *lǎoshī* refers to white-collar professionals; *yuán* 員／员 in *yùndòngyuán, jiùhuǒyuán, yǎnyuán,* and *fúwùyuán* implies a degree of physicality or refers to a member of a team or troupe, while *jiā* 家 in *zuòjiā, yīnyuèjiā,* and *yìshùjiā* denotes creativity.

What's in a job?

In traditional China, the primary occupations were gentry, peasant, artisan, and merchant, with the gentry (scholar-officials who achieved their positions by studying hard and passing exams) at the top rung of society, and merchants at the bottom (because they produced nothing but merely lived off the labor of others). The greatest proportion of the population was involved in farming and crafts. In modern China, people like to comment that this order has been flipped upside down. Nowadays, businesspeople have the potential to earn the greatest wealth and social power, whereas the erudite scholarly class (e.g., teachers, writers) is generally less well paid. Although farmers in China still make up the bulk of the population, this proportion is shrinking rapidly as modernization leads to urbanization.

What's in a job?

To check comprehension of this FYI, stimulate discussion by asking, "What were the four primary occupations in traditional China? Which was considered the most prestigious? and the least? Why were they ranked in this way? What is the ranking of these occupations in modern China?"

6.13 • Write *Qǐngwèn . . . zěnme shuō?* on the board for students to use as a tool to elicit new words from you.

• If students have questions about the word *huòzhě*, direct them to read the Grammar Bits section on this page.

6.13 *What professions would you like to pursue? Write at least three terms in pinyin. If the profession you seek is not among those already introduced, ask your teacher for help, or try to find a translation online.*

Wǒ jiānglái xiǎng dāng _____, huòzhě _____,
huòzhě _____.

(*huòzhě* 或者 means "or"; *jiānglái* 將來／将来 means "in the future")

Grammar Bits 语法点滴

Expressing "or" one way OR the other

Háishi 還是／还是, meaning "or," introduces alternatives in a question.

Nǐ niànshū háishi gōngzuò? *(Do you work or study?)*
Nǐ yào zhèi ge háishi nèi ge? *(Do you want this one or that one?)*

Huòzhě 或者, also meaning "or," introduces alternatives in a statement.

Niànshū huòzhě gōngzuò dōu kěyǐ. *(Either studying or working is fine.)*
Zhèi ge huòzhě nèi ge dōu xíng. *(Either this one or the other one will do.)*

6.14 • Direct students' attention to the model dialogue in the speech balloons.

• Invite a confident pair to do a demonstration for the class.

• Mingle among your students as they engage in conversation. Observe and assist, as necessary.

• Do not interrupt students to correct pronunciation unless the errors severely alter the meaning they are trying to get across.

6.14 *Mingling: Find out something about the career goals of as many of your classmates as you can in the time given.*

Nǐ xiǎng dāng shénme?

Wǒ xiǎng dāng . . .

Encounter 3 Talking about occupations of family and friends

6.15 *Getting ready: If someone asks about the occupations of people in your family, what would you say?*

_____

_____

6.16 *Watch and listen to the video segment. For each speaker, identify the relationship between the speaker and the persons mentioned, as well as the professions named. Write in English or pinyin.*

a. _____

_____

b. _____

_____

c. _____

_____

Wǒ māma shì jūnrén.

Wǒ de péngyou Todd shì yǎnyuán.

6.15 • Possible answers: *My dad is a politician; he gives a lot of speeches. My mom is a math teacher. My sister is a lawyer, but she wants to quit.*

• Have volunteers add items to the list they started in exercise 6.2.

6.16 • You may want to give students a sample answer before playing the video, so they will know what to listen for; for example, mother = lawyer, older brother = actor.

• Have students watch the video once or twice all the way through, focusing on meaning, and then ask them to write down the occupations mentioned in English. Verify answers as a class.

• As the next step, if students are up for the challenge, have them write down these occupations in pinyin. You may need to pause the video, or repeat these words out loud yourself to help students.

6.16 Key:

a. mother = architect: *jiànzhùshī* father = engineer: *gōngchéngshī*

b. father = soldier: *jūnrén* mother = athlete: *yùndòngyuán* the speaker = athlete: *yùndòngyuán*

c. the speaker = waiter/attendant/ clerk: *fúwùyuán* husband = firefighter: *jiùhuǒyuán* child #1 = student: *xuéshēng* child #2 = singer: *gēxīng*

6.17 • Direct students' attention to the sample sentences in the speech balloons.

• Have students work in pairs to assist each other.

6.17 *Are any of your family members or friends engaged in one of the occupations you've learned to say so far? Write at least five sentences, following the examples.*

_____

_____

_____

_____

_____

6.18 • Provide enough time for students to read and understand the sample questions. Check for understanding by asking the class a question and inviting students to "popcorn" appropriate answers. Note that there are no standard answers to these questions. There are multiple ways to answer each question. For example, 我爸爸是老师 or 我爸爸是做老师的.

• To demonstrate, invite the class to interview you.

• Remind students to take notes in English, as the point of this exercise is speaking and listening.

• During the activity, mingle with your students to observe and assist. Do not interrupt students to correct pronunciation unless the errors severely alter the intended meaning.

6.18 *Mingling: Find out something about the occupations of several of your classmates' family members. Ask and answer questions such as the following.*

Nǐ fùmǔ shì zuò shénme de?

你父母是做甚麼的？／你父母是做什么的？

Nǐ yǒu xiōngdìjiěmèi ma? Tāmen shì zuò shénme de?

你有兄弟姐妹嗎？他們是做甚麼的？／你有兄弟姐妹吗？他们是做什么的？

Nǐ jiālǐ yǒu méiyǒu rén dāng yīshēng?

你家裡有沒有人當醫生？／你家里有没有人当医生？

Take some notes about what your classmates tell you.

_____

_____

_____

_____

Encounter 4 — Discussing reasons behind your career choice

6.19 • You might need to help your students "jump start" the brainstorming process by asking them to think about their intended or dream career path. Stimulate their thinking by asking, "Why do you think people choose to be doctors or teachers? Do you want to be one? Why or why not? What do you want to be later in life? Why?"

• Possible answers: *I want to be a nurse, because I want to help people. I want to be a flight attendant, because I want to travel. I liked the show ER, so I want to become a doctor.*

• Have volunteers add items to the list the class started in exercise 6.2.

6.20 • Have students write their own answers first, and then have them share and compare with their partners. See if anyone can guess the meaning of *wèishénme* ("why") and *dāng* ("to work as, to serve as").

• Invite volunteers to share the answers on the board.

6.20 Key:
Why do you want to be a teacher?

6.19 *Getting ready: If someone were to ask why you chose your career, what would you say?*

_____

6.20 *Watch and listen to the video. What do you think is the meaning of* Nǐ wèishénme xiǎng dāng lǎoshī? 你為甚麼想當老師？／你为什么想当老师？ *Write the English below.*

_____

6.21 *Watch and listen to the video again. Match each reason with the person who said it.*

1. ____　　　　　　　2. ____　　　　　　　3. ____

4. ____　　　　　　　5. ____　　　　　　　6. ____

a. Yīnwèi dāng ____ hěn zhuàn qián.

因為當____很賺錢。／因为当____很赚钱。

Because being a ___ can earn you a lot of money.

b. Yīnwèi dāng ____ hěn yǒu yìsi.

因為當____很有意思。／因为当____很有意思。

Because being a ___ is very interesting.

c. Yīnwèi dāng ____ néng bāng biéren.

因為當____能幫別人。／因为当____能帮别人。

Because being a ___ enables you to help others.

d. Yīnwèi wǒ mǔqīn shì ____, suǒyǐ wǒ yě xiǎng dāng ____.

因為我母親是____, 所以我也想當____。／
因为我母亲是____, 所以我也想当____。

Because my mother is a ____; therefore I'd like to be a ____ too.

e. Yīnwèi wǒ fùmǔ yào wǒ dāng ____.

因為我父母要我當____。／因为我父母要我当____。

Because my parents want me to be a ____.

f. Wǒ bù zhīdào wèishénme.

我不知道為甚麼。／我不知道为什么。

I don't know why.

6.22 *Complete the following conversation with your own career choice and the reasons behind it, using pinyin.*

Q: Nǐ jiānglái xiǎng dāng shénme?

A: Wǒ xiǎng dāng _____.

Q: Nǐ wèishénme xiǎng dāng _____?

A: _____.

6.23 *Mingling: Speak to several of your classmates, using the dialogue in exercise 6.22 as a model. Learn about their career choices and the reasons behind those choices. Take some notes below.*

_____

_____

_____

FYI 供你参考

From "work unit" to want ads: Changes in modern China

As globalization pushes change in China, as Chinese socialism becomes influenced by Western capitalism, and as technology "flattens" the entire world, the life and career choices of the average Chinese citizen are changing as well. It was not so long ago that words like *dānwèi* ([assigned] work unit/place of work) and *tiě fànwǎn* (iron rice bowl—signifying guaranteed lifelong employment) were used to describe the lives and aspirations of all people on the Chinese mainland. Both phrases have now become part of an increasingly long list of things that "used to be" in China. The *dānwèi*, or work unit to which each person was assigned, used to be every citizen's source of assigned employment, health care, housing, and a host of other social benefits. The "iron rice bowl" guaranteed benefits from the *dānwèi* for life. Today, the "iron rice bowl" has cracked, and the work unit's importance in the average person's life has almost vanished. Looking for a job suitable to one's interests and training has become part of the fabric of working in modern China. Where there was previously no private enterprise, entrepreneurship is now thriving. Today, roughly 10 percent of the world's billionaires are Chinese. Very likely, this figure will increase steadily as China's standard of living surges upward.

♫ Unit Rap

Go to the **Encounters** *website at* www.EncountersChinese.com *and listen to the song to review key expressions from Unit 6. Listen again and sing along!*

Encounter 5 Reading and writing

▶ Reading familiar sentences in Chinese characters

Note: In modern Mandarin (PRC), a distinction is made in writing between "he" 他, "she" 她, and "it" 它, all of which are pronounced *tā*. In Taiwan, 它 is further distinguished from 牠, used for animals, and also pronounced *tā*. Beginning here, the three forms used in Mainland China—他, 她, and 它—will appear in reading exercises.

6.24 Pair work: *Read the following dialogues (written in traditional characters) aloud with a partner, using the English as a guide.*

1 甲：你是學生嗎？ (*Are you a student?*)
乙：是的。我念高中二年級。 (*Yes. I'm a sophomore in high school.*)
甲：才高二啊！ (*Only a high school sophomore!*)
乙：你呢？你念幾年級？ (*How about you? What grade are you in?*)
甲：我讀大一！ (*I'm a college freshman!*)

2 甲：你有弟弟妹妹嗎？ (*Do you have younger brothers and sisters?*)
乙：有，兩個妹妹。 (*I do, two younger sisters.*)
甲：都上學了嗎？ (*Have they both started school [by now]?*)
乙：上學了。我大妹妹上初中一年級，小妹妹上小學二年級。
(*Yes, they have. The older one is in grade 7, and the younger one is in grade 2.*)

3 甲：你是大學生還是研究生？ (*Are you an undergraduate or graduate student?*)
乙：大學生。我明年想上研究生院。 (*Undergrad. I'd like to go to graduate school next year.*)

4 甲：你將來想當甚麼？ (*What do you want to be in the future?*)
乙：我想當演員或者運動員。可是我父母要我當醫生。你呢？ (*I'd like to be an actor or an athlete. But my parents want me to be a doctor. What about you?*)
甲：我還不知道呢。 (*I don't know yet.*)

5 甲：你父母是做甚麼的？ (*What do your parents do?*)
乙：我爸爸是老師，我媽媽是律師。 (*My father is a teacher, and my mother is a lawyer.*)
甲：哦，我爸爸也是律師。 (*Oh, my father is a lawyer too.*)
乙：那麼你媽媽呢？ (*What about your mother then?*)
甲：我媽媽不工作。 (*My mother doesn't work.*)

6.24 • Before releasing students to read the character dialogues in pairs, have the class read the notes on *tā* for understanding.
• Avoid reading the dialogue aloud for your students or having them repeat after you. Tell them to use the English and familiar characters as bridges to determine the meaning and pronunciation for unknown characters.
• Keep in mind that reading fluency is not the goal of this activity. Tell students to not get discouraged if they have trouble reading quickly and accurately.
• Have students complete this exercise multiple times before they move on to 6.25 and 6.26.

6 甲：警察，救火員，還是經理……當哪個最好？ *(Which is best: a police officer, firefighter, or business manager?)*

乙：我怎麼知道呢？為甚麼要問這個？ *(How would I know? Why do you ask?)*

甲：我爺爺，伯伯，和爸爸都是警察。我兩個舅舅都是救火員。我媽媽是經理。我不知道我要當甚麼。 *(My grandfather, uncle, and father are all police officers. My mother's brothers are both firefighters. My mother is a business manager. I don't know what I want to be.)*

乙：我呢，我想當司機！ *(Me, I want to be a driver!)*

甲：司機有甚麼好？ *(What's good about being a driver?)*

乙：司機很賺錢！ *(Drivers make [a lot of] money!)*

甲：是嗎？ *(They do?)*

乙：是啊！我姐姐的男朋友是個歌星的司機，他一個月賺的錢可不少啊！ *(Yes! My sister's boyfriend is the chauffeur for a famous singer; he makes quite a lot of money every month!)*

7 甲：你先生是做甚麼的？ *(What does your husband do?)*

乙：他是個軍人。你的呢？ *(He's a soldier. What about yours?)*

甲：我沒有先生，有男朋友。他是個服務員。 *(I don't have a husband; I have a boyfriend. He's a waiter.)*

8 甲：王老師，您家人都是做甚麼的？ *(Professor Wang, what do the people in your family do?)*

乙：他們都是農民。 *(They're all farmers.)*

9 甲：你有沒有秘書？ *(Do you have a secretary?)*

乙：我是工人，我沒有秘書！ *(I'm a laborer; I don't have a secretary!)*

甲：你不是工程師嗎？ *(Aren't you the engineer?)*

乙：我太太才是工程師。她有秘書。 *(My wife is the engineer. She has a secretary.)*

10 甲：我不知道我將來要當甚麼！ *(I don't know what I want to be in the future!)*

乙：你想賺錢還是想幫別人還是…… *(Do you want to make money or help others or . . .)*

甲：都要！又想賺錢又想幫別人又要有意思的工作。 *(I want it all! To make money and help people and have an interesting job.)*

乙：那你去當醫生或者護士吧。 *(Then go be a doctor or a nurse.)*

甲：不，不。我不想當醫生或者護士。 *(No. I don't want to be a doctor or a nurse.)*

乙：為甚麼不？　　*(Why not?)*

甲：不知道。我就是不要。　　　*(I don't know. I just don't want to.)*

6.25 Pair work: *Read the dialogues aloud with a partner, this time without any English.*

6.25–6.26

• Have students read these dialogues multiple times, focusing on reading fluency.

• Encourage students *not* to refer to exercise 6.24 for help. Instead, ask them to rely on the dialogue context and their partners to help them read new characters.

• After students practice reading the dialogues a few times, play the audio and have them check their pronunciation.

1 甲：你是學生嗎？

　　乙：是的。我念高中二年級。

　　甲：才高二啊！

　　乙：你呢？你念幾年級？

　　甲：我讀大一！

2 甲：你有弟弟妹妹嗎？

　　乙：有，有兩個妹妹。

　　甲：都上學了嗎？

　　乙：上學了。我大妹妹上初中一年級，小妹妹上小學二年級。

3 甲：你是大學生還是研究生？

　　乙：大學生。我明年想上研究生院。

4 甲：你將來想當甚麼？

　　乙：我想當演員或者運動員。可是我父母要我當醫生。
　　　　你呢？

　　甲：我還不知道呢。

5 甲：你父母是做甚麼的？

　　乙：我爸爸是老師，我媽媽是律師。

　　甲：哦，我爸爸也是律師。

　　乙：那麼你媽媽呢？

　　甲：我媽媽不工作。

6 甲：警察，救火員，還是經理……當哪個最好？

　　乙：我怎麼知道呢？為甚麼要問這個？

　　甲：我爺爺，伯伯，和爸爸都是警察。我兩個舅舅都是救火
　　　　員。我媽媽是經理。我不知道我要當甚麼。

　　乙：我呢，我想當司機！

　　甲：司機有甚麼好！

　　乙：司機很賺錢！

甲：是嗎？

乙：是啊！我姐姐的男朋友是個歌星的司機，他一個月賺的錢可不少啊！

7 甲：你先生是做甚麼的？

乙：他是個軍人。你的呢？

甲：我沒有先生，有男朋友。他是個服務員。

8 甲：王老師，您家人都是做甚麼的？

乙：他們都是農民。

9 甲：你有秘書嗎？

乙：我是工人，我沒有秘書。

甲：你不是工程師嗎？

乙：我太太才是工程師。她有秘書。

10 甲：我不知道我將來要當甚麼！

乙：你想賺錢還是想幫別人還是……

甲：都要！又想賺錢又想幫別人又要有意思的工作。

乙：那你去當醫生或者護士吧。

甲：不，不。我不想當醫生或者護士。

乙：為甚麼不？

甲：不知道。我就是不要。

6.26 *Pair work: Now try it once again, this time in simplified characters.*

1 甲：你是学生吗？

乙：是的。我念高中二年级。

甲：才高二啊！

乙：你呢？你念几年级？

甲：我读大一！

2 甲：你有弟弟妹妹吗？

乙：有，有两个妹妹。

甲：都上学了吗？

乙：上学了。我大妹妹上初中一年级，小妹妹上小学二年级。

3 甲：你是大学生还是研究生？
乙：大学生。我明年想上研究生院。

4 甲：你将来想当什么？
乙：我想当演员或者运动员。可是我父母要我当医生。
你呢？
甲：我还不知道呢。

5 甲：你父母是做什么的？
乙：我爸爸是老师，我妈妈是律师。
甲：哦，我爸爸也是律师。
乙：那么你妈妈呢？
甲：我妈妈不工作。

6 甲：警察，救火员，还是经理……当哪个最好？
乙：我怎么知道呢？为什么要问这个？
甲：我爷爷，伯伯和爸爸都是警察。我两个舅舅都是救火
员。我妈妈是经理。我不知道我要当什么。
乙：我呢，我想当司机！
甲：当司机有什么好！
乙：司机很赚钱！
甲：是吗？
乙：是啊！我姐姐的男朋友是个歌星的司机，他一个月赚的
钱可不少啊！

7 甲：你先生是做什么的？
乙：他是个军人。你的呢？
甲：我没有先生，有男朋友。他是服务员。

8 甲：王老师，您家人都是做什么的？
乙：他们都是农民。

9 甲：你有秘书吗？
乙：我是工人，我没有秘书。
甲：你不是工程师吗？
乙：我太太才是工程师。她有秘书。

10 甲：我不知道我将来要当什么！

乙：你想赚钱还是帮别人还是……

甲：都要！又想赚钱又想帮别人又要有意思的工作。

乙：那你去当医生或者护士吧。

甲：不，不。我不想当医生或者护士。

乙：为什么不？

甲：不知道。我就是不要。

6.27 *Match the corresponding simplified characters, traditional characters, and English.*

a. 帮别人	1. 老師	A. *in the future*
b. 几年级	2. 將來	B. *which year in school*
c. 读书	3. 運動員	C. *be in what job/profession*
d. 小学	4. 醫生	D. *doctor*
e. 大学生	5. 演員	E. *athlete*
f. 将来	6. 幾年級	F. *undergraduate student*
g. 当什么	7. 護士	G. *nurse*
h. 演员	8. 大學生	H. *help others*
i. 运动员	9. 幫別人	I. *actor*
j. 医生	10. 當甚麼	J. *teacher*
k. 老师	11. 讀書	K. *elementary school*
l. 护士	12. 小學	L. *attend school*

6.28 *Match the corresponding simplified characters, traditional characters, and English.*

a. 律师	1. 律師	A. *farmer*
b. 救火员	2. 服務員	B. *or [in questions]*
c. 还是	3. 經理	C. *earn money*
d. 经理	4. 還是	D. *driver/chauffeur*
e. 司机	5. 秘書	E. *waiter/attendant/clerk*
f. 赚钱	6. 軍人	F. *manager*
g. 军人	7. 農民	G. *engineer*
h. 服务员	8. 賺錢	H. *lawyer*
i. 农民	9. 救火員	I. *secretary*
j. 秘书	10. 司機	J. *firefighter*
k. 工程师	11. 工程師	K. *soldier*

▶ Reading real-life texts

6.29 *Look at the employment agency ad. Fill in the blanks in the English version of this ad.*

上海第一职业介绍所

正规职介: 国家批准
服务保证: 高效，周到，诚心
求职／找工作: 021 - 62342534
免费代理招聘: 021 - 62342645

浦东投资公司急招会计师，5000元
实业有限公司招建筑师，6388元
贸易公司急招司机，2200元

_____ **Number One Employment Agency**

Proper placements: government certified

Service guaranteed to be effective, considerate, and honest

Career/job seekers: 021-62342534

Free service to potential employers: 021-62342645

Pudong Investment Company urgently seeks _____, 5000 _____

Enterprise Corporation seeks _____, 6388 _____

Trade Company urgently seeks _____, 2200 _____

6.29–6.31
• If possible, copy exercises 6.29–6.31 to transparencies and project them on the board for easier viewing.
• Tell students to consult the vocabulary list on page 161–162 for help, if necessary.

6.30 *Look at the photo and answer the following questions.*

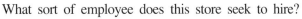

a. What does the sign above the door say? Apartments for _____

b. At what time is the front entrance locked at night? _____

6.31 *Look at the help wanted sign.* 招聘 *zhāopìn literally means "seek to hire."*

What sort of employee does this store seek to hire? _____

6.29 • Students may not be able to recognize the characters for *Shànghǎi* as a chunk, but they should recognize the first character 上 (they learned it in Unit 3). Once students identify 上, give hints by telling students that this is the name of a big city in eastern China. They should be able to guess what the second character is with ease.

• This employment agency is advertising that it is properly certified to conduct business by the appropriate government agency, and not a "fly-by-night" operation.

6.29 Key:

Shanghai
accountant, yuan
architect, yuan
driver, yuan

6.30 Key:

a. graduate students
b. 24:00 (12:00 A.M.)

6.31 Key:

waiter

6.33 • Encourage students to complete this exercise independently, but allow them to work in pairs if necessary. Suggest that they write their notes in pinyin first, then "translate" their writing into characters. When they finish writing, students should proofread their partners' writing before handing in their drafts.

• Encourage students to be creative. Give them the question frames *Qǐngwèn . . . zěnme shuō?* and *Qǐngwèn . . . zěnme xiě?* as tools to elicit new language items from you.

• For these new language items/ characters, tell students to write pinyin next to them so their peer readers can understand the notes when proofreading.

• A sample note: 我上大学一年级。我以后想做摄影师，因为我想看世界。我爸爸妈妈都是老师，因为他们很喜欢帮助人。

▶ Learning to write characters

6.32 *For stroke order and other useful information about each of the following characters from this unit, go to the* **Character Writing Workbook**. *Choose either traditional or simplified characters and practice writing them until you can reproduce them on demand.*

做，將／将，來／来，想，要，念，級／级，為／为，因，當／当，也，意，思，賺／赚，錢／钱，幫／帮，別，或，者，還／还，知，道，她

▶ Writing a note

6.33 *Write a brief self-introduction in your choice of traditional or simplified Chinese characters. Include information about what you do or what you would like to do and why; also include what members of your family and your friends do.*

Cultural Bits 文化点滴

Education and careers

View the video segment "Education and careers" and then discuss the following questions with your classmates.

• Do you agree with the commentary that going to college is much more important to the future of a young person in China than in the United States?

• Summarize what you know about the Chinese 高考 *gāokǎo* (college entrance exam).

• Discuss some differences in the process of getting into college in China compared to the process in the United States.

• What are some changes underway in the Chinese educational system and in its link to today's marketplace for careers?

Recap

▶ Grammar

Verb-object (VO) combinations

Certain verbs are combined with an object to express a generalized verbal action.

niànshū *(study)*

shàngxué *(attend school)*

zhuànqián *(earn money)*

All verb-object combinations can have their object shifted or modified.

shàngxué *(attend school)* ⇒ shàng gāozhōng *(attend high school)* ⇒ shàng yì suǒ zhùmíng de gāozhōng *(attend a famous high school)*

Háishi vs. huòzhě

Use *háishi* in a question to state alternatives.

Nǐ xiǎng shàng dàxué háishi xiǎng gōngzuò? *(Do you intend to go to college or work?)*

Use *huòzhě* in a statement to state alternatives.

Shàng dàxué huòzhě gōngzuò dōu hǎo. *(Going to college or working—either is fine.)*

▶ Vocabulary

Schools

chūzhōng 初中 middle school

dàxué 大學／大学 college, university

gāozhōng 高中 high school

xiǎoxué 小學／小学 elementary school

yánjiūshēngyuàn 研究生院 graduate school

Professions

fúwùyuán 服務員／服务员 waiter, attendant, salesclerk

gēxīng 歌星 singer

gōngchéngshī 工程師／工程師 engineer

gōngrén 工人 laborer

hùshi 護士／护士 nurse

jiànzhùshī 建築師／建筑師 architect

jiàoshòu 教授 professor

jǐngchá 警察 police officer

jīnglǐ 經理／经理 manager

jiùhuǒyuán 救火員／救火员 firefighter

jūnrén 軍人／军人 soldier

kuàijìshī 會計師／会计師 accountant

lǎoshī 老師／老师 teacher

lǜshī 律師／律師 lawyer

mìshū 秘書／秘书 secretary

nóngmín 農民／农民 farmer

sījī 司機／司机 driver, chauffeur

yǎnyuán 演員／演员 actor, actress

yīnyuèjiā 音樂家／音乐家 musician

yīshēng 醫生／医生 doctor

yìshùjiā 藝術家／艺术家 artist

yùndòngyuán 運動員／运动员 athlete

zuòjiā 作家 writer

Verbs

bāng 幫／帮 help, assist

dāng 當／当 be (in position of), serve as

dú 讀／读 study

dú (gāozhōng) 讀高中／读高中 attend (high school)

dú (sān niánjí) 讀三年級／读三年级 be in (Grade 3)

dúshū 讀書／读书 attend school

gōngzuò 工作 work

niàn 念 study

niàn (gāozhōng) 念高中／念高中 attend (high school)

niàn (sān niánjí) 念三年級／念三年级 be in (Grade 3)

niànshū 念書／念书 attend school

shàng 上 go to (school)

shàng (gāozhōng) 上高中 attend (high school)

yào 要 want, want to

zhuàn 賺／赚 earn (money)

zuò 做 do

Stative verbs

méi(yǒu) yìsi 没（有）意思
    unintcrcsting, dull
yǒu yìsi 有意思 interesting, fun
zuìhǎo 最好 best

Adverbs

cái 才 only
hái 還／还 still, yet
zuì 最 most

Auxiliary (helping) verbs

xiǎng 想 would like to, intend to
yào 要 want to, will

Nouns

biéren 别人 other people
niánjí 年級／年级 year (in school)
qián 錢／钱 money

Verb phrases and conjunctions

suǒyǐ 所以 therefore
wèishénme 為甚麼／为什么 why
yīnwèi 因為／因为 because

▶ Checklist of "can do" statements

After completing this unit, you should be able to perform each of the following tasks.

Listening and speaking

- [ ] Tell someone that you're a student and specify what school you attend.
- [ ] Specify your year or grade level.
- [ ] Ask someone what he or she does for a living.
- [ ] Specify two occupations in which you are now interested.
- [ ] Introduce family members and friends by their profession.
- [ ] Ask a friend what he or she wants to be in the future.
- [ ] Describe your career aspirations.
- [ ] State your reasons for selecting a particular career.
- [ ] Ask a friend why he or she has chosen a particular career.

Checklist
• Have students work in pairs to go through this checklist and demonstrate selected skills to the class. Reserve 20–30 minutes for students to complete this activity. Tell students that putting check marks in each box is NOT the point. The point is to check if they can really do the things on the list.

• Finally, lead the class to revisit the list they made for exercise 6.2, 6.10, 6.15, and 6.19 to see if they have learned enough Chinese to say everything on the list.

Reading and writing

- [ ] Read and understand simple statements about year or grade level.
- [ ] Read and understand simple statements about professional affiliations.
- [ ] Read and understand professional affiliations in advertisements.
- [ ] Write a simple statement about family members, giving their ages and occupations/professions.

Understanding culture

- [ ] State one difference between the Chinese school system and your own.
- [ ] Comment on the difference between traditional social classes in China and modern job realities.
- [ ] Explain the impact of globalization on the career choices of modern Chinese youth.

"Meeting our needs"

各有所求

Gèyǒusuǒqiú

Discussing personal needs

In this unit, you will learn how to:

- talk about physical and mental conditions.

- ask about someone's well-being.

- make and respond to suggestions about specific physical or mental conditions.

- express urgency.

- interpret signs for food, drink, sanitary facilities, etc.

- interpret simple declarative statements about physical perceptions and needs.

- write simple declarative statements about physical needs and responses to those needs.

Encounter 1 Stating how you feel

As a homework assignment before starting Unit 7, ask students to flip through the unit to preview the content.

7.1 • Before watching Episode 7, ask students what they remember from previous episodes. Encourage them to respond in Chinese and English.

• Play the video clip twice, if necessary.

• Allow time for students to discuss the video among themselves. Understanding the plot is crucial for students to complete the unit's exercises.

7.2 • Possible answers: *I was hungry last night. I was cold this morning.* Have students work in pairs and write a mini-journal of the physical sensations they have had in the past two days. Make it clear that students need to think of physical sensations, not emotions. The goal of this activity is to get students thinking about how people really talk about how they feel physically.

• After students have completed this unit, have them revisit their mini-journals to see if they have learned enough Chinese to say everything on the list. The purpose of this activity is to help students connect what they're learning with real-life communication needs.

7.3 • Tell students to use the two key words--*lěng* and *rè*--and the speakers' body language as clues to understanding the content.

• Feel free to play video multiple times and pause to give hints, if necessary. Make sure you give time for students to discuss and compare answers.

7.3 Key:

a. lěng *(cold)*
b. rè *(hot)*

7.4 • Have students work in pairs. They should write their own answers first, then share and compare with their partners.

• See if anyone can guess the meaning of the word *juéde.* ("to feel")

7.4 Key:

Do you **feel cold**? I don't really **feel cold**. I (actually) **feel** rather hot.

7.1 *View Episode 7 of the dramatic series.*

7.2 *Getting ready: What are some physical sensations you have had in the past day or two? Have you felt hot, cold, hungry, or tired? Take some notes about these sensations.*

_____

_____

7.3 *Watch and listen to the video segment. Then circle how each person is feeling.*

a.

lěng *(cold)*   rè *(hot)*

b.

lěng *(cold)*   rè *(hot)*

7.4 *What do you think the following sentences mean? Fill in the blanks in the English translations.*

Nǐ juéde lěng ma? Wǒ bìng bù juéde lěng. Wǒ juéde tǐng rè ne.

你覺得冷嗎？我並不覺得冷。我覺得挺熱呢。／
你觉得冷吗？我并不觉得冷。我觉得挺热呢。

Do you _____? I don't really _____. I (actually) _____ rather hot.

7.5 *Number the English sentences below to match the order of the Chinese sentences.*

Nǐ bìng le ma?
你病了嗎？／你病了吗？

Fāshāo le ma?
發燒了嗎？／发烧了吗？

Wǒ méi bìng!
我没病！

Nǐ yào bu yao hē diǎnr rè de?
你要不要喝點兒熱的？／
你要不要喝点儿热的？

Qù chīfàn?
去吃飯／去吃饭？

_4_ Do you want to drink something hot?

_1_ Are you sick?

_2_ Do you have a fever?

_5_ Do you want to go eat?

_3_ I'm not sick!

7.5 • Write *bìng, fāshāo, hē,* and *chīfàn* on the board. After students have completed the matching exercise, play the video again and have them guess the meaning of these key words in context.

• If students ask why *Qù chīfàn?* is a question, direct them to read the Grammar Bit on page 165.

Grammar Bits 语法点滴

The noun that is and isn't there

You have already learned that *de* helps to describe or modify the noun that it precedes. Examples include:

> wǒ de péngyou (*my friend*)
>
> wǒ de dōngxi (*my things*)
>
> Měiguó de xuéxiào (*American schools*)

In all of these examples, the noun is present. However, *de* also plays a role when the noun is missing or implied. For example:

> rè de dōngxi (*something that's hot*) ⇒ rè de (*something hot*)
>
> lěng de (*something that's cold, something cold*)
>
> wǒ de (*something belonging to me, mine*)
>
> hǎo de (*something that's good, a good one*)
>
> shéi de? (*of who ⇒ whose?*)
>
> chī de (*something to eat*)
>
> hē de (*something to drink*)

"Rising intonation" questions without *ma*

You've already learned that, in Chinese, you can turn a statement into a question by adding the particle *ma* to the end of it. The overall intonation in a *ma* question is higher than in the statement. In addition, just as in English, questions in Chinese can also be formed without *ma*—simply by saying a phrase, in the proper context, in a higher and rising intonation, as in the video segment for exercise 7.3: *Qù chīfàn?* ([Shall we] go eat?)

 7.6 *Watch and listen to the video segment. Then match the corresponding items below.*

a. rè 熱	1. *hungry*	A. 高兴
b. lěng 冷	2. *sleepy*	B. 饱
c. lèi 累	3. *full*	C. 忙
d. è 餓	4. *hot*	D. 热
e. kě 渴	5. *happy*	E. 着急
f. bǎo 饱	6. *worried*	F. 累
g. kùn 睏	7. *cold*	G. 生气
h. máng 忙	8. *angry*	H. 渴
i. gāoxìng 高興	9. *thirsty*	I. 困
j. zháojí 着急	10. *busy*	J. 饿
k. shēngqì 生氣	11. *tired*	K. 冷

7.7 • Do a demonstration by acting out a few physical sensations while the class guesses.

• Write *Nǐ . . . ma?*, *Bú duì*, and *Duì! Duì! Wǒ hěn . . .* on the board.

• Remind students to use the words in exercise 7.6.

• Mingle among students and assist as necessary.

7.8 • Prepare copies of the class roster to give to students.

• Tell students to take notes in English.

• After students have finished mingling, bring the activity to a conclusion by asking the class, for example:

Wǒmen yǒu jǐ ge rén juéde hěn rè? *(How many of us feel hot?)*

Wǒmen yǒu jǐ ge rén juéde hěn è? *(How many of us feel hungry?)*

7.9 Key:

le *(in all blanks)*

Grammar Bits

• Exercises 7.10–7.12 are designed to help students master the usage of *le* by applying it in a meaningful context. You may wish to have students do these exercises first, before they read this Grammar Bit.

• Check comprehension by asking the class:

1. In Chinese, we put *le* at the end of a sentence to indicate a . . . ? *(change)*

2. "I am hungry," *zěnme shuō?* *(Wǒ hěn è.)*

3. "I am hungry now./I have become hungry," *zěnme shuō?* *(Wǒ è le.)*

4. "I am not hungry," *zěnme shuō?* *(Wǒ bú è.)*

5. "I am no longer hungry," *zěnme shuō?* *(Wǒ bú è le.)*

7.7 Pair work: *With a partner, drill these vocabulary items by playing "charades" or "twenty questions." The person guessing could ask, for example, "Nǐ rè ma?" or "Nǐ máng ma?" The person pantomiming would say "Bú duì" until the correct question is asked. The response would then be, "Duì! Duì! Wǒ hěn ___!"*

7.8 Mingling: *Fill in the blank below to express how you are feeling right now. Then walk around the room asking how everyone is; address your classmates by name and take notes (on a class roster) on each person's response.*

Q: Nǐ xiànzài juéde zěnmeyàng? *(How are you feeling right now?)*

A: Wǒ hěn _____.

7.9 *Watch and listen to the video segment. Fill in the blanks (in pinyin) with the words you hear.*

Husband: È _____ ma?

Wife: Wǒ è _____. Zánmen chīfàn ba. *(Let's eat.)*

Zhao: Chībǎo _____ ma?

Alejandro: Chībǎo _____.

Zhao: Yào bu yao huíqù shuì yí ge wǔjiào? *(Do you want to go back and take an afternoon nap?)*

April: Bú yào. *(No.)*

Grammar Bits 语法点滴

Le: Review and extension

You've probably noticed that the sentence particle *le* is used throughout the exchange in this video segment. It roughly means "to have become _____ (when you weren't before)." In other words, *le* indicates a change in status: You weren't this way before, but now you are.

> Wǒ è le. *(I'm hungry.)* *(Literally: I've gotten hungry. I wasn't before.)*
>
> Bǎo le ma? *(Full?)* *(Literally: Have you become full now? You were hungry before.)*

You may recall this construction from Unit 1: *Wǒ dǒng le.* (Now I understand [after your explanation].)

If you want to answer a *le* question in the negative—in other words, when there's NO change in status—you can use *bù* or *méi*. Consider these examples:

> Xiànzài è le ma? *(Are you hungry now?)*
>
> Bú è. Háishi bú è. *(No, I'm not. I'm still not hungry.)*
>
> Bìng le ma? *(Are you sick?)*   Méi bìng. *(I'm not sick.)*
>
> Dǒng le ma? *(Do you understand now?)*
>
> Háishi bù dǒng. *(I still don't understand.)*

The negative form *bù . . . le*, on the other hand, indicates a status that once existed but no longer does.

> Wǒ gāngcái hěn kùn, xiànzài bú kùn le. *(I was sleepy just now; now I'm not sleepy anymore.)*
>
> Wǒ gāngcái hěn lěng, xiànzài bù lěng le. *(I was cold just now; now I'm not cold anymore.)*

7.10 *Match the corresponding items below.*

a. Wǒ dǒng le.   1. *She's become angry.*   A. 我好了。

b. Wǒ bìng le.   2. *He's gotten worried.*   B. 我懂了。

c. Wǒ hǎo le.   3. *I've gotten sick.*   C. 她生氣了。／她生气了。

d. Tā shēngqì le.   4. *Now I understand.*   D. 他著急了。／他着急了。

e. Tā zháojí le.   5. *I'm well now.*   E. 我病了。

7.10 Key:
a. 4. B
b. 3. E
c. 5. A
d. 1. C
e. 2. D

7.11 *Write the English meanings of the sentences below.*

a. Wǒ bù dǒng.   _____

b. Wǒ méi bìng.   _____

c. Wǒ bú tài *(too)* hǎo. _____

d. Tā bù shēngqì.   _____

e. Tā bù zháojí.   _____

7.11 Key:
a. I don't understand.
b. I'm not sick.
c. I am not (feeling) too good.
d. He/she is not angry.
e. He/she is not worried/anxious.

7.12 *Fill in the blanks with pinyin to match the English sentences.*

a. *I'm no longer angry.*   Wǒ bù _____ le.

b. *I'm no longer hungry.*   Wǒ bú _____ le.

c. *I'm no longer tired.*   Wǒ bú _____ le.

d. *I'm no longer cold.*   Wǒ bù _____ le.

7.13 *Fill in the blanks below with the last time you felt the following way.*

   Examples: Wǒ jīntiān zǎoshang è le.
              Wǒ liǎng ge xīngqī yǐqián bìng le.
              Wǒ zuótiān wǎnshang shēngqì le.

a. Wǒ _____ è le.

b. Wǒ _____ bìng le.

c. Wǒ _____ shēngqì le.

d. Wǒ _____ zháojí le.

e. Wǒ _____ lèi le.

f. Wǒ _____ dǒng le. [*Try using* xiànzài *(now).*]

7.14 *Pair work: Work with a partner. Compare each sentence you wrote with each of your partner's. If the time you wrote is earlier, give your partner a thumbs-up sign. If the time your partner wrote is earlier, he or she gives you a thumbs-up sign. If you and your partner wrote the same time, shake hands.*

7.14 • Invite a confident pair to perform a demonstration for the class.

• If time allows, have students do this activity with multiple classmates.

Encounter 2 Asking about someone's well-being

7.15 Before playing the video, have students work in pairs to guess the pinyin for as many of these expressions as possible. Remind students to use the English translations and known characters as clues. Next, play the video and have students complete exercise 7.15. Upon completion, tell students to compare their predictions to their final answers.

7.15 Key:

Asking about someone's well-being

a. Nǐ zěnme yàng? Hǎo ma?
b. Yǒu shénme shì ma?
c. Zěnme le?
d. Nǐ ne? Nǐ zěnme yàng?

Stating one's own well-being

a. Hái hǎo. Mǎma hūhū.
b. Méishì, méishì.
c. Méishì, méishì, zhēnde.
d. Méishì. Hěn hǎo. Lǎo yàngzi.

7.15 *Watch and listen to the video segment. Using the English as a guide, write the pinyin for the following expressions. (Note: Not all the expressions below appear in the video segment.)*

Asking about someone's well-being

a. 你怎麼樣？好嗎？ _____
   (How are you? [Are] things OK?)

b. 有甚麼事嗎？ _____
   (Is anything wrong?)

c. 怎麼了？ _____
   (What's going on?)

d. 你呢？你怎麼樣？ _____
   (What about you? What's up with you?)

Stating one's own well-being

a. 還好。馬馬虎虎。 _____
   (OK. So-so.)

b. 没事，没事。 _____
   (No, nothing's wrong.)

c. 没事，没事，真的。 _____
   (No, nothing's wrong. Really.)

d. 没事。很好。老樣子。 _____
   (Nothing's up. Things are fine. The same as ever.)

FYI 供你参考

Restraint as a social virtue

Stimulate class discussion by asking, "When you have a problem, is it a good idea to complain about it to people around you in China? Why or why not? According to this FYI, how do Chinese people value and treat people's personal feelings?"

If harmony within a group is a key social objective, then it often behooves an individual to downplay personal feelings. Not complaining about one's own problems can be a sign of maturity, or it can be an indication that one has learned to put the needs of others or of a group before one's own needs. Furthermore, there is the expectation that with increasing age, one becomes more skillful in cooperating with others and maintaining harmony (including within one's own physical body). Complaints can sometimes be seen as an admission of failure, leading to disharmony. Of course, struggling to maintain a reasonable balance between the needs of the individual and those of others is a challenge in any society. In the video segment you just watched, while one person resists burdening another with his personal issues, the other presses out of concern for the well-being of her friend. The reluctance to "unburden oneself" may be more pronounced in China than in many Western societies. However, as with many other issues, change is in the air.

7.16 *Match the corresponding traditional and simplified characters.*

a. 你呢？你怎麼樣？

b. 你怎麼樣？好嗎？

c. 還好。馬馬虎虎。

d. 有甚麼事嗎？

e. 老樣子。

f. 怎麼了？

1. 你怎么样？好吗？

2. 还好。马马虎虎。

3. 怎么了？

4. 你呢？你怎么样？

5. 有什么事吗？

6. 老样子。

▶ Reading practice

7.17 *Pair work: Work together with your partner. The following dialogue is written in simplified characters. Practice reading it aloud with your partner. Then change roles and read it again.*

甲：嗨，老朋友。你怎么样？好吗？

乙：还好。马马虎虎。

甲：有什么事吗？

乙：没事，没事。

甲：怎么了？

乙：没事，没事，真的。你呢？你怎么样？

甲：没事。很好。老样子。

Now try reading it in traditional characters.

甲：嗨，老朋友。你怎麼樣？好嗎？

乙：還好。馬馬虎虎。

甲：有甚麼事嗎？

乙：沒事，沒事。

甲：怎麼了？

乙：沒事，沒事，真的。你呢？你怎麼樣？

甲：沒事。很好。老樣子。

7.18 *Tang Yuan in the previous video segment wasn't feeling happy but didn't want to admit it at first. If he had been really unwell, he might have used one or more of the following phrases. Watch and listen to the video. Then number the English translations below in the order in which the Chinese statements appear in the segment.*

_____ *I have a headache.*

_____ *I'm not feeling well.*

_____ *I'm angry.*

_____ *I've gotten sick.*

_____ *I'm in a bad mood.*

_____ *I'm not doing too well.*

_____ *I'm worried.*

7.19 *Now complete the pinyin transcription of each statement.*

a. Wǒ _____ shūfu.

b. Wǒ _____ le.

c. Wǒ _____.

d. Wǒ xīnqíng _____ _____.

e. Wǒ hěn _____.

f. Wǒ hěn _____.

g. Wǒ bú _____ _____.

7.20 *Match the corresponding English, pinyin, and characters.*

a. *I'm not feeling well.*   1. Wǒ tóu téng.   A. 我心情不好。

b. *I've gotten sick.*   2. Wǒ bù shūfu.   B. 我病了。

c. *I have a headache.*   3. Wǒ hěn shēngqì.   C. 我很生氣。／我很生气。

d. *I'm in a bad mood.*   4. Wǒ bìng le.   D. 我不舒服。

e. *I'm worried.*   5. Wǒ xīnqíng bù hǎo.   E. 我不太好。

f. *I'm angry.*   6. Wǒ bú tài hǎo.   F. 我頭疼。／我头疼。

g. *I'm not doing too well.*   7. Wǒ hěn zháojí.   G. 我很著急。／我很着急。

7.21 *Pair work:* Work together with your partner. Write a dialogue of at least four exchanges between you and your partner, making small talk about how you are feeling. Write the script in pinyin below.

甲：_____

乙：_____

甲：_____

乙：_____

甲：_____

乙：_____

甲：_____

乙：_____

7.22 Using the dialogue from exercise 7.21, perform a skit for another pair or the entire class.

Nǐ zěnme yàng? Hái hǎo ma?

Hái hǎo. Nǐ ne?

Encounter 3 Suggesting a course of action

 7.23 *Watch and listen to the video segment. Check the actions illustrated below that you hear mentioned.*

☐ chī dōngxi ☐ hē kāfēi huò chá ☐ sànbù ☐ liáotiānr ☐ huíjiā

☐ xǐzǎo ☐ shuìjiào ☐ dǎ diànhuà ☐ guàngjiē ☐ xiūxi

7.23 Key:

chī dōngxi
hē kāfēi huò chá
sànbù
liáotiānr
huíjiā
xǐzǎo
shuìjiào
dǎ diànhuà
xiūxi

7.24 Key:

a. 8
b. 5
c. 7
d. 9
e. 10
f. 2
g. 3
h. 1
i. 4
j. 6

7.24 *Match the pinyin and traditional characters with the corresponding English equivalents.*

a. sànbù 散步

b. chī dōngxi 吃東西

c. hē kāfēi huò chá 喝咖啡或茶

d. liáotiānr 聊天兒

e. huíjiā 回家

f. xǐzǎo 洗澡

g. shuìjiào 睡覺

h. guàngjiē 逛街

i. dǎ diànhuà 打電話

j. xiūxi 休息

1. *go shopping*

2. *take a shower/bath*

3. *go to sleep*

4. *make a phone call*

5. *eat something*

6. *rest*

7. *drink coffee or tea*

8. *take a walk*

9. *chat*

10. *go home*

7.25 *Match the corresponding traditional and simplified characters.*

a. 散步	1. 吃东西
b. 吃東西	2. 聊天儿
c. 喝咖啡或茶	3. 洗澡
d. 聊天兒	4. 打电话
e. 回家	5. 逛街
f. 洗澡	6. 休息
g. 睡覺	7. 回家
h. 逛街	8. 散步
i. 打電話	9. 睡觉
j. 休息	10. 喝咖啡或茶

7.25 Key:
a. 8
b. 1
c. 10
d. 2
e. 7
f. 3
g. 9
h. 5
i. 4
j. 6

Grammar Bits 语法点滴

"Duping" your verbs: Review and extension

Sometimes in conversation a speaker will "soften" or minimize an action by duplicating the verb or by adding *yìdiǎnr* "a little" (or its shortened form *diǎnr*) before the object.

- duplicating a one-syllable verb:
  - wèn *(ask)* ⇒ wènwen *(pose a question)*
  - kàn *(look)* ⇒ kànkan *(take a look)*
- duplicating a verb-object combination:
  - sànbù *(take a walk)* ⇒ sànsanbù *(take a little walk)*
  - liáotiānr *(chat)* ⇒ liáoliaotiānr *(have a little chat)*
- with [yì]diǎnr:
  - chī dōngxi *(eat something)* ⇒ chī diǎnr dōngxi *(have a little something to eat)*
  - hē kāfēi *(drink coffee)* ⇒ hē diǎnr kāfēi *(drink a bit of coffee)*

One cannot "dup" all verbs. The verb must denote an action over which you have some control, such as *kàn* (look) => *kànkan* (take a look); that is, the action must be volitional. Therefore, you can choose to *kànkan* (take a look), but you cannot *wàngwang* (forget-forget) because you have no real control over forgetting.

By the way, the *r* sound in *(yì)diǎnr* is a Beijing habit. Don't pronounce the *n*. When *r* is added to a word, the *n* sound disappears, but the letter is retained in standard pinyin spelling.

Grammar Bits

- Although this textbook is designed so that teachers do not need to explicitly teach grammar, it might be helpful to spend some time discussing the material in this section with your students.
- After students have read this section, check comprehension by asking:

Why do we "dup" verbs in Chinese?

How do we "dup" verbs in Chinese? Work with a partner to come up with three examples to share with the class.

Can we "dup" the verb *wàng* ("to forget")? Why (not)?

- Have the class work in small groups to "dup" the words listed in exercise 7.25. Encourage students to say these words aloud:

sànbù → sànsanbù
chī dōngxi → chīchi dōngxi
hē kāfēi huò chá → hēhe kāfēi huò chá
liáotiānr → liáoliaotiānr
xǐzǎo → xǐxizǎo
shuìjiào → shuìshuijiào
guàngjiē → guàngguangjiē
dǎ diànhuà → dǎda diànhuà

Make sure to point out the exception: *xiūxi → xiūxixiūxi*. Also point out that *huíjiā* is generally not "duped."

7.26 • Encourage students to apply the information they learned in the Grammar Bits on page 173.
• Invite a volunteer to do a demonstration with you for the class.
• As students engage in their conversations, circulate around the classroom and provide assistance, as necessary.

7.26 *Pair work: Working with a partner, make a list of four to six terms that describe how you feel right now (hungry, tired, worried, etc.). Then tell your partner how you feel: for example,* Wǒ hěn lèi. *Your partner should respond by making a suggestion:* Nà nǐ xiūxixiūxi ba. *(Remember to add the particle* ba *for suggestions.) Switch roles and continue until you have both used all your terms. Practice two or three of your favorite exchanges to perform for another pair or the entire class.*

Grammar Bits

• Check comprehension by asking clarification questions, such as:

"Let's go for walk," *zěnme shuō?* (Zánmen sànsanbù ba.)

"Let's take a break," *zěnme shuō?* (Zánmen xiūxixiūxi ba.)

• Have students apply the usage of *zánmen* by doing exercise 7.26 again. This time, have them make suggestions with *zánmen*. For example, *Zánmen xiūxixiūxi ba.*

Grammar Bits 语法点滴

Zánmen 咱們／咱们 **vs.** *wǒmen* 我們／我们

You've already learned the pronoun *wǒmen* (we). *Zánmen* also means "we," but it is a narrower sense of "we" in that it includes only the speaker and the person(s) being addressed. It is equivalent to "you and I."

Zánmen zǒu ba! *(Let's [you and I] go!)*

Wǒmen, on the other hand, has a wider application. *Wǒmen* includes the speaker and others, but not necessarily the person being addressed.

Wǒmen zǒu le, zàijiàn a! *(We are leaving now. Good-bye then!)*

Zánmen is particularly suited to suggesting a shared course of action because of its narrower focus. It also creates a more intimate feeling between the speaker and the person(s) addressed. However, keep in mind that although *zánmen* is widely used in northern China, it is less used in the south. By the way, the first *n* in *zánmen* is silent but is still retained in the pinyin spelling.

Encounter 4 Expressing urgency

7.27 Key:
3
2
4
1

7.27 *Watch and listen to the video. Focus only on what the second person says. Then number the terms below from the least urgent (1) to the most urgent (4).*

_____ děi

_____ yào

_____ bìxū

_____ xiǎng

7.28 *Match the corresponding items below.*

a. Wǒ xiǎng shàng cèsuǒ.

1. 我必须上廁所。/
   我必须上厕所。

A. I want to go to the bathroom.

b. Wǒ yào shàng cèsuǒ.

2. 我想上廁所。/
   我想上厕所。

B. I must go to the bathroom!

c. Wǒ děi shàng cèsuǒ.

3. 我得上廁所。/
   我得上厕所。

C. I'd like to go to the bathroom.

d. Wǒ bìxū shàng cèsuǒ.

4. 我要上廁所。/
   我要上厕所。

D. I have to go to the bathroom.

Of course, if you don't need to go to the bathroom, you can say:

Wǒ bú yòng shàng cèsuǒ.   我不用上廁所。／我不用上厕所。

Write a sentence (in pinyin) stating your degree of urgency regarding a trip to the bathroom.

_____

Chinese terms for "restroom"

As in other countries, the issue of the toilet is a delicate one in China. There are various ways of referring to this place; some are direct and some are more polite. Some of the more popular expressions, in addition to *cèsuǒ* 廁所／厕所 (toilet), include *wèishēngjiān* 衛生間／卫生间 (literally, "hygienic room"), *xǐshǒujiān* 洗手間／洗手间 (literally, "washroom" or "room to wash your hands"), and *huàzhuāngshì* 化妆室／化妆室 (literally, "makeup room" or "powder room"). Public toilets are usually called *gōnggòng cèsuǒ* 公共廁所／公共厕所 (public toilet) and are usually separated by gender: *nán* 男 (male) and *nǚ* 女 (female). Just as in the United States and elsewhere, a visit to a *gōnggòng cèsuǒ* can be an adventure.

7.29 • Have students work in pairs to write their own sentences.

• In addition to the words provided in the word bank, encourage students to use words from exercise 7.23.

7.29 *Complete the following sentences to state your own "degree of urgency" right now.*

> chī dōngxi   hē shuǐ   shuìjiào   sànbù   shàng cèsuǒ   qù guàngjiē
>
> huíjiā   qù zhǎo ge péngyou *(call on a friend)*   chī yào *(take medicine)*

1. Wǒ xiǎng _____.
2. Wǒ yào _____.
3. Wǒ děi _____.
4. Wǒ bìxū _____.
5. Wǒ bú yòng _____.

7.30 • Direct students' attention to the model dialogue in the speech balloons. (By now, students should know the design of *Encounters* well enough to understand that they should use the provided model sentences to carry on their own dialogues. Therefore, a quick reminder should be sufficient.)

• Mingle among students to observe performance and provide assistance, if necessary.

7.30 *Pair work: Find out what your partner wrote about his or her "degree of urgency." Take some notes below.*

_____

_____

Nǐ xiànzaì xiǎng zuò shénme?

Wǒ xiànzaì xiǎng . . .

7.31 • Tell students that they need to accomplish this task by speaking as little English as possible. By now, students should have a large enough Chinese vocabulary to complete this exercise. Mingle among the groups to observe student performance. If too much English is spoken, bring the whole class together to brainstorm appropriate language items, for example, *Nǐ xiǎng qù cèsuǒ ma? Duì, wǒ yě xiǎng qù cèsuǒ. Nǐ bìxū qù zuò shénme?* This negotiation process in Chinese will take some time, so make sure to leave 10–15 minutes for students to work this out among themselves.

• When they have finished writing their sentences, groups should take turns sharing their sentences with the class. Enforce the rule that one person cannot speak again until all group members have gotten a chance to talk.

• As the rest of the class listens to the group presentations, they should excitedly yell out *Duì, wǒmen yě shì!* ("Right, we feel that way, too!") when they hear a statement that their group also wrote.

7.31 *Group work: Work with two or three classmates to come up with five sentences that you all agree on, regarding urgent (or not so urgent) things you want to do right now.*

Example: Wǒmen dōu hěn xiǎng qù chī diǎnr dōngxi! *(We'd all really like to go eat something!)*

_____

_____

_____

_____

_____

♫ **Unit Rap**

Go to the **Encounters** *website at www.EncountersChinese.com and listen to the song to review key expressions from Unit 7. Listen again and sing along!*

Encounter 5 Reading and writing

▶ Reading familiar sentences in Chinese characters

7.32 *Pair work: Read the following dialogues (written in traditional characters) aloud with a partner, using the English as a guide.*

1 甲：哎 (ài)，冷啊，冷啊。　*(Wow, it's cold, it's cold.)*

乙：冷嗎？我不覺得冷。要不要喝點熱的？　*(Is it? I'm not cold. You want to drink something hot?)*

甲：要要要。我們去喝點熱的吧！　*(Yes, yes, yes. Let's go get something hot to drink!)*

2 甲：累了嗎？　*(Tired?)*

乙：不累。就是有點兒餓。你餓了嗎？　*(No. I'm just a little hungry. Are you hungry yet?)*

甲：我並 (bìng) 不餓。有點兒渴。　*(I'm not really hungry. I'm a little thirsty.)*

乙：那我們去喝點兒東西？　*(Then shall we go get something to drink?)*

甲：好啊。你也可以吃點兒東西。　*(OK. And you can eat something too.)*

3 甲：我飽了。你吃飽了嗎？　*(I'm full. Are you full yet?)*

乙：我也吃飽了。吃飽了就 (jiù) 睏！　*(I'm full too. As soon as I'm full, I get sleepy!)*

4 甲：忙不忙？　*(Are you busy?)*

乙：很忙，很忙。我姐姐跟他先生要回來了！　*(I'm really very busy. My sister and her husband are coming back very soon!)*

甲：甚麼時候來？　*(When are they returning?)*

乙：後天來。我真 (zhēn) 高興！　*(The day after tomorrow. I'm really happy!)*

7.32 • Avoid reading the dialogue aloud for your students or having them repeat after you. Tell them to use the English and familiar characters as bridges to determine the meaning and pronunciation for unknown characters.

• Keep in mind that reading fluency is not the goal of this activity. Tell students to not get discouraged if they have trouble reading quickly and accurately.

• Have students complete this exercise multiple times before they move on to 7.33 and 7.34.

5 甲：你是著急還是生氣？ *(Are you worried or are you angry?)*

乙：生氣。我女兒還沒回家。我叫她早回來…… *(I'm angry. My daughter's not home yet. I told her to come back early . . .)*

甲：哦，你著急嗎？ *(Oh, are you worried?)*

乙：也著急。 *(Yes, I'm worried too.)*

6 甲：昨天晚上我媽媽生氣了。 *(My mother got angry last night.)*

乙：為甚麼？ *(Why?)*

甲：我回家晚了。我就是不懂她為甚麼會那麼著急。 *(I got home late. I just don't understand why she gets so worried.)*

乙：父母嘛 (ma—*pause marker*)……都會著急的！ *(They're parents . . . all parents worry!)*

7 甲：嗨，老朋友。你最近怎麼樣？還好嗎？ *(Hi, old friend. How have you been? [Are] things OK?)*

乙：不太好。我心情不好。 *(Not too good. I'm in a bad mood.)*

甲：甚麼事啊？ *(Is something wrong?)*

乙：我生我男朋友的氣。真頭疼！ *(I'm angry at my boyfriend. [He's a] real headache!)*

甲：不要生氣啦！我們去散散步，聊聊天兒，好不好？ *(Don't be mad! Let's go for a walk and have a chat, OK?)*

乙：好吧。我先給我男朋友打個電話…… *(OK. Let me call my boyfriend first . . .)*

甲：生你男朋友的氣，為甚麼還要給他打電話呢？ *(If you're mad at your boyfriend, why would you want to call him?)*

8 甲：我今天晚上有事，要見個朋友。我得回家洗澡。對不起，我走了！ *(I have something to do tonight. I'm meeting with a friend. I have to go home and take a bath/shower. Sorry, I'm leaving now!)*

乙：我也走了。 *(I'll leave too.)*

甲：你去哪兒？ *(Where are you going?)*

乙：先必須上個衛生間，然後回家睡覺！我累了！明天見。 *(First I have to go to the bathroom, and then I'm going home to bed! I'm tired! See you tomorrow.)*

7.33–7.34

- Have students read these dialogues multiple times, focusing on reading fluency.

- Encourage students *not* to refer to exercise 7.32 for help. Instead, ask them to rely on the dialogue context and their partners to help them read new characters.

- After students practice reading the dialogues a few times, play the audio and have them check their pronunciation.

7.33 *Pair work:* *Read the dialogues aloud with a partner, this time without any English.*

1 甲：哎 (ài)，冷啊，冷啊。

乙：冷嗎？我不覺得冷。要不要喝點熱的？

甲：要要要。我們去喝點熱的吧！

2 甲：累了嗎？

乙：不累。就是有點兒餓。你餓了嗎？

甲：我並 (bìng) 不餓。有點兒渴。

乙：那我們去喝點兒東西？

甲：好啊。你也可以吃點兒東西。

3 甲：我飽了。你吃飽了嗎？

乙：我也吃飽了。吃飽了就 (jiù) 睏！

4 甲：忙不忙？

乙：很忙，很忙。我姐姐跟他先生要回來了！

甲：甚麼時候來？

乙：後天來。我真 (zhēn) 高興！

5 甲：你是著急還是生氣？

乙：生氣。我女兒還沒回家。我叫她早回來……

甲：哦，你著急嗎？

乙：也著急。

6 甲：昨天晚上我媽媽生氣了。

乙：為甚麼？

甲：我回家晚了。我就是不懂她為甚麼會那麼著急。

乙：父母嘛 (ma) ……都會著急的！

7 甲：嗨，老朋友。你最近怎麼樣？還好嗎？

乙：不太好。我心情不好。

甲：甚麼事啊？

乙：我生我男朋友的氣。真頭疼！

甲：不要生氣啦！我們去散散步，聊聊天兒，好不好？

乙：好吧。我先給我男朋友打個電話……

甲：生你男朋友的氣，為甚麼還要給他打電話呢？

8 甲：我今天晚上有事，要見個朋友。我得回家洗澡。對不起，我走了！

乙：我也走了。

甲：你去哪兒？

乙：先必須上個衛生間，然後回家睡覺！我累了！明天見。

7.34 Pair work: *Now try it once again, this time in simplified characters.*

1 甲：哎 (ài)，冷啊，冷啊。

乙：冷吗？我不觉得冷。要不要喝点热的？

甲：要要要。我们去喝点热的吧！

2 甲：累了吗？

乙：不累。就是有点儿饿。你饿了吗？

甲：我并 (bìng) 不饿。有点儿渴。

乙：那我们去喝点儿东西？

甲：好啊。你也可以吃点儿东西。

3 甲：我饱了。你吃饱了吗？

乙：我也吃饱了。吃饱了就 (jiù) 困！

4 甲：忙不忙？

乙：很忙，很忙。我姐姐跟他先生要回来了！

甲：什么时候来？

乙：后天来。我真 (zhēn) 高兴！

5 甲：你是着急还是生气？

乙：生气。我女儿还没回家。我叫她早回来……

甲：哦，你着急吗？

乙：也着急。

6 甲：昨天晚上我妈妈生气了。

乙：为什么？

甲：我回家晚了。我就是不懂她为什么会那么着急。

乙：父母嘛 (ma)……都会着急的！

7 甲：嗨，老朋友。你最近怎么样？还好吗？

乙：不太好。我心情不好。

甲：什么事啊？

乙：我生我男朋友的气。真头疼！

甲：不要生气啦！我们去散散步，聊聊天儿，好不好？

乙：好吧。我先给我男朋友打个电话……

甲：生你男朋友的气，为什么还要给他打电话呢？

8 甲：我今天晚上有事，要见个朋友。我得回家洗澡。对不
　　　起，我走了！

　　乙：我也走了。

　　甲：你去哪儿？

　　乙：先必须上个卫生间，然后回家睡觉！我累了！明天见。

7.35 *Match the corresponding simplified characters, traditional characters, and English.*

a. 觉得	1. 吃點東西	A. *a little hungry*
b. 喝点热的	2. 有點餓	B. *really happy*
c. 有点饿	3. 飽了	C. *full (after eating)*
d. 吃点东西	4. 喝點熱的	D. *feel*
e. 饱了	5. 真高興	E. *become sleepy*
f. 困了	6. 生氣	F. *angry*
g. 真高兴	7. 覺得	G. *drink something hot*
h. 生气	8. 睏了	H. *meet with a friend*
i. 头疼	9. 見朋友	I. *have a headache*
j. 见朋友	10. 上衛生間	J. *eat something*
k. 上卫生间	11. 頭疼	K. *go to the bathroom*

▶ Reading real-life texts

7.36 飲／饮 yǐn *means "drink." What kinds of drinks are being advertised?*

Answer: _____ and _____

7.37 *Match the photos with the captions. Write the letter on the line.*

a.

b.

c.

___ Open for business   ___ Restroom   ___ Men's room/Women's room

7.38 *Read the following note and fill in the blanks.*

7.38 Key:
not well; a headache

李华：

我不舒服. 发烧.

头疼. 先回去了.

姚丽

Li Hua:

I'm _____. I have a fever

and _____. I've gone home early.

Yao Li

▶ Learning to write characters

7.39 *For stroke order and other useful information about each of the following characters from this unit, go to the* Character Writing Workbook. *Choose either traditional or simplified characters and practice writing them until you can reproduce them on demand.*

熱／热，冷，累，餓／饿，飽／饱，忙，怎，樣／样，吧，吃
飯／饭，東／东，西，坐，走，回，高，興／兴，著／着，急

▶ Writing a note

7.40 *Write a brief description of yourself in your choice of traditional or simplified Chinese characters. Include information about how you feel at different times, and what you do in response to these feelings.*

Cultural Bits 文化点滴

Meeting our needs

View the video segment "Meeting our needs" and then discuss the following questions with your classmates.

- What are some challenges you might face in China?
- What might be easier in China than in your home country?
- What are some steps you might take to "get underway" in China?
- What are some things you might need to be careful about?

7.40 • If you find it necessary, help students brainstorm and review the language items they need to construct their paragraphs. Invite students to offer their suggestions "popcorn style." Have volunteers take notes on the board in both pinyin and English.

• If you feel students would benefit, allow them to write their paragraphs in pinyin before "translating" them into characters.

• When they finish writing, partners should proofread each other's writing before handing in their drafts.

• A sample paragraph: 我今天早上不舒服，所以我得喝热水。今天下午我头痛，所以我想回家。现在我发烧，所以我必须睡觉。

Recap

▶ Grammar

Sentence-ending particles: Review

Use *ba* to make a suggestion or mild command or to express agreement.

> Zánmen zǒu ba! (*Let's go, OK?*)
> Hǎo ba. (*OK then.*)

Use *a* to soften a question.

> Lǎoshī, nín hǎo a? (*How are you, Teacher?*)

Use *ma* to ask a question.

> Nǐ lěng ma? (*Are you cold?*)

Use *ne* to ask a follow-up question.

> Tāmen hěn máng. Nǐmen ne? (*They're busy. How about you [all]?*)

Use *le* to show a change in the situation.

> Wǒ zuótiān bìng le. Jīntiān hǎo le. (*Yesterday I was sick. I'm better today.*)

Rising intonation questions without *ma*

Questions in Chinese can be formed without *ma* at the end of the inquiry by simply using rising intonation, just as you do in English.

> Chīfàn? (*[Shall we go] eat?*)
> Rè? (*[You're] hot?*)

Possessive *de* with and without nouns

The possessive *de* modifies the noun it precedes.

> wǒ de shǒujī (*my cell phone*)

When the noun modified by *de* is understood or implied, it can be omitted.

> Nǐ yào hē diǎnr rè de ma? (*Will you have a little [something] hot to drink?*)

Zánmen vs. *wǒmen*

Zánmen is used when the speaker refers to himself or herself and the person(s) addressed.

> Zánmen zǒu ba! (*Let's [you and I] go.*)

Wǒmen includes the speaker and others, but not necessarily the person(s) addressed.

> Wǒmen zuótiān qù guàngjiē le, nǐ wèishénme méiyǒu lái? (*We [all] went shopping yesterday; why didn't you come?*)

"Softening" an action

In conversation, you can "soften" or minimize the impact of an action by duplicating the verb or adding (*yì*)*diǎnr*.

> Zánmen qù kànkan, hǎo ma? (*Let's go take a look, OK?*)
> Zánmen qù chī diǎnr dōngxi, xíng bu xíng? (*Let's go have a bite to eat, OK?*)

▶ Vocabulary (*Starred items are for review.*)

Physical and mental states
(*all stative verbs*)

bǎo 飽／饱 full, not hungry
è 餓／饿 hungry
gāoxìng* 高興／高兴 happy, pleased, in good spirits
hǎo* 好 well, in good health
kě 渴 thirsty
kùn 睏／困 sleepy

lèi 累 tired, weary
lěng 冷 cold (in temperature)
máng 忙 busy
rè 熱／热 hot (in temperature, not flavor)
shēngqì 生氣／生气 angry, upset
shūfu 舒服 feeling well, comfortable

wǎn* 晚 late
zháojí 著急／着急 worried, anxious

Verb objects
(*verbs with generalized objects*)

chīfàn 吃飯／吃饭 have a meal, eat
fāshāo 發燒／发烧 have a fever

guàngjiē 逛街　go shopping

liáotiānr 聊天兒／聊天儿　have a chat

sànbù 散步　take a walk/stroll

shuìjiào 睡覺／睡觉　sleep, go to sleep

tóuténg 頭疼／头疼　have a headache

xǐzǎo 洗澡　take a bath/shower

Verbs

bìng le 病了　become ill, sick

chī 吃　eat

chībǎo 吃飽／吃饱　eat to fullness

dǎ diànhuà 打電話／打电话　make a phone call

děng 等　wait

hē 喝　drink

huíjiā 回家　return home

huíqu 回去　return

jiàn (péngyou) 見(朋友)／见(朋友)　meet, meet up with (a friend)

qù 去　go to

shàng 上　go to

shuì 睡　sleep

shuō 說／说　speak, say

xiūxi 休息　rest, take a rest, take it easy

zǒu 走　leave/depart from (a place)

Auxiliary (helping) verbs

bìxū 必須／必须　must

búyòng 不用　no need to

děi 得　have to

huì 會／会　be likely to, will

juéde 覺得／觉得　feel, think

xiǎng* 想　would like to, feel like

yào* 要　want to, will, be about to

Adverbs

bú yào 不要　don't; don't want

hái 還／还　still, yet; fairly

jiù 就　right after, then

tài 太　too, extremely

tǐng 挺　very, rather, quite (stronger than *hěn*)

zhēn 真　really, truly, indeed

Time words

gāngcái* 剛才／刚才　a moment ago, just now

ránhòu 然後／然后　thereafter, then

xiān 先　first, in advance of

xiànzài* 現在／现在　now, at present

Conjunctions

háishi* 還是／还是　or (in questions)

huòzhě* 或者　or (in statements)

nà 那　in that case, then

suǒyǐ* 所以　therefore, so

yīnwèi* 因為／因为　because

Nouns

cèsuǒ 廁所／厕所　toilet

chá 茶　tea

diànhuà* 電話／电话　telephone; phone call

dōngxi 東西／东西　(material) thing, things

kāfēi 咖啡　coffee

nánpéngyou* 男朋友　boyfriend

nǚpéngyou* 女朋友　girlfriend

shì 事　matter, affair

tiānqi 天氣／天气　weather

wǔjiào 午覺／午觉　afternoon nap

xīnqíng 心情　mood, feeling, state of mind

xuéxiào 學校／学校　school

yào 藥／药　medicine

Phrases

Bìng bu lěng/rè. 並不冷／熱。‖ 并不冷／热。Not really cold/hot.

Chī diǎnr dōngxi. 吃點兒東西。／吃点儿东西。Have something to eat.

Hái hǎo. 還好。／还好。I'm OK. I'm fairly well.

Mǎma-hūhū. 馬馬虎虎。／马马虎虎。Fair to middling. So-so.

Méishì. 沒事。Nothing's wrong; it doesn't matter; never mind.

Wǒ lǎo yàngzi. 我老樣子。／我老样子。I'm the same as usual.

Xīngqīyī jiàn! 星期一見!／星期一见! See you Monday!

Zánmen zǒu ba! 咱們走吧!／咱们走吧! Let's (you and I) go/leave!

Zěnme le? 怎麼了?／怎么了? What's going on? What happened?

Zěnmeyàng? 怎麼樣?／怎么样? How's it going?

Zěnme zhème lěng/rè? 怎麼這麼冷／熱?‖ 怎么这么冷／热? How come it's so cold/hot?

Zhēn de ma? 真的嗎?／真的吗? Really? Is that true?

❱ **Checklist of "can do" statements**

After completing this unit, you should be able to perform each of the following tasks.

Listening and speaking

- ☐ Find out how someone is feeling.
- ☐ Respond to questions about your own physical condition.
- ☐ Ask and respond to questions about mental states (worried, anxious, etc.).
- ☐ Be able to suggest a remedy for specific physical or mental conditions.
- ☐ Be able to express degrees of urgency of action. (For example, "I have to go to the bathroom.")
- ☐ Courteously express your need to take leave of a friend.

Reading and writing

- ☐ Demonstrate your ability to read simple signs indicating sources of food, drink, and sanitary facilities.
- ☐ Be able to read simple statements regarding the physical needs of others.
- ☐ Write simple statements expressing your physical needs and mental state.

Understanding culture

- ☐ Explain why one might wish to demonstrate restraint in expressing personal feelings.

Checklist

• Have students work in pairs to go through this checklist and demonstrate selected skills to the class. Reserve 20–30 minutes for students to complete this activity. Tell students that putting check marks in each box is NOT the point. The point is to check if they can really do the things on the list.

• Finally, lead the class to revisit the list they made for exercise 7.2 to see if they have learned enough Chinese to say everything on the list.

"Early to bed, early to rise . . . "

早睡早起身體好

Zǎo shuì zǎo qǐ shēntǐ hǎo

Discussing daily routines

In this unit, you will learn how to:

- discuss daily routines for weekdays.
- discuss daytime and evening activities.
- discuss weekend activities.
- talk about when and how often you do things.
- express actions that occur before, during, or after other actions.

- read key items on signs advertising services around town.
- read simple written statements regarding daily routines.
- write a simple note describing your own daily routines.

Encounter 1   Discussing morning routines

As a homework assignment before starting Unit 8, ask students to flip through the unit to preview the content.

8.1 • Before watching Episode 8, ask students what they remember from previous episodes. Encourage them to respond in Chinese and English.

• Play the video clip twice, if necessary.

• Allow time for students to discuss the video among themselves. Understanding the plot is crucial for students to complete the unit's exercises.

8.2 • Possible answers: *take a shower, brush my teeth, wash my face.* The goal of this activity is to get students to think about the routine things we do every day and how people really talk about them.

• Invite volunteers to write the suggestions on a poster. Hang the poster on the wall. After students have completed the unit, make sure to revisit this poster and check if they have learned enough Chinese to say everything on the poster. The purpose of this activity is to help students connect what they're learning with real-life communication needs.

8.3–8.4

• Have students glance at exercises 8.3 and 8.4 before playing the video.

• Tell students to use the body language and context in the video to access meaning. Feel free to pause the video to give hints. You may also want to play the video multiple times, but make sure to allow time for students to answer the questions and compare their answers with classmates.

8.3 Key:

a. What do you do in the morning? (If students ask about the meaning of *dōu . . . xiē,* have them turn to page 198 and read the *Grammar Bits.*)

b. What time do you get up?

8.4 Key:

a. 5:30

b. 7:00, 8:00, or 9:00

c. doesn't say

8.5 Key:

Answers will vary based on students' real-life situations.

8.1 *View Episode 8 of the dramatic series.*

8.2 Getting ready: *What do you do in the morning to get ready for the day?*

_____

_____

8.3 *Watch and listen to the video segment. What do you think the following questions mean? Write the English below.*

a. Nǐ zǎoshang dōu zuò xiē shénme?

你早上都做些甚麼？／你早上都做些什么？

_____

b. Nǐ jǐ diǎn zhōng qǐ chuáng?

你幾點鐘起床？／你几点钟起床？

_____

8.4 *Watch and listen to the video segment again. Circle the appropriate time each person gives in response.*

a.

5:30
7:00, 8:00, or 9:00
doesn't say

b.

5:30
7:00, 8:00, or 9:00
doesn't say

c.

5:30
7:00, 8:00, or 9:00
doesn't say

8.5 *How would you answer for yourself? Fill in the blanks below.*

Wǒ měitiān _____ diǎn qǐ chuáng.

我每天_____點起床。／我每天_____点起床。

8.6 *Pair work: Tell your partner what time you get up in the morning, and then listen to what time he or she tells you. If you have time, ask other classmates as well.*

> Nǐ měitiān jǐ diǎn qǐ chuáng?

> Wǒ měitiān . . .

8.6 • Have students read the model dialogue in the speech balloons before they begin this activity.

• If necessary, invite a confident pair to demonstrate the dialogue before students do it in pairs.

• Remind students that they can take notes in English, as the focus of this exercise is on speaking, not writing.

Grammar Bits 语法点滴

Expressing how an action was done

To express how an action is performed, use "adverbs of manner"—get up <u>early</u>, run <u>fast</u>, sing <u>well</u>, etc.—with the particle *de* (得). Here is the basic pattern:

subject + verb + *de* **(得) + adverb**

Nǐ qǐ de hěn zǎo. 你起得很早。 *(You get up early.)*

Nǐ shuō de hěn hǎo. 你說得很好。／你说得很好。 *(You speak well.)*

• Nǐ shuō de bú gòu màn. 你說得不夠慢。／你说得不够慢。 *(You don't speak slowly enough.)* (夠 gòu = enough)

Note that this *de* (得) is NOT the same as the possessive particle *de* (的).

Grammar Bits

• Divide the class into three or four small groups. Tell groups to read this section for understanding and then come up with 3–4 sample sentences that use an "adverb of manner."

• Have students write the sentences on a poster; if possible hang the poster on the wall for future reference.

8.7 *Guess what the following phrases mean, and then match the corresponding Chinese and English phrases. Hint:* bǐ *(比) means "compared to."*

a. Māma zǎoshang qǐ de hěn zǎo: tā liù diǎn jiù qǐ le.

媽媽早上起得很早：她六點就起了。／
妈妈早上起得很早：她六点就起了。

b. Bàba měitiān qǐ de hěn wǎn: tā shí diǎn cái qǐ.

爸爸每天起得很晚：他十點才起。／
爸爸每天起得很晚：他十点才起。。

c. Mā bǐ wǒ qǐ de zǎo, Bà bǐ wǒ qǐ de wǎn.

媽比我起得早，爸比我起得晚。／
妈比我起得早，爸比我起得晚。

1. *Dad gets up very late every day—not until ten.*

2. *Mom gets up earlier (while) Dad gets up later than I do.*

3. *Mom gets up very early; she's already up at six.*

8.7 • If necessary, have students work in pairs to assist each other.

• Make sure students understand the key words *zǎo* and *wǎn*.

• Invite volunteers to share the answers with the class.

8.7 Key:

a. 3
b. 1
c. 2

8.8 • Before mingling, make sure students know the language they need in order to conduct such an "interview." If necessary, have them refer to the model dialogue in exercise 8.6.

• Also make sure students understand the format of the table and of the notes they will take. Students should still be familiar with the pinyin phrases in this table from exercise 8.7.

• If students would benefit from the exposure, invite a confident pair to demonstrate the dialogue.

• Mingle around the classroom and provide assistance as necessary.

8.8 Mingling: *Find out what time everyone in your class gets up. Write your classmates' names in the first column and then check the appropriate boxes in the chart below, based on their answers.*

姓名	bǐ wǒ qǐ de zǎo	bǐ wǒ qǐ de wǎn	gēn wǒ yíyàng shíjiān qǐ *(gets up the same time as I)*
	☐	☐	☐
	☐	☐	☐
	☐	☐	☐
	☐	☐	☐
	☐	☐	☐

Grammar Bits

• Before students read this *Grammar Bits*, ask them to review exercises 8.7 and 8.8 to determine which sentence patterns make comparisons. Invite volunteers to write these patterns on the board.

• Divide the class into three or four groups, and provide each group with the same task: Read the material for understanding and come up with three sample sentences that express similarities and differences. The sentences should meet the following criteria:

1. The first sentence must use an adjective to compare people or things. For example, *Nǐ bǐ wǒ hǎo* (You are better than I am), or *Zhèi ge bǐ nèi ge hǎo* (This one is better than that one).

2. The second sentence must use a verb to compare how people do things. For example, *Tā yújiā zuò de bǐ wǒ hǎo* (She does yoga better than I do).

3. The third sentence must express how *A* and *B* are the same, or how they do things similarly. For example, *Zhèi ge gēn nèi ge yíyàng hǎo* (This one is as good as that one), or *Nǐ yújiā zuò de gēn tā yíyàng hǎo* (You do yoga as well as she does).

• If possible, hang the poster on the wall for future reference.

Grammar Bits 语法点滴

Expressing similarities and differences

To talk about similarities and differences, use:

X gēn Y (bù) yíyàng

Gēn 跟 means "and, with, as" and *yíyàng* 一樣／一样 means "the same." Thus:

Wǒ gēn nǐ yíyàng. *(I am the same as you.)*

Zhōngwén gēn Yīngwén bù yíyàng. *(Chinese and English are different.)*

Wǒ gēn nǐ yíyàng shíjiān qǐ chuáng. *(I get up at the same time as you.)*

To compare one thing to another, use:

X bǐ Y + stative verb or other verbal expression

Wǒ bǐ nǐ hǎo. *(I'm better than you.)*

Jīntiān bǐ zuótiān lěng. *(Today is colder than yesterday.)*

Wǒ bǐ nǐ qǐ de zǎo. *(I get up earlier than you.)*

To negate a comparison, there are two alternatives, one with *bù* (preceding *bǐ*) and the other with *méiyǒu* (. . . *nàme*) (replacing *bǐ*). However, note that the meanings are significantly different.

Wǒ bù bǐ nǐ hǎo. *(I am not better than you.)*

Wǒ méiyǒu nǐ hǎo. *(I am not as good as you.)*

Wǒ bù bǐ nǐ zǎo qǐ chuáng. *(I don't get up earlier than you.)*

Wǒ méiyǒu nǐ nàme zǎo qǐ chuáng. *(I don't get up as early as you.)*

8.9 *Watch and listen to the video segment. The words beneath the ten illustrations below describe typical morning activities, some of which are mentioned in the segment, some not. Under the picture of each speaker at the bottom of the page, circle the letters that correspond to the activities he or she mentions.*

a. xǐ liǎn

b. shuāyá

c. shū tóufa

d. guā húzi

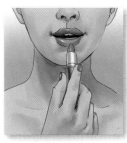

e. huàzhuāng

f. pǎobù

g. zuò zǎocāo

h. zuò yújiā

i. xǐzǎo

j. chī zǎofàn

1. a b c d e
   f g h i j

2. a b c d e
   f g h i j

8.9 • Before they watch the video, have students read the pinyin words aloud to their partners.

• As always, feel free to play the video multiple times, pause to give hints, and allow time for students to compare answers with one another.

• Invite volunteers to share their answers with the class.

8.9 Key:

1. f, i, j
2. i, j

8.10 *Check the activities you do every morning. Then match the corresponding items in the columns.*

a. ☐ xǐ liǎn 洗臉	1. 梳头发	A. *jog*
b. ☐ shuāyá 刷牙	2. 化妆	B. *do yoga*
c. ☐ shū tóufa 梳頭髮	3. 做早操	C. *eat breakfast*
d. ☐ guā húzi 刮鬍子	4. 刷牙	D. *do morning calisthenics*
e. ☐ huàzhuāng 化妝	5. 做瑜珈	E. *comb hair*
f. ☐ pǎobù 跑步	6. 吃早饭	F. *wash face*
g. ☐ zuò zǎocāo 做早操	7. 洗脸	G. *shave (a beard)*
h. ☐ zuò yújiā 做瑜珈	8. 洗澡	H. *brush teeth*
i. ☐ xǐzǎo 洗澡	9. 跑步	I. *bathe / take a shower*
j. ☐ chī zǎofàn 吃早飯	10. 刮胡子	J. *put on makeup*

8.11 *Match the corresponding Chinese and English phrases.*

a. měitiān pǎobù 每天跑步　　　　　　　　1. *bathes twice a day*

b. cónglái bù xǐzǎo 從來不洗澡／从来不洗澡　　2. *jogs every day*

c. yì tiān xǐ liǎng cì zǎo 一天洗兩次澡／一天洗两次澡　3. *never takes a bath/shower*

Based on the previous exercise, fill in each blank with an appropriate English equivalent.

d. měitiān 每天 = _____

e. yì tiān liǎng cì 一天兩次／一天两次 = _____

f. cónglái bù 從來不／从来不 = _____

Grammar Bits 语法点滴

Counting nouns—and now, counting verbs!

You have learned that nouns are counted in Chinese with measure words: *sān běn shū* (three books); *sān ge rén* (three people); *sān wèi lǎoshī* (three teachers). The word order is: number + measure word + noun. Verbal actions can be "counted" as well. In this unit, you will practice this using *cì* (times). For example:

Wǒ yì zhōu zuò yí cì yújiā. *(I do yoga once a week.)*

Wǒ yì tiān xǐ liǎng cì zǎo. *(I shower twice a day.)*

In these examples, the verbal form is verb + object, as in *xǐzǎo* and *zuò yújiā*. In this construction, *zǎo* (bath) and *yújiā* (yoga) are the objects of the verbs *xǐ* (wash) and *zuò* (do), respectively. With VO (verb-object) combinations, the pattern to express number of occurrences is:

verb + number + measure word (*cì* 次) + noun

xǐ + sān + cì + zǎo　　　*take three showers*

8.12 *Check the appropriate boxes or fill in the blanks to indicate how often you do each of the following activities. Remember:* yì zhōu 一週／一周 = *"one week."*

	從來不／从来不	一週／一周 __X__ 次	每天
梳頭髮／梳头发	☐	____ 次	☐
化妝／化妆	☐	____ 次	☐
做早操	☐	____ 次	☐
刷牙	☐	____ 次	☐
做瑜珈	☐	____ 次	☐
吃早飯／吃早饭	☐	____ 次	☐
洗臉／洗脸	☐	____ 次	☐
洗澡	☐	____ 次	☐
跑步	☐	____ 次	☐
刮鬍子／刮胡子	☐	____ 次	☐

8.12 • If necessary, have students work in pairs to assist each other.
• Remind students to use exercises 8.10 and 8.11 for vocabulary help.
• Students' answers will vary based on their real-life situations.

8.13 *Pair work: Choose the best response to answer your partner, based on what you checked in the previous exercise.*

Q: Nǐ duō cháng shíjiān shū yí cì tóufa? *(How often do you comb your hair?)*

A:　a. Wǒ měitiān shū tóufa.

　　b. Wǒ yì zhōu shū (sān) cì tóufa.

　　c. Wǒ cónglái bù shū tóufa.

Now find out how often your partner does the activities listed in the previous exercise, using this Q & A as a model. Record your partner's answers, using a different color pen or pencil to distinguish them from your own answers.

8.13 • Make sure students know how to "split" verbs to make sentences such as: *Wǒ yì zhōu pǎo jǐ cì bù.* You may need to explain how this happens explicitly in English. Have the class "split" the verbs listed in exercise 8.12 to make sure they all can do it.
• During this activity, mingle among your students to observe their performance and provide assistance.

8.14 *Fill in each blank with an appropriate English translation. Then check the sentence that best corresponds to your own habits.*

a. ☐ 我早上洗澡。　　_____

b. ☐ 我晚上洗澡。　　_____

c. ☐ 我早上洗一次，晚上洗一次。　_____

d. ☐ 我不是每天洗澡。　_____

8.14 Key:
a. I take a shower in the morning.
b. I take a shower in the evening.
c. I take a shower in the morning, and again in the evening.
d. I don't take a shower every day.

8.15 *Mingling:* Go around the room and ask your classmates the following questions:

Nǐ yì tiān xǐ jǐ cì zǎo? 你一天洗幾次澡？／你一天洗几次澡？
Nǐ shénme shíhou xǐzǎo? 你甚麼時候洗澡？／你什么时候洗澡？

While you're at it, find out one other detail about their daily routines. Note their answers on your copy of the class roster.

Encounter 2 | Discussing daytime activities

8.16 • Possible answers: *go to school, attend English class, go to work,* etc. The point of this exercise is to get students to think about the things we often do on weekdays and how we talk about them.

• Brainstorm activities as a class, and invite students to offer answers "popcorn style."

• Invite volunteer scribes to write these suggestions on a poster. Make sure to revisit this poster after exercise 8.18 to see if students have learned enough Chinese to say everything on the poster.

8.17 • This activity may be difficult for some students. Tell students to use the sound of these words, not their meanings, to determine the correct answers. Have the class read the pinyin words aloud.

• Make sure that students also understand the characters used as column headings in this exercise before they watch the video.

8.17 Key:
爸爸: a, e
女兒／女儿: b, d
兩個都／两个都: c, f

8.18 • In this exercise, students are asked to connect sound to meaning. Play the video again. This time, tell students to focus on the meaning of these words by paying attention to the speakers' body language and the context in which they interact.

• Encourage students to use familiar characters as clues.

• Revisit the poster students began in exercise 8.16 and see if they need to know any additional Chinese words to complete the vocabulary list. Act as a "live dictionary" to teach these words.

8.18 Key:
a. 5. D
b. 6. B
c. 4. F
d. 3. A
e. 1. C
f. 2. E

8.16 *Getting ready:* What do you generally do during the day on a weekday? Write your answer below in English.

_____

_____

8.17 *Watch and listen to the video segment. Check which of the speakers is doing, or intends to do, each of the activities listed below: the father, the daughter, or both.*

	爸爸	女兒／女儿	兩個都／两个都
a. shàngbān	☐	☐	☐
b. shàngxué	☐	☐	☐
c. chī zhōngfàn (wǔfàn)	☐	☐	☐
d. fàngxué	☐	☐	☐
e. xiàbān	☐	☐	☐
f. huíjiā	☐	☐	☐

Note: The final two entries in the table are not in the segment, but you should be able to guess what they mean.

8.18 *Match the corresponding items below.*

a. *go to work*   1. xiàbān 下班   A. 放学
b. *go to school*   2. huíjiā 回家   B. 上学
c. *eat lunch*   3. fàngxué 放學   C. 下班
d. *get out of school* 4. chī zhōngfàn (wǔfàn) 吃中飯（午飯） D. 上班
e. *get out of work*   5. shàngbān 上班   E. 回家
f. *return home*   6. shàngxué 上學   F. 吃中饭（午饭）

8.19 *Using the vocabulary in exercise 8.18 and following the pattern below, write five sentences about your schedule or about that of someone in your family.*

Example: **subject + time expression + verb phrase**

Wǒ Xīngqīyī hé Xīngqīsān qī diǎn bàn shàngxué.

subject	+ time expression	+ verb phrase

1. _____

2. _____

3. _____

4. _____

5. _____

8.19 This exercise is designed for students to notice correct Chinese word order. It is a good idea to bring students' attention to it after they have completed writing their own sentences. Ask the class: "What do you notice about the word order in the sentences you just wrote? Do English sentences share the same word order?"

8.20 *Pair work: Find out five facts about your partner's daily schedule or about that of someone in his or her family, and write them down below.*

Nǐ měitiān jǐ diǎn zhōng chī zhōngfàn?

8.20 • Direct students' attention to the sample question in the speech balloon.

• Have the class brainstorm other questions they can ask to conduct this interview. Invite students to offer their suggestions "popcorn style." You can assess how ready your students are by the answers they offer.

• Remind students to take notes in English, as this exercise emphasizes speaking and listening, not writing.

1. _____

2. _____

3. _____

4. _____

5. _____

Encounter 3 | Discussing evening activities

8.21 • Possible answers: *relax, watch TV, walk my dog,* etc. The point of this exercise is to get students thinking about the activities people do after school, after work, and in the evenings.

• Add all reasonable student suggestions to a class poster, and make sure to revisit this poster after exercise 8.23.

8.22 Key:

1. b
2. c, h
3. c, d
4. e, g

8.21 *Getting ready:* What do you generally do in the evening?

_____

_____

8.22 *Watch and listen to the video segment. Then check the appropriate activities, according to what each person says he or she does.*

	1.	2.	3.	4.
a. kànbào *read the paper*	☐	☐	☐	☐
b. zuò wǎnfàn (nòng wǎnfàn) *make dinner*	☐	☐	☐	☐
c. chī wǎnfàn *eat dinner*	☐	☐	☐	☐
d. zuò gōngkè (xiě zuòyè) *do homework*	☐	☐	☐	☐
e. kànshū *read*	☐	☐	☐	☐
f. tīng yīnyuè *listen to music*	☐	☐	☐	☐
g. kàn diànshì *watch TV*	☐	☐	☐	☐
h. shàngwǎng (chá e-mail) *go online (check e-mail)*	☐	☐	☐	☐
i. wán diànzǐ yóuxì *play video games*	☐	☐	☐	☐

8.23 *Match the corresponding items below.*

a. kànbào 看報   1. 上网

b. zuò wǎnfàn 做晚飯   2. 看电视

c. chī wǎnfàn 吃晚飯   3. 看书

d. zuò gōngkè 做功課   4. 做晚饭

e. kànshū 看書   5. 听音乐

f. tīng yīnyuè 聽音樂   6. 做功课

g. kàn diànshì 看電視   7. 看报

h. shàngwǎng 上網   8. 玩电子游戏

i. wán diànzǐ yóuxì 玩電子遊戲   9. 吃晚饭

8.23 After students finish this exercise, revisit the poster they began in exercise 8.21 and see if they need to know any additional Chinese words to complete the vocabulary list. Act as a "live dictionary" to teach these words.

8.23 Key:
a. 7
b. 4
c. 9
d. 6
e. 3
f. 5
g. 2
h. 1
i. 8

FYI 供你参考

Many terms for meals

There are a number of alternative terms for the meals of the day. For each of the following terms, the parenthetical English translations are literal. Breakfast is *zǎofàn* 早飯／早饭 ("early rice"), *zǎodiǎn* 早點／早点 ("early tidbits"), or *zǎocān* 早餐 ("early meal"). Lunch is *wǔfàn* 午飯／午饭 ("noon rice"), *zhōngfàn* 中飯／中饭 ("middle rice") or *wǔcān* 午餐 ("noon meal"). Dinner is *wǎnfàn* 晚飯／晚饭 ("late rice") or *wǎncān* 晚餐 ("late meal"). There are no "tidbits" for lunch or dinner. *Fàn* and *diǎn* are more conversational; *cān* is used more in writing. Interestingly, *zhōngcān* 中餐 means "Chinese food" rather than "lunch."

Many terms for meals

Divide the class into four groups. Before students read this FYI, give each group a different task:

1. Read the FYI and identify two ways to say "breakfast" in Chinese. Then teach the class.

2. Read the FYI and identify two ways to say "lunch" in Chinese. Then teach the class. Can lunch be called *zhōngcān*?

3. Read the FYI and identify two ways to say "dinner" in Chinese. Then teach the class.

4. Read the FYI and identify the difference between *fàn* and *cān*. Then teach the class.

Note: Although the character 餐 has not formally been simplified—there is no simplified form listed in standard dictionaries, for example—in daily usage many people (including restaurant owners) write the much more expedient 歺.

8.24 *What do you do during the evening on weekdays? Using pinyin, fill in the blanks below with activities from the previous list or any other activities you know how to say in Chinese.*

a. Wǒ měitiān wǎnshang huíjiā yǐhòu děi _____.

我每天晚上回家以後得……／我每天晚上回家以后得……

Every evening after I get home, I have to . . .

b. Wǒ měitiān wǎnshang huíjiā yǐhòu xǐhuan _____.

我每天晚上回家以後喜歡……／我每天晚上回家以后喜欢……

Every evening after I get home, I like to . . .

c. Wǒ měitiān wǎnshang huíjiā yǐhòu huì _____.

我每天晚上回家以後會……／我每天晚上回家以后会……

Every evening after I get home, I will . . .

8.24 Key:
Answers will vary based on students' real-life situations.

8.25 • Tell students to take notes in pinyin.

• If students have questions about the meaning of *dōu . . . xiē*, tell them to review the Grammar Bits below.

8.25 Pair work: *Find out what your partner does during the evening on weekdays. Ask:*

Q: Nǐ wǎnshang dōu zuò xiē shénme?

你晚上都做些甚麼？／你晚上都做些什么？

What (all) do you do in the evening?

A: (write your partner's name in the blank on the left)

_____ děi _____, _____, _____;

xǐhuan _____, _____, _____;

huì _____, _____, _____.

Grammar Bits 语法点滴

Yes, you can signal the plural in Chinese!

You've learned that to make the plural form in Chinese, you don't change the noun (for example, "book" to "books"). Instead, you just indicate the plural with a number. "Three books" in Chinese is "three (measure word) book"—*sān běn shū*. The plural, however, can be signaled with the measure word *xiē* (several), as well. The question *Nǐ wǎnshang dōu zuò xiē shénme?* expects plurality in the answer. The plural signal *xiē* is supported in this question by *dōu* (all), which also indicates that the person asking the question expects several things in a listed answer.

Encounter 4 Discussing weekend activities

8.26 • Possible answers: *play with friends, spend time with family, play sports*, etc.

• Brainstorm answers as a class, and invite volunteer scribes to write the suggestions on a poster.

• Revisit this poster after exercise 8.28 to see if students have learned enough Chinese to say everything on this list.

8.26 Getting ready: *What do you generally do during weekends and holidays?*

_____

_____

_____

_____

8.27 *Watch and listen to the video segment. Then check the appropriate activities, according to what each person says he or she does.*

	1.	2.	3.	4.	5.
a. shuì lǎnjiào *sleep in*	☐	☐	☐	☐	☐
b. kàn diànyǐng *go to the movies*	☐	☐	☐	☐	☐
c. guàng shāngchǎng *go to the mall*	☐	☐	☐	☐	☐
d. qù sànsanbù *go for a walk*	☐	☐	☐	☐	☐
e. gēn péngyou yìqǐ chūqu wánr *go out with friends*	☐	☐	☐	☐	☐
f. dāizai jiāli *stay at home*	☐	☐	☐	☐	☐
g. zuò jiāwù *do housework*	☐	☐	☐	☐	☐
h. gēcǎo *mow the lawn (literally, "cut grass")*	☐	☐	☐	☐	☐
i. dǎgōng *do (part-time) work*	☐	☐	☐	☐	☐
j. zuò gōngkè *do homework*	☐	☐	☐	☐	☐

8.27 Key:

1. e
2. a
3. b, c, d, e
4. f, g, h
5. i, j

Note: The answer to #1 is tricky. The speakers in the video episode mention *dǎqiú* (play ball), *hējiǔ* (drink), *chàng kǎlā OK* (sing karaoke). They do not actually say *gēn péngyou yìqǐ chūqu wánr* (go out with friends), but this is implied.

8.28 After students finish this exercise, revisit the poster they began in exercise 8.26 and see if they need to know any additional Chinese words to complete the vocabulary list. Act as a "live dictionary" to teach these words.

8.28 Key:

a. 6
b. 8
c. 9
d. 2
e. 4
f. 1
g. 3
h. 10
i. 5
j. 7

8.28 *Match the corresponding items in the columns below.*

a. shuì lǎnjiào 睡懶覺

b. kàn diànyǐng 看電影

c. guàng shāngchǎng 逛商場

d. qù sànsanbù 去散散步

e. gēn péngyou yìqǐ chūqu wánr 跟朋友一起出去玩兒

f. dāizai jiāli 呆在家裡

g. zuò jiāwù 做家務

h. gēcǎo 割草

i. dǎgōng 打工

j. zuò gōngkè 做功課

1. 呆在家里

2. 去散散步

3. 做家务

4. 跟朋友一起出去玩儿

5. 打工

6. 睡懒觉

7. 做功课

8. 看电影

9. 逛商场

10. 割草

8.29 *What do you do on weekends and holidays? Fill in the blanks below with choices from the list above, using pinyin.*

a. Wǒ zhōumò xǐhuan _____.

　我週末喜歡……／我周末喜欢……

　(On) weekends I like to . . .

b. Wǒ zhōumò yě děi _____.

　我週末也得……／我周末也得……

　(On) weekends I also have to . . .

8.30 *Pair work: Find out your partner's answers to the questions above. Ask:*

Q: Nǐ zhōumò dōu zuò xiē shénme?

　你週末都做些甚麼？／你周末都做些什么？

　What (all) do you do on weekends?

A: (write your partner's name in the blank on the left)

　_____ xǐhuan _____, yě xǐhuan _____ ;

　děi _____, yě děi _____.

Encounter 5 Expressing actions that occur before, during, or after other actions

8.31 Getting ready: *What do you do before dinner, during dinner (besides eating), and after dinner?*

8.31 • Possible answers: *set the table, talk with my family, go for a walk*, etc.
• Brainstorm answers as a class, and have students offer their suggestions "popcorn style."

_____

_____

8.32 *Watch and listen to the video segment. Then, using pinyin, write what the speaker says she likes to do during the time specified.*

8.32 Key:
before dinner: *pǎobù*
during dinner: *kàn diànshì*
after dinner: *shàngwǎng*

a. before dinner   b. during dinner   c. after dinner

_____   _____   _____

8.33 *Match the corresponding items.*

8.33 Key:
a. 2. A
b. 3. C
c. 1. B

a. chī wǎnfàn yǐqián   1. 吃晚飯以後   A. 吃晚饭以前

b. chī wǎnfàn de shíhou   2. 吃晚飯以前   B. 吃晚饭以后

c. chī wǎnfàn yǐhòu   3. 吃晚飯的時候   C. 吃晚饭的时候

8.34 *In pinyin, write one thing you like to do before, during, and after dinner.*

8.34-8.35
• Remind students to use words they've learned in previous exercises.
• If students want to use vocabulary they don't already know, remind them to use the pattern *Qǐngwèn ... zěnme shuō?* Write new words on the board in pinyin and English.

a. Chī wǎnfàn yǐqián, wǒ xǐhuan _____.

b. Chī wǎnfàn de shíhou, wǒ xǐhuan _____.

c. Chī wǎnfàn yǐhòu, wǒ xǐhuan _____.

8.35 *Now complete each of the following sentences to state one thing you do before doing homework, while you do it, and after you do it.*

8.34-8.35 Key:
Answers will vary based on students' real-life situations.

a. Wǒ zuò gōngkè yǐqián _____.

b. Wǒ zuò gōngkè de shíhou_____.

c. Wǒ zuò gōngkè yǐhòu_____.

8.36 • Tell students that, for this
activity, they are to share something
they think is remarkable, interesting,
or unique that they do every day.

• Have partners proofread each
other's sentences.

8.36 Key:

Answers will vary based on
students' real-life situations.

8.36 *Is there something notable about your daily activities? See the following examples.*

> Wǒ chīfàn yǐhòu děi shuāyá.
> Wǒ qǐ chuáng yǐhòu zuò yújiā.
> Wǒ bù xǐhuan zuò gōngkè de shíhou kàn diànshì.
> Wǒ xǐhuan chīfàn de shíhou kànshū.

Write three sentences about something that is notable about your daily activities. Use the terms yǐqián, yǐhòu, *and* de shíhou, *if appropriate.*

_____

_____

_____

8.37 • Pair students with different
partners from exercise 8.36.

• Tell students to take notes in
English.

8.37 *Pair work: Share your sentences with your partner. Take notes about what your partner tells you.*

_____

_____

_____

8.38 • Review the language
items students will need in order to
conduct this interview. For example:
*Nǐ jǐ diǎn qǐchuáng? Nǐ shuìjiào
yǐqián xǐzǎo ma?*

• Use this exercise as a capstone
speaking activity to evaluate
students' speaking and listening
performance for this unit.

When are teeth best brushed?

• Check comprehension by
stimulating a mini-discussion in
English. Ask the class, "Is breakfast
in bed a good idea in China? Why or
why not?"

8.38 *Mingling: Interview someone in the class. Find out six to ten facts about his or her daily routine. Take notes on your copy of the class roster.*

FYI 供你参考

When are teeth best brushed?

While "breakfast in bed" is a luxury many in the West would welcome, the idea is not appealing to most Chinese. Why? In China, people tend to brush their teeth shortly after getting out of bed, to rid their mouths of the staleness built up overnight. Surely, they feel, the "debris" from the night's sleep should be eliminated before ingesting food. Many Americans, on the other hand, prefer to brush their teeth after breakfast, not before, to follow the habit of brushing after every meal. Small habits such as these tend to be deeply ingrained and hard to change over the course of a lifetime, and people can become quite vehement in defending their choice of habit.

♫ Unit Rap

*Go to the **Encounters** website at www.EncountersChinese.com and listen to the song to review key expressions from Unit 8. Listen again and sing along!*

Encounter 6 Reading and writing

▶ Reading familiar sentences in Chinese characters

8.39 Pair work: *Read the following dialogues (written in traditional characters) aloud with a partner, using the English as a guide.*

8.39 • Avoid reading the dialogue aloud for your students or having them repeat after you. Tell them to use the English and familiar characters as bridges to determine the meaning and pronunciation of unknown characters.

• Keep in mind that reading fluency is not the goal of this activity. Tell students not to get discouraged if they have trouble reading quickly and accurately.

• Have students complete this exercise multiple times before they move on to 8.40 and 8.41.

1 甲：你每天幾點起床？   *(What time do you get up every day?)*

乙：我每天六點就起床了。你呢？   *(I'm up as early as six every day. And you?)*

甲：我七點半才起。你比我起得早。   *(I don't get up until seven thirty. You get up earlier than I do.)*

2 甲：我們明天早上一起去吃早飯，好嗎？   *(Let's go have breakfast together tomorrow morning, OK?)*

乙：好啊。幾點？   *(OK. What time?)*

甲：你幾點起床？   *(What time do you get up?)*

乙：跟你一樣時間。七點，七點半。   *(The same time as you. Seven, seven thirty.)*

甲：那我們八點見，怎麼樣？   *(Then let's meet up at eight, how about it?)*

乙：行。老地方？   *(Fine. The usual place?)*

甲：好。明天八點見。   *(OK. See you at eight tomorrow.)*

乙：好，不見不散！   *(Fine. Let's wait for each other.)*

3 甲：小明！去洗臉刷牙！要吃早飯了！   *(Xiao Ming! Go wash your face and brush your teeth! We're about to have breakfast!)*

乙：知道，知道。   *(I know, I know.)*

甲：別忘了梳頭髮！   *(Don't forget to brush your hair!)*

乙：知道了，知道了。   *(I know, I know.)*

甲：小明！你在做甚麼？   *(Xiao Ming! What are you doing?)*

乙：來了！來了！   *(I'm coming! I'm coming!)*

甲：快點啊！吃飯了！   *(Hurry up! We're eating!)*

乙：知道了。   *(I know, I know.)*

4 甲：你跑步嗎？   *(Do you jog?)*

乙：不，我做瑜珈。   *(No, I do yoga.)*

甲：天天都做嗎？   *(Do you do it every day?)*

乙：不，一週三次。你呢？   *(No, three times a week. And you?)*

甲：我每天都跑步。   *(I jog every day.)*

5 甲：我們家人都是晚上洗澡。你們家人呢？ *(My whole family bathes at night. What about yours?)*

乙：我爸爸媽媽也是晚上洗，可是我喜歡早上洗。我哥哥呢，早上晚上都洗！ *(My father and mother also bathe at night, but I like to shower in the morning. As for my brother, he takes a shower both morning and night!)*

甲：哇，一天洗兩次澡啊！ *(Wow, two baths a day!)*

乙：對。 *(Right.)*

6 甲：你們家誰做晚飯？ *(Who cooks in your family?)*

乙：我爸爸或者我媽媽。看 (kàn) 誰先回家。你們家呢？ *(My father or my mother, depending on [kàn] who comes home first. How about in your family?)*

甲：我，我姐姐或者我弟弟。看誰在家。 *(Me, my sister, or my brother, depending on who is at home.)*

7 甲：你早上幾點出門？ *(What time do you leave the house in the morning?)*

乙：七點五十分。我跟我妹妹一起走。我上大學去，妹妹上小學去。 *(Seven fifty. I go with my younger sister. I go to college, and my younger sister goes to grade school.)*

甲：我六點半就出門了。我跟我媽媽走。媽上班，我上學。 *(I'm already out by six thirty. I leave with my mom. Mom goes to work, and I go to school.)*

8 甲：爸爸，您明天幾點下班？ *(Dad, what time do you get off work tomorrow?)*

乙：五點半。你為甚麼問這個？ *(Five thirty. Why do you ask?)*

甲：爸，您回來吃晚飯嗎？ *(Are you coming back for dinner, Dad?)*

乙：對，回家吃飯。為甚麼問？ *(Yes, I'm coming home for dinner. Why do you ask?)*

甲：我只是問問。 *(I'm just asking.)*

乙：你幾點放學？ *(What time do you get out of school?)*

甲：四點半。 *(Four thirty.)*

乙：想不想出去吃飯？ *(Want to go out for dinner?)*

甲：想！ *(I do!)*

9 甲：你們大家都在做甚麼？ *(What are you all doing?)*

乙：媽媽在上網，爸爸在看電視，妹妹在做功課。 *(Mom's online, Dad's watching TV, and my younger sister's doing homework.)*

甲：你在做甚麼？ *(What are you doing?)*

乙：沒做甚麼。我在聽音樂。為甚麼問呢？ *(Not much. Listening to music. Why do you ask?)*

甲：要不要過來玩電子遊戲？ *(Want to come over and play video games?)*

乙：不了。我還要做功課呢。你過來我們一起做吧。 *(Better not. I still have to do homework. You come over and we'll do it together.)*

甲：好吧。做好功課就玩電子遊戲，行不行？ *(OK. After we're done we can play video games, all right?)*

乙：行！做好功課以後還有時間嗎？你幾點睡覺？ *(Fine. Will we still have time after finishing our homework? What time do you go to sleep?)*

甲：我很晚睡覺。 *(I go to bed really late.)*

乙：我是早睡早起。玩一會兒吧！ *(I go to sleep early and get up early. Let's have some fun for a while, then!)*

⑩ 甲：週末到了！可以睡懶覺了！ *(The weekend's here! We can sleep in!)*

乙：別睡覺了。出去走走吧。 *(Don't sleep. Let's go out!)*

甲：去哪兒？ *(Go where?)*

乙：逛逛商場，看看電影…… *(We could cruise the mall, see a movie . . .)*

甲：做做家務…… *(Do some housework . . .)*

乙：別做家務了！你老想呆在家裡！ *(No more housework! You always want to stay home!)*

甲：家裡有甚麼不好？ *(What's wrong with being at home?)*

乙：老呆在家裡沒意思！ *(Always staying home is boring.)*

甲：好吧好吧。出去吧。 *(OK, OK. Let's go out.)*

乙：我們可以早一點回家，好不好？ *(We can come back early, OK?)*

甲：好好好。 *(Fine, fine, fine.)*

8.40 Pair work: *Read the dialogues aloud with a partner, this time without any English.*

❶ 甲：你每天幾點起床？

乙：我每天六點就起床了。你呢？

甲：我七點半才起。你比我起得早。

❷ 甲：我們明天早上一起去吃早飯，好嗎？

乙：好啊。幾點？

甲：你幾點起床？

乙：跟你一樣時間。七點，七點半。

甲：那我們八點見，怎麼樣？

乙：行。老地方？

甲：好。明天八點見。

乙：好，不見不散！

8.40–8.41 🎧

• Have students read these dialogues multiple times, focusing on reading fluency.

• Encourage students *not* to refer to exercise 8.39 for help. Instead, ask them to rely on the dialogue context and their partners to help them read new characters.

• After students practice reading the dialogues a few times, play the audio and have them check their pronunciation.

3 甲：小明！去洗臉刷牙！要吃早飯了！

乙：知道，知道。

甲：別忘了梳頭髮！

乙：知道了，知道了。

甲：小明！你在做甚麼？

乙：來了！來了！

甲：快點啊！吃飯了！

乙：知道了。

4 甲：你跑步嗎？

乙：不，我做瑜珈。

甲：天天都做嗎？

乙：不，一週三次。你呢？

甲：我每天都跑步。

5 甲：我們家人都是晚上洗澡。你們家人呢？

乙：我爸爸媽媽也是晚上洗，可是我喜歡早上洗。我哥哥
　　呢，早上晚上都洗!

甲：哇，一天洗兩次澡啊！

乙：對。

6 甲：你們家誰做晚飯？

乙：我爸爸或者我媽媽。看 (kàn) 誰先回家。你們家呢？

甲：我，我姐姐或者我弟弟。看誰在家。

7 甲：你早上幾點出門？

乙：七點五十分。我跟我妹妹一起走。我上大學去，妹妹上
　　小學去。

甲：我六點半就出門了。我跟我媽媽走。媽上班，我上學。

8 甲：爸爸，您明天幾點下班？

乙：五點半。你為甚麼問這個？

甲：爸，您回來吃晚飯嗎？

乙：對，回家吃飯。為甚麼問？

甲：我只是問問。

乙：你幾點放學？

甲：四點半。

乙：想不想出去吃飯？

甲：想！

9 甲：你們大家都在做甚麼？

乙：媽媽在上網，爸爸在看電視，妹妹在做功課。

甲：你在做甚麼？

乙：沒做甚麼。我在聽音樂。為甚麼問呢？

甲：要不要過來玩電子遊戲？

乙：不了。我還要做功課呢。你過來我們一起做吧。

甲：好吧。做好功課就玩電子遊戲，行不行？

乙：行！做好功課以後還有時間嗎？你幾點睡覺？

甲：我很晚睡覺。

乙：我是早睡早起。玩一會兒吧！

10 甲：週末到了！可以睡懶覺了！

乙：別睡覺了。出去走走吧。

甲：去哪兒？

乙：逛逛商場，看看電影……

甲：做做家務……

乙：別做家務了！你老想呆在家裡！

甲：家裡有甚麼不好？

乙：老呆在家裡沒意思！

甲：好吧好吧。出去吧。

乙：我們可以早一點回來，好不好？

甲：好好好。

8.41 Pair work: *Now try it once again, this time in simplified characters.*

1 甲：你每天几点起床？

乙：我每天六点就起床了。你呢？

甲：我七点半才起。你比我起得早。

2 甲：我们明天早上一起去吃早饭，好吗？

乙：好啊。几点？

甲：你几点起床？

乙：跟你一样时间。七点，七点半。

甲：那我们八点见，怎么样？

乙：行。老地方？

甲：好。明天八点见。

乙：好，不见不散！

3 甲：小明！去洗脸刷牙！要吃早饭了！
乙：知道，知道。
甲：别忘了梳头发！
乙：知道了，知道了。
甲：小明！你在做什么？
乙：来了！来了！
甲：快点啊！吃饭了！
乙：知道了。

4 甲：你跑步吗？
乙：不，我做瑜珈。
甲：天天都做吗？
乙：不，一周三次。你呢？
甲：我每天都跑步。

5 甲：我们家人都是晚上洗澡。你们家人呢？
乙：我爸爸妈妈也是晚上洗，可是我喜欢早上洗。我哥哥呢，早上晚上都洗！
甲：哇，一天洗两次澡啊！
乙：对。

6 甲：你们家谁做晚饭？
乙：我爸爸或者我妈妈。看 (kàn) 谁先回家。你们家呢？
甲：我，我姐姐或者我弟弟。看谁在家。

7 甲：你早上几点出门？
乙：七点五十分。我跟我妹妹一起走。我上大学去，妹妹上小学去。
甲：我六点半就出门了。我跟我妈妈走。妈上班，我上学。

8 甲：爸爸，您明天几点下班？
乙：五点半。你为什么问这个？
甲：爸，您回来吃晚饭吗？
乙：对，回家吃饭。为什么问？
甲：我只是问问。
乙：你几点放学？
甲：四点半。
乙：想不想出去吃饭？
甲：想！

9 甲：你们大家都在做什么？

乙：妈妈在上网，爸爸在看电视，妹妹在做功课。

甲：你在做什么？

乙：没做什么。我在听音乐。为什么问呢？

甲：要不要过来玩电子游戏？

乙：不了。我还要做功课呢。你过来我们一起做吧。

甲：好吧。做好功课就玩电子游戏，行不行？

乙：行！做好功课以后还有时间吗？你几点睡觉？

甲：我很晚睡觉。

乙：我是早睡早起。玩一会儿吧！

10 甲：周末到了！可以睡懒觉了！

乙：别睡觉了。出去走走吧。

甲：去哪儿？

乙：逛逛商场，看看电影……

甲：做做家务……

乙：别做家务了！你老想呆在家里！

甲：家里有什么不好？

乙：老呆在家里没意思！

甲：好吧好吧。出去吧。

乙：我们可以早一点回来，好不好？

甲：好好好。

8.42 *Match the corresponding simplified characters, traditional characters, and English.*

a. 洗脸	1. 上大學	A. *wash (one's) face*	
b. 梳头发	2. 回家吃飯	B. *go out to eat*	
c. 你在做什么	3. 在網上	C. *what are you doing*	
d. 一周三次	4. 梳頭髮	D. *cook*	
e. 做饭	5. 一週三次	E. *be online*	
f. 出门	6. 做飯	F. *return home and eat*	
g. 上大学	7. 你在做甚麼	G. *go to college*	
h. 放学	8. 出門	H. *comb (one's) hair*	
i. 回家吃饭	9. 出去吃飯	I. *three times a week*	
j. 出去吃饭	10. 洗臉	J. *leave the house*	
k. 在网上	11. 放學	K. *get out of school (for the day)*	

8.43 *Match the corresponding simplified characters, traditional characters, and English.*

a. 看电视	1. 週末到了	A. *play video games*
b. 做功课	2. 聽音樂	B. *go to sleep; sleep*
c. 听音乐	3. 睡懶覺	C. *watch a movie*
d. 过来	4. 逛商場	D. *the weekend is here*
e. 玩电子游戏	5. 看電視	E. *do homework*
f. 有时间	6. 做家務	F. *do housework*
g. 睡觉	7. 看電影	G. *sleep in*
h. 周末到了	8. 有時間	H. *listen to music*
i. 睡懒觉	9. 做功課	I. *stroll the shopping center*
j. 逛商场	10. 玩電子遊戲	J. *watch TV*
k. 看电影	11. 睡覺	K. *come over*
l. 做家务	12. 過來	L. *have the time*

▶ Reading real-life texts

8.44 *Look at the photo.* 吧 ba *is normally used as a particle indicating a suggestion, with a neutral tone. Here it means "bar" and is pronounced* bā. *In the United States, similar establishments tend to use the word "café." Of the three activities below, check the two that you can do in this establishment.*

a. ☐ 上網／上网

☐ 跑步

☐ 吃東西／吃东西

b. How many hours (小時／小时) is this establishment open for business (*yíngyè* 營業／营业)? Answer: _____

8.45 *Look at the photo.* 便利 *biànlì means "convenient," and a* 店 *diàn is a shop or store.*

a. What kind of establishment is this?

_____

b. The last two items on the sign advertise that you can buy cell phone numbers and a rechargeable phone card here: 充 *chōng* "recharge" + 值 *zhí* "value" + 卡 *kǎ* "card." What do the first two items advertise? _____ and

_____

8.46 *Look at the photo. If you go out strolling in Beijing, you might see this sign.*

a. 愛／爱 *ài* means "love." What is the name of this store? _____

b. Look at the logo. How do you think "5i5j" is related to the name of the store?

8.47 *Look at the photo. This is a sign over a sink outside a cafeteria.* 温馨提示 *wēnxīn tíshì means "a friendly reminder." Fill in the blanks below with pinyin and English separately.*

Wèi le _____ _____ jiànkāng

_____ _____ _____ _____ _____ shǒu.

For the sake of your health,

please _____ hands before _____.

8.46 a. I Love My Home/Family (Students may be interested to know that this store "stole" its name from the title of a very popular sitcom in China.)
b. 5i5j = 我爱我家, wǒ ài wǒ jiā. You can introduce a bit of contemporary Chinese culture via this exercise. When sending text messages, Chinese people use numbers and letters to represent characters—to save time typing. For example, 918＝加油吧 (jiāyóu ba, "Pour it on! Keep up the good work"), 246 = 饿死了 (è sǐ le, "I'm starving"), 530 = 我想你 (wǒ xiǎng nǐ, "I miss you"). One can easily find the latest "slang" by doing a quick search on the Internet.

8.47 Students might not be able to recognize 先 (xiān) because they have never seen it before. If so, just give them the answer directly.

8.47 Key:
Wèi le nín de jiànkāng
fàn qián qǐng xiān xǐ shǒu.
For the sake of your health, please wash hands before eating.

▶ Learning to write characters

8.48 *For stroke order and other useful information about each of the following characters from this unit, go to the Character Writing Workbook. Choose either traditional or simplified characters and practice writing them until you can reproduce them on demand.*

每，洗，手，看，電／电，視／视，網／网，玩，睡，覺／觉，週／周，末，門／门，班，影，以，前，後／后

▶ Writing a note

8.49 *Write a note to a friend, briefly describing a typical day during the week and on the weekend, and suggesting some opportunities when you could get together.*

Cultural Bits 文化点滴

Daily routines

View the video segment "Daily routines" and then discuss the following questions with your classmates.

- What are some differences between the daily routines described here and yours? Name some things the speakers do that you never do.

- What are some things that the speakers do after work or school that you also do?

8.49 • If students would benefit, allow them to write their paragraphs in pinyin before "translating" them into characters. However, if they are ready, do encourage them to skip this intermediate step and write their paragraphs in characters directly.
• Remind students to use the vocabulary list on pages 212–213 for help.
• When they finish writing, partners should proofread each other's drafts before handing them in.

Recap

▶ Grammar

Commenting on how an action is performed

Use *de* after the verb and follow the verb with a comment.

Tā shuō de hěn hǎo/kuài/màn/búcuò/bù hǎo. (*He speaks well/fast/slowly/quite well/badly.*)

Expressing similarities and differences

Use *gēn* (with) and *yíyàng* (same) to talk about similarities and differences.

When A and B are the same:

Wǒ gēn nǐ yíyàng, dōu xǐhuan chīfàn. (*I'm the same as you—we both like to eat.*)

When A and B are different:

Wǒ gēn nǐ bù yíyàng, nǐ hěn máng, wǒ bù máng. (*I'm different from you; you're busy, I'm not.*)

Use *bǐ* to compare two people, things, etc.

Duì a! Wǒ bǐ nǐ máng yìdiǎnr. (*Right! I'm a bit busier than you.*)

To negate, use *bù* or *méiyǒu*.

Wǒ bù bǐ nǐ máng. (*I'm not busier than you.*)
Wǒ méiyǒu nǐ máng. (*I'm not as busy as you.*)

Counting verbs with *cì*

Use *cì* with a verbal phrase to express how many times an action happens.

Wǒ měitiān xǐ liǎng cì zǎo. (*I shower twice a day.*)
Wǒ yào qù sān cì. Jīntiān yí cì. Míngtiān yí cì. Hòutiān yí cì. (*I intend to go three times. Once today, once tomorrow, and once the day after tomorrow.*)
Wǒ qùguo liǎng cì Fēizhōu. (*I've been to Africa twice.*)

Signaling the plural with *xiē*

Use the measure word *xiē* to signal the plural.

Nǐ wǎnshang dōu zuò xiē shénme? (*What [all] do you do in the evening?*)
Zuò gōngkè, tīng yīnyuè, wán diànzǐ yóuxì—wǒ wǎnshang dōu zuò. (*Doing homework, listening to music, playing video games—I do all these things in the evening.*)

▶ Vocabulary

Daily routines

chī zǎofàn/zhōngfàn/wǎnfàn 吃早飯／中飯／晚飯 ‖ 吃早饭／中饭／晚饭 eat breakfast/lunch/dinner

chūmén 出門／出门 leave home

fàngxué 放學／放学 get out of school

guā húzi 刮鬍子／刮胡子 shave (a beard)

huàzhuāng 化妝／化妆 put on makeup

huíjiā 回家 return home

pǎobù 跑步 run, jog

qǐ chuáng 起床 get up (from bed)

shàngbān 上班 go to work/office

shàngxué 上學／上学 go to school

shuāyá 刷牙 brush (one's) teeth

shuìjiào 睡覺／睡觉 sleep; go to bed

shūtóufa 梳頭髮／梳头发 comb (one's) hair

xiàbān 下班 get off work

xǐliǎn 洗臉／洗脸 wash (one's) face

xǐzǎo 洗澡 take a bath/shower

zuò zǎocāo 做早操 do morning calisthenics

zuò zǎofàn/zhōngfàn/wǎnfàn
做早飯／中飯／晚飯 ‖
做早饭／中饭／晚饭
cook breakfast/lunch/dinner

Evening and weekend activities

chūqu wánr 出去玩兒／出去玩儿 go out for some fun

dǎgōng 打工 do part-time work

dāizai jiāli 呆在家裡／呆在家里 stay at home

gēcǎo 割草 cut the grass, mow the lawn

guàng shāngchǎng 逛商場／逛商场 go to the mall

kànbào 看報／看报 read a newspaper

kàn diànshì 看電視／看电视 watch TV

kàn diànyǐng 看電影／看电影 see a movie

kànshū 看書／看书 read, read a book

qù sànsanbù 去散散步 take a walk/stroll

shàngwǎng 上網／上网 go online

shuì lǎnjiào 睡懶覺／睡懒觉 sleep in

tīng yīnyuè 聽音樂／听音乐 listen to music

wán diànzǐ yóuxì 玩電子遊戲／玩电子游戏 play video games

xiě zuòyè 寫作業／写作业 do homework

zuò gōngkè 做功課／做功课 do homework

zuò jiāwù 做家務／做家务 do housework

zuò yújiā 做瑜珈 do yoga

Time expressions

měitiān 每天 every day, daily

tiāntiān 天天 every day, day after day

yì tiān liǎng cì 一天兩次 twice a day

yì zhōu jǐ cì 一周幾次／一周几次 several times a week

Nouns

bào 報／报 newspaper

cǎo 草 grass, lawn

diànshì 電視／电视 television

diànyǐng 電影／电影 movie, film

diànzǐ yóuxì 電子遊戲／电子游戏 video game

gōngkè 功課／功课 homework, schoolwork

húzi 鬍子／胡子 beard

jiāwù 家務／家务 household chores/duties

shāngchǎng 商場／商场 mall, market, bazaar

shíhou 時候／时候 (duration of) time; moment

shíjiān 時間／时间 time; duration

shū 書／书 book

tóufa 頭髮／头发 hair (on human head)

wǎnfàn 晚飯／晚饭 dinner, supper

wǔfàn 午飯／午饭 lunch

yīnyuè 音樂／音乐 music

yújiā 瑜珈 yoga

zǎocān 早餐 breakfast

zǎocāo 早操 morning calisthenics

zǎofàn 早飯／早饭 breakfast

zhōngfàn 中飯／中饭 lunch

zhōngtou 鐘頭／钟头 hour (of time)

More verbs

chá 查 check on, examine

chī 吃 eat

chūqu 出去 go out

dāi (zai) 呆 (在) stay (at)

huílai 回来 come back, return

kàn 看 read; see

mǎi 買／买 buy, purchase

nòng 弄 make

qǐ 起 get up (from bed); rise

qù 去 go (to)

tīng 聽／听 listen (to)

wán 玩 play, have fun, amuse oneself

xǐ 洗 wash, bathe, shower

zhīdào 知道 know, realize, be aware of

zuò 做 do; engage in

Stative verbs

ài 愛／爱 love, like

wǎn 晚 late

xǐhuan 喜歡／喜欢 like, prefer

zǎo 早 early

Auxiliary (helping) verbs

děi 得 must, need to

huì 會／会 be sure to, be likely to

kěyǐ 可以 can, may

néng 能 can, be capable of

xǐhuan 喜歡／喜欢 like to (but not "would like to")

yào 要 want to, will

Coverbs

bǐ 比 compared to

gēn 跟 with

zài 在 in, on, at

Adverbs

cái 才 then and only then, not until, until

cónglái bù/méi 從來不／没 ||
从来不／没 never

yìqǐ 一起 together

Measure words

cì 次 times, occurrences

xiē 些 (for a small amount) several

▶ Checklist of "can do" statements

After completing this unit, you should be able to perform each of the following tasks.

Listening and speaking

☐ Express what you do in the morning to get ready for your day; find out similar information from a friend.

☐ Tell a friend how often and at what time you do a certain activity.

☐ Tell a friend what you generally do after coming home from school or after classes.

☐ Give some details about your evening activities before, during, and after dinner.

☐ Say how you spend a holiday, a day off, or a weekend.

☐ Find out similar information from a friend.

Reading and writing

☐ Read simple statements concerning daily routines.

☐ Read key items on signs advertising services around town.

☐ Write a simple note describing some aspects of your daily routine.

Understanding culture

☐ Name some similarities and differences between your daily routines and those of many young people in China.

Checklist

• Have students work in pairs to go through this checklist and demonstrate selected skills to the class. Reserve 20–30 minutes for students to complete this activity. Tell students that putting check marks in each box is NOT the point. The point is to check if they can really do the things on the list.

"You get what you pay for"

一分價錢一分貨

Yì fēn jiàqian yì fēn huò

Shopping and bargaining

In this unit, you will learn how to:

- handle simple money transactions involved in shopping.
- inquire about the price of an item and bargain for it, if appropriate.
- make simple statements indicating what you wish to buy.
- make simple statements specifying colors and sizes.

- understand key information on signs and promotional material related to products for sale.
- read simple statements about purchases made or planned.
- write simple statements about purchases made or planned.

Encounter 1 Handling money

As a homework assignment before starting Unit 9, ask students to flip through the unit to preview the content.

9.1 • Before watching Episode 9, ask students what they remember from previous episodes. Encourage them to respond in Chinese and English.

• Play the video clip twice, if necessary.

• Allow time for students to discuss the video among themselves. Understanding the plot is crucial for students to complete the unit's exercises.

9.2 • Possible answers: *How much is it? It's $12.99*, etc. The goal of this activity is to get students to think about the basic language items needed to go shopping in China.

• Invite volunteers to write the suggestions on a poster. Hang the poster on the wall. After students have completed the unit, make sure to revisit this poster and check if they have learned enough Chinese to say everything on the poster. The purpose of this activity is to help students connect what they're learning with real-life communication needs.

9.3–9.6

• Have students glance at all these exercises before playing the video.

• Encourage students to first work on exercises 9.3, 9.5, and 9.6. They could then return to 9.4.

• Tell students to use body language and context in the video to access meaning. Feel free to pause the video to give hints. You may also want to play the video multiple times, but make sure to allow time between repeats for students to answer the questions and compare their answers with classmates.

9.3 Key:

How much is this? / How much does this cost?

Dollars and cents in China

• If you prefer, you can have students read this FYI *after* they have completed exercise 9.6.

• Divide the class into four groups, and provide each group with the same task: Read this FYI to understand Chinese currency. Prepare a class presentation to teach your peers this information. Specifically, make sure to mention how the words for *Rénmínbì* units differ in spoken and written contexts. Provide several good examples.

 9.1 *View Episode 9 of the dramatic series.*

9.2 *Getting ready:* How do you complete simple transactions when shopping, and what questions might you ask?

 9.3 *Watch and listen to the video segment. Write the English translation of* Zhèi ge duōshao qián? 這個多少錢？／这个多少钱？

FYI 供你参考

Dollars and cents in China

Chinese currency is called *Rénmínbì (RMB)* 人民幣／人民币 (the people's currency). The basic monetary unit is the *yuán* 元, more or less equivalent in usage (if not in value) to the U.S. dollar. The term *yuán* is most often used in the written language; its spoken equivalent is *kuài* 塊／块 (piece, lump). *Kuài* is a measure word, so it is preceded by a number and (usually) followed by the noun *qián* (meaning "money"): *liǎng kuài qián* 兩塊錢／两块钱 (two yuán/"dollars"). 1/10 of a *yuán* is a *jiǎo* 角; colloquially, 1/10 of a *kuài* is a *máo* 毛; and 1/10 of a *jiǎo*, or *máo*, is a *fēn* 分. Here's a summary:

written Chinese	spoken Chinese
yuán 元 ("*dollar*")	kuài 塊／块 ("*dollar*")
jiǎo 角 ("*dime*")	máo 毛 ("*dime*")
fēn 分 ("*cent*")	fēn 分 ("*cent*")

So, *jiǔshíjiǔ kuài jiǔ máo jiǔ fēn qián* (as spoken) = 九十九元九角九分 (as written) = ¥99.99

Here are some things to keep in mind:

• In speech, the last unit (*máo* 毛 or *fēn* 分) is often unexpressed. Thus:

  liǎng kuài wǔ = "two fifty" or ¥2.50 (The *wǔ* refers to *máo*.)

  liǎng máo wǔ = "twenty-five cents" or ¥0.25 (The *wǔ* refers to *fēn*.)

• The noun *qián* is, by custom, usually used for single-digit sums but is often dropped for double-digit figures and larger. So: *wǔ kuài qián tài shǎo le!* BUT *wǔshí kuài tài duō le!*

• In written Chinese, prices (as well as other numbers) are often given in Arabic numerals, followed by the character 元 or the symbol ¥. So: 9元 or ¥ 9.

• If possible, bring real Chinese money to class. Provide them as realia for students to use in their group presentations.

• If time allows, have students make a "Money Dictionary" poster to hang on the wall for future reference.

• Make sure students understand that *jiǎo* and *máo* are equivalent in denomination, but not in value, to the dime; *fēn* is comparable in denomination, but not in value, to the penny or cent.

9.4 *Fill in the blanks with the correct numbers to express the prices given in both pinyin and characters. Some answers have been provided as examples.*

a. sì kuài qián 四塊錢／四块钱   __ __ 4 . 0 0

b. qī kuài qián 七塊錢／七块钱   __ __ __ . __ __

c. sān máo qián 三毛錢／三毛钱   __ __ . 3 0

d. wǔ máo qián 五毛錢／五毛钱   __ __ . __ __

e. liù fēn qián 六分錢／六分钱   __ __ . 0 6

f. jiǔ fēn qián 九分錢／九分钱   __ __ . __ __

g. shíjiǔ kuài jiǔ máo jiǔ 十九塊九毛九／十九块九毛九 __ __ __ . __ __

h. sì kuài sān máo jiǔ 四塊三毛九／四块三毛九 __ __ . __ __

i. wǔ kuài 五塊／五块   __ __ . __ __

j. liù máo yī 六毛一   __ __ . __ __

k. yìbǎi kuài 一百塊／一百块   __ __ __ . __ __

9.5 *How do you say, "How much altogether?" Complete the sentence below in pinyin.*

Yígòng _____ qián? 一共多少錢？／一共多少钱？

9.6 *Match the corresponding items below.*

a. *That's right.*   1. Cuò le.   A. 錯了／错了

b. *That's not right.*   2. Duì le.   B. 對了／对了

c. *That's wrong.*   3. Bú duì.   C. 沒錯／没错

d. *There's no mistake.*   4. Méi cuò.   D. 不對／不对

9.7 Pair work: *Work with a partner. Place three items on your desk (for example, a watch, a pen, and a calculator). Write a private note indicating how much each item costs. Now ask your partner how much each of his or her items costs, and then answer your partner's questions in return. Arrange the items in order of most expensive* (zuì guì) *to least expensive* (zuì piányi). *Then figure out the total cost of all the items together. Be sure to check each other's calculations and say whether they are right or wrong. Finally, share the total cost of your items with another pair (or with the class).*

 9.8 *Watch and listen to the video segment. Then fill in the blanks with the appropriate pinyin.*

a. Měiguórén _____ Měijīn.

美國人用美金。／美国人用美金。

Americans use U.S. dollars.

b. Zhōngguórén _____ Rénmínbì, Táibì, Àomén yuán, háiyǒu Gǎngbì.

中國人用人民幣，台幣，澳門元，還有港幣。／
中国人用人民币，台币，澳门元，还有港币。

Chinese people use RMB, New Taiwan dollars, Macau patacas, and Hong Kong dollars.

9.9 *Match the corresponding items.*

a. *People's Republic of China (RMB)*

b. *Taiwan (New Taiwan dollar)*

c. *Hong Kong (Hong Kong dollar)*

d. *Macau (pataca)*

e. *United States (U.S. dollar)*

f. *European Union (euro)*

g. *England (pound)*

h. *Japan (yen)*

i. *Australia (Australian dollar)*

j. *Canada (Canadian dollar)*

k. *India (rupee)*

1. _____ Rìyuán
   日元

2. _____ Ōuyuán
   歐元／欧元

3. _____ Jiānádà yuán
   加拿大元

4. _____ Lúbǐ
   盧比／卢比

5. _____ Gǎngbì
   港幣／港币

6. _____ Àomén yuán
   澳門元／澳门元

7. _____ Rénmínbì
   人民幣／人民币

8. _____ Àoyuán
   澳元

9. _____ Táibì
   台幣／台币

10. _____ Měijīn
    美金

11. _____ Yīngbàng
    英鎊／英镑

9.9 If you discover students have difficulties, help them by suggesting three strategies:

1. Use the images.
2. Say the currency names out loud to hear the similarity in sound across languages.
3. Use process of elimination.
4. Play the video clip from exercise 9.8, if necessary.

9.9 Key:

a. 7
b. 9
c. 5
d. 6
e. 10
f. 2
g. 11
h. 1
i. 8
j. 3
k. 4

9.10 *Write the pinyin term for the currency in your home country here:* _____.
(If the currency of your home country does not appear on p. 218, consult your teacher.)
Then search the Internet for a currency conversion site (e.g., www.xe.com*) and complete
the following statements for "your" currency. For convenience, round to the nearest
whole number.*

Yí kuài Měijīn néng (kěyǐ) huàn qī kuài Rénmínbì.

一塊美金能（可以）換七塊人民幣。／
一块美金能（可以）换七块人民币。

(One U.S. dollar converts into seven RMB.)

a. Yí kuài _____ néng (kěyǐ) huàn _____ Rénmínbì.
　　　　　(YOUR CURRENCY)　　　　　　　　(AMOUNT)

b. Yí kuài _____ néng (kěyǐ) huàn _____ Táibì.
　　　　　(YOUR CURRENCY)　　　　　　　　(AMOUNT)

c. Yí kuài _____ néng (kěyǐ) huàn _____ Gǎngbì.
　　　　　(YOUR CURRENCY)　　　　　　　　(AMOUNT)

d. Yí kuài _____ néng (kěyǐ) huàn _____ Àomén yuán.
　　　　　(YOUR CURRENCY)　　　　　　　　(AMOUNT)

9.11 *Pair work: Take the three items you used in exercise 9.7. Relabel the prices in RMB.
How would you respond if someone were to point at one of the items and ask,* Zhèi ge
Rénmínbì duōshao qián? *Fill in the blank below for your first item.*

_____ kuài Rénmínbì.

Now repeat exercise 9.7 using prices in Rénmínbì.

9.12 *Pair work: Do the exercise again using prices in New Taiwan dollars. The question
would be* Zhèi ge Táibì duōshao qián? *Your answer:* _____ kuài Táibì.

9.13 *Pair work: Do it again using prices in Hong Kong dollars. The question would be*
Zhèi ge Gǎngbì duōshao qián? *Your answer:* _____ kuài Gǎngbì.

9.14 *Pair work: Do it one more time using prices in Macau patacas. The question would
be* Zhèi ge Àomén yuán duōshao qián? *Your answer:* _____ kuài Àomén yuán.

Encounter 2 Braining

Encounter 2 **Bargaining**

9.15 • Possible answers: *That's too much. How about 10? 12?* The goal of this activity is to get students to think about the language people use to bargain.

• Brainstorm as a class, and invite students to offer answers "popcorn style."

• Invite volunteer scribes to write these suggestions on the poster the class began in exercise 9.2.

• Make sure to revisit this poster at the end of the unit to check if students have learned enough Chinese to say everything on the list.

9.16 Key:

¥50	¥10
¥45	¥20
¥40	¥25
¥35	¥30 (The Chinese friend

makes this counter-offer.)

Final price: ¥65
Number of items purchased: 2

9.17 Key:

a. How much are you selling this for?
b. Too expensive!
c. It's not expensive. It's very cheap.
d. It's too much!
e. It's too low!
f. What about ¥30?
g. OK, OK. Let's go with ¥30.

9.15 Getting ready: *You can sometimes bargain at a garage sale or flea market. What would you say if you wanted the seller to lower his or her price?*

_____

_____

9.16 *Watch and listen to the video segment. Fill in the blanks to accurately reflect the progression between offer and counter-offer.*

Vendor: ¥ 50   Customer: _____

Vendor: _____   Customer: _____

Vendor: _____   Customer: _____

Vendor: _____   Customer: _____

Final price: _____

Number of items purchased: _____

9.17 *What do you think each of the following expressions means? Write the English equivalents of each.*

(Note: *mǎi* 買／买 = "buy" and *mài* 賣／卖 = "sell")

a. Nǐ zhèi ge mài duōshao qián? 你這個賣多少錢？／你这个卖多少钱？

_____

b. Tài guì le! 太貴了！／太贵了！ _____

c. Bú guì, bú guì. Hěn piányi. 不貴，不貴。很便宜。／
不貴，不貴。很便宜。

_____

d. Tài duō le! 太多了！ _____

e. Tài shǎo le! 太少了！ _____

f. 30 kuài zěnmeyàng? ３０塊怎麼樣？／３０块怎么样？

_____

g. Xíng le, xíng le. Jiù 30 kuài ba. 行了，行了。就３０塊吧。／就３０块吧。

_____

9.18 *Pair work: Draw an item on an index card and give it a price (make it higher than what you would actually be willing to sell it for). Work with your partner. He or she should "bargain" for your item and try to get it as cheaply as possible; you, of course, would like to keep your price as high as possible. Reverse roles after you have reached an agreement.*

9.18 Remind students to use the phrases introduced in exercise 9.17 to "bargain" with their classmates.

FYI 供你参考

Haggling over price

An astute observer of Chinese culture has remarked that bargaining is an "art form much beloved by the Chinese." However, it's not all about getting a lower price. Of course price is important, but establishing a relationship between buyer and seller that is friendly, not adversarial, is also important. Neither side wants to take advantage of the other; rather, a solution that is pleasing to both is usually the goal of each side. This is entirely within the tradition of seeking harmony, something that lies at the core of Chinese culture. When you're in China, take time to watch how people bargain. If possible, bring a Chinese friend with you when you go shopping, as Alejandro did in the video. You'll have fun, maybe walk away with a bargain, and also have a better opportunity to interact with the vendor who might ask you to come again!

Your bargaining "chips":

- Keep the negotiations good-natured and friendly.
- Know when to bargain and when not to. If you are in doubt, watch Chinese shoppers, or ask a Chinese friend.
- Start by offering less than you are willing to pay and go up slowly.
- If you're getting nowhere by bargaining, consider turning away, feigning disinterest, and then returning later.
- Think of "outside-the-box" bargaining solutions, such as buying multiple items for a lower price, getting a second item thrown in for free or at a significant discount, or getting a service added for free.
- Keep in mind this handy opening line: *Néng bu néng piányi yìdiǎnr?* (Can it be a little bit cheaper?)

Adapted from May-lee and Winberg Chai, *China A to Z: Everything You Need to Know to Understand Chinese Customs and Culture* (New York: Plume/Penguin, 2007), 13.

Haggling over price

- Divide the class into four groups, and give each group the same task: Read the FYI and then come up with four true/false statements in English to test your peers' understanding of the material. Example: True or false? Make sure you show disinterest and walk away when you don't get your price. (Answer: False. You have to bargain a bit first.)
- Encourage students to make their statements tricky and fun. They should test their peers' understanding of the details in this FYI.

Encounter 3   Comparing prices

9.19 *Getting ready: What are some items that you most often shop for?*

_____

_____

9.19 • Possible answers: *clothes, video games, books*, etc. The goal of this activity is to get students to think about everyday items that people shop for.

• Brainstorm as a class, and invite students to offer answers "popcorn style."

9.20 *Listen to the audio segment. Then match the traditional and simplified characters.*

a. yì píng shuǐ 一瓶水

1. 一条长裤

b. yì xiē táng 一些糖

2. 一条短裤

c. yì xiē yīfu 一些衣服

3. 一件T-恤衫

d. yì dǐng màozi 一顶帽子

4. 一些衣服

e. yí jiàn T-xù shān 一件 T-恤衫

5. 一瓶水

f. yì tiáo duǎnkù 一條短褲

6. 一顶帽子

g. yì tiáo chángkù 一條長褲

7. 一些糖

9.21 *What is the maximum amount that you would spend for each of the following items? Fill in the blanks below.*

9.21 Answers will vary based on students' own estimates.

(Note: *kěn* 肯 = "be willing" and *huā* 花 = "spend")

a. Mǎi yì píng shuǐ, wǒ zuì duō kěn huā _____ kuài qián. *(For one bottle of water, I'd be willing to spend at most _____ [units of currency].)*

b. Mǎi yì xiē táng, wǒ zuì duō kěn huā _____ kuài qián.

c. Mǎi yì dǐng màozi, wǒ zuì duō kěn huā _____ kuài qián.

d. Mǎi yí jiàn T-xù shān, wǒ zuì duō kěn huā _____ kuài qián.

e. Mǎi yì tiáo duǎnkù, wǒ zuì duō kěn huā _____ kuài qián.

f. Mǎi yì tiáo chángkù, wǒ zuì duō kěn huā _____ kuài qián.

9.22 *Pair work: Ask your partner,* Mǎi yì píng shuǐ, nǐ zuì duō kěn huā duōshao qián? *Compare his or her answer with your own. Now pretend that each of you bought the item in question for the amount you stated. Whose item would be more expensive?*

9.22–9.23
• Have students work with different partners for each exercise.
• Invite several confident pairs to demonstrate the exchange.
• Mingle with your students to observe, or join the activity and play along.

• If yours is more expensive, say *Wǒ de bǐ nǐ de guì.* 我的比你的貴。／我的比你的贵。 (Mine is more expensive than yours.)

• If your partner's is more expensive, say *Wǒ de méiyǒu nǐ de nàme guì.* 我的沒有你的那麼貴。／我的没有你的那么贵。 (Mine is not as expensive as yours.)

• If your items are the same price, say *Wǒ de gēn nǐ de yíyàng guì.* 我的跟你的一樣貴。／我的跟你的一样贵。 (Mine is just as expensive as yours.)

9.23 *Mingling: Go around the room and compare your height with each of your classmates'.*

• If you are taller, say *Wǒ bǐ nǐ gāo.* 我比你高。 (I am taller than you.)

• If you are shorter, say *Wǒ méiyǒu nǐ nàme gāo.* 我沒有你那麼高。／我没有你那么高。 (I am not as tall as you.)

• If you are the same height, say *Wǒ gēn nǐ yíyàng gāo.* 我跟你一樣高。／我跟你一样高。 (I am the same height as you.)

Grammar Bits 语法点滴

Another "round" with the comparison pattern

Recall the following patterns from Unit 8:

> Wǒ de gēn nǐ de yíyàng guì. *(Mine is just as expensive as yours.)*
> Wǒ de bǐ nǐ de guì. *(Mine is more expensive than yours.)*

We can also compare by degrees:

> Wǒ de bǐ nǐ de guì yìdiǎnr. *(Mine is a bit more expensive than yours.)*
> Wǒ de bǐ nǐ de guì de duō. *(Mine is much more expensive than yours.)*

To express the negative, it's most common to use *méiyǒu . . . nàme.*

> Wǒ de méiyǒu nǐ de nàme guì. *(Mine is not as expensive as yours.)*

Note: Never use *hěn* (very) when making comparisons.

Encounter 4 | Specifying colors and sizes

9.24 • Have students share and compare their lists with partners.

• After students complete exercise 9.26, revisit these lists to see if students can say all of their favorite colors in Chinese. If they do not know the Chinese for one or more of their colors, encourage them to use a bilingual dictionary to look up and learn the appropriate vocabulary.

9.24 *Getting ready: What are your favorite colors? List four.*

_____   _____

_____   _____

9.25 **Key:**

What color?

9.25 *Watch and listen to the video segment. What does the following mean? Fill in the blank with the appropriate English equivalent.*

Shénme yánsè? 甚麼顏色？／什么颜色？_____

Grammar Bits 语法点滴

Making your Chinese "colorful"

The Chinese word for "color" is *yánsè*, or just *sè* when used in combinations; thus, "the color red" is *hóng yánsè*, or *hóngsè* for short. You can say either *Wǒ xǐhuan hóng yánsè* or *Wǒ xǐhuan hóngsè* to mean "I like the color red." Similarly, you can say *Wǒ xǐhuan T-xù shān*, which means "I like T-shirts." If you want to say "I like red T-shirts," you can do so in several ways. You could say *Wǒ xǐhuan hóng T-xù shān* (I like red T-shirts), *Wǒ xǐhuan hóngsè de T-xù shān* (I like T-shirts that are the color red), or *Wǒ xǐhuan hóng yánsè de T-xù shān* (I like T-shirts that are the color red).

The particle *de* is sandwiched between a noun (*T-xù shān*) and the word or phrase that describes it. If the descriptive element consists of a single syllable (*hóng*), *de* is often omitted (*hóng T-xù shān*). However, if the descriptive element consists of more than one syllable (*hóngsè*), *de* is almost always included (*hóngsè de T-xù shān*).

If the topic is known—in this case, "T-shirts"—you can drop the noun. Thus, *Wǒ xǐhuan hóng de, Wǒ xǐhuan hóngsè de,* and *Wǒ xǐhuan hóng yánsè de* all mean "I like red ones."

Grammar Bits

• Have students study this Grammar Bits *after* they have completed exercise 9.26.

• Divide the class into four groups, and give each group one of the following tasks:

Group 1: Read the Grammar Bits with your group and come up with four ways to say, "I like yellow jackets." Be ready to share your sentences with the class.

Group 2: Read the Grammar Bits with your group and come up with four ways to say, "I don't like blue hats." Be ready to share your sentences with the class.

Group 3: Read the Grammar Bits with your group and come up with four ways to say, "I like red T-shirts." Be ready to share your sentences with the class.

Group 4: Read the Grammar Bits with your group and come up with four ways to say, "I don't like black pants." Be ready to share your sentences with the class.

9.26 *Match the corresponding items.*

a. ▪ *black*	1. hóngsè 红色	A. 金色
b. ▪ *red*	2. jīnsè 金色	B. 银色
c. ▪ *blue*	3. hēisè 黑色	C. 红色
d. ▪ *green*	4. júhóngsè 橘红色	D. 咖啡色
e. ▪ *yellow*	5. mǐsè 米色	E. 黄色
f. ▪ *orange*	6. lánsè 藍色	F. 绿色
g. ▪ *brown*	7. zǐsè 紫色	G. 米色
h. ▪ *purple*	8. huángsè 黄色	H. 黑色
i. ▪ *white*	9. huīsè 灰色	I. 紫色
j. ▪ *beige*	10. lǜsè 綠色	J. 橘红色
k. ▪ *pink*	11. yínsè 銀色	K. 灰色
l. ▪ *gold*	12. kāfēisè 咖啡色	L. 藍色
m. ▪ *silver*	13. fěnhóngsè 粉红色	M. 白色
n. ▪ *gray*	14. báisè 白色	N. 粉红色

9.26 Key:
a. 3. H
b. 1. C
c. 6. L
d. 10. F
e. 8. E
f. 4. J
g. 12. D
h. 7. I
i. 14. M
j. 5. G
k. 13. N
l. 2. A
m. 11. B
n. 9. K

Note: "Orange" can be said one of several ways:

• júhóngsè 橘红色 *(the red of the tangerine)*

• júsè 橘色 *(the color of the tangerine)*

• chéngsè 橙色 *(the color of the orange)*

Similarly, "brown" can be expressed as follows:

• kāfēisè 咖啡色 *(the color of coffee)*

• chásè 茶色 *(the color of tea)*

• zōngsè 棕色 *(the color of bark)*

9.27 • Prepare colored pencils, markers, or crayons for students to use in class.

• Demonstrate the activity with the class. Leave the room briefly so the class can come up with a secret color palette.

• Reenter the room to take the color dictation. Make sure you play a monolingual Chinese speaker. Do not predict what the students are trying to say. If what they say doesn't make sense, respond, *"Wǒ bù dǒng."* Let students figure out how to fix their sentences to clarify meaning.

• As students do this exercise in pairs, remind them to make their own color palettes in secret and keep them hidden from their partners.

9.27 Pair work: *Work with a partner. You'll need a set of pens, pencils, or crayons for each of the 14 colors on the preceding page. Fill in each of the boxes below with a color of your choice. Use a different color for each box.*

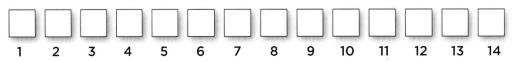

Note: Ordinal numbers are as follows: *dì-yī* 第一, *dì-èr* 第二, *dì-sān* 第三, *dì-sì* 第四, etc. A "box" (on a form, such as an application, or in an activity, as above) is a *gézi* 格子. So, *dì-qī ge gézi* means "the seventh box."

Sit back to back with your partner so that you can't see each other's books, and tell how you've colored your boxes. Then, following your partner's descriptions, duplicate his or her row below.

For example, say Dì-yī ge gézi shì hóng de. Dì-èr ge gézi shì hēi de.

Practice asking questions such as Dì-wǔ ge gézi shì shénme yánsè? Dì-qī ge gézi shì lán de ma?

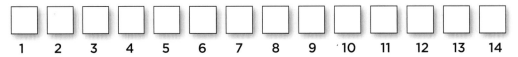

When you're done, compare your rows. If you did the exercise correctly, your second row should match your partner's first row, and vice versa.

9.28 If time allows, have students perform exercise 9.28 with multiple classmates.

9.28 Pair work: *Work with a partner. Identify the color of each clothing item you and your partner are wearing. Use the following pattern. Then reverse roles.*

Q *(tugging at an article of your clothing, ask)*: Zhè shì shénme yánsè?

A: Nà shì hóngsè de.

9.29 *Watch and listen to the video segment. Then match the corresponding items below.*

a. XS

b. S

c. M

d. L

e. XL

1. dàhào 大號

2. zhōnghào 中號

3. xiǎohào 小號

4. jiādàhào 加大號

5. jiāxiǎohào 加小號

A. 中号

B. 加大号

C. 大号

D. 加小号

E. 小号

Note: In Taiwan, XL is *tèdàhào* 特大号 (especially large size) and XS is *tèxiǎohào* 特小号 (especially small size).

9.30 *Mingling: This exercise works perfectly if you and your classmates are wearing T-shirts. If you are not, pretend that you are. What size do you wear? Walk around and engage in a dialogue similar to the one below, but adjust the details to match your specific situation.*

A: Nǐ chuān jǐ hào de T-xù shān? (*chuān* = wear)

B: Wǒ chuān zhōnghào de. Nǐ ne?

A: Wǒ chuān dàhào de.

B: Nǐ de bǐ wǒ de dà.

A: Nǐ de bǐ wǒ de xiǎo.

B: Nǐ de duōshao qián?

A: Shíwǔ kuài. Nǐ de ne?

B: Bǐ nǐ de guì yìdiǎnr. / Bǐ nǐ de guì de duō. *OR* Gēn nǐ de yíyàng guì. *OR*
　　Méiyǒu nǐ de nàme guì.

9.31 *Mingling: Draw a T-shirt in one of the colors introduced in this unit. Write a size on the front of the shirt. This is the T-shirt you have available "for sale." On the back of the paper, write a different size and list two different colors. These are sizes and colors that are "also available." Decide which T-shirt you wish to "buy," and then write its size and two possible colors below.*

_____　_____　_____

Now walk around the classroom. How many of your classmates are "selling" the exact shirt you want? You might use dialogue such as the following to determine if someone has the shirt you want.

A: Zhèi jiàn T-xù shān yǒu xiǎohào de ma?

B: Duìbuqǐ, méiyǒu. Kěshì lán de yǒu xiǎohào de. Yào ma?

A: Duìbuqǐ, bú yào. Wǒ bú yào lán de. Yǒu bái de ma?

B: Yǒu!

A: Yǒu xiǎohào de ma?

B: Yǒu! Báisè de xiǎohào.

A: Tài hǎo le!

▶ Putting it all together

9.32 *Work in pairs or small groups of three to four people. Write a one-minute script about shopping, using language you've learned in this unit. Practice performing the script (make sure each person gets approximately equal talking time), and then perform it for your class.*

🎵 Unit Rap

Go to the **Encounters** *website at* www.EncountersChinese.com *and listen to the song to review key expressions from Unit 9. Listen again and sing along!*

Encounter 5	Reading and writing

9.32 • Remind students that they can use vocabulary from the entire unit.

• Ask students to exchange completed scripts with their partners and proofread each other's work. Remind the "editors" to consult with the writers for clarification on any confusing language.

• Have students prepare one or two questions they can use to quiz the class after they perform their script.

9.33 • Avoid reading the dialogue aloud for your students or having them repeat after you. Tell them to use the English and familiar characters as bridges to determine the meaning and pronunciation of unknown characters.

• Keep in mind that reading fluency is not the goal of this activity. Tell students not to get discouraged if they have trouble reading quickly and accurately.

• Have students complete this exercise multiple times before they move on to 9.34 and 9.35.

▶ Reading familiar sentences in Chinese characters

9.33 *Pair work: Read the following dialogues (written in traditional characters) aloud with a partner, using the English as a guide.*

1 甲：老闆(lǎobǎn)，這個多少錢？ *(Owner, how much is this?)*

乙：我看看……那個十塊錢。 *(Let me see . . . that's ten "dollars.")*

甲：這個呢？ *(How about this one?)*

乙：五塊五。 *(Five "dollars" and fifty "cents.")*

甲：這個呢？ *(How about this one?)*

乙：九毛五。 *(Ninety-five "cents.")*

甲：好。我都要。一共多少錢？ *(Fine. I'll take them all. How much altogether?)*

乙：一共十六塊九毛五分錢。 *(Altogether, that's sixteen "dollars" and ninety-five "cents.")*

甲：不對吧…… *(I don't think that's right . . .)*

乙：哦，錯了。是十六塊四毛五。對不起！ *(Oh, that's wrong. It's sixteen "dollars" and forty-five "cents." Sorry!)*

2 甲：一塊美金能換六塊人民幣，對不對？ *(One U.S. dollar can convert into six RMB, is that right?)*

乙：差不多。 *(Approximately.)*

甲：一塊歐元呢？ *(How about one euro?)*

乙：對不起，我不知道。 *(Sorry, I don't know.)*

3 甲：英國用的是甚麼錢？　*(What currency does England use?)*

乙：英鎊。　*(The pound.)*

甲：加拿大呢？　*(How about Canada?)*

乙：加拿大元。　*(Canadian dollars.)*

甲：澳大利亞呢？　*(And Australia?)*

乙：澳元。你為甚麼問這些？　*(Australian dollars. Why are you asking all this?)*

甲：沒甚麼。只是問問。　*(No reason. I'm just asking.)*

4 甲：我要去歐洲。得去換些歐元。　*(I have to go to Europe. I have to exchange some "dollars" for euros.)*

乙：你想換多少歐元？　*(How many euros are you thinking of getting?)*

甲：七百塊夠不夠？　*(Is seven hundred enough?)*

乙：你去幾天？　*(How many days are you going for?)*

甲：一個星期。　*(A week.)*

乙：差不多。夠了吧。　*(That's about right. [That] should be enough.)*

5 甲：這是甚麼錢啊？　*(What kind of money is this?)*

乙：是盧比嗎？　*(Are these rupees?)*

甲：不是吧。　*(I don't think so.)*

乙：哦，我知道了，是日元。　*(Oh, I know. These are Japanese yen.)*

甲：是嗎？不對吧。　*(Are they? I don't think that's right.)*

乙：是不是港幣？　*(Are they Hong Kong dollars?)*

甲：對了，對了。是港幣。　*(Right, right. They're Hong Kong dollars.)*

6 甲：老闆，你這個賣多少錢？　*(Owner, how much are you selling this for?)*

乙：兩百塊。　*(Two hundred "dollars.")*

甲：兩百塊太貴了！怎麼那麼貴？　*(Two hundred is too expensive. How come it's so expensive?)*

乙：不貴！這是好東西啊！　*(It's not expensive! This is really good stuff!)*

甲：一百塊行嗎？　*(Is one hundred OK?)*

乙：一百塊太少了！你看看，多好的東西。　*(One hundred is too little! Look! Such fine stuff!)*

甲：你賣得太貴了。不買不買。　*(You sell things at too high a price. I'm not buying.)*

7 甲：我要買一些衣服。 *(I want to buy some clothes.)*

乙：甚麼衣服？ *(What clothes?)*

甲：想買一條長褲，一條短褲，還想買件T-恤衫。 *(I'd like to buy a pair of pants, a pair of shorts, and I'd also like to buy a T-shirt.)*

乙：哦，好。我跟你一起去買。走吧。 *(Oh, OK. I'll go shopping with you. Let's go.)*

8 甲：有沒有紅帽子？ *(Do you have red hats?)*

乙：對不起，沒有紅的。黑的或白的行不行？也有灰色的和米色的。 *(Sorry, we don't have red. Is black or white OK? We also have gray or beige.)*

甲：有藍的嗎？ *(Do you have blue?)*

乙：對不起，藍的也沒有。 *(Sorry, we don't have blue either.)*

甲：那我就要那頂米色的吧。有大號的嗎？ *(Then I'll take that beige one. Do you have it in large?)*

乙：有有有。這是大號的。這是加大號的。 *(Yes, yes, yes. This is large, and this is extra large.)*

甲：好，我買一頂大號的。 *(Good. I'll take the large.)*

9 甲：我有三塊糖：一塊橘紅色的、一塊咖啡色的、一塊黃色的。給你一塊。你要哪塊？ *(I have three pieces of candy: an orange-colored one, a brown one, and a yellow one. I'll give you one. Which one do you want?)*

乙：我要第一塊。 *(I'll take the first one.)*

甲：第一塊是橘紅色的。好，給你。 *(The first one is the orange-colored one. OK, here.)*

10 甲：這兩瓶水，怎麼大的便宜，小的貴？ *(These two bottles of water—how come the big one is cheaper and the small one is more expensive?)*

乙：對啊！小瓶比大瓶貴。我也不知道為甚麼。 *(Right, the small one is more expensive than the big one. I don't know why either.)*

甲：那我們去問問老闆吧！ *(Let's go ask the owner!)*

乙：好啊。 *(Fine.)*

9.34 *Pair work: Read the dialogues aloud with a partner, this time without any English.*

9.34–9.35

• Have students read these dialogues multiple times, focusing on reading fluency.

• Encourage students *not* to refer to exercise 9.33 for help. Instead, ask them to rely on the dialogue context and their partners to help them read new characters.

• After students practice reading the dialogues a few times, play the audio and have them check their pronunciation.

1 甲：老闆(lǎobǎn)，這個多少錢？

乙：我看看……那個十塊錢。

甲：這個呢？

乙：五塊五。

甲：這個呢？

乙：九毛五。

甲：好。我都要。一共多少錢？

乙：一共十六塊九毛五分錢。

甲：不對吧……

乙：哦，錯了。是十六塊四毛五。對不起！

2 甲：一塊美金能換六塊人民幣，對不對？

乙：差不多。

甲：一塊歐元呢？

乙：對不起，我不知道。

3 甲：英國用的是甚麼錢？

乙：英鎊。

甲：加拿大呢？

乙：加拿大元。

甲：澳大利亞呢？

乙：澳元。你為甚麼問這些？

甲：沒甚麼。只是問問。

4 甲：我要去歐洲。得去換些歐元。

乙：你想換多少歐元？

甲：七百塊夠不夠？

乙：你去幾天？

甲：一個星期。

乙：差不多。夠了吧。

5 甲：這是甚麼錢啊？

乙：是盧比嗎？

甲：不是吧。

乙：哦，我知道了，是日元。

甲：是嗎？不對吧。

乙：是不是港幣？

甲：對了，對了。是港幣。

6 甲：老闆，你這個賣多少錢？

乙：兩百塊。

甲：兩百塊太貴了！怎麼那麼貴？

乙：不貴！這是好東西啊！

甲：一百塊行嗎？

乙：一百塊太少了！你看看，多好的東西。

甲：你賣得太貴了。不買不買。

7 甲：我要買一些衣服。

乙：甚麼衣服？

甲：想買一條長褲，一條短褲，還想買件T-恤衫。

乙：哦，好。我跟你一起去買。走吧。

8 甲：有沒有紅帽子？

乙：對不起，沒有紅的。黑的或白的行不行？也有灰色的和米色的。

甲：有藍的嗎？

乙：對不起，藍的也沒有。

甲：那我就要那頂米色的吧。有大號的嗎？

乙：有有有。這是大號的。這是加大號的。

甲：好，我買一頂大號的。

9 甲：我有三塊糖：一塊橘紅色的、一塊咖啡色的、一塊黃色的。給你一塊。你要哪塊？

乙：我要第一塊。

甲：第一塊是橘紅色的。好，給你。

10 甲：這兩瓶水，怎麼大的便宜，小的貴？
乙：對啊！小瓶比大瓶貴。我也不知道為甚麼。
甲：那我們去問問老闆吧！
乙：好啊

9.35 Pair work: *Now try it once again, this time in simplified characters.*

1 甲：老板(lǎobǎn)，这个多少钱？
乙：我看看……那个十块钱。
甲：这个呢？
乙：五块五。
甲：这个呢？
乙：九毛五。
甲：好。我都要。一共多少钱？
乙：一共十六块九毛五分钱。
甲：不对吧……
乙：哦，错了。是十六块四毛五。对不起！

2 甲：一块美金能换六块人民币，对不对？
乙：差不多。
甲：一块欧元呢？
乙：对不起，我不知道。

3 甲：英国用的是什么钱？
乙：英镑。
甲：加拿大呢？
乙：加拿大元。
甲：澳大利亚呢？
乙：澳元。你为什么问这些？
甲：没什么。只是问问。

4 甲：我要去欧洲。得去换些欧元。
乙：你想换多少欧元？
甲：七百块够不够？
乙：你去几天？
甲：一个星期。
乙：差不多。够了吧。

5 甲：这是什么钱啊？

乙：是卢比吗？

甲：不是吧。

乙：哦，我知道了，是日元。

甲：是吗？不对吧。

乙：是不是港币？

甲：对了，对了。是港币。

6 甲：老板，你这个卖多少钱？

乙：两百块。

甲：两百块太贵了！怎么那么贵？

乙：不贵！这是好东西啊！

甲：一百块行吗？

乙：一百块太少了！你看看，多好的东西。

甲：你卖得太贵了。不买不买。

7 甲：我要买一些衣服。

乙：什么衣服？

甲：想买一条长裤，一条短裤，还想买件T-恤衫。

乙：哦，好。我跟你一起去买。走吧。

8 甲：有没有红帽子？

乙：对不起，没有红的。黑的或白的行不行？
也有灰色的和米色的。

甲：有蓝的吗？

乙：对不起，蓝的也没有。

甲：那我就要那顶米色的吧。有大号的吗？

乙：有有有。 这是大号的。这是加大号的。

甲：好，我买一顶大号的。

9 甲：我有三块糖：一块橘红色的、一块咖啡色的、
一块黄色的。给你一块。你要哪块？

乙：我要第一块。

甲：第一块是橘红色的。好，给你。

10 甲：这两瓶水，怎么大的便宜，小的贵？

乙：对啊！小瓶比大瓶贵。我也不知道为什么。

甲：那我们去问问老板吧！

乙：好啊。

9.36 *Match the corresponding simplified characters, traditional characters, and English.*

a. 多少钱	1. 不對	A. *how much (money)*
b. 两百一十块	2. 台幣	B. *RMB*
c. 不对	3. 澳大利亞元	C. *Hong Kong dollar*
d. 对吗	4. 港幣	D. *British pound*
e. 错了	5. 錯了	E. *euro*
f. 澳门元	6. 盧比	F. *Australian dollar*
g. 人民币	7. 英鎊	G. *Macau pataca*
h. 欧元	8. 對嗎	H. *rupee*
i. 英镑	9. 歐元	I. *It's wrong.*
j. 澳大利亚元	10. 兩百一十塊	J. *210 "dollars" [yuan]*
k. 卢比	11. 澳門元	K. *not right*
l. 台币	12. 人民幣	L. *Is that right?*
m. 港币	13. 多少錢	M. *New Taiwan dollar*

9.36 Key:
a. 13. A
b. 10. J
c. 1. K
d. 8. L
e. 5. I
f. 11. G
g. 12. B
h. 9. E
i. 7. D
j. 3. F
k. 6. H
l. 2. M
m. 4. C

9.37 *Match the corresponding simplified characters, traditional characters, and English.*

a. 买	1. 買	A. *long pants*
b. 卖	2. 短褲	B. *the color blue*
c. 贵	3. 長褲	C. *give*
d. 长裤	4. 貴	D. *large size*
e. 短裤	5. 紅色	E. *extra-small size*
f. 一顶帽子	6. 大號	F. *sell*
g. 红色	7. 一頂帽子	G. *buy*
h. 蓝色	8. 給	H. *shorts*
i. 大号	9. 加小號	I. *the color red*
j. 加小号	10. 藍色	J. *expensive*
k. 给	11. 賣	K. *a hat/cap*

9.37 Key:
a. 1. G
b. 11. F
c. 4. J
d. 3. A
e. 2. H
f. 7. K
g. 5. I
h. 10. B
i. 6. D
j. 9. E
k. 8. C

▶ Reading real-life texts

9.38 *Look at the photos. What does each sign mean? Write the letter on the line.*

a.

b.

_____ Closed (literally "Resting")

_____ Open for business

9.39 *Look at the photos. Match the signs with their pinyin.*

a.

b.

c.

_____ Chángtú líng diǎn èr yuán fēn zhōng

_____ Yuán tǒng bīngqílín sān yuán

_____ Xǐ jiǎn chuī shí yuán, jiē fà liù bǎi yuán

Now fill in the blanks to complete the English translation of the signs.

d. Ice cream cone: ¥ _____

e. _____, cut, and blow-dry: _____ 10; _____ extensions: _____ 600

f. Long-distance calls: _____ per _____

9.40 *Look at the photo. What does the sign say about the price of the product? Fill in the blanks.*

Chāo dī tèjià 78 yuán/píng

Extra low special price _____

per _____

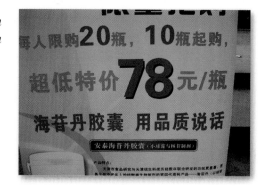

9.41 *Look at the photo. The Chinese word for "club" is jùlèbù* 俱樂部／俱乐部. *Circle the characters for "five color," which also means "multicolored."*

9.41 Key:

five color, multicolored: 五色

▶ Learning to write characters

9.42 *For stroke order and other useful information about each of the following characters from this unit, go to the* Character Writing Workbook. *Choose either traditional or simplified characters and practice writing them until you can reproduce them on demand.*

買／买，賣／卖，黑，紅／红，白，金，銀／银，少，元，太，
貴／贵，便，宜，夠／够，能，比，跟，給／给

▶ Writing a note

9.43 *Write a few sentences to a friend, telling him or her about some recent purchases you made; include details such as price, color, and size.*

9.43 • If students are ready, encourage them to write their paragraphs in characters, skipping the pinyin step.

• Remind students to use the vocabulary list on pages 238–239.

• When they finish writing, partners should proofread each other's drafts before handing them in.

• If time allows (and with students' consent), collect and randomly distribute students' notes in class. Have students write short responses to the letters they receive.

Cultural Bits 文化点滴

Shopping and handling money

View the video segment "Shopping and handling money" and then discuss the following questions with your classmates.

- *Zuì dī jiàgé* 最低價格／最低价格 means "the lowest price." How would you use this phrase in bargaining?

- Discuss different situations in which you might or might not bargain.

- Make a list of everything you might say while bargaining.

Recap

▶ Grammar

Money measure words

Here are some examples of money measure words. Pinyin words in parentheses may be omitted in speech.

wǔ kuài (qián) (*five "dollars," ¥5.00*)
wǔ kuài wǔ (máo qián) (*five "dollars" and fifty "cents," ¥5.50*)
wǔ kuài wǔ máo wǔ (fēn qián) (*five "dollars" and fifty-five "cents," ¥5.55*)

In the written language—on signs indicating prices, receipts, etc.—the word *yuán* is used in place of *kuài*, and the word *jiǎo* is used in place of *máo*.

三元三角三分 OR 3.33元

Comparison: Review and expansion

Use *bǐ* + *yìdiǎnr* or *de duō* to compare two things.

Zhèige bǐ nèige dà yìdiǎnr. (*This one is a bit bigger than that one.*)
Zhèige bǐ nèige dà de duō. (*This one is much bigger than that one.*)

Use *gēn . . . yíyàng* to say that two things are the same or similar.

Zhèige gēn nèige yíyàng dà. (*This one and that one are the same size.*)

To express the negative, it's most common to use *méiyǒu . . . nàme.*

Zhèige méiyǒu nèige nàme dà. (*This one is not as big as that one.*)

Remember, don't use *hěn* when making comparisons.

~~Zhèige bǐ nèige hěn dà.~~

More "colorful" grammar

Note the various ways of expressing colors.

báisè (*the color white*)
bái yánsè (*the color white*)
bái de (*white [ones]*)

Remember that if a color is used to describe a noun, add the modifying particle *de* before the noun if the color term is more than one syllable. Thus, "a black cap/hat" can be:

hēi màozi
hēisè de màozi
hēi yánsè de màozi

▶ Vocabulary (*Starred items are for review.*)

Money

fēn 分 a measure word for 1/100 of the primary monetary unit; "cent"

jiǎo 角 written form of the measure word for 1/10 of the primary monetary unit; "dime"

kuài 塊／块 spoken form of the measure word for the primary monetary unit; "dollar"

máo 毛 spoken form of the measure word for 1/10 of the primary monetary unit; "dime"

qián 錢／钱 money

yuán 元 written form of the measure word for the primary monetary unit; "dollar"

Currencies

Àomén yuán 澳門元／澳门元 Macau pataca

Àoyuán 澳元 Australian dollar

Gǎngbì 港幣／港币 Hong Kong dollar

Jiānádà yuán 加拿大元 Canadian dollar

Lúbǐ 盧比／卢比 rupee (India and Pakistan)

Měijīn 美金 U.S. dollar

Ōuyuán 歐元／欧元 euro

Rénmínbì 人民幣／人民币 People's money (People's Republic of China)

Rìyuán 日元 Japanese yen

Táibì 台幣／台币 New Taiwan dollar

Yīngbàng 英鎊／英镑 British pound

Consumer items (with measure words)

chángkù (tiáo) 長褲／长裤 (條／条) pants, trousers

duǎnkù (tiáo) 短褲／短裤 (條／条) shorts

màozi (dǐng) 帽子 (頂／顶) hat/cap

shuǐ (píng, bēi) 水 (瓶，杯) water (bottle, glass)

táng (xiē, kuài) 糖 (些，塊／块) candy (some, piece)

T-xù shān (jiàn) T-恤衫 (件) T-shirt

yīfu (jiàn) 衣服 (件) clothing

Colors

báisè 白色 white

fěnhóngsè 粉紅色／粉红色 pink

hēisè 黑色 black

hóngsè 紅色／红色 red

huángsè 黃色 yellow

huīsè 灰色 gray

jīnsè 金色 gold

júhóngsè 橘紅色／橘红色 orange

kāfēisè 咖啡色 brown, coffee color

lánsè 藍色／蓝色 blue

lǜsè 綠色／绿色 green

mǐsè 米色 beige

yínsè 銀色／银色 silver

zǐsè 紫色 purple

Sizes

dàhào 大號／大号 large

jiādàhào 加大號／加大号 extra large

jiāxiǎohào 加小號／加小号 extra small

xiǎohào 小號／小号 small

zhōnghào 中號／中号 medium

Question words

duōshao* 多少 how many, how much (usually more than ten)

jǐ* 幾／几 how many (usually fewer than ten)

zěnme* 怎麼／怎么 how, how could

zěnmeyàng* 怎麼樣／怎么样 how, how does that sound to you (after a proposal or suggestion)

Stative verbs (adjectives)

duō 多 many, much

gāo* 高 tall, high

guì 貴／贵 expensive

piányi 便宜 inexpensive, cheap

shǎo 少 few

xíng* 行 OK, all right, acceptable

yíyàng* 一樣／一样 same, identical, alike

Verbs

chuān 穿 wear, put on, dress

gěi 給／给 give to

huā 花 spend

huàn 換／换 exchange, change

mǎi 買／买 buy

mài 賣／卖 sell

Coverbs

bǐ* 比 compare to (used to compare)

gēn* 跟 with, and (used to compare)

Adverbs

jiù 就 only

tài . . . (le) 太……(了) too, overly, extremely

yígòng 一共 altogether, in all, in total

Auxiliary (helping) verbs

děi* 得 must, have to

huì* 會／会 can (do a learned activity); will, might

kěn 肯 willing to

kěyǐ* 可以 may, permit to

néng* 能 able to, can (if circumstances permit)

xiǎng* 想 would like to

yào* 要 going to, will, want to

Pronouns

nèige* 那個／那个 that, that one

zhèige* 這個／这个 this, this one

Prefixes

dì 第 (for ordinal numbers)

▶ Checklist of "can do" statements

After completing this unit, you should be able to perform each of the following tasks.

Listening and speaking

☐ Indicate your interest in a particular item for sale.

☐ Ask the price of an item.

☐ Understand prices that are given to you.

☐ Express your desire, or lack of desire, to purchase an item.

☐ Indicate specific characteristics (color, size, etc.) of your desired purchase.

☐ Ask the total price of several items.

☐ Say how much you are paying in a transaction.

☐ Close a transaction appropriately.

☐ Understand various terms for currency.

☐ Use appropriate bargaining expressions.

Reading and writing

☐ Understand simple declarative sentences related to money and shopping.

☐ Understand key information on signs related to products for sale.

☐ Write a brief note listing purchases that were made or are planned.

Understanding culture

☐ Visit a local Chinese grocery store or shop and buy something using your Chinese.

Checklist

• Have students work in pairs to go through this checklist and demonstrate selected skills to the class. Reserve 20–30 minutes for students to complete this activity. Tell students that putting check marks in each box is NOT the point. The point is to check if they can really do the things on the list.

• Once students have completed the checklist, revisit the lists they made for exercises 9.2 and 9.15. Have they learned enough Chinese to say everything?

UNIT 10

"Good quality at a low price"

价廉物美

Jiàliánwùměi

Getting around town to shop

In this unit, you will learn how to:

- state where you go to shop for certain things.
- ask for and interpret directions to stores and within stores.
- provide simple directions as requested.
- understand and follow directions as given.
- handle basic shopping transactions.
- understand key information on signs related to shopping.
- discuss modes of transportation.
- read and write simple sentences regarding purchases.

Encounter 1 | Picking a store

As a homework assignment before starting Unit 10, ask students to flip through the unit to preview the content.

 10.1 *View Episode 10 of the dramatic series.*

10.2 *Getting ready: What do you most often shop for, and where do you go to shop?*

_____

10.1 • Before watching Episode 10, ask students what they remember from previous episodes. Encourage them to respond in Chinese and English.

• Play the video clip twice, if necessary.

• Allow time for students to discuss the video among themselves. Understanding the plot is crucial for students to complete the unit's exercises.

10.3 *Watch and listen to the video segment. What do you think is the meaning of* Zuìhǎo dào nǎr qù mǎi yīfu? 最好到哪兒去買衣服？／最好到哪儿去买衣服？ *Write the English translation below.*

_____

10.2 • Have the class create a poster with two lists: "I like to buy . . ." and "I often shop at . . ."

• Hang the poster on the wall. After students have completed the unit, revisit the poster and check if they have learned enough Chinese to say everything on the poster.

10.4 *Match the corresponding items.*

a. gòuwù zhōngxīn   1. 商店   A. *store*

b. shāngdiàn   2. 百貨商店／百货商店   B. *shopping center*

c. bǎihuò shāngdiàn   3. 購物中心／购物中心   C. *department store*

Note: A group of *shāngdiàn* 商店 clustered together is called a *shāngchǎng* 商場／商场—a shopping mall. A larger shopping mall becomes a *bǎihuò shāngchǎng* 百貨商場／百货商场, which is similar to a *gòuwù zhōngxīn* 購物中心／购物中心.

10.3–10.4

• Have students glance at these two exercises before they watch the video.

• If students have difficulties with exercise 10.3, see if anyone can guess the meaning of *zuìhǎo* ("the best") and *dào . . . qù* ("to go to . . .").

• For exercise 10.4, tell students to pay attention to the buildings in the video to determine the meaning of these words.

FYI 供你参考

Shopping in China: Then and now

Gone are the days when travelers visiting China from abroad were advised to shop in what were known as Friendship Stores. Called *Yǒuyì Shāngdiàn* 友誼商店／友谊商店, these stores were for foreigners only; they are now only a faint reminder of the socialist China that existed before the country became a shopper's paradise. With the rapid economic growth China has experienced during the past generation, both overseas visitors and Chinese citizens can now afford to shop for almost anything imaginable. The country has witnessed a veritable explosion of Chinese department stores, malls, and markets, as well as a wide variety of foreign stores, ranging from Walmart all the way up to Christie's and Sotheby's.

Gone also is the special currency (*wàihuìjuàn* 外匯卷／外汇卷) issued by the government for use by foreigners; it's now *Rénmínbì* 人民幣／人民币 for all. The change in currency regulations that permitted visitors free access to buy anything anywhere sounded the closing bell for most of China's Friendship Stores. Indeed, Beijing's Friendship Store has since given way to a modern luxury hotel.

So where should one shop? The most interesting places are the bustling local markets and shopping alleys. They are also where you can find the best prices. Great deals and wonderful treasures are usually only as far away as the next pushcart, hastily set up stall, or tattered blanket laid on the ground. Visit these local places, use your Chinese, and bargain for the best price. You'll be rewarded, not only with a cheaper price but also with an invaluable learning experience. Buy Chinese and learn Chinese!

10.3 Key:

Where is the best place to buy clothes?

10.4 Key:

a. 3. B
b. 1. A
c. 2. C

Shopping in China: Then and now

To check comprehension of this material, stimulate a class discussion by asking clarification questions, such as: What are *Yǒuyì Shāngdiàn* and *wàihuìjuàn*? Do they still exist in China today? Where should today's visitors to China go shopping for the best prices or variety? What are some shopping tips you have learned from this FYI?

Alternatively, you may choose to explore a local department store or convenience store. These are likely to be full of both familiar and unfamiliar goods. Many Western and Japanese products are available to Chinese consumers. You'll notice that no one bargains at these places. These stores are staffed by employees earning a monthly salary who have no authority to set or adjust prices. If you ask for a price reduction, you'll quickly be refused.

Some shopping tips:

- Don't be surprised if fellow shoppers take a good deal of interest in you, especially in smaller towns or in the countryside. Appreciate their interest and try out a bit of your Chinese. You may occasionally feel as if your personal space is being invaded, but do your best to remain calm and accommodating. Enjoy the experience!

- If possible, shop in the company of local friends. They can give you a sense of where to shop, how much things should cost, what to look for in quality, and how and where to bargain.

- If you spot something you really want in a local market, buy it immediately; you may not be able to find it again later. You can ship it home, if necessary.

- You can use your credit card (*xìnyòngkǎ* 信用卡) and swipe your card (*shuākǎ* 刷卡) at most major stores.

- If you shop in hotel gift shops and upscale department stores for comfort and convenience, bear in mind that prices will probably be inflated.

- Wherever and whenever you shop, remember that a smile will buy you more good-will than any amount of *Rénmínbì*, *Gǎngbì*, or *Táibì* ever can.

 10.5 *Listen to the audio segment. Then match the traditional and simplified characters.*

a. chènshān 襯衫   1. 运动服

b. jiákè 夾克   2. 外套

c. yùndòngfú 運動服   3. 衬衫

d. qúnzi 裙子   4. 毛衣

e. máoyī 毛衣   5. 夹克

f. wàitào 外套   6. 裙子

10.6 *Where do you like to shop for shirts? Fill in the blanks below, in English, with the name of your favorite store.*

Wǒ xǐhuan dào _____ qù mǎi chènshān.

我喜歡到_____去買襯衫。 ╱

我喜欢到_____去买衬衫。

Following the pattern above, list places where you like to shop for different clothing items. If you like to shop online, use a variation of the following:

Wǒ xǐhuan shàngwǎng mǎi jiákè.

我喜歡上網買夾克。 ╱我喜欢上网买夹克。

_____

_____

_____

_____

Grammar Bits 语法点滴

Readying the action: Using coverbs

Although "going places" can be expressed quite simply in Chinese in a **subject + qù + place** format (e.g., *Wǒ qù shāngdiàn.* = "I'm going to the store."), a coverb is just as often used, particularly in more complex sentences involving purpose or follow-up activities.

Coverbs precede the main verb in a sentence. There are many coverbs in Chinese, and they can all be translated by English prepositions such as "to," "from," "on," "at," etc.

To express motion to an intended place, use the coverb *dào* (to) plus the destination with the verbs *qù* (go) or *lái* (come).

Thus: **Subject + *dào* + place + *qù/lái* + purpose**

Examples:

Tā dào shāngdiàn qù mǎi yīfu. *(She is going to the store to buy some clothes.)*

Tā dào xuéxiào lái kàn wǒmen. *(She is coming to school to see us.)*

If you're not "going there," add the negative *bù* to the coverb.

Tā búdào shāngdiàn qu. *(She is not going to the store.)*

Other adverbs and auxiliary verbs can also appear directly before the coverb.

Tā yào dào Zhōngguó qù kàn qīnqi. *(She wants/intends/will go to China to see her relatives.)*

Tā bù xiǎng dào Zhōngguó qù gōngzuò. *(She doesn't feel like going to China to work.)*

Usually when you "go" or "come," your action is purposeful. The position of the purpose in the Chinese sentence reflects something important about Chinese grammar: sentences are usually arranged in chronological order. In other words, you have to arrive at a place before you can achieve your purpose; thus, the "purpose" follows the action of going or coming.

Note that the verbs *lai* and *qu* are usually toneless when used at the end of a sentence. Additional coverbs will be introduced later in this unit.

10.7 *Pair work:* Ask your partner, Nǐ xǐhuan dào nǎr qù mǎi yīfu? 你喜歡到哪兒去買衣服？／你喜欢到哪儿去买衣服？ *Take notes on his or her response.*

_____

_____

_____

Compare your partner's answers with your own. Together, pick two stores where both of you have shopped for clothes, and list them below (you can write the names in English). Your answers should match your partner's.

A: _____　　B: _____

Think about your experiences at these stores, and pick the most appropriate choice below.

☐ Wǒ juéde (A) bǐ (B) hǎo.
我觉得A比B好。／
我覺得A比B好 。

☐ Wǒ juéde (A) méiyǒu (B) hǎo.
我覺得A沒有B好。／
我觉得A没有B好。

☐ Wǒ juéde (A) gēn (B) yíyàng hǎo.
我覺得A跟B一樣好。／
我觉得A跟B一样好。

Check to see which sentence your partner picked. Report your conclusions to another pair or to the class. Try to give a reason for your conclusion (for example, A de dōngxi duō. B de dōngxi piányi).

10.7 • Tell students to take notes in English, as this exercise focuses on listening and speaking, not on reading and writing.

• For the last task, you may need to prepare your students by having them brainstorm possible reasons for why one store is better than another. If necessary, list relevant adjectives on the board for students to use.

• Challenge students to share their reasons aloud in complete sentences. For example: *Wǒ juéde* Old Navy *bǐ* Gap *hǎo, yīnwèi* Old Navy *de yīfu yòu duō yòu piányi.* Have the class listen and respond with agreement or disagreement: *Wǒ tóngyì* or *Wǒ bù tóngyì.*

10.8 *Listen to the audio segment. Match the corresponding items below.*

a.  *athletic shoes*   1. liángxié 涼鞋   A. 高跟鞋

b. *leather [dress] shoes*   2. gāogēnxié 高跟鞋   B. 皮鞋

c. *high-heeled shoes*   3. yùndòngxié 運動鞋   C. 拖鞋

d. *sandals*   4. tuōxié 拖鞋   D. 运动鞋

e. *slippers*   5. píxié 皮鞋   E. 涼鞋

10.9 *Point out that students should supply specific store names as answers. They should write store names in English.*

10.9 Nǐ xǐhuan dào nǎr qù mǎi xié? 你喜歡到哪兒去買鞋？／你喜欢到哪儿去买鞋？ *Fill in the blanks below, in English, with your favorite stores.*

Wǒ xǐhuan dào _____ qù mǎi liángxié, gāogēnxié, hé píxié. (hé = *and*)
我喜歡到_____去買涼鞋、高跟鞋和皮鞋。／
我喜欢到_____去买涼鞋、高跟鞋和皮鞋。

Wǒ xǐhuan dào _____ qù mǎi yùndòngxié.
我喜歡到_____去買運動鞋。／
我喜欢到_____去买运动鞋。

Wǒ xǐhuan dào _____ qù mǎi tuōxié.
我喜歡到_____去買拖鞋。／
我喜欢到_____去买拖鞋。

FYI 供你参考

Chinese taste in clothing: Then and now

Over the past couple decades, the pace of cultural change in China has been dizzying. Perhaps the most obvious change has been in the way Chinese people dress. In the 1960s and 1970s, practically everyone wore the so-called Mao suit, a combination of a close-fitting, high-collared jacket and baggy pants, usually gray, green, or blue. Called *Zhōngshān zhuāng*, curiously named after Sun Yat-Sen (*Sūn Zhōngshān*), "father" of the 1911 revolution that overthrew the imperial system, this outfit was intended to promote egalitarianism. After Mao passed away in 1976, China "opened" to the West, bringing rapid economic growth, an expansion of the middle class, and the end of the Mao suit. Nowadays, Chinese are just as fashionable, chic, and hip as any other citizens of the world. Generally speaking, however, Chinese dress more formally than people in the West. Men favor slacks and button-down shirts, while women prefer skirts, blouses, and dresses. However, as in the rest of the world, jeans are everywhere. Shorts, on both women and men, are becoming more visible, but it is still a good idea not to show too much skin in China. A short stroll down Beijing's most famous shopping street, Wangfujing Avenue, will give you a good idea of what's appropriate and what's not.

Chinese taste in clothing: Then and now

Divide the class into three groups, and provide each group with a guiding question:

1. What are *Zhōngshān zhuāng*? Discuss the history and background of this outfit. If time allows, do a quick Internet search to find relevant pictures and information to present to the class.

2. What do people wear in China today? If time allows, do a quick Internet search to find relevant pictures and information to present to the class.

3. What and where is Wangfujing Avenue? If time allows, do a quick Internet search to find relevant pictures and information to present to the class.

10.10 *Pair work: Ask your partner,* 你喜歡到哪兒去買鞋？／你喜欢到哪儿去买鞋？ *Take notes on his or her answers and then compare them with your own.*

_____

_____

_____

Based on your partner's answers, follow up by saying that your favorite stores are better, by agreeing that your partner's stores are better, or by recognizing that the stores are equal in quality. Give a reason or two to support your response. (For example, you can suggest that a particular store's shoes are better [hǎo 好], cheaper [piányi 便宜], or more numerous [duō 多].)

10.10 • For the last task, you may need to prepare your students by having them brainstorm possible reasons for why one store is better than another. If necessary, list relevant adjectives on the board for students to use.

• Challenge students to share their reasons aloud in complete sentences.

10.11 *Listen to the audio segment. Then match the traditional and simplified characters.*

a.  féizào 肥皂

1. 卫生纸

b.  yáshuā 牙刷

2. 牙膏

c. 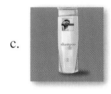 xǐfàshuǐ 洗髮水

3. 牙线

d.  wèishēngzhǐ 衛生紙

4. 牙刷

e.  hùfàsù 護髮素

5. 梳子

f.  shūzi 梳子

6. 洗发水

g.  yáxiàn 牙線

7. 护发素

h.  yágāo 牙膏

8. 毛巾

i.  máojīn 毛巾

9. 肥皂

10.12 *What do you think is the meaning of* Nǐ tōngcháng zài nǎr mǎi rìyòngpǐn? 你通常在哪兒買日用品？／你通常在哪儿买日用品？ *Complete the following English translation.*

Where do you generally _____?

Fill in the blank below with the English name of a store where you usually shop.

Wǒ tōngcháng zài _____ mǎi yágāo.

我通常在_____買牙膏。／我通常在_____买牙膏。

Based on the model above, write three more sentences about where you might shop for various items for everyday use (assuming you wouldn't shop for everything at the same store).

_____

_____

_____

10.13 *Pair work: Ask your partner,* 你通常在哪兒買日用品？／你通常在哪儿买日用品？ *Compare his or her answer with your own.*

_____

_____

_____

Based on your partner's answer, say that your favorite store is better, agree that his or her favorite store is better, or say that the two stores are the same. Then give a reason or two to support your response. If you shop at the same store, be sure to indicate this by saying Wǒmen zài tóngyàng de dìfang mǎi rìyòngpǐn.

10.12 • Make sure students understand the meaning of the question and can correctly complete the English translation. (Where do you generally buy products for everyday use?)

• Ask students to glean the meaning of *tōngcháng* from the English translation. ("generally")

• Tell students to write their store names in English.

• Remind students to refer to previous exercises for language items they can use in this exercise.

10.13 Encourage students to use language items they used in exercises 10.7 and 10.10 to complete this task..

10.14 *Listen to the audio segment. Then match the traditional and simplified characters.*

a.  bǐjìběn 筆記本　　1. 电脑

b.  zhǐ 紙　　2. 笔记本

c.  bǐ 筆　　3. 纸

d.  míngxìnpiàn 明信片　　4. 笔

e.  diànnǎo 電腦　　5. 明信片

f.  jìniànpǐn 紀念品　　6. 纪念品

10.15 Remind students that this exercise is asking for specific store names in English.

10.15 Nǐ tōngcháng dào nǎr qù mǎi diànnǎo, wénjù hé jìniànpǐn? 你通常到哪兒去買電腦、文具和紀念品？／你通常到哪儿去买电脑、文具和纪念品？ *Fill in the blanks below with the names, in English, of your favorite stores for these items. Note:* Qítā 其他 *means "other."* Wénjù 文具 *means "stationery."*

Wǒ tōngcháng dào _____ qù mǎi bǐjìběn, zhǐ, bǐ hé qítā wénjù.

我通常到_____去買筆記本、紙、筆和其他文具。／
我通常到_____去买笔记本、纸、笔和其他文具。

Wǒ tōngcháng dào _____ qù mǎi diànnǎo.

我通常到_____去買電腦。／
我通常到_____去买电脑。

Wǒ tōngcháng dào _____ qù mǎi míngxìnpiàn hé qítā jìniànpǐn.

我通常到_____去買明信片和其他紀念品。／
我通常到_____去买明信片和其他纪念品。

10.16 *Pair work: Ask your partner,* 你通常到哪兒去買電腦、文具和紀念品？／你通常到哪儿去买电脑、文具和纪念品？ *Compare his or her answers with your own from the previous exercise.*

Based on these answers, you may want to follow up by saying that your favorite stores are better, by agreeing that your partner's stores are better, or by saying that they are the same. Then give a reason or two to support your response.

10.16 • Tell students that their task here is the same as in exercises 10.7, 10.10, and 10.13.

• Encourage students to recycle and use the language items introduced in previous exercises.

Grammar Bits 语法点滴

The measure of the thing

You already know measure words such as *ge* 個／个 (general use), *tiáo* 條／条 (used for long, thin things like pants), *jiàn* 件 (used for general clothing), and *dǐng* 頂／顶 (used for hats). For all the objects introduced in this Encounter, the standard rule applies: if you don't know the specific measure word, use *ge* 個／个, but if you can manage, learn the specific measure word and use it in conjunction with the noun. The following are some more specific measure words you will find useful as your vocabulary develops.

All the clothing items in this Encounter use *jiàn* 件, except *qúnzi* (skirt) and *kùzi* (pants), which use *tiáo* 條／条. Since shoes come in pairs, they take the measure word *shuāng* 雙／双 (pair), unless you are specifically talking about only one shoe (i.e., "Where's my left shoe? I've lost a shoe!"), in which case you would use *zhī* 隻／只. (Note that the traditional character is half of the traditional character for "pair.")

Personal grooming items are more complex. Toothbrushes and toothpaste (like pencils and pens) are stick-like objects and take the measure word *zhī* 支 (twig). Shampoo and conditioner come in bottles and take the measure word *píng* 瓶 (bottle). Soap (like candy and metal coins) is made in a big vat, hardened, and then processed into usable pieces, and therefore is matched with the measure word *kuài* 塊／块 (piece). Toilet paper comes in a roll and therefore takes the measure word *juǎn* 卷 (roll). A comb (as well as an umbrella and the Olympic torch) is held in your fist, and is measured with *bǎ* 把 (to grab). Most Chinese towels are narrow and long and, like pants, are matched with *tiáo* 條／条. As for dental floss, the measure word depends on how the floss is sold: if it's in a hard, box-like container as in the United States, the measure word is *hé* 盒 (box); if it's in a plastic bag as in China, the measure word is *bāo* 包 (packet). However, if you are talking about a length of floss you have broken off and are holding in your hands, you have a *gēn* 根 (root) of floss.

Office supplies, paper, and name cards (as well as photographs and pictures) are flat sheets and measured with *zhāng* 張／张. A notebook, like a book, is measured with *běn* 本, and computers are measured with *tái* 台.

These measure words are a lot to remember, but give yourself time. If you get them wrong, don't worry; you'll still be comprehensible, but you might sound funny, as if you were talking about a "flock of children feeding a group of chickens" or a "herd of soldiers walking by a platoon of cattle."

Grammar Bits

• Measure words were briefly introduced in Units 3 and 5 (pages 72 and 119). This section explores the topic in greater depth and aims to give students a better grasp on its usage.

• Review the concept of measure words by asking, "Do we use measure words in English? What are some examples?" (an ear of corn, a cup of coffee, etc.) "Do we use measure words in Chinese? What are some examples?" (*yī běn shū, yī ge zhōngtóu*, etc.) "What is the difference between the usage of measure words in English and Chinese?" (Chinese uses a measure word for every noun.)

• After students have read this Grammar Bits section, have the class make a collaborative "measure word dictionary" on poster paper. Divide the class into three groups, and tell them to identify measure words for clothing, personal grooming products, and stationery items, respectively.

• Hang the poster on the classroom wall for future reference.

Encounter 2 Giving and following directions

10.17 *Getting ready: How do you give someone directions to somewhere?*

_____

_____

10.18 *Watch and listen to the video segment. Then match the corresponding items.*

a. *turn left*

b. *turn right*

c. *go straight ahead*

d. *go two blocks*

e. *It's not far from here.*

f. *It's very close to here.*

g. *It's one mile (away).*

h. *the third traffic light*

i. *two blocks away*

1. wǎng zuǒ guǎi 往左拐

2. wǎng qián zǒu 往前走

3. dì sān ge hónglǜdēng 第三個紅綠燈

4. lí zhèr yì lǐ lù 離這兒一里路

5. lí zhèr hěn jìn 離這兒很近

6. wǎng yòu guǎi 往右拐

7. lí zhèr bù yuǎn 離這兒不遠

8. guò liǎng tiáo jiē 過兩條街

9. lí zhèr liǎng tiáo jiē 離這兒兩條街

A. 离这儿不远

B. 离这儿很近

C. 往左拐

D. 往前走

E. 往右拐

F. 过两条街

G. 离这儿两条街

H. 第三个红绿灯

I. 离这儿一里路

Note: *lǐ* 里 (Chinese mile) is about 1/3 of an English mile.

Grammar Bits 语法点滴

More about coverbs and the locative verb *zài*

Use the coverb *wǎng*, meaning "toward," with verbs such as *zǒu* (go) and *guǎi* (turn) to indicate motion in the direction of a place that is not one's final destination.

> Wǎng zuǒ/yòu zǒu. *(Go to the left/right.)*
> Wǎng zuǒ/yòu guǎi. *(Turn to the left/right.)*

Use *cóng*, meaning "from," to indicate from where an action originates.

> Cóng zhèr wǎng qián zǒu. *(Go straight from here.)*
> Cóng shūdiàn wǎng zuǒ guǎi. *(Turn left from/at the bookstore.)*

Use the verb *zài*, meaning "at, in, on," to express location at a place, following this pattern:

Subject + *zài* + place

"The subject is at the place."

> Shāngdiàn zài zhèr. *(The store is here.)*
> Tā bú zài nàr. *(She's not over there.)*
> Nǐ zài nǎr? *(Where are you?)*

Use the coverb *lí*, meaning "separated/distant from," to separate one place from another, following this pattern:

Place 1 + *lí* + place 2 + *yuǎn* / *jìn* / (number) *lǐ lù*

"Place 1 is far from Place 2." /

"Place 1 is near Place 2." /

"Place 1 is (number) miles from Place 2."

Caution: Qualifying adverbs (*hěn*, *bù*, etc.) are placed before the stative verb (*yuǎn*, *jìn*).

> Wǒ jiā lí shāngchǎng bù yuǎn. *(My home is not far from the mall.)*
> Běijīng lí Huáshèngdùn hěn yuǎn. *(Beijing is very far away from Washington, D.C.)*
> Wǒ jiā lí gòuwù zhōngxīn yì lǐ lù. *(My house is a mile from the shopping center.)*

Grammar Bits

• Divide the class into four groups, and assign one of the coverbs from this section (*wǎng, cóng, zài, lí*) to each group. Groups should become "experts" on their assigned coverb and teach the class how to use the words in a sentence.

• Have groups create a collaborative class poster titled "Coverb Dictionary." Hang the poster on the wall for future reference.

• If necessary, model using one of the words in a complete sentence. For example: *Wǒ dào shāngdiàn qù mǎi yágāo.*

10.19 *Pair work:* *Work with a partner. Look at the map, pick a destination, and write it here:*

_____

Give your partner directions to this destination without naming it. If your partner follows your directions and arrives at the destination you intended, then you both did well! If not, go over your directions together and see where you went wrong. Then reverse roles and repeat the process.

1. Dì-wǔ Xiǎoxué
   第五小學／第五小学
   (No. 5 Elementary School)

2. Dì-yī Zhōngxué
   第一中學／第一中学
   (No. 1 High School)

3. Hépíng Gòuwù Zhōngxīn
   和平購物中心／和平购物中心
   (Peace Shopping Center)

4. Rénrén Biànlìdiàn
   人人便利店
   (Everyone's Convenience Store)

5. Sānxīng Chāoshì
   三星超市
   (Three Stars Supermarket)

6. Yǒuyì Shāngdiàn
   友誼商店／友谊商店
   (Friendship Store)

7. Yuǎndōng Bǎihuò Shāngchǎng
   遠東百貨商場／远东百货商场
   (Far East Shopping Mall)

8. Zhōngguó Yínháng
   中國銀行／中国银行
   (Bank of China)

9. Zhōng-Měi Fúzhuāng Gōngsī
   中美服裝公司／中美服装公司
   (China-U.S. Apparel Company)

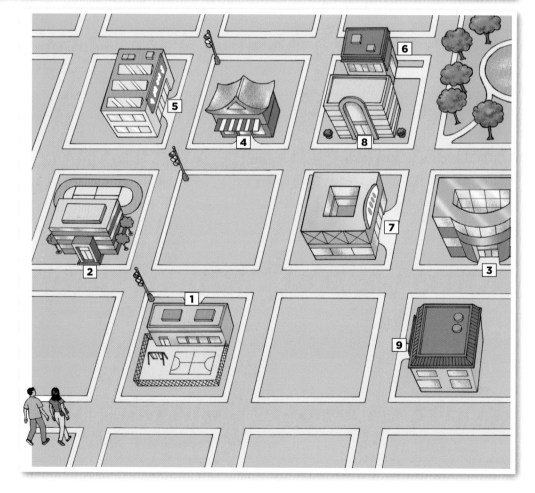

Bonus: What do you think is the meaning of wǎng húi zǒu 往回走*?*

Answer: _____

Encounter 3 Managing directions

10.20 *Watch and listen to the video segment. Then match the corresponding items.*

a.   1. dōngběi 東北   A. 东

b.   2. nán 南   B. 西

c.   3. běi 北   C. 西南

d.   4. dōng 東   D. 东南

e.   5. dōngnán 東南   E. 南

f.   6. xī 西   F. 北

g.   7. xīběi 西北   G. 东北

h.   8. xīnán 西南   H. 西北

10.20 Preteach the word *tàiyáng* ("sun") before students watch the video. It may help them to better understand the context of the new vocabulary.

10.20 Key:
a. 4. A
b. 2. E
c. 6. B
d. 3. F
e. 1. G
f. 5. D
g. 8. C
h. 7. H

10.21 *Write the English meaning of* Qǐng gàosu wǒ zěnme zǒu 請告訴我怎麼走／请告诉我怎么走。

10.21 Key:
Please tell me how to get there.

10.22 *Pair work: Work with a partner. Choose one of the destinations shown below. Have your partner start at the X, and then give him or her directions to the destination. Your partner will first ask* Zěnme zǒu? *and you should reply with* Wǎng [direction] zǒu. *Your partner should then answer with* Dào [place] le. *If this is right, say* Duì le, *and then switch roles. If this is wrong, start over. Repeat the activity several times.*

(Note: Don't try to memorize the names of the destinations now. These terms are the subject of a later lesson.)

diànyǐngyuàn

yīyuàn

xuéxiào

gōngyuán

X

fànguǎn

huǒchēzhàn

jiāyóuzhàn

chāojí shìchǎng

Encounter 4 | Discussing modes of transportation

10.23 *Getting ready: How do you move around town? Make a list of a few modes of transportation.*

_____

_____

_____

_____

10.24 *Watch and listen to the video segment. Then match the corresponding items.*

a.    1. zuò gōnggòngqìchē 坐公共汽車   A.开车

b.    2. kāichē 開車   B.走路

c.    3. zǒulù 走路   C.打的

d.    4. qí zìxíngchē 騎自行車   D.坐火车

e.    5. qí mótuōchē 騎摩托車   E.坐地铁

f.    6. zuò dìtiě 坐地鐵   F.騎自行车

g.    7. dǎdī 打的   G.坐公共汽车

h.    8. zuò huǒchē 坐火車   H.騎摩托车

Modes of transportation

Divide the class into three groups, and give each group one of the following tasks:

• Read the FYI to become a "taxi expert." Teach the class all the ways to say *taxi* in Chinese, including the origin of different variations and when to use each one.

• Read the FYI to become a "bus expert." Teach the class all the ways to say *bus* in Chinese, including the origin of different variations and when to use each one.

• Read the FYI to become a "bicycle expert." Teach the class all the ways to say *bicycle* in Chinese, including the origin of different variations and when to use each one.

FYI 供你参考

Modes of transportation

Gōnggòngqìchē 公共汽車／公共汽车 (public bus) is often shortened to *gōngchē* 公車／公车. The term *dǎdī* 打的 (take a cab) comes into Mandarin from Cantonese, in which "*diksi*" 的士 (pronounced like the English word "Dixie") is the transliteration of "taxi." The Cantonese "*dik*" 的 is in this case pronounced *dī* in Mandarin. As you know, it is usually pronounced *de*, as in *wǒ de* 我的. *Dǎ* 打 (literally, "to hit") is the equivalent of the English verb "to catch." The more formal term for "take a taxi" is different in the PRC and Taiwan. In the PRC, the formal term for "taxicab" is *chūzūqìchē* 出租汽車／出租汽车 (literally, "car for rent"), whereas in Taiwan it is *jìchéngchē* 計程車／计程车 (literally, "the car [in which the fare] is calculated based on distance"). "To take" is *zuò* 坐 (literally, "to sit"), but *dǎdī* is far easier and more hip, so this term has become much more popular than either *zuò chūzūqìchē* or *zuò jìchéngchē*.

Also, in the PRC a bicycle is known as a *zìxíngchē* 自行車／自行车—a "self-propelled vehicle"—whereas in Taiwan it is a *jiǎotàchē* 腳踏車／脚踏车—a "foot-pedaled vehicle." Same animal, different coat!

Grammar Bits

• Divide the class into three groups, and assign one of the coverbs from this section (*zuò, dā, qí*) to each group. Groups should become "experts" on their assigned coverb and teach the class how to use the word in a sentence.

• Have groups add these words (and example sentences) to the coverb dictionary poster.

Grammar Bits 语法点滴

Taking a ride with more coverbs—*zuò, dā, qí*

Most of the time when you travel, you travel with the coverb *zuò* 坐 (to ride in a conveyance). Since *zuò*, as a verb (rather than a coverb), means "to sit," it is used with many nouns linked to travel, although in some instances you may not be literally sitting down. Like other coverbs, it is used along with main verbs, such as *qù* (go).

> zuò diàntī *(take an elevator)*
> zuò huǒchē *(take the train)*
> zuò gōngchē qù *(go by bus)*
> zuò dìtiě qù *(go by subway)*

For mass transit, the coverb *dā* 搭 (ride) is used interchangably with *zuò*.

> dā gōngchē *(ride the bus)*
> dā dìtiě *(ride the subway)*

When you ride a bicycle, motorcycle, or horse, you ride astraddle with *qí* 騎／骑.

> qí zìxíngchē *(ride a bike)*

When *zuò* is used with *dào* (to), elements of the sentence are lined up in chronological order.

> Wǒ xiǎng zuò gōnggòngqìchē dào shāngdiàn qù mǎi dōngxi. *(I'd like to take the bus to the store to buy some stuff.)*

10.25 *What do you think is the meaning of* zǒulù yào yí ge zhōngtóu? *Complete the English translation below.*

a. ____________ takes an hour.

b. *Now write the English for the following:* Kāichē zhǐ yào shí fēn zhōng.

____

c. *Write the term for "one hour" in pinyin.* ________________________

d. *Write the term for "one minute" in pinyin.* ________________________

10.25 • Have students use context to guess the meaning of *yào* in this sentence ("need"). Point out that it does not mean "would like to," as they learned in Unit 7.

• Have students use context to guess the meaning of *zhōngtóu* ("hour"). Encourage them to identify a synonym (*xiǎoshí*).

• Have students use context to guess the meaning of *zhǐ* ("only").

10.25 Key:

a. Walking (there) takes an hour.
b. Driving (there) only takes ten minutes.
c. yí ge zhōngtóu / yí ge xiǎoshí
d. yī fēnzhōng

10.26 ***Pair work:*** *How often do you use each of the following modes of transportation? Check the appropriate boxes in the chart below.*

	每天	每個星期／每个星期	每個月／每个月	從來不／从来不
a. 坐公共汽車／坐公共汽车	☐	☐	☐	☐
b. 開車／开车	☐	☐	☐	☐
c. 走路	☐	☐	☐	☐
d. 騎自行車／骑自行车	☐	☐	☐	☐
e. 騎摩托車／骑摩托车	☐	☐	☐	☐
f. 打的	☐	☐	☐	☐
g. 坐地鐵／坐地铁	☐	☐	☐	☐
h. 坐火車／坐火车	☐	☐	☐	☐

10.26 Make sure students understand the meaning of the phrases at the top of each column and of the vocabulary in each row.

10.27 • Point out the sample dialogue in the illustration, and tell students to model their questions and answers on this exchange.

• If necessary, have a confident pair do a demonstration for the class.

• Circulate in the classroom as students complete the activity, and provide guidance and assistance as necessary.

10.27 *Pair work:* Ask your partner how often he or she uses certain modes of transportation. Note his or her answers below.

Nǐ duō cháng shíjiān qí yí cì zìxíngchē?

Wǒ měi tiān qí zìxíngchē.

_____

_____

_____

_____

_____

10.28 • Remind students that the group discussion should be conducted in Chinese *only*.

• To prepare students, brainstorm a list of appropriate language items. Give some suggestions to begin the discussion. For example, they need to know how to ask what others want to buy, state their own preferences, make suggestions, and state disagreements.

• Have groups prepare an oral report of their final appointments and present it to the class.

10.28 *Group work:* Work in groups of three or four. Make an appointment to go shopping. Decide on specifics about: (1) date and time; (2) three items you will shop for; (3) where you are going; (4) how far away your destination is (how many miles); and (5) how you are going to get there. Take notes about your appointments below. Be prepared to report to your group or to the class.

Date and time: _____

Items to shop for: _____ _____ _____

Where: _____

How far: _____

How to get there: _____

FYI供你参考

From bicycle-to-bicycle to bumper-to-bumper

It wasn't too long ago that China was known as the *Zìxíngchē Wángguó* 自行車王國／自行车王国, or the "Kingdom of Bicycles." An entire family riding a single bicycle down the street; someone moving house with seemingly his or her entire life's possessions balanced precariously on board; a farmer pedaling an ancient bicycle to tug a cart loaded down with live chickens from the countryside—all were common sights on the bicycle-crowded streets of Beijing. People from all walks of life in China relied on the humble bicycle, now extolled, at least in the United States, as a "green solution" to sky-high gas prices and environmental pollution, as well as a sure road to fitness and good health. However, in China's capital today, the streets are crowded with another sort of vehicle: the automobile. As the rapidly emerging Chinese middle class embraces four wheels instead of two, China is signaling the beginning of the end of its status as the bicycle kingdom. In Beijing alone, some ten million bicycles now compete with two million cars. China is the fastest-growing market for cars in the world. Gridlock—*sāichē* 塞車／塞车—has officially become part of the Chinese vocabulary, reflecting changes in Chinese life and culture. A word of advice: traveling by bicycle is still the best way to see and experience China, but watch out for other vehicles vying for your space.

From bicycle-to-bicycle . . .

Check comprehension by stimulating a class discussion. Ask:

1. *Zìxíngchē Wángguó* is used to refer to what phenomenon in China?

2. What does *sāichē* mean? Why does it happen in China?

10.29 • Play the video once through without interruption. Have students watch to get the gist: where are the two characters in the video and what are they doing? (In a department store, shopping.)

• Play the video again. Have students watch for details to answer these questions: What specific tasks are

Encounter 5 Moving around within a department store

10.29 *Watch and listen to the video segment. Match the corresponding items below.*

a. *in front*	1. zuǒbian 左邊	A. 前面	10.29 Key:
b. *in back*	2. qiánmian 前面	B. 中间	a. 2. A
c. *in the center*	3. yòubian 右邊	C. 后面	b. 5. C
d. *to the left*	4. zhōngjiān 中間	D. 左边	c. 4. B
e. *to the right*	5. hòumian 後面	E. 右边	d. 1. D
			e. 3. E

the characters trying to accomplish in the department store? (They try to figure out where things are in the store, discuss which floor to go to, find items on sale, and decide how to make a payment.)

• Lead a discussion in English about the plot. Understanding the plot (gist and details) will help students complete the exercises in this Encounter.

10.30 *Pair work: Work with a partner. Take five blocks (or squares of colored paper) in five different colors, and sit back-to-back with your partner. Position four blocks on each side of the fifth, central block, like this:*

X

X X X

X

Describe your color pattern for your partner, so that he or she can re-create it with his or her blocks. For example, say Hóng de zài zhōngjiān, huáng de zài zuǒbian, bái de zài qiánmian. *If your partner is successful in re-creating your pattern, reverse roles. If your patterns aren't identical, do the exercise over!*

10.30 • Prepare sets of colored paper/blocks, as described in the exercise, for students to use.

• Demonstrate this activity before asking students to do it in pairs. Tell students that they will organize the blocks/paper into a pattern and tell you how they should be positioned.

• Leave the room briefly so students can secretly discuss and agree on a pattern.

• Have students give you instructions "popcorn style." Make sure not to predict what your students are trying to say. Pretend you are a monolingual Chinese speaker. If their instructions don't make sense, respond with, "*Wǒ bù dǒng.*" Students should work together to correct their mistakes and help you create the intended pattern.

• After the demonstration, have students perform this activity multiple times.

10.31 Remind students that they encountered *shàng* and *xià* in the Unit 3 vocabulary words *shàngwǔ* and *xiàwǔ*. See if they can make some associations to guess the meaning for *shàngmian* and *xiàmian*.

10.31 Key:
above
below

10.32 Key:
a. 2. A
b. 1. B

10.31 *Can you guess what the following terms mean? Write the English.*

a. shàngmian 上面 _____

b. xiàmian 下面 _____ _____

10.32 *Match the corresponding items below.*

| a. *fifth floor* | 1. wǔ céng 五層 | A. 五楼 |
| b. *five floors* | 2. wǔ lóu 五樓 | B. 五层 |

Fill in the blanks using numerals, and then write the English meanings of the sentences.

c. Wǒ sùshè (dorm) yǒu _____ céng. Wǒ zhù _____ lóu.

_____

d. Wǒmen de jiàoxuélóu (classroom building) yǒu _____ céng. Wǒ zài _____ lóu shàngkè.

_____

Note: Don't be confused. *Sān lóu* 三樓／三楼 means "the third floor," even without the ordinal prefix *dì* 第. (Remember *dì sān cì* 第三次 "the third time"?) Example: "Go to the third floor" 到三樓去／到三楼去.

10.33 Pair work: *Ask your partner,* Nǐ jiā yǒu jǐ céng? Nǐ zhù jǐ lóu? 你家有幾層？你住幾樓？／你家有几层？你住几楼？ *Then compare your answers. If there's time, repeat with other people in your class. Take notes on everyone's answers.*

10.34 This exercise demonstrates how sale prices are calculated and represented in China. If students are confused, you may need to provide more examples (write the ones below on the board) to help them see the underlying pattern.

40% off = dǎ liù zhé
30% off = dǎ qī zhé
25% off = dǎ qīwǔ zhé
15% off = dǎ bāwǔ zhé

10.34 Key:
a. 1. B
b. 2. A

10.34 *Watch and listen to the video segment from exercise 10.29 again. Figure out the sales, and match the corresponding items.*

| a. *big sale* | 1. dà jiǎnjià 大減價 | A. 打六折 |
| b. *40 percent off* | 2. dǎ liù zhé 打六折 | B. 大减价 |

Note: You might have noticed that, in Chinese, the amount of a discount is expressed in reverse ratio to the English. Thus, *bā zhé* 八折 means "20 percent off," and *èr zhé* 二折 means "80 percent off."

10.35 *Look at the clothes you are wearing and other items in your possession. Think of three items that you bought on sale and try to remember how much the sale price was discounted. Complete the chart below. Write in English if you don't know how to say the items in Chinese. Fill in the discounted amount according to the "Chinese style" by writing a figure in the blank between the Chinese characters.*

Item   **Discount**

_____   打_____折

_____   打_____折

_____   打_____折

10.36 *Pair work: Tell your partner about your three items. For example, you might say Zhèi ge dǎ qī-wǔ zhé (This was 25 percent off) or Zhèi ge dǎ jiǔ zhé (This was 10 percent off). Take notes about your partner's items below.*

_____

Compare your answers to see who obtained the biggest discount.

10.37 *Figure out payments. Match the corresponding items below.*

a. *pay*
b. *cash*
c. *pay in cash*
d. *credit card*
e. *pay with a credit card*

1. xìnyòngkǎ 信用卡
2. xiànjīn 现金
3. fùqián 付錢
4. fù xiànjīn 付现金
5. shuākǎ 刷卡

A. 现金
B. 付现金
C. 刷卡
D. 信用卡
E. 付钱

10.37 You may want to play the video for this Encounter again before students do this exercise. Have students preview the listed words before they watch the video so they will know what to watch and listen for.

10.37 Key:
a. 3. E
b. 2. A
c. 4. B
d. 1. D
e. 5. C

10.38 Have the class brainstorm/review ways to state payment preferences. Invite students to offer their suggestions "popcorn style." Possibilities include:

Wǒ xǐhuan shuākǎ.
Wǒ tōngcháng dōu fù xiànjīn.
Wǒ juéde yòng xìnyòngkǎ zuì fāngbiàn.

10.38 *Write three sentences (in pinyin) about your preferred method of payment. For example:* Wǒ hěn shǎo shuākǎ.

_____
_____
_____

10.39 *Pair work: Share your sentences with your partner. Write your partner's sentences below.*

_____
_____
_____

🎵 **Unit Rap**

Go to the **Encounters** *website at www.EncountersChinese.com and listen to the song to review key expressions from Unit 10. Listen again and sing along!*

Encounter 6 Reading and writing

▶ Reading familiar sentences in Chinese characters

10.40 • Avoid reading the dialogue aloud for your students or having them repeat after you. Tell them to use the English and familiar characters as bridges to determine the meaning and pronunciation of unknown characters.

• Keep in mind that reading fluency is not the goal of this activity. Tell students to not get discouraged if they have trouble reading quickly and accurately.

• Have students complete this exercise multiple times before they move on to 10.41 and 10.42.

10.40 *Pair work: Read the following dialogues (written in traditional characters) aloud with a partner, using the English as a guide.*

1 甲：我想去買些衣服。你說到哪兒去買最好？ *(I'd like to go shopping for clothes. Where do you say is the best place to go?)*

乙：甚麼樣的衣服？ *(What kind of clothes?)*

甲：我要一條短褲，一件T-恤衫。 *(I want a pair of shorts and a T-shirt.)*

乙：你T-恤衫不是很多嗎？為甚麼還要買？ *(Don't you have a lot of T-shirts? Why do you want to buy more?)*

甲：不够，不够…… *(Not enough, not enough . . .)*

乙：那我跟你一起去吧。走！我們去遠東百貨商店。 *(Then I'll go with you. Let's go! We'll go to the Far East Department Store.)*

2 甲：你覺得這件外套好看嗎？ *(Do you like how this coat looks?)*

乙：還可以。 *(It's OK.)*

甲：這件呢？ *(How about this one?)*

乙：嗯。這件比剛才那件好看。 *(Uh-huh. This one is better than the one just now.)*

甲：那這件呢？ *(How about this one, then?)*

乙：那件沒有第二件好看。 *(It doesn't look as nice as the second one.)*

甲：可是第二件最貴…… *(But the second one is the most expensive . . .)*

乙：價錢 (jiàqian) 貴一點，可是東西好多了。一分價錢一分貨。 *(It's a little more in price, but it's a much better item. You get what you pay for. [Literally: Pay a penny and get a penny's worth of goods.])*

3 甲：你要買甚麼樣的鞋？ *(What kinds of shoes do you want to buy?)*

乙：運動鞋。你呢？ *(Athletic shoes. And you?)*

甲：高跟涼鞋。 *(High-heeled sandals.)*

乙：涼鞋也有高跟的嗎？　　*(Are there sandals with high heels?)*

甲：有啊！高跟才好看。　　*(There are! They only look good if they have high heels!)*

乙：好吧！你去買你的高跟涼鞋，我去找 (zhǎo) 運動鞋！　　*(Well then! You go buy your high-heeled sandals, and I'll go look for athletic shoes!)*

4 甲：先生，請問，日用品是在三樓嗎？　　*(Sir, may I ask, are the personal grooming products [items for daily use] on the third floor?)*

乙：對，三樓。可以坐 扶手電梯 (fúshǒu diàntī) 上去。　　*(Right, the third floor. You can take the escalator up.)*

甲：扶手電梯在哪兒呢？　　*(Where is the escalator?)*

乙：在後面。你從 這兒往右走，就在那兒。　　*(In the back. Turn right here, and it's over there.)*

甲：三樓賣牙膏，牙刷，肥皂，洗髮水嗎？　　*(On the third floor, do they sell toothpaste, toothbrushes, soap, and shampoo?)*

乙：都有，都有。　　*(Yes, yes, they have all that.)*

5 甲：哪兒有電腦賣？　　*(Where are there computers for sale?)*

乙：離這兒不遠有一家商店賣電腦的。不到一里路。　　*(Not too far from here is a store that sells computers. Less than a mile away.)*

甲：怎麼走？　　*(How do I get there?)*

乙：往前走，前面那兒往左拐，就看到了。很近。叫美德電腦商店。　　*(Go straight, and up ahead turn left, and you'll see it. It's really close. It's called the Meide Computer Store.)*

甲：好，謝謝。我等一會兒就去。　　*(OK, thanks. I'll go in just a little while.)*

6 甲：你家離這兒還有多遠？　　*(How much farther is your home from here?)*

乙：很近。再走兩里路就到了。　　*(It's close. Another two miles and we'll be there.)*

甲：我們現在往西走，對嗎？　　*(We're going west now, right?)*

乙：不，我們是往南走。我家在北京南邊兒。　　*(No, we're going south. My home is in south Beijing.)*

甲：哦。　　*(Oh.)*

7 甲：我們今天晚上怎麼去小王家？　　*(How are we getting to Xiao Wang's home tonight?)*

乙：坐公共汽車？　　*(By bus?)*

甲：太慢了。打的吧。　　*(That's too slow. Let's take a cab.)*

乙：打的好貴啊！ *(It's really expensive to take a cab!)*

甲：可是比坐公共汽車快多了！ *(But it's a lot faster than taking a bus!)*

乙：那這樣：我們騎自行車，好不好？ *(Then let's do this: we'll ride bikes, OK?)*

甲：騎自行車跟坐公共汽車一樣慢。沒關係，我們早一點兒出門吧！ *(Riding bikes is just as slow as taking the bus. No matter, let's leave a little earlier!)*

8 甲：你喜歡坐地鐵嗎？ *(Do you like to ride the subway?)*

乙：我從來不坐地鐵。我愛走路。從這兒走路回家只要半個鐘頭。 *(I never ride the subway. I like to walk. It only takes a half hour to walk home from here.)*

甲：哇，你每天都走路回家嗎？ *(Wow, do you walk home every day?)*

乙：對啊！你呢？你怎麼回家？ *(That's right! And you? How do you get home?)*

甲：我跟我姐姐一起回家。她開車。 *(I go home with my sister. She drives.)*

9 甲：我坐左邊，小王坐右邊，你坐中間，好不好？ *(I'll sit on the left, Young Wang will sit on the right, and you sit in the middle, OK?)*

乙：為甚麼？ *(Why?)*

甲：因為我們兩個人都想跟你說話！ *(Because we both want to talk to you!)*

10 甲：我們去購物中心吧。今天衣服大減價。 *(Let's go to the shopping center. There's a big sale on clothing today.)*

乙：是嗎？毛衣也減價嗎？ *(Really? Are sweaters on sale too?)*

甲：有些毛衣打五折呢！ *(Some sweaters are 50 percent off!)*

乙：那走吧！去看看。別忘了帶信用卡。 *(Let's go then! Let's take a look. Don't forget to bring your credit card.)*

甲：我沒有信用卡。我都是付現金。 *(I don't have a credit card. I always pay cash.)*

乙：真的？我只刷卡。 *(Really? I only charge.)*

11 甲：你看！我今天在日月商場買了很多好東西，都很便宜。一條褲子，兩條裙子，一雙拖鞋和一雙皮鞋，三條毛巾，兩本筆記本，一包白紙，還有一些筆：紅的，黑的，還有藍的。 *(Look! I bought a lot of nice things at Sun-Moon Mall today, all very inexpensive. A pair of pants, two skirts, a pair of slippers and a pair of leather shoes, three towels, two notebooks, a ream of white paper, and some pens: red ones, black ones, and blue ones.)*

乙：你買了多少錢啊？　*(How much did it cost to buy all of this?)*

甲：不多，不多。都是減價的東西。　*(Not much, not much. It was all stuff on sale.)*

10.41 Pair work: *Read the dialogues aloud with a partner, this time without any English.*

10.41–10.42

• Have students read these dialogues multiple times, focusing on reading fluency.

• Encourage students *not* to refer to exercise 10.40 for help. Instead, ask them to rely on the dialogue context and their partners to help them read new characters.

• After students practice reading the dialogues a few times, play the audio and have them check their pronunciation.

1 甲：我想去買些衣服。你説到哪兒去買最好？

乙：甚麼樣的衣服？

甲：我要一條短褲，一件T-恤衫。

乙：你T-恤衫不是很多嗎？為甚麼還要買？

甲：不夠，不夠……

乙：那我跟你一起去吧。走！我們去遠東百貨商店。

2 甲：你覺得這件外套好看嗎？

乙：還可以。

甲：這件呢？

乙：嗯。這件比剛才那件好看。

甲：那這件呢？

乙：那件沒有第二件好看。

甲：可是第二件最貴……

乙：價錢 (jiàqian) 貴一點，可是東西好多了。一分價錢一分貨。

3 甲：你要買甚麼樣的鞋？

乙：運動鞋。你呢？

甲：高跟涼鞋。

乙：涼鞋也有高跟的嗎？

甲：有啊！高跟才好看。

乙：好吧！你去買你的高跟涼鞋，我去找 (zhǎo) 運動鞋！

4 甲：先生，請問，日用品是在三樓嗎？

乙：對，三樓。可以坐 扶手電梯 (fúshǒu diàntī) 上去。

甲：扶手電梯在哪兒呢？

乙：在後面。你從 這兒往右走，就在那兒。

甲：三樓賣牙膏，牙刷，肥皂，洗髮水嗎？

乙：都有，都有。

5 甲：哪兒有電腦賣？

乙：離這兒不遠有一家商店賣電腦的。不到一里路。

甲：怎麼走？

乙：往前走，前面那兒往左拐，就看到了。很近。叫美德電腦商店。

甲：好，謝謝。我等一會兒就去。

6 甲：你家離這兒還有多遠？

乙：很近。再走兩里路就到了。

甲：我們現在往西走，對嗎？

乙：不，我們是往南走。我家在北京南邊兒。

甲：哦。

7 甲：我們今天晚上怎麼去小王家？

乙：坐公共汽車？

甲：太慢了。打的吧。

乙：打的好貴啊！

甲：可是比坐公共汽車快多了！

乙：那這樣：我們騎自行車，好不好？

甲：騎自行車跟坐公共汽車一樣慢。沒關係，我們早一點兒出門吧！

8 甲：你喜歡坐地鐵嗎？

乙：我從來不坐地鐵。我愛走路。從這兒走路回家只要半個鐘頭。

甲：哇，你每天都走路回家嗎？

乙：對啊！你呢？你怎麼回家？

甲：我跟我姐姐一起回家。她開車。

9 甲：我坐左邊，小王坐右邊，你坐中間，好不好？

乙：為甚麼？

甲：因為我們兩個人都想跟你說話！

10 甲：我們去購物中心吧。今天衣服大減價。

乙：是嗎？毛衣也減價嗎？

甲：有些毛衣打五折呢！

乙：那走吧！去看看。別忘了帶信用卡。

甲：我沒有信用卡。我都是付現金。

乙：真的？我只刷卡。

11 甲：你看！我今天在日月商場買了很多好東西，都很便宜。一條褲子，兩條裙子，一雙拖鞋和一雙皮鞋，三條毛巾，兩本筆記本，一包白紙，還有一些筆：紅的，黑的，還有藍的。

乙：你買了多少錢啊？

甲：不多，不多。都是減價的東西。

10.42 *Pair work: Read the dialogues aloud with a partner, this time in simplified characters.*

1 甲：我想去买些衣服。你说到哪儿去买最好？

乙：什么样的衣服？

甲：我要一条短裤，一件T-恤衫。

乙：你T-恤衫不是很多吗？为什么还要买？

甲：不够，不够……

乙：那我跟你一起去吧。走！我们去远东百货商店。

2 甲：你觉得这件外套好看吗？

乙：还可以。

甲：这件呢？

乙：嗯。这件比刚才那件好看。

甲：那这件呢？

乙：那件没有第二件好看。

甲：可是第二件最贵……

乙：价钱 (jiàqian) 贵一点，可是东西好多了。一分价钱一分货。

3 甲：你要买什么样的鞋？

乙：运动鞋。你呢？

甲：高根凉鞋。

乙：凉鞋也有高根的吗？

甲：有啊！高根才好看。

乙：好吧！你去买你的高跟凉鞋，我去找 (zhǎo) 运动鞋！

4 甲：先生，请问，日用品是在三楼吗？

乙：对，三楼。可以坐扶手电梯 (fúshǒu diàntī) 上去。

甲：扶手电梯在哪儿呢？

乙：在后面。你从 这儿往右走，就在那儿。

甲：三楼卖牙膏，牙刷，肥皂，洗发水吗？

乙：都有，都有。

5 甲：哪儿有电脑卖？

乙：离这儿不远有一家商店卖电脑的。不到一里路。

甲：怎么走？

乙：往前走，前面那儿往左拐，就看到了。很近。叫美德电脑商店。

甲：好，谢谢。我等一会儿就去。

6 甲：你家离这儿还有多远？

乙：很近。再走两里路就到了。

甲：我们现在往西走，对吗？

乙：不，我们是往南走。我家在北京南边儿。

甲：哦。

7 甲：我们今天晚上怎么去小王家？

乙：坐公共汽车？

甲：太慢了。打的吧。

乙：打的好贵啊！

甲：可是比坐公共汽车快多了！

乙：那这样：我们骑自行车，好不好？

甲：骑自行车跟坐公共汽车一样慢。没关系，我们早一点儿出门吧！

8 甲：你喜欢坐地铁吗？

乙：我从来不坐地铁。我爱走路。从这儿走路回家只要半个钟头。

甲：哇，你每天都走路回家吗？

乙：对啊！你呢？你怎么回家？

甲：我跟我姐姐一起回家。她开车。

9 甲：我坐左边，小王坐右边，你坐中间，好不好？

乙：为什么？

甲：因为我们两个人都想跟你说话！

10 甲：我们去购物中心吧。今天衣服大减价。

乙：是吗？毛衣也减价吗？

甲：有些毛衣打五折呢！

乙：那走吧！去看看。别忘了带信用卡。

甲：我没有信用卡。我都是付现金。

乙：真的？我只刷卡。

11 甲：你看！我今天在日月商场买了很多好东西，都很便宜。一条裤子，两条裙子，一双拖鞋和一双皮鞋，三条毛巾，两本笔记本，一包白纸，还有一些笔：红的，黑的，还有蓝的。

乙：你买了多少钱啊！

甲：不多，不多。都是减价的东西。

10.43 *Match the corresponding simplified characters, traditional characters, and English.*

a. 购物中心	1. 涼鞋	A. *shopping center*
b. 买东西	2. 運動鞋	B. *the most expensive*
c. 卖东西	3. 電梯	C. *third floor*
d. 一条短裤	4. 洗髮水	D. *buy things, shop*
e. 最贵	5. 買東西	E. *three floors*
f. 运动鞋	6. 後面	F. *shampoo*
g. 凉鞋	7. 三層樓	G. *sandals*
h. 三楼	8. 購物中心	H. *notebook*
i. 三层楼	9. 最貴	I. *a pair of shorts*
j. 电梯	10. 三樓	J. *elevator*
k. 后面	11. 電腦	K. *athletic shoes*
l. 洗发水	12. 一條短褲	L. *computer*
m. 电脑	13. 賣東西	M. *sell things*
n. 笔记本	14. 筆記本	N. *in the back, behind*

10.43 Key:
a. 8. A
b. 5. D
c. 13. M
d. 12. I
e. 9. B
f. 2. K
g. 1. G
h. 10. C
i. 7. E
j. 3. J
k. 6. N
l. 4. F
m. 11. L
n. 14. H

10.44 *Match the corresponding simplified characters, traditional characters, and English.*

a. 白纸	1. 一樣慢	A. *far from here*
b. 黑笔	2. 付現金	B. *black pen*
c. 离这儿远	3. 南邊兒	C. *ride a bike*
d. 南边儿	4. 黑筆	D. *the south*
e. 坐公共汽车	5. 大減價	E. *drive*
f. 骑自行车	6. 白紙	F. *the right-hand side*
g. 坐地铁	7. 中間	G. *white paper*
h. 开车	8. 坐地鐵	H. *ride the subway*
i. 半个钟头	9. 騎自行車	I. *ride the bus*
j. 一样慢	10. 左邊	J. *the left-hand side*
k. 左边	11. 坐公共汽車	K. *just as slow*
l. 右边	12. 半個鐘頭	L. *pay cash*
m. 中间	13. 開車	M. *a half hour*
n. 大减价	14. 右邊	N. *the middle*
o. 付现金	15. 離這兒遠	O. *a big sale*

10.44 Key:
a. 6. G
b. 4. B
c. 15. A
d. 3. D
e. 11. I
f. 9. C
g. 8. H
h. 13. E
i. 12. M
j. 1. K
k. 10. J
l. 14. F
m. 7. N
n. 5. O
o. 2. L

▶ Reading real-life texts

10.45 *Look at the photo. Fill in the blanks.*

Yóu cǐ shàng lóu. = _____

_____ from here.

Where do you think this sign was posted? Check one.

a. ☐ in front of a flight of stairs

b. ☐ by an exit

10.46 *Look at the photo.* 特 tè *is an abbreviated form of* 特别 tèbié, *which means "special." What do you think this sign says?*

Write the English:

_____

10.47 *Look at the photo. What items of clothing do you think might be offered here, at ¥25 each? Check one.*

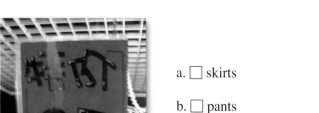

a. ☐ skirts

b. ☐ pants

c. ☐ shirts

10.48 *What is the price reduction on these shoes? Check one.*

10.48 Key:
b

a. ☐ 5% off

b. ☐ 50% off

c. ☐ 15% off

10.49 *Look at the sign. What do you think* 向前约50米／向前约50米 Xiàng qián yuē 50 mǐ *means? Take a guess; fill in the blank below.*

10.49 Key:
50 meters ahead

Answer: approximately _____

10.50 *Look at the sign. What is being offered for sale here?*

10.50 Key:
women's pants

Answer: _____

▶ Learning to write characters

10.51 *For stroke order and other useful information about each of the following characters from this unit, go to the* Character Writing Workbook*. Choose either traditional or simplified characters and practice writing them until you can reproduce them on demand.*

到，用，心，百，貨／货，商，場／场，店，離／离，遠／远，
近，路，左，右，南，北，面，邊／边，開／开，車／车

▶ Writing a note

10.52 *Write a paragraph (perhaps as part of an e-mail message to a friend) about your shopping habits, such as where you like to shop for what. Mention a few things you have purchased recently.*

Cultural Bits 文化点滴

Shopping and finding specific items

View the video segment "Shopping and finding specific items" and then discuss the following questions with your classmates.

• What are some challenges you might face in asking for directions? How might you deal with these challenges?

• Think of three things you can tell someone about the 塤／埙 *xūn* (ocarina).

• List several cultural items you might be interested in shopping for in China.

Recap

▶ Grammar

Coverbs

Coverbs are transitive verbs that precede the main verb and provide an "environment" for the main verbal action.

Use *dào* to indicate "to" a place.

> Wǒ dào shāngchǎng qù mǎi dōngxi. (*I'm going to the mall to shop.*)

Use *cóng* to indicate "from" a place.

> Wǒ cóng xuéxiào lái jiàn nǐ. (*I'm coming from school to meet you.*)

Use *wǎng* to indicate "toward" a place.

> Wǎng zuǒ zǒu jiù dào le. (*Go left and you'll be right there.*)

Use *zài* to indicate "at" a place.

> Wǒ zài chāojí shìchǎng mǎi shuǐguǒ. (*I buy fruit at the supermarket.*)

Use *lí* to indicate "the distance from" a place.

> Wǒ jiā lí Xiǎo Wáng jiā sān lǐ lù. (*My house is three miles from Xiao Wang's.*)

Use *zuò* to indicate "taking a vehicle to" a place.

> Wǒ zuò diàntī shànglóu. (*I'm taking the elevator upstairs.*)

Use *dā* to indicate "riding a mode of public transport."

> Wǒ tiāntiān dā gōngchē shàngbān. (*I ride the bus to work every day.*)

Use *qí* to indicate "riding something astraddle."

> Wǒ qí zìxíngchē qù. (*I'll go by bicycle.*)

Measure words
(Starred items are for review.)

Every Chinese noun is "marked" by its appropriate measure word. This listing here reinforces the measure words you've encountered to date.

bǎ 把 things you grab in your fist (e.g., combs)

bàn* 半 halves (e.g., half an hour)

bāo 包 things that come in a packet (e.g., dental floss)

běn 本 things that come in volumes (e.g., books, notebooks)

céng 層／层 stories (in a building)

cì* 次 times, occurrences

dǐng 頂／顶 hats

fēn* 分 "cent" (spoken)

fēn* 分 minutes of clock time

ge* 個／个 (general use)

gēn 根 root-like things (e.g., a strand of dental floss)

hé 盒 things that come in a box (e.g., matches)

jiā 家 stores

jiàn 件 clothing (e.g., shirts, jackets, sweaters)

juǎn 卷 things that come in rolls (e.g., toilet paper)

kè* 刻 quarters of an hour

kuài* 塊／块 "dollar" (spoken)

kuài* 塊／块 things that come in pieces (e.g., soap)

lǐ (lù) 里（路） "Chinese mile"

lóu 樓／楼 floors (in a building)

máo* 毛 "dime" (spoken)

píng 瓶 things that come in bottles (e.g., shampoo, conditioner)

shuāng 雙／双 things that come in pairs (e.g., shoes)

suì* 歲／岁 years of age

tái 台 electronic items put on a table (e.g., computers, TVs)

tiān* 天 days

tiáo 條／条 long, rope-like things (e.g., pants, skirts, towels)

wèi* 位 persons with standing (e.g., teachers, guests)

xiē* 些 small amount, several

zhāng 張／张 things that come in sheets (e.g., paper, postcards)

zhī 支 stick-like things (e.g., toothbrush, toothpaste)

▶ Vocabulary

Things to buy (*with measure words*)

diànnǎo (tái) 電腦／电脑 (台) computer

dōngxi (ge, xiē) 東西／东西 (個／个，些) thing(s), articles

jìniànpǐn (ge) 紀念品／纪念品 (個／个) souvenir

Clothing (*with measure words*)

kùzi (tiáo) 褲子／裤子 (條／条) pants, trousers

chènshān (jiàn) 襯衫／衬衫 (件) shirt

duǎnkù (tiáo) 短褲／短裤 (條／条) shorts

jiákè (jiàn) 夾克／夹克 (件) jacket

máoyī (jiàn) 毛衣 (件) sweater, jumper

qúnzi (tiáo) 裙子 (條／条) skirt

wàitào (jiàn) 外套 (件) overcoat

yīfu (jiàn) 衣服 （件） clothes, clothing

yùndòngfú (jiàn) 運動服／运动服 （件） athletic clothes

Shoes (*with measure words*)

gāogēnxié (shuāng) 高跟鞋 （雙／双） high-heeled shoes

liángxié (shuāng) 涼鞋／凉鞋 （雙／双） sandals

píxié (shuāng) 皮鞋 (雙／双) leather (dress) shoes

tuōxié (shuāng) 拖鞋 (雙／双) slippers

yùndòngxié (shuāng) 運動鞋／运动鞋 （雙／双） athletic shoes

Products for daily use (*with measure words*)

féizào (kuài) 肥皂 (塊／块) soap

hùfàsù (píng) 護髮素／护发素 (瓶) conditioner

máojīn (tiáo) 毛巾 (條／条) towel

shūzi (bǎ) 梳子 （把） comb

wèishēngzhǐ (juǎn) 衛生紙／卫生纸 (卷) toilet paper

xǐfàshuǐ (píng) 洗髮水／洗发水 (瓶) shampoo

yágāo (zhī) 牙膏 (支) toothpaste

yáshuā (zhī) 牙刷 (支) toothbrush

yáxiàn (hé, bāo, gēn) 牙線／牙线 (盒，包，根) floss

Stationery (*with measure words*)

bǐ (zhī) 筆／笔 (支) pen

bǐjìběn (ge) 筆記本／笔记本 (個／个) notebook

míngxìnpiàn (zhāng) 明信片 (張／张) postcard

wénjù (xiē) 文具 （些） stationery

zhǐ (zhāng) 紙／纸 (張／张) paper

Places to shop

bǎihuò shāngdiàn 百貨商店／百货商店 department store

gòuwù zhōngxīn 購物中心／购物中心 shopping center

shāngchǎng 商場／商场 shopping mall

shāngdiàn 商店 store

Locations and directions

běi(bian) 北(邊)／北(边) north (side/direction)

dōng(bian) 東(邊)／东(边) east (side/direction)

dōngběi 東北／东北 northeast

dōngnán 東南／东南 southeast

hòu(bian) 後(邊)／后(边) back, behind

lóushàng 樓上／楼上 upstairs

lóuxià 樓下／楼下 downstairs

nán(bian) 南(邊)／南(边) south (side/direction)

nǎr 哪兒／哪儿 where

nàr 那兒／那儿 there

qián(bian) 前(邊)／前(边) front, in front

shàng(mian) 上(面) top, above

xī(bian) 西(邊)／西(边) west (side/direction)

xià(mian) 下(面) bottom, below

xīběi 西北 northwest

xīnán 西南 southwest

yòu(bian) 右(邊)／右(边) right

zhèr 這兒／这儿 here

zhōng(jiān) 中間／中间 middle

zuǒ(bian) 左(邊)／左(边) left

Nouns

diàntī 電梯／电梯 elevator

dìtiě 地鐵／地铁 subway

dìtiězhàn 地鐵站／地铁站 subway stop/station

fúshǒu diàntī 扶手電梯／扶手电梯 escalator

gōnggòngqìchē (gōngchē) 公共汽車 (公車)／公共汽车 (公车) public bus

hónglǜdēng 紅綠燈／红绿灯 red (traffic) light

huǒchē 火車／火车 train

jiàoxuélóu 教學樓／教学楼 classroom building

jiàqian 價錢／价钱 price

lóu 樓／楼 a multistoried building

mótuōchē (liàng) 摩托車／摩托车（輛／辆）motorcycle, motorbike

rìyòngpǐn 日用品 articles of daily use

sùshè 宿舍 dormitory, dorm

xiànjīn 現金／现金 cash

xìnyòngkǎ 信用卡 credit card

zhàn 站 stop, station

zhōngtóu 鐘頭／钟头 hour

Coverbs

cóng 從／从 from

dā 搭 ride on/take (a form of public transportation)

dào 到 to

lí 離／离 from, away from

qí 騎／骑 ride (something astraddle)

wǎng 往 toward, to

zài 在 in, at, on

zuò 坐 ride on/take (a form of transportation)

Verbs and verbal expressions

chūmén 出門／出门 leave/go out of the house

dǎdī 打的 take a cab

dǎ diànhuà 打電話／打电话 make a phone call, phone

Dào le! 到了！(We're) there!

dǎzhé 打折 give a discount

fùqián 付錢／付钱 pay (in money)

fù xiànjīn 付現金／付现金 pay cash

gàosu 告訴／告诉 tell, let know, inform

guǎi 拐 turn (in the direction of)

guò 過／过 pass by/over

jiǎnjià 減價／减价 be on sale

jiē 接 meet, pick up

juéde 覺得／觉得 feel, think

kāichē 開車／开车 drive a car

mǎi 買／买 buy, purchase

mài 賣／卖 sell

mǎi dōngxi 買東西／买东西 shop (literally, "buy things")

Nǐ kàn! 你看！Take a look! Look!

qí 騎／骑 ride (a bike, horse)

qí zìxíngchē 騎自行車／骑自行车 ride a bicycle/go by bicycle

shàngkè 上課／上课 attend class, go to class, hold class

shuākǎ 刷卡 charge, swipe a credit card

yào 要 need, require (in time or effort)

yòng 用 use

yǒu 有 have

zhǎo 找 look for

zǒulù 走路 walk (on the road)

zuò dìtiě 坐地鐵／坐地铁 take the subway

zuò gōnggòngqìchē (gōngchē) 坐公共汽車(公車)／坐公共汽车(公车) go by bus

Stative Verbs

duō 多 more (in number), numerous

hǎo 好 better (in comparisons)

jìn 近 near

lèi 累 tired

piányi 便宜 cheap, inexpensive

yuǎn 遠／远 far

Adverbs

chángcháng 常常 often, frequently

dāngrán 當然／当然 certainly, of course, naturally

hǎo 好 very (precedes stative verbs)

hěn shǎo 很少 rarely

jiù 就 exactly, precisely; then, in that case

nàme 那麼／那么 then, in that case

tài 太 too, exceedingly

tōngcháng 通常 generally, in general, normally

zuìhǎo 最好 best

Conjunctions

háiyǒu 還有／还有 furthermore, in addition, what's more

hé 和 and (links nouns and nominal expressions, not clauses)

ránhòu 然後／然后 and then, after that

Other words and expressions

búdào 不到 less than (followed by a number expression)

duō 多 how/how much... (before a stative verb)

Ò 哦 Oh

qítā 其他 others, the rest

Wà 哇 Wow

▌Checklist of "can do" statements

After completing this unit, you should be able to perform each of the following tasks.

Listening and speaking

☐ Find out where a certain item can be purchased.

☐ After making a comparison between items, express your preference for one.

☐ Handle ways to express prices and bargain appropriately.

☐ Tell a friend where you like to shop and give a reason why.

☐ Ask for and understand directions (including compass points) to a particular place.

☐ Ask about various modes of transportation.

☐ Find your way around a large store.

☐ Manage a sales transaction (i.e., ask about prices, discounts, methods of payment).

Checklist

• Have students work in pairs to go through this checklist and demonstrate selected skills to the class. Reserve 20–30 minutes for students to complete this activity. Tell students that putting check marks in each box is NOT the point. The point is to check if they can really do the things on the list.

• Once students have completed the checklist, revisit the posters they made for exercise 10.2 and the Grammar Bits sections.

Reading and writing

☐ Interpret directional signs.

☐ Interpret key information on retail ads regarding prices and sales.

☐ Read and write simple sentences regarding purchases.

Cultural understanding

☐ Demonstrate an understanding of the different sources of goods and products available for sale in China, from roadside vendors to upscale shopping centers.

☐ Demonstrate an understanding of appropriate and inappropriate behavior in each of the above locations, and an ability to effectively conclude transactions based on need.

REFERENCE

Glossaries

The Chinese-English and English-Chinese glossaries list the words introduced in *Encounters* and additional words that are useful to the beginning learner. Look upon this section as a sort of mini-dictionary. In the glossaries, most nouns are accompanied by their appropriate measure word in square brackets. Traditional characters for each entry are given first, followed by simplified characters.

The following grammatical abbreviations are used throughout the glossaries:

A	adverb	PH	phrase
AV	auxiliary verb	PR	pronoun
C	conjunction	PREF	prefix
CV	coverb	PW	place word
EV	equative verb	QW	question word
I	interjection	S	suffix
IE	idiomatic expression	SP	specifier
M	measure word	SV	stative verb
N	noun	TW	time word
NP	noun phrase	V	verb
NU	number	VO	verb object
P	particle	VP	verbal phrase

Chinese-English Glossary

A

ǎi short (*height or stature*) 矮 SV

ài love; like 愛／爱 V

àiren spouse 愛人／爱人 N

āiyā Oh; Oh my goodness! 哎呀 I

Àodàlìyà Australia 澳大利亚／澳大利亚 PW

Àomén Macau 澳門／澳门 PW

Àomén yuán Macau pataca (*currency*) 澳門元／澳门元 N

Àoyuán Australian dollar 澳元 N

āyí aunt (*mother's sister*) 阿姨 N

B

ba (*particle of suggestion*) 吧 P

bā eight 八 NU

bàba dad; father 爸爸 N

bǎihuò shāngdiàn department store 百货商店／百货商店 N

báisè white 白色 N

bāng help; assist 幫／帮 V

bàn ge zhōngtóu a half hour 半個鐘頭／半个钟头 TW

bāngzhù help; assist 幫助／帮助 V

bànyè midnight 半夜 TW

bǎo full; not hungry 飽／饱 SV

bào [fèn] newspaper 報 [份]／报 [份] N

bāshí eighty 八十 NU

bāshì bus 巴士 N

Bāyuè August 八月 N

(yì)bēi ... a cup of; a glass of (一)杯...... N/M

běibian(r) north (*side, direction*) 北邊(兒)／北边(儿) PW

Běijīng Beijing 北京 PW

Běi Měizhōu North America 北美洲 PW

bēizi [ge] glass; cup 杯子 [個]／杯子 [个] N

bǐ than, compare; in comparison 比 CV

bǐ [zhī] pen 筆 [枝]／笔 [枝] N

bian(r) side (*left, right, north, etc.*) 邊(兒)／边(儿) PW

biǎo [kuài] watch; timepiece 錶 [塊]／表 [块] N

bié do not (*imperative*) 別 A

biéde another; different one 別的 SP

bié kèqi you're welcome; don't be so polite 別客氣／別客气 IE

biéren other people; others 別人 N

bǐjìběn [běn] notebook 筆記本 [本]／笔记本 [本] N

bìng sickness; illness 病 N

bìng le become ill/sick 病了 VP

bìxū must (*matter of obligation*) 必須／必须 AV

bóbo uncle (*father's older brother*) 伯伯 N

bómǔ aunt (*wife of father's older brother*) 伯母 N

bówùguǎn museum 博物館／博物馆 N

bù no; not 不 A

bùcháng seldom; not often 不常 A

búcuò not bad; pretty good 不錯／不错 SV

búdào ... less than (*followed by number expression*) 不到...... VP

bú shì no; that's not the case 不是 EV

bù shūfu slightly sick; uncomfortable 不舒服 SV

bú yào don't; don't want 不要 V/AV

búyòng need not 不用 A

búyòng xiè you're welcome 不用謝／不用谢 IE

C

cái then; not until; until 才 A

cāicai kàn take a guess 猜猜看 VP

cāntīng cafeteria 餐廳／餐厅 N

cǎo grass 草 N

céng story (*in a building*) 層／层 M

cèsuǒ bathroom; toilet 廁所／厕所 N

chá check (*examine*) 查 V

chá [bēi] tea [cup of] 茶 [杯] N

chà lack(ing) ("*before the hour*") 差 V

cháng long 長／长 SV

chàng sing 唱 V

chángcháng often; frequently 常常 A

chànggē(r) sing a song 唱歌(兒)／唱歌(儿) VO

Cháng Jiāng Yangtze River 長江／长江 PW

chángkù [tiáo] pants; trousers 長褲 [條]／长裤 [条] N

chē vehicle; car 車／车 N

chènshān [jiàn] shirt; blouse 襯衫 [件]／衬衫 [件] N

chēzhàn bus stop 車站／车站 N

chī have a meal; eat a meal; eat 吃 V

chībǎo eat to fullness 吃飽／吃饱 V

chīfàn have a meal; eat a meal; eat 吃飯／吃饭 V/VO

chuān wear; dress; put on clothes 穿 V/VO

chuán [tiáo] boat; ship 船 [條]／船 [条] N

chuáng [zhāng] bed 床 [張]／床 [张] N

chuān yīfu wear; dress; put on clothes 穿衣服 V/VO

chūguó go abroad 出國／出国 VO

chūmén leave; go out of 出門／出门 VO

chūqu go out 出去 V

chūqu wánr go out for some fun 出去玩兒／出去玩兒 VP

chūshēngzài be born in 出生在 VP

chūzhōng junior high school 初中 N

chūzūqìchē [liàng] taxi 出租汽車 [輛]／出租汽车 [辆] N

cì times; occurrences 次 M

cóng from (*a place, a time, etc.*) 從／从 CV

cóng . . . lái come from . . . 從……來／从……来 VP

cónglái bù never 從來不／从来不 A

D

dà old (*age*); big; large 大 SV

dà (érzi, nǚér) eldest (son, daughter) 大(兒子, 女兒)／大(儿子, 女儿) N

dǎdī take a cab 打的 VO

dǎ diànhuà make a phone call; phone 打電話／打电话 VO

dǎgōng do part-time work; do odd jobs 打工 VO

dàhào large; big (*size in clothing, etc.*) 大號／大号 N

dài wear (*hat, glasses, etc.*) 戴 V

dāizai stay (at) 呆在 VP

dāizai jiāli remain at home; stay at home 呆在家裏／呆在家里 VP

dàizi [ge] bag 袋子 [個]／袋子 [个] N

dàjiā everyone 大家 N

dāng to be; act as; work as; serve as 當／当 V

dāngrán of course; naturally 當然／当然 A

dào to (*a place or time*) 到 CV

dàoguo been to (*a place*) 到過／到过 V

dào le to have arrived 到了 VP

dào . . . qù go to . . . (*a place*) 到……去 VP

dàxué university; college 大學／大学 N

dàxuéshēng college student 大學生／大学生 N

dǎzhé give a discount 打折 VO

Déguó Germany 德國／德国 PW

Déguóhuà German (*language*) 德國話／德国话 N

Déguórén German (*person/people*) 德國人／德国人 N

děi have to; must 得 AV

děng wait; wait for; await 等 V

děngyú equal(s) 等于 V

de shíhou when (*at the time of*) 的時候／的时候 TW

Déwén German (*language*) 德文 N

Déyǔ German (*language*) 德語／德语 N

dì (*ordinal prefix*) 第 PREF

diǎn (zhōng) o'clock; time on the clock 點(鐘)／点(钟) M

diànhuà [ge] telephone 電話 [個]／电话 [个] N

diànhuà hàomǎ telephone number 電話號碼／电话号码 N

diànnǎo [tái] computer 電腦 [台]／电脑 [台] N

diànshì [tái] television; TV 電視 [台]／电视 [台] N

diàntī elevator 電梯／电梯 N

diànxìn [fēng] e-mail message 電信 [封]／电信 [封] N

diànyǐng [bù] film; movie 電影 [部]／电影 [部] N

diànyǐngyuàn movie theater 電影院／电影院 N

diànyóu e-mail 電郵／电邮 N

diànzǐ yóuxì [ge] video game 電子遊戲 [個]／电子游戏 [个] N

dìbā (ge) eighth (one) 第八(個)／第八(个) N/NU

dìdi younger brother 弟弟 N

dìèr (ge) second (one) 第二(個)／第二(个) N/NU

dìfang [ge] place 地方 [個]／地方 [个] N

dìjiǔ (ge) ninth (one) 第九(個)／第九(个) N/NU

dìliù (ge) sixth (one) 第六(個)／第六(个) N/NU

dìqī (ge) seventh (one) 第七(個)／第七(个) N/NU

dìsān (ge) third (one) 第三(個)／第三(个) N/NU

dìshí (ge) tenth (one) 第十(個)／第十(个) N/NU

dìshí'èr (ge) twelfth (one) 第十二(個)／第十二(个) N/NU

dìshíyī (ge) eleventh (one) 第十一(個)／第十一(个) N/NU

dìsì (ge) fourth (one) 第四(個)／第四(个) N/NU

dìtiě subway 地鐵／地铁 N

dìtiězhàn subway stop/station 地鐵站／地铁站 N

dìtú [zhāng] map 地圖 [張]／地图 [张] N

dìwǔ (ge) fifth (one) 第五(個)／第五(个) N/NU

dìyī (ge) first (one) 第一(個)／第一(个) N/NU

dìzhǐ address; location; mailing address 地址 N

dǒng understand 懂 V

dōngběibian(r) northeast 東北邊(兒)／东北边(儿) PW

dōngbian(r) east (*side, direction*) 東邊(兒)／东边(儿) PW

dōngnán southeast 東南／东南 PW

dōngxi [ge] object; thing; stuff 東西 [個]／东西 [个] N

dōu both; all 都 A

dòufu tofu 豆腐 N

dú study 讀／读 V

duǎn short (*length*) 短 SV

duǎnkù [tiáo] shorts/short pants [pair of] 短褲 [條]／短裤 [条] N

duì right; correct 對／对 SV

duìbuqǐ I'm sorry; excuse me; sorry 對不起／对不起 IE

duì le yes; that's right 對了／对了 IE

duō how; to what extent 多 A

duō many; much; numerous 多 SV

duōshao how many (*more than ten*) 多少 QW

dúshēngnǚ only child (*girl*) 獨生女／独生女 N

dúshēngzǐ only child (*boy*) 獨生子／独生子 N

dúshū attend school 讀書／读书 VO

E

è hungry 餓／饿 SV
Éguó Russia 俄國／俄国 PW
Éguóhuà Russian (*language*) 俄國話／俄国话 N
Éguórén Russian (*person/people*) 俄國人／俄国人 N
èr two 二 NU
èrshí twenty 二十 NU
èrshíyī twenty-one 二十一 NU
Èryuè February 二月 N
érzi son 兒子／儿子 N
Éwén Russian (*language*) 俄文 N
Éyǔ Russian (*language*) 俄語／俄语 N

F

Fǎguó France 法國／法国 PW
Fǎguóhuà French (*language*) 法國話／法国话 N
Fǎguórén French (*person/people*) 法國人／法国人 N
fàn [wǎn] cooked rice [bowl of] 飯 [碗]／饭 [碗] N
fàngjià have or be on a holiday 放假 VO
fángjiān [ge] room 房間 [個]／房间 [个] N
fànguǎn(r) restaurant 飯館兒／饭馆儿 N
fāngxiàng way/direction 方向 N
fàngxué get out of school; dismiss school 放學／放学 VO
fángzi [dòng] house 房子 [棟／栋] N
fántǐzì traditional character 繁體字／繁体字 N
fāshāo have a fever 發燒／发烧 VO
Fǎwén French (*language*) 法文 N
Fǎyǔ French (*language*) 法語／法语 N
fēicháng extremely; very; rather; quite 非常 A
fēijī [jià] airplane 飛機 [架]／飞机 [架] N
féizào [kuài] soap [bar of] 肥皂 [塊]／肥皂 [块] N
Fēizhōu Africa 非洲 PW
Fēizhōurén African (*person/people*) 非洲人 N
fēn 1/100 of the primary monetary unit; "cent" 分 M
fēn minute (*clock time*) 分 M
fěnhóngsè pink 粉紅色／粉红色 N
fùmǔ parents 父母 N
fùqián pay money 付錢／付钱 VO
fùqin father; dad 父親／父亲 N
fúshǒu diàntī escalator 扶手電梯／扶手电梯 N
fúwùyuán waiter; waitress; service person; attendant; salesclerk 服務員／服务员 N
fù xiànjīn pay in cash 付現金／付现金 VO

G

gāng just; only a short time ago 剛／刚 A
Gǎngbì Hong Kong dollar 港幣／港币 N
gāngcái just now; just a moment ago 剛才／刚才 A
gāo tall; (*also a surname*) 高 SV
gāogēnxié [shuāng] high-heeled shoes [pair of] 高跟鞋 [雙]／高跟鞋 [双] N
gàosu tell; inform 告訴／告诉 V

gāoxìng happy; pleased 高興／高兴 SV
gāozhōng senior high school 高中 N
gēcǎo cut the grass; mow the lawn 割草 VO
gēge older brother 哥哥 N
gěi give 給／给 V
gēn with; and 跟 C
gèng still; even more (*in comparisons*) 更 A
gēxīng singing star 歌星 N
gōng (gòngqì) chē [liàng] public bus 公(共汽)車 [輛]／公(共汽)车 [辆] N
gōngchéngshī engineer 工程師／工程师 N
gōngkè homework; schoolwork; assignment 功課／功课 N
gōngrén laborer; worker 工人／工人 N
gōngyuán(r) public park 公園(兒)／公园(儿) N
gōngzuò job; work 工作 N/V
gǒu dog (*Chinese zodiac*) 狗 N
gòuwù zhōngxīn shopping center 購物中心／购物中心 N
guā húzi shave (one's) beard 刮鬍子／刮胡子 VO
guǎi turn (*in the direction of*) 拐 V
guàngjiē go shopping 逛街 VO
guàng shāngchǎng go to the mall 逛商場／逛商场 VO
Guǎngzhōu Canton (*old name for Guangzhou*) 廣州／广州 PW
gūgu aunt (*father's sister*) 姑姑 N
guì expensive; costly 貴／贵 SV
Guìlín Guilin (*city in southwestern China*) 桂林 PW
guìxìng what's your surname? 貴姓／贵姓 IE
guo (*experiential verbal suffix*) 過／过 S
guó country (*suffix to names of countries*) 國／国 N/S
guò exceed; past (*the clock hour*) 過／过 V
guò pass by (*on the way*) 過／过 V
guò yìhuǐr after a little while 過一會兒／过一会儿 VP

H

hái still; yet 還／还 A
hài Hi! 嗨 I
hái hǎo I'm OK; I'm fairly well 還好／还好 IE
hái méi not yet (*in a negative sentence*) 還沒／还没 A
hái shi still; yet 還是／还是 A
háishi or (*when offering alternatives*) 還是／还是 C
háiyǒu furthermore; in addition; what's more 還有／还有 C
háizi kid; child 孩子 N
háizimen children 孩子們／孩子们 N
hànbǎobāo [ge] hamburger 漢堡包 [個]／汉堡包 [个] N
Hánguó Korea 韓國／韩国 PW
Hánguóhuà Korean (*language*) 韓國話／韩国话 N
Hánguórén Korean (*person/people*) 韓國人／韩国人 N
Hánwén Korean (*language*) 韓文／韩文 N

Hànyǔ　Korean (*language*)　韓語／韩语　N

hǎo　OK; good; fine; nice; well　好　SV

hào　number (*in a series*)　號／号　M

hào　day of the month　號／号　M

hào　size (*small, medium, large, etc.*)　號／号　M

hǎochī　delicious; good-tasting　好吃　SV

hǎokàn　attractive; good-looking; pretty　好看　SV

hàomǎ　number (*telephone number, etc.*)　號碼／号码　N

hē　drink　喝　V

hé　with (*in the company of*); and　和　C

hēisè　black　黑色　N

hěn　very (*usually light in sense*)　很　A

hěn gāoxìng rènshi nǐ/nín　happy to meet you　很高興認識你(您)／很高兴认识你(您)　IE

hěn shǎo　rarely　很少　A

hóngdēng　red light (*traffic*)　紅燈／红灯　N

hónglǜdēng　traffic light　紅綠燈／红绿灯　N

hóngsè　red　紅色／红色　N

hóu　monkey (*Chinese zodiac*)　猴　N

hòubian(r)　back; behind; in back of　後邊(兒)／后边(儿)　PW

hòumian　back; behind; in back of　後面／后面　PW

hòunián　year after next　後年／后年　PW

hòutiān　day after tomorrow　後天／后天　TW

hǔ　tiger (*Chinese zodiac*)　虎　N

huā　spend (*money*)　花　V

huà　talk; speech; words　話／话　N

huàjiā　painter; artist　畫家／画家　N

huàn　exchange; change　換／换　V

Huáng Hé　Yellow River　黃河　PW

huángsè　yellow　黃色　N

huànqián　exchange; change currency　換錢／换钱　VO

huāqián　spend money　花錢／花钱　V/VO

huàzhuāng　put on makeup　化妝／化妆　VO

huàzhuāngpǐn　makeup　化妝品／化妆品　N

huàzhuāngshì　bathroom　化妝室／化妆室　N

hùfàsù [píng]　conditioner (*for hair*) [bottle of]　護髮素 [瓶]／护发素 [瓶]　N

huí　return (*to a place*)　回　V

huì　likely to; will likely; sure to　會／会　AV

huì　can, know (*how to*)　會／会　V

huíjiā　go; return home　回家　VO

huílai　come back to; return　回來／回来　V

huíqu　return　回去　V

huīsè　gray　灰色　N

huǒchē [liàng]　train　火車 [輛]／火车 [辆]　N

huòzhě　or (*in statements*)　或者　C

hùshi　nurse　護士／护士　N

húzi　beard　鬍子／胡子　N

J

jī　rooster; chicken (*Chinese zodiac*)　雞／鸡　N

jǐ (ge)　how many (*less than ten*)　幾(個)／几(个)　QW

jiā　plus; add to　加　V

jiā　home; family　家　N

jiādàhào　size extra large　加大號／加大号　N

jiákè [jiàn]　jacket　夾克 [件]／夹克 [件]　N

jiālǐrén　family members　家裏人／家里人　N

jiǎn　subtract　減／减　V

jiàn　see/meet up with (*someone*)　見／见　V

Jiānádà　Canada　加拿大　PW

Jiānádàrén　Canadian (*person/people*)　加拿大人　N

Jiānádà yuán　Canadian dollar　加拿大元　N

jiǎngjià　bargain (*for a better price*)　講價／讲价　VO

jiānglái　future; in the future　將來／将来　TW/N

jiǎnjià　be on sale　減價／减价　VO

jiǎntǐzì　simplified character　簡體字／简体字　N

jiànzhùshī　architect　建築師／建筑师　N

jiāo　teach　教　V

jiǎo　1/10 of the primary monetary unit (*written*); "dime"　角　M

jiào　tell (*someone to do something*)　叫　V

jiào　called; be called (*by a given name*); be named　叫　EV

jiàoshòu [wèi]　professor　教授 [位]／教授 [位]　N

jiāoshū　teach　教書／教书　VO

jiàoxuélóu　classroom building　教學樓／教学楼　N

jiàqian　price　價錢／价钱　N

jiāwù　household chores/duties　家務／家务　N

jiāxiǎohào　size extra small　加小號／加小号　N

Jiāzhōu　California　加州　PW

jiē　meet up with; pick up (*someone*)　接　V

jiē [tiáo]　street　街 [條]／街 [条]　N

jiějie　elder sister　姐姐　N

jiěmèi　sisters　姐妹　N

jìfù　stepfather　繼父／继父　N

jíle (hǎojíle, kuàijíle . . .)　extremely (good, fast, etc.)　極了(好極了, 快極了……)／极了(好极了,快极了……)　S

jìmǔ　stepmother　繼母／继母　N

jìn　near　近　SV

jǐngchá　police officer　警察　N

jīnglǐ　manager (*of business, etc.*)　經理／经理　N

jìniànpǐn [ge]　souvenir　紀念品 [個]／纪念品 [个]　N

jīnnián　this year　今年　TW

jìnqu　go in　進去／进去　V

jīnsè　gold (*color*)　金色　N

jīntiān　today　今天　TW

jīntiān wǎnshang　tonight; this evening　今天晚上　TW

jiǔ　nine　九　NU

jiǔ　wine; alcoholic beverage　酒　N

jiù　only; exactly; precisely; then　就　A

jiùhuǒyuán　firefighter　救火員／救火员　N

jiùjiu　uncle (*mother's brother*)　舅舅　N

Jiǔyuè　September　九月　N

juéde　feel/think that　覺得／觉得　V

júhóngsè　orange (*color*)　橘紅色　N

jūnrén　soldier　軍人／军人　N

K

kāfēi [bēi]   coffee [cup of]   咖啡 [杯]   N

kāfēisè   coffee-colored/brown   咖啡色   N

kāichē   drive a car; go by car   開車／开车   VO

kāishǐ   begin; start   開始／开始   V

kàn   watch; look; see (*a movie, etc.*)   看   V

kàn   read (*a book, etc.*)   看   V

kànbào   read a newspaper   看報／看报   VO

kàn diànshì   watch TV   看電視／看电视   VO

kàn diànyǐng   see a movie   看電影／看电影   VO

kànjian   see   看見／看见   V

kàn (yí) kàn   look; take a look   看(一)看   VP

kànshū   read; read a book; reading   看書／看书   VO/N

kǎoshì   test; give or take a test   考試／考试   N/V

kě   thirsty   渴   SV

kè   lesson; class   课／课   N/M

kěn   willing to   肯   AV

kěnéng   probably; maybe   可能   A

kèqi   polite   客氣／客气   SV

kěshì   but; yet; however   可是   C

kěyǐ   can; may (*permission to*)   可以   AV

kòng   free time   空   N

kǒu   mouth (*the radical*)   口   N

kuài   quick; quickly; fast   快   SV

kuài   primary monetary unit (*spoken*); denomination equivalent to a "dollar"   塊／块   M

kuàijìshī   accountant   會計師／会计师   N

kuài yào + *verb*   soon; about to; before long   快要   A

kuàizi [shuāng]   chopsticks [pair of]   筷子 [雙]／筷子 [双]   N

kùn   sleepy   睏／困   SV

kùzi [tiáo]   pants/trousers [pair of]   褲子 [條]／裤子 [条]   N

L

lái   come   來／来   V

lánsè   blue   藍色／蓝色   N

lǎodà   oldest child   老大   N

lǎoèr   second child (*in a family*)   老二   N

lǎogōng   husband   老公   N

lǎolao   maternal grandmother   姥姥   N

lǎopo   wife   老婆   N

lǎoshī [wèi]   teacher   老師 [位]／老师 [位]   N

lǎoxiǎo   youngest child   老小   N

lǎoyāo   youngest child   老么／老幺   N

lǎoye   maternal grandfather   姥爺／姥爷   N

lèi   tired; weary   累   SV

lěng   cold (*temperature*)   冷   SV

lí   from (*distant from*)   離／离   CV

(yì) lǐ   one mile (*Chinese mile*)   (一)里   N/M

liǎng (ge)   two; a couple of   兩(個)／两(个)   NU

liángxié [shuāng]   sandals [pair of]   涼鞋 [雙]／凉鞋 [双]   N

liáotiān(r)   chat   聊天兒／聊天儿   VO

lǐbianr   in; inside   裏邊兒／里边儿   PW

líng   zero   零   NU

línjū   neighbor   鄰居／邻居   N

liù   six   六   NU

liùshí   sixty   六十   NU

Liùyuè   June   六月

lóng   dragon (*Chinese zodiac*)   龍／龙   N

lóu   floor (*in a building*)   樓／楼   M

lóu [dòng]   building (*multi-storied*)   樓 [棟]／楼 [栋]   N

lóushàng   upstairs   樓上／楼上   PW

lóuxià   downstairs   樓下／楼下   PW

lù [tiáo]   path; road   路 [條]／路 [条]   N

Lúbǐ   rupee (*India and Pakistan*)   盧比／卢比   N

Luòshānjī   Los Angeles   洛杉磯／洛杉矶   PW

lùdēng   green light (*traffic*)   綠燈／绿灯   N

lùsè   green   綠色／绿色   N

lùshī   lawyer   律師／律师   N

lǚxíng   travel   旅行   V

M

ma   (*question particle*)   嗎／吗   P

mā   mom; mother   媽／妈   N

mǎ   horse (*Chinese zodiac*)   馬／马   N

mǎi   purchase; buy   買／买   V

mài   sell   賣／卖   V

mǎi dōngxi   shop (*buy things*)   買東西／买东西   VO

māma   mom; mother   媽媽／妈妈   N

mǎma-hūhū   fair to middling; so-so   馬馬虎虎／马马虎虎   IE

màn   slow   慢   SV

máng   busy; have something to do   忙   SV

máo   1/10 of the primary monetary unit (*spoken*); "dime"   毛   M

máobǐ [zhī]   writing brush   毛筆 [枝]／毛笔 [枝]   N

máojīn [tiáo]   towel   毛巾 [條]／毛巾 [条]   N

máoyī [jiàn]   sweater   毛衣 [件]   N

màozi [dǐng]   hat; cap   帽子 [頂]／帽子 [顶]   N

méi   (*negator for* **yǒu**)   没   A

měi (ge)   each   每(個)／每(个)   PR

měi ge rén   everyone   每個人／每个人   N

méi guānxi   that's all right; no problem   没關係／没关系   IE

Měiguó   America; U.S.   美國／美国   PW

Měiguórén   American (*person/people*)   美國人／美国人   N

Měijīn   U.S. money   美金   N

mèimei   younger sister   妹妹   N

méi shì   nothing's wrong; it doesn't matter; never mind   没事   IE

měitiān   daily; every day   每天   TW

méi yìsi uninteresting; dull 没意思 SV

méiyǒu not have; be without 没有 V

míngnián next year 明年 TW

míngtiān tomorrow 明天 TW

míngxìnpiàn [zhāng] postcard 明信片 [張]／明信片 [张] N

míngzi [ge] name; first name; given name 名字 [個]／名字 [个] N

mǐsè beige 米色 N

mìshu secretary 秘書／秘书 N

mótuōchē [liàng] motorcycle; motorbike 摩托車 [輛]／摩托车 [辆] N

mù tree; wood (the radical) 木 N

mǔqin mother; mom 母親／母亲 N

N

nà in that case; then 那 C

nà that; that one 那 PR/SP

nǎinai paternal grandmother 奶奶 N

nàli there 那裏／那里 PW

nǎli, nǎli (polite rejection of a compliment) 哪裡, 哪裡／哪里, 哪里 IE

nàme then, in that case 那麼／那么 C

nán difficult 難／难 SV

nánbian(r) south (side/direction) 南邊(兒)／南边(儿) PW

nánháir boy 男孩兒／男孩儿 N

nánháizi boy 男孩子 N

Nán Měizhōu South America 南美洲 PW

nánpéngyou boyfriend 男朋友 N

nǎr where 哪兒／哪儿 QW

nàr there 那兒／那儿 PW

ne and what about X 呢 P

něi which 哪 QW

nèi that; that one 那 PR/SP

nèige that, that one 那個／那个 PR/SP

néng able to; can (circumstances permitting) 能 AV

nèr there 那兒／那儿 PW

nǐ you (informal) 你 PR

nián year 年 N/M

niàn study 念 V

niánjí year (in school); grade 年級／年级 N

niànshū attend school 念書／念书 VO

nǐ de your(s) 你的 PR

Nǐ duō dà? How old are you? 你多大 PH

nǐ hǎo hello; how do you do? 你好 IE

Nǐ jǐ suì? How old are you? 你幾歲／你几岁 PH

Nǐ kàn! Take a look! 你看！ PH

nǐmen you (plural) 你們／你们 PR

nǐmen zìjǐ yourselves 你们自己 PR

nín you (formal) 您 PR

nín guìxìng what's your (honorable) name 您貴姓／您贵姓 IE

nín hǎo hello; how do you do? 您好 IE

nín zǎo good morning 您早 IE

niú ox (Chinese zodiac) 牛 N

Niǔyuē New York 紐約／纽约 PW

niúzǎikù [tiáo] blue jeans; jeans 牛仔褲 [條]／牛仔裤 [条] N

nǐ zǎo good morning 你早 IE

nǐ zìjǐ yourself 你自己 PR

nòng make, cook 弄 V

nóngmín farmer 農民／农民 N

nuǎnhuo warm 暖和 SV

nǚ'ér daughter 女兒／女儿 N

nǚháir girl 女孩兒／女孩儿 N

nǚháizi girl 女孩子 N

nǚpéngyou girlfriend 女朋友 N

O

Ò oh (sudden understanding) 噢 I

Ōuyuán Euro (currency) 歐元／欧元 N

Ōuzhōu Europe 歐洲／欧洲 PW

Ōuzhōurén European (person/people) 歐洲人／欧洲人 N

P

pá climb; crawl 爬 V

pàng fat 胖 SV

pǎo run 跑 V

pǎobù run; jog 跑步 VO

péngyou friend 朋友 N

piányi inexpensive; cheap 便宜 SV

píjiǔ [píng] beer [bottle of] 啤酒 [瓶] N

píng bottle 瓶 N/M

píngcháng generally 平常 A

píxié [shuāng] leather shoes [pair of] 皮鞋 [雙]／皮鞋 [双] N

Pǔtōnghuà Standard Mandarin 普通話／普通话 N

Q

qī seven 七 NU

qí ride astride (a bike, horse, etc.) 騎／骑 V

qǐ get up (from bed); rise 起 V

qián [kuài] money 錢 [塊]／钱 [块] N

qián(bian) front; in front 前(邊)／前(边) PW

qiánmian front; in front 前面 PW

qiánnián year before last 前年 TW

qiántiān day before yesterday 前天 TW

qìchē [liàng] car 汽車 [輛]／汽车 [辆] N

qǐchuáng get up from bed 起床 VO

qǐng please (used in polite requests) 請／请 V

qǐng invite; treat somebody to a meal 請／请 V

qǐngwèn may I ask (followed by inquiry) 請問／请问 IE

qīnqi relative(s) 親戚／亲戚 N

qīshí seventy 七十 NU

qítā (de) others (the rest, what remains) 其他(的) PR

qiú [ge] ball 球 [個]／球 [个] N

Qīyuè July 七月 N

qīzi wife 妻子／妻子 N

qí zìxíngchē ride a bicycle 騎自行車／骑自行车 VO

qù go 去 V

qùguo gone to 去過／去过 VP

qù lǚxíng go on a journey 去旅行 VP

qù mǎi dōngxi go shopping 去買東西／去买东西 VP

qùnián last year 去年 TW

qúnzi [tiáo] skirt 裙子 [條]／裙子 [条] N

qù sànsanbù take a walk/stroll 去散散步 VP

qù wánr go have some fun 去玩兒／去玩儿 VP

R

ránhòu after(ward); and then; after that 然後／然后 TW

rè hot (temperature) 熱／热 SV

règǒu [ge] hot dog 熱狗 [個]／热狗 [个] N

rén [ge] person 人 [個]／人 [个] N

Rénmínbì [kuài] People's money (PRC currency) 人民幣 [塊]／人民币 [块] N

rènshi know a person 認識／认识 V

rènshi zì recognize/know Chinese characters; be literate 認識(字)／认识(字) V

rì sun; day (the radical) 日 N

Rìběn Japan 日本 PW

Rìběnhuà Japanese (language) 日本話／日本话 N

Rìběnrén Japanese (person/people) 日本人 N

Rìwén Japanese (language) 日文 N

rìyòngpǐn articles of everyday use 日用品 N

Rìyǔ Japanese (language) 日語／日语 N

Rìyuán Japanese yen 日元 N

róngyì easy 容易 SV

rúguǒ unless; if 如果 C

S

sān three 三 NU

sànbù take a walk/stroll 散步 VO

sānshí thirty 三十 NU

Sānyuè March 三月 N

shān [zuò] mountain 山 [座]／山 [座] N

shàng go to; attend (school) 上 V

shàngbān(r) go to work/the office 上班(兒)／上班(儿) VO

shàngbiānr up; above 上邊兒／上边儿 PW

shàng cèsuǒ use the toilet 上廁所／上厕所 VO

shāngchǎng mall; market; bazaar; shopping mall 商場／商场 N

shāngdiàn [ge] store; shop 商店 [個]／商店 [个] N

shàng ge yuè last month 上個月／上个月 last month TW

Shànghǎi Shanghai 上海 PW

shàngkè attend class; start a class; go to class; hold class 上課／上课 VO

shàngmian top; above 上面 PW

shàngwǎng go on the web; go online; go on the Internet 上網／上网 VO

shàngwǔ morning (from about 10 A.M. to noon) 上午 PW

shàng xīngqī last week 上星期 TW

shàngxué go to school 上學／上学 VO

shǎo few (in number) 少 SV

shé snake (Chinese zodiac) 蛇 N

shéi who 誰／谁 QW

shēng be born; give birth to 生 V

shēng háizi give birth to a child 生孩子 VO

shēnghuó fāngshì lifestyle 生活方式 N

shēngfù birth father 生父 N

shēngmǔ birth mother 生母 N

shēngqì angry; upset; mad 生氣／生气 SV

shēngrì birthday 生日 N

shēngzài born in 生在 VP

shénme what 什麼／什么 QW

shénme shíhou when 什麼時候／什么时候 QW

shí ten 十 NU

shì to be 是 EV

shì room (as in apartment unit) 室 N

shì [jiàn] matter; affair 事 [件] N

shì de yes; that's right 是的 IE

shí'èr twelve 十二 NU

shí'èr shēngxiào the twelve animals of the Chinese zodiac 十二生肖 N

Shí'èryuè December 十二月 N

shīfu master craftsman; skilled worker 師傅／师傅 N

shíhou time; moment 時候／时候 N

shíjiān time 時間／时间 N

shìqing [jiàn] matter; affair 事情 [件] N

shíyī eleven 十一 NU

Shíyīyuè November 十一月 N

Shíyuè October 十月 N

shòu thin; slender 瘦 SV

shǒubiǎo [kuài] watch; wristwatch 手錶 [塊]／手表 [块] N

shòuhuòyuán sales clerk 售貨員 N

shǒujī [ge] cell phone 手機 [個]／手机 [个] N

shǒujī hàomǎ cell phone number 手機號碼／手机号码 N

shū [běn] book 書 [本]／书 [本] N

shǔ to belong to one of 12 zodiac signs 屬／属 V

shǔ rat/mouse (Chinese zodiac) 鼠 N

shuākǎ charge; swipe a credit card 刷卡 VO

shuāng　a pair of [something]　雙／双　M
shuāyá　brush (one's) teeth　刷牙　VO
shūbāo [ge]　bookbag　書包 [個]／书包 [个]　N
shūdiàn　bookstore　書店／书店　N
shūfu　feel well; comfortable　舒服　SV
shuǐ [bēi/píng]　water [glass/bottle of]　水 [杯／瓶]　N
shuì　sleep; go to sleep　睡　V/VO
shuìjiào　sleep; go to sleep　睡覺／睡觉　V/VO
shuì lǎnjiào　sleep in/late　睡懶覺／睡懒觉　VO
shuō　talk; speak; say　說／说　V/VO
shuōhuà　talk; speak; say　說話／说话　V/VO
shuō Zhōngguóhuà　speak Chinese　說中國話／说中国话　VP
shūshu　uncle (father's younger brother)　叔叔　N
shūtóufa　comb (one's) hair　梳頭髮／梳头发　VO
shūzi [bǎ]　comb　梳子 [把]　N
sì　four　四　NU
sījī　driver; chauffeur　司機／司机　N
Sìyuè　April　四月　N
suì　age　歲／岁　M
suìshu　age　歲數／岁数　N
suǒyǐ　so; therefore　所以　C
sùshè　dormitory　宿舍　N
Sūzhōu　Suzhou (city in eastern China)　蘇州／苏州　PW

T

tā　he　他　PR
tā　she　她　PR
tā　it (most often not translated)　它　PR
tài . . . (often takes **le**)　too; exceedingly; extremely　太......(了)　A
Táiběi　Taipei　台北　PW
Táibì　Taiwan dollar　台幣／台币　N
Tàiguó　Thailand　泰國／泰国　PW
Tàiguórén　Thai (person/people)　泰國人／泰国人　N
tàitai　wife (formal)　太太　N
Táiwān　Taiwan　台灣／台湾　PW
tāmen　they; them　他們；她們；它們／他们；她们；它们　PR
táng [kuài]　candy [piece of]　糖 [塊]／糖 [块]　N
tiān　day　天　N/M
tiān a　good grief; my heavens　天啊　IE
tiānqì　weather　天氣／天气　N
tiāntiān　daily; every day　天天　TW
tīng　listen to　聽／听　V
tǐng　very; rather; quite　挺　A
tīng yīnyuè　listen to music　聽音樂／听音乐　VO
tōngcháng　usually　通常　A

(tóngfù) yìmǔ de xiōngdìjiěmèi　half sibling (same father)　(同父)異母的兄弟姐妹／(同父)异母的兄弟姐妹　N
(tóngmǔ) yìfù de xiōngdìjiěmèi　half sibling (same mother)　(同母)異父的兄弟姐妹／(同母)异父的兄弟姐妹　N
tóngshì　colleague; fellow worker　同事　N
tóngshìmen　colleagues; fellow workers　同事們／同事们　N
tóngxué　schoolmate; classmate　同學／同学　N
tóngxuémen　classmates; fellow students　同學們／同学们　N
tóufa　hair (on human head)　頭髮／头发　N
tóuténg　have a headache　頭疼／头疼　VO
tǔ　soil; earth　土　N
tù　rabbit (Chinese zodiac)　兔　N
tuōxié [shuāng]　slippers [pair of]　拖鞋 [雙]／拖鞋 [双]　N
túshūguǎn [ge]　library　圖書館／图书馆　N
T-xù shān [jiàn]　T-shirt　T-恤衫 [件]　N

W

wà　wow　哇　I
wàigōng　maternal grandfather　外公　N
wàiguó　foreign country　外國／外国　N
wàiguóhuà　foreign language　外國話／外国话　N
wàiguórén　foreigner　外國人／外国人　N
wàipó　maternal grandmother　外婆　N
wàitào [jiàn]　jacket; coat; overcoat　外套 [件]　N
wàiyǔ　foreign language　外語／外语　N
wǎn　late　晚　SV
wǎn　bowl　碗　N
wǎncān　supper; dinner　晚餐　N
wǎnfàn　supper; dinner　晚飯／晚饭　N
wǎng　toward(s)　往　CV
wǎng . . . guǎi　turn (in direction of)　往......拐　VP
wàng le　forgot　忘了　VP
wǎng qián zǒu　go straight　往前走　VP
wán(r)　play; have fun; amuse oneself　玩(兒)／玩(儿)　V
wán(r) diànzǐ yóuxì　play video games　玩(兒)電子遊戲／玩(儿)电子游戏　VP
wǎnshang　night; evening (6 P.M. until midnight)　晚上　TW
wàzi [shuāng]　socks [pair of]　襪子 [雙]／袜子 [双]　N
wèi　(polite measure word for people)　位　M
wèishēngzhǐ　toilet paper　衛生紙／卫生纸　N
wèishénme　why　為什麼／为什么　QW
wèn　ask; inquire　問／问　V
wénjù [xiē]　stationery　文具 [些]　N
wèntí [ge]　question; problem　問題 [個]／问题 [个]　N

wènwen   ask; inquire   問問／问问   V
wǒ   I; me   我   PR
wǒ de   my; mine   我的   PR
Wǒ lǎo yàngzi.   I'm the same as usual.   我老樣子／我老样子   PH
wǒmen   we; us   我們／我们   PR
wǒmen de   our(s)   我們的／我们的   PR
wǔ   five   五   NU
wǔcān   lunch   午餐   N
wǔfàn   lunch   午飯／午饭   N
wǔjiào   afternoon nap   午覺／午觉   N
wǔshuì   afternoon nap; take a nap   午睡   N/V
Wǔyuè   May   五月   N

X

xǐ   wash   洗   V
xià(chē, huǒchē . . .)   get off (a bus, train, etc.)   下(車,火車……)／下(车,火车……)   V
xiàbān   get off work   下班   VO
xiàcì   next time   下次   N
xià (ge)   next (in a series)   下 (個)／下 (个)   SP
xià (ge) xīngqī   next week   下(個)星期／下(个)星期   TW
xià ge yuè   next month   下個月／下个月   TW
xiàkè   get out of class   下課／下课   VO
xiàmian   under; bottom; below; underneath   下面   PW
xiān   first; in advance of   先   A
xiǎng   think; want to; feel like; intend to   想   AV
Xiāng Gǎng   Hong Kong   香港   PW
xiànjīn   cash   現金／现金   N
xiānsheng   husband; Mister, Mr.   先生   N
xiànzài   now; at present; at this moment   現在／现在   TW
xiǎo   small; little   小   SV
xiǎo háizi   kid; child   小孩子   N
xiǎohào   size small   小號／小号   N
xiǎojiě   young lady; Miss   小姐   N
xiǎoxué   elementary school   小學／小学   N
xiàozhǎng [wèi]   principal   校長 [位]／校长 [位]   N
xiàwǔ   afternoon   下午   TW
xiàyǔ   to rain   下雨   VO
Xībānyá   Spain   西班牙   PW
Xībānyáhuà   Spanish (language)   西班牙話／西班牙话   N
Xībānyárén   Spanish (person/people)   西班牙人   N
Xībānyáwén   Spanish (language)   西班牙文／西班牙话文   N
Xībānyáyǔ   Spanish (language)   西班牙語／西班牙语   N
xīběi   northwest   西北   PW
xībian(r)   west (side; direction)   西邊(兒)／西边(儿)   PW
xiē   (for a small amount)   些   M
xié [shuāng]   shoes [pair of]   鞋 [雙]／鞋 [双]   N

xiě   write   寫／写   V
xiè   thank; (also a surname)   謝／谢   V/N
Xièxie nǐ/nín   thank you   謝謝你／您 ‖ 谢谢你／您   PH
xiězì   write   寫字／写字   VO
xiě zuòyè   do homework   寫作業／写作业   VO
xǐfàshuǐ [píng]   shampoo [bottle of]   洗髮水 [瓶]／洗发水 [瓶]   N
xīguā   watermelon   西瓜   N
xǐhuan   like; prefer   喜歡／喜欢   V
xǐliǎn   wash one's face   洗臉／洗脸   VO
xīnán   southwest   西南   PW
xíng   be OK; all right   行   V
xìng   surname   姓   N
xìng   be surnamed   姓   V
xīngqī   week   星期   TW
Xīngqī'èr   Tuesday   星期二   TW
Xīngqīliù   Saturday   星期六   TW
xīnqíng   mood; state of mind   心情   N
Xīngqīrì   Sunday   星期日   TW
Xīngqīsān   Wednesday   星期三   TW
Xīngqīsì   Thursday   星期四   TW
Xīngqītiān   Sunday   星期天   TW
Xīngqīwǔ   Friday   星期五   TW
Xīngqīyī   Monday   星期一   TW
xìnyòngkǎ [zhāng]   credit card   信用卡 [張]／信用卡 [张]   N
xiōngdì   brothers   兄弟   N
xiōngdìjiěmèi   brothers and sisters   兄弟姐妹   N
xiūxi   rest; take a rest; take it easy   休息   V
xǐ yīfu   do the laundry   洗衣服   VO
xǐzǎo   bathe; take a bath/shower   洗澡   VO
xué   study; learn how to   學／学   V
xuésheng   student   學生／学生   N
xuéxiào   school   學校／学校   N

Y

yágāo [zhī]   toothpaste [tube of]   牙膏 [支]   N
yáng   sheep/ram (Chinese zodiac)   羊   N
yàng   kind; type; shape   樣／样   M
yǎngfù   adoptive father   養父／养父   N
yǎngmǔ   adoptive mother   養母／养母   N
Yángshuò   Yangshuo (city in southern China)   陽朔／阳朔   PW
yánjiūshēngyuàn   graduate school   研究生院   N
yánsè   color   顏色／颜色   N
yǎnyuán   actor   演員／演员   N
yào   have a desire to; want to; going to; will   要   AV
yào   medicine   藥／药   N
yàoshi   if   要是   C
yáshuā [zhī]   toothbrush   牙刷 [支]   N
yáxiàn   dental floss   牙線／牙线   N
yáyī   dentist   牙醫／牙医   N
Yàzhōu   Asia   亞洲／亚洲   PW

Yàzhōurén   Asian (*person/people*)   亞洲人／亚洲人   N

yě   too; also; as well   也   A

yèli   at night; during the night; nighttime   夜裏／夜里   TW/N

yěxǔ   perhaps; might; maybe   也许／也許   A

yéye   paternal grandfather; Grandpa (*respectful form of address*)   爺爺／爷爷   N

yī   one (*the number*)   一   NU

yìbǎi, èrbǎi . . .   one hundred, two hundred, etc.   一百，二百……   NU

yìbān   generally   一般   A

yìbān lái shuō   generally speaking   一般來说／一般来说   VP

yícì   once; one time   一次   NU/M

Yìdàlì   Italy   意大利   PW

Yìdàlìhuà   Italian (*language*)   意大利話／意大利话   N

Yìdàlìrén   Italian (*person/people*)   意大利人   N

Yìdàlìwén   Italian (*language*)   意大利文   N

Yìdàlìyǔ   Italian (*language*)   意大利語   N

yìdiǎnr   a bit; a little; some   一點兒／一点儿   NU/M

yídìng   certainly; for sure   一定   A

yídìng děi   certainly must   一定得   A/AV

yīfu [jiàn]   clothing [article of]   衣服 [件]   N

yí ge   a; one of   一個／一个   NU/M

yígòng   altogether; in all; in total   一共   A

yǐhòu   later; afterwards   以後／以后   TW

yìhuǐr   in a little while   一會兒／一会儿   TW

yìhuǐr jiàn   see you in a little while   一會兒見／一会儿见   IE

yǐjing   already   已經／已经   A

yí kèzhōng   quarter of an hour   一刻鐘／一刻钟   N

yíkuàir   together   一塊兒／一块儿   A

yīlóu   first floor   一樓／一楼   N

Yìndù   India   印度   PW

Yìndùhuà   Hindi (*language*)   印度話／印度话   N

Yìndùrén   Indian (*person/people*)   印度人   N

Yìndùwén   Hindi (*language*)   印度文   N

Yìndùyǔ   Hindi (*language*)   印度語   N

Yīngbàng   British pound   英鎊／英镑   N

yīnggāi   should; ought to   應該／应该   AV

Yīngguó   Britain; England   英國／英国   PW

Yīngguórén   British (*person/people*)   英國人／英国人   N

Yīngwén   English (*language*)   英文   N

Yīngyǔ   English (*language*)   英语   N

yínháng   bank   銀行／银行   N

yínsè   silver (*color*)   銀色／银色   N

yīnwéi   because; because of   因為／因为   C

yīnyuè   music   音樂／音乐   N

yīnyuèjiā   musician   音樂家／音乐家   N

yìqǐ   together   一起   A

yǐqián   ago; before; previously   以前   TW

yīshēng   physician; doctor   醫生／医生   N

yìshùjiā   artist   藝術家／艺术家   N

yì tiān liǎng cì   twice a day   一天兩次／一天两次   TW

yìxiē   a few; several; some   一些   NU/M

yíyàng   same; identical; alike   一樣／一样   SV

Yīyuè   January   一月   N

yìzhí   all along (*in time or place*)   一直   A

yìzhí zǒu   go straight ahead   一直走   VP

yì zhōu jǐ cì   several times a week   一周幾次／一周几次   TW

yòng   use; utilize; make use of   用   V

yǒu   there is/are; have; possess   有   V

yòu . . . yòu   both . . . and   又……又   C

yòubian(r)   right side   右邊(兒)／右边(儿)   PW

yǒude shíhou   sometimes   有的時候／有的时候   TW

yǒukòng   be free, have free time   有空   VO

yǒushì   busy; have something to do   有事   VO

yǒu yìsi   interesting; fun   有意思   SV

yǒuyòng   useful   有用   SV

yú [tiáo]   fish   魚 [條]／鱼 [条]   N

yǔ   rain   雨   N

yuán   primary monetary unit (*written*); "dollar"   元   M

yuǎn   far   遠／远   SV

yuè   month (*in words designating the months*)   月   N

yújiā   yoga   瑜珈   N

yùndòngfú [jiàn]   athletic clothes   運動服／运动服 [件]   N

yùndòngxié [shuāng]   sneakers/athletic shoes [pair of]   運動鞋 [雙]／运动鞋 [双]   N

yùndòngyuán   athlete   運動員／运动员   N

Z

zài   on; at; in; be located at   在   V

zài . . . de shíhou   during   在……的時候／在……的时候   TW

zàijiàn   good-bye; see you again   再見／再见   IE

zài shuō yícì   repeat what was said   再说一次／再说一次   VP

zài wàibian   outside   在外邊／在外边   VP/PW

zǎo   early   早   SV

zǎo   morning (*as a greeting*)   早   IE

zǎocān   breakfast   早餐   N

zǎocāo   morning calisthenics   早操   N

zǎodiǎn   breakfast   早點／早点   N

zǎofàn   breakfast   早飯／早饭   N

zǎoshang   morning (*until about 9–10 A.M.*)   早上   TW

zǎoshang hǎo   good morning   早上好   IE

zěnme   how; how come   怎麼／怎么   QW

zěnme le   what's the matter   怎麼了／怎么了   VP

zěnmeyàng   how does that sound to you (*after a suggestion*)   怎麼樣／怎么样   QW

zěnmeyàng   how's it going   怎麼樣／怎么样   IE

zhàn [ge] station/stop (*of a bus, train, etc.*) 站 [個]／站 [个] N

zhǎngdà grow up 長大／长大 V

zhàngfu husband 丈夫 N

zhǎo look for 找 V

zháojí worried; nervous; anxious 著急／着急 V

zhǎoqián make change; give in change 找錢／找钱 VO

zhàoyàng as usual; as before 照樣／照样 A

zhè this; this one 這／这 PR/SP

zhège this one 這個／这个 PR/SP

zhèi this; this one 這／这 PR/SP

zhèige this one 這個／这个 PR/SP

zhèlǐ here 這裏／这里 PW

zhème (to) this extent; such; so 這麼／这么 A

zhēn really; truly; indeed 真 A

zhēn de ma really; is that true? 真的嗎／真的吗 IE

zhèr here 這兒／这儿 PW

zhèxiē these 這些／这些 PR

zhèyàng so; like this 這樣／这样 A

zhǐ only 只 A

zhǐ [zhāng] paper [sheet of] 紙 [張]／纸 [张] N

zhīdao know (*have knowledge of*) 知道 V

zhōngfàn lunch 中飯／中饭 N

Zhōngguó China 中國／中国 PW

Zhōngguóhuà Chinese (*language*) 中國話／中国话 N

Zhōngguórén Chinese (*person/people*) 中國人／中国人 N

zhōnghào size medium 中號／中号 N

zhōngjiānr between; center; middle 中間兒／中间儿 PW

zhōngtóu [ge] hour 鐘頭 [個]／钟头 [个] N

Zhōngwén Chinese (*language*) 中文 N

zhōngwǔ noon; midday 中午 TW

zhōngxué middle school; secondary school 中學／中学 N

zhōumò weekend 週末／周末 N

Zhōurì Sunday 週日／周日 TW

zhū pig/boar (*Chinese zodiac*) 豬／猪 N

zhù stay at; reside; live 住 V

zhuǎn turn in direction of 轉／转 V

zhuànqián earn money 賺錢／赚钱 VO

zhuōzi [zhāng] table 桌子 [張]／桌子 [张] N

zhùzai reside (at); live (at) 住在 VP

zì [ge] character; word 字 [個]／字 [个] N

zìdiǎn [běn] dictionary 字典 [本] N

zìjǐ myself; by myself; oneself 自己 PR

zǐsè purple 紫色 N

zìxíngchē [liàng] bicycle 自行車 [輛]／自行车 [辆] N

zǒu go by way of; walk 走 V

zǒu leave (*depart from a place*) 走 V

zǒulù walk; walk on the road 走路 VO

zuì most; exceedingly (*superlative prefix*) 最 A/PREF

zuìhǎo best 最好 SV

zuìhòu finally; at the end 最後／最后 A

zuìjìn recently 最近 TW

zuò ride on; take; go by (*a bus, train, etc.*) 坐 V/CV

zuò make; cook; do; engage in 做 V

zuǒbian(r) left side 左邊(兒)／左边(儿) PW

zuò dìtiě take the subway 坐地鐵／坐地铁 VO

zuòfàn do the cooking; cook food; prepare a meal 做飯／做饭 VO

zuò gōngchē qù go by bus 坐公車去／坐公车去 VP

zuò gōngkè do homework 做功課／做功课 VO

zuòjiā writer 作家 N

zuò jiāwù do housework 做家務／做家务 VO

zuótiān yesterday 昨天 TW

zuò wǎnfàn cook dinner 做晚飯／做晚饭 VO

zuòyè homework 作業／作业 N

zuò yújiā do yoga 做瑜伽 VO

zuò zǎocāo work out in the morning 做早操 VO

zuò zǎofàn cook breakfast 做早飯／做早饭 VO

zuò zhōngfàn cook lunch 做中飯／做中饭 VO

English-Chinese Glossary

A

a (one of) yí ge 一個／一个 NU

a bit yìdiǎnr 一點兒／一点儿 NU/M

a couple of liǎng ge 兩個／两个 NU

a little yìdiǎnr 一點兒／一点儿 NU/M

able to néng; huì 能;會／能;会 AV

above shàngbian; shàngmian 上邊;上面／上边;上面 PW

accountant kuàijìshī 會計師／会计师 N

actor yǎnyuán 演員／演员 N

add to jiā 加 V

address dìzhǐ 地址 N

adoptive father yǎngfù 養父／养父 N

adoptive mother yǎngmǔ 養母／养母 N

affair (*business*) shì(qing) [jiàn] 事(情) [件] N

Africa Fēizhōu 非洲 PW

African (*person/people*) Fēizhōurén 非洲人 N

after yǐhòu 以後／以后 TW

after(ward/s) ránhòu 然後／然后 TW

afternoon xiàwǔ 下午 TW

afternoon nap wǔshuì 午睡 N

age suì; suìshu 歲;歲數／岁;岁数 M/N

ago yǐqián 以前 TW

ah āi yā 哎呀 INT

airplane fēijī [jià] 飛機 [架]／飞机 [架] N

alcoholic beverage jiǔ 酒 N

alike yíyàng 一樣／一样 SV

all dōu 都 A

all along (*in time or place*) yìzhí 一直 A

all right hǎo; xíng 好;行 SV

already yǐjing 已經／已经 A

also yě 也 A

altogether (*in total*) yígòng 一共 A

A.M. shàngwǔ 上午 TW

America Měiguó 美國／美国 PW

American (*person/people*) Měiguórén 美國人／美国人 N

American dollar Měijīn; Měiyuán 美金;美元 N

and gēn; hé 跟;和 C

and then ránhòu 然後／然后 TW

and what about ... ... ne ......呢 P

angry shēngqì 生氣／生气 SV

another (*a different one*) biéde 別的 SP

anxious zháojí 著急／着急 SV

April Sìyuè 四月 N

architect jiànzhùshī 建築師／建筑师 N

arrived, to have dào le 到了 VP

articles of daily use rìyòngpǐn 日用品 N

artist yìshùjiā 藝術家／艺术家 N

as before zhàoyàng 照樣／照样 A

as usual zhàoyàng 照樣／照样 A

Asia Yàzhōu 亞洲／亚洲 PW

Asian (*person/people*) Yàzhōurén 亞洲人／亚洲人 N

ask wèn; wènwen 問;問問／问;问问 V

assignment (*school*) gōngkè 功課／功课 N

assist bāng; bāngzhù 幫;幫助／帮;帮助 V

at (*the location of*) zài 在 V

at night yèli; wǎnshang 夜裏;晚上／夜里;晚上 TW

at the time of/when ... de shíhou ......的時候／......的时候 TW

athlete yùndòngyuán 運動員／运动员 N

athletic clothes yùndòngfú [jiàn] 運動服／运动服 [件] N

athletic shoes yùndòngxié 運動鞋／运动鞋 N

attend (*school, class*) shàng 上 V

attend class shàngkè 上課／上课 VO

attend school dúshū; niànshū 讀書;念書／读书;念书 VO

attractive hǎokàn 好看 SV

August Bāyuè 八月 N

aunt (*father's sister*) gūgu 姑姑 N

aunt (*mother's sister*) āyí 阿姨 N

aunt (*wife of father's older brother*) bómǔ 伯母 N

aunt (*wife of father's younger brother*) shěnshen 嬸嬸 N

aunt (*wife of mother's brother*) jiùmā 舅媽／舅妈 N

Australia Àodàlìyà 澳大利亞／澳大利亚 PW

Australian dollar Àoyuán 澳元 N

automobile qìchē [liàng] 汽車 [輛]／汽车 [辆] N

await děng 等 V

B

back hòumian; hòubian(r) 後面;後邊(兒)／后面;后边(儿) PW

bag dàizi [ge] 袋子 [個]／袋子 [个] N

ball qiú [ge] 球 [個]／球 [个] N

bank yínháng 銀行／银行 N

bargain (*for a better price*) jiǎngjià 講價／讲价 VO

bathe xǐzǎo 洗澡 VO

bathroom cèsuǒ 廁所／厕所 N

bazaar shāngchǎng 商場／商场 N

be shì 是 EV

beard húzi 鬍子／胡子 N

because yīnwèi 因為／因为 C

become ill/sick bìng le 病了 VP

bed chuáng [zhāng] 床 [張]／床 [张] N

been to (*a place*) dàoguo; qùguo 到過; 去過／到过; 去过 VP

beer [bottle of] píjiǔ [píng] 啤酒 [瓶] N

before (*in advance of*) xiān 先 A

before (*in the past*) yǐqián 以前 TW

before noon shàngwǔ 上午 TW

begin kāishǐ 開始／开始 V

behind hòumian; hòubian(r) 後面; 後邊(兒)／后面; 后边(儿) PW

beige mǐsè 米色 N

Beijing Běijīng 北京 PW

belong to (*one of 12 zodiac signs*) shǔ 屬/属 V

below xiàmian 下面 PW

best zuìhǎo 最好 SV

better hǎo yìdiǎnr 好一點兒／好一点儿 SV

between zhōngjiānr 中間兒／中间儿 PW

bicycle zìxíngchē [liàng] 自行車 [輛]／自行车 [辆] N

big dà 大 SV

big (*size in clothing, etc.*) dàhào 大號／大号 N

birth father shēngfù 生父 N

birth mother shēngmǔ 生母 N

birthday shēngrì 生日 N

bit (yì)diǎn(r) (一)點(兒)／(一)点(儿) N/M

black hēisè 黑色 N

blouse chènshān [jiàn] 襯衫 [件]／衬衫 [件] N

blue lánsè 藍色／蓝色 N

blue jeans [pair of] niúzǎikù [tiáo] 牛仔褲 [條]／牛仔裤 [条] N

boar (*Chinese zodiac*) zhū 豬／猪 N

boat chuán [tiáo] 船 [條]／船 [条] N

book shū [běn] 書 [本]／书 [本] N

bookbag shūbāo [ge] 書包 [個]／书包 [个] N

bookstore shūdiàn 書店／书店 N

born, be shēng 生 V

born in shēng zài 生在 VP

both dōu 都 A

both . . . and yòu . . . yòu 又……又 C

bottle of (*something*) yì píng . . . 一瓶…… N/M

bottom xiàmian 下面 PW

bowl wǎn 碗 N/M

bowl of (*something*) yì wǎn . . . 一碗…… N/M

boy nánháir; nánháizi 男孩兒; 男孩子／男孩儿; 男孩子 N

boyfriend nánpéngyou 男朋友 N

breakfast zǎofàn; zǎocān; zǎodiǎn 早飯; 早餐; 早點／早饭; 早餐; 早点 N

Britain Yīngguó 英國／英国 PW

British (*person/people*) Yīngguórén 英國人／英国人 N

British pound Yīngbàng 英鎊／英镑 N

brother (*older*) gēge 哥哥 N

brother (*younger*) dìdi 弟弟 N

brothers xiōngdì 兄弟 N

brothers and sisters xiōngdìjiěmèi 兄弟姐妹 N

brown (*coffee-colored*) kāfēisè 咖啡色 N

brush (one's) teeth shuāyá 刷牙 VO

building (*multistoried*) lóu [dòng] 樓 [棟]／楼 [栋] N

bus gōng (gòng qì) chē; bāshì 公(共汽)車; 巴士／公(共汽)车; 巴士 N

bus stop chēzhàn 車站／车站 N

business matter shì(qing) [jiàn] 事(情) [件] N

busy yǒushì; máng 有事; 忙 VP/SV

but kěshì 可是 C

buy mǎi 買／买 V

by myself zìjǐ 自己 P

C

cafeteria cāntīng 餐廳／餐厅 N

California Jiāzhōu 加州 PW

called (*by a given name*) jiào 叫 EV

can (*know how to*) huì 會／会 AV

can (*may*) kěyǐ 可以 AV

can (*be capable of*) néng 能 AV

Canada Jiānádà 加拿大 PW

Canadian (*person/people*) Jiānádàrén 加拿大人 N

Canadian dollar Jiānádà yuán 加拿大元 N

candy [piece of] táng [kuài] 糖 [塊]／糖 [块] N

Canton (*old name for Guangzhou*) Guǎngzhōu 廣州／广州 PW

cap màozi [dǐng] 帽子 [頂]／帽子 [顶] N

car qìchē [liàng] 汽車 [輛]／汽车 [辆] N

cash xiànjīn 現金／现金 N

cell phone shǒujī [ge] 手機 [個]／手机 [个] N

cell phone number shǒujī hàomǎ 手機號碼／手机号码 N

cent (yì) fēn (qián) (一)分(錢)／(一)分(钱) N

center zhōngjiānr 中間兒／中间儿 PW

certainly yídìng 一定 A

change huàn 換／换 V

change currency huànqián 換錢／换钱 VO

character (*Chinese word*) zì [ge] 字 [個]／字 [个] N

charge (*on a credit card*) shuākǎ 刷卡 VO

chat liáotiān(r) 聊天(兒)／聊天(儿) VO

chauffeur sījī 司機／司机 N

cheap piányi 便宜 SV

check (*examine*) chá 查 V

chicken (*Chinese zodiac*) jī 雞／鸡 N

child háizi [ge] 孩子 [個]／孩子 [个] N

children háizimen 孩子們／孩子们 N

China Zhōngguó 中國／中国 PW

Chinese (*language*) Zhōngguóhuà; Zhōngwén 中國話; 中文／中国话; 中文 N

Chinese (*person/people*) Zhōngguórén 中國人／中国人 N

chopsticks [pair of] kuàizi [shuāng] 筷子 [雙]／筷子 [双] N

class (*in school*) kè 課／课 N

classmate tóngxué 同學／同学 N

classroom building jiàoxuélóu 教學樓／教学楼 N

climb (*stairs, etc.*) pá 爬 V

clothes, put on chuān yīfu 穿衣服 V/VO

clothing [article of] yīfu [jiàn] 衣服 [件] N

coat wàitào [jiàn]; jiákè [jiàn] 外套 [件]；夾克 [件]／夹克 [件] N

coffee [cup of] kāfēi [bēi] 咖啡 [杯] N

coffee-colored kāfēisè 咖啡色 N

cold (*temperature*) lěng 冷 SV

colleague tóngshì 同事 N

college dàxué 大學／大学 N

college student dàxuéshēng 大學生／大学生 N

color yánsè 顏色／颜色 N

comb shūzi [bǎ] 梳子 [把] N

comb (*one's*) **hair** shūtóufa 梳頭髮／梳头发 VO

come lái 來／来 V

come back huílai 回來／回来 V

come from . . . cóng . . . lái 從……來／从……来 VP

comfortable shūfu 舒服 SV

compare bǐ 比 CV

computer diànnǎo [tái] 電腦 [台]／电脑 [台] N

conditioner [bottle of] (*for hair*) hùfàsù [píng] 護髮素 [瓶]／护发素 [瓶] N

cook breakfast zuò zǎofàn 做早飯／做早饭 VO

cook dinner zuò wǎnfàn 做晚飯／做晚饭 VO

cook food zuòfàn 做飯／做饭 VO

cook lunch zuò zhōngfàn 做中飯／做中饭 VO

correct duì 對／对 SV

costly guì 貴／贵 SV

country (*suffix for names of countries*) guó 國／国 N/S

crawl pá 爬 V

credit card xìnyòngkǎ [zhāng] 信用卡 [張]／信用卡 [张] N

cup bēizi [ge] 杯子 [個]／杯子 [个] N

cup of (*something*) yì bēi . . . 一杯…… N/M

cut the grass/lawn gēcǎo 割草 VO

D

dad bàba 爸爸 N

daily měitiān; tiāntiān 每天；天天 TW

daily-use articles rìyòngpǐn 日用品 N

daughter nǚ'ér 女兒／女儿 N

day tiān 天 N/M

day after tomorrow hòutiān 後天／后天 TW

day before yesterday qiántiān 前天 TW

day of the month hào 號／号 M

December Shí'èryuè 十二月 N

delicious hǎochī 好吃 SV

delighted gāoxìng 高興／高兴 SV

dentist yáyī 牙醫／牙医 N

depart zǒu 走 V

department store bǎihuò shāngdiàn 百貨商店／百货商店 N

dictionary zìdiǎn [běn] 字典 [本] N

different one biéde 別的 SP

difficult nán 難／难 SV

dime (*spoken*) (yì) máo (qián) (一)毛(錢)／(一)毛(钱) N

dime (*written*) jiǎo 角 N

dinner wǎnfàn; wǎncān 晚飯；晚餐／晚饭；晚餐 N

direction fāngxiàng 方向 N

disembark (*from a train, car, bus, etc.*) xiàchē 下車／下车 VO

dislike bù xǐhuan 不喜歡／不喜欢 VP

dismiss school fàngxué 放學／放学 VO

do zuò 做 V

do homework zuò gōngkè ‖ xiě zuòyè 做功課／做功课 ‖ 寫作業／写作业 VO

do housework zuò jiāwù 做家務／做家务 VO

do morning calisthenics zuò zǎocāo 做早操 VO

do not (*imperative*) bié; bú yào 別；不要 V/AV

do odd jobs dǎgōng 打工 VO

do part-time work dǎgōng 打工 VO

do the cooking zuòfàn 做飯／做饭 VO

do the laundry xǐ yīfu 洗衣服 VO

doctor yīshēng 醫生／医生 N

dog (*Chinese zodiac*) gǒu 狗 N

dollar, American Měijīn; Měiyuán 美金；美元 N

dollar (*spoken*) (yí) kuài (qián) (一)塊(錢)／(一)块(钱) N

dollar (*written*) yuán 元 N

don't (*imperative*) bié; bú yào 別；不要 V/AV

don't be so polite bié kèqi 別客氣／别客气 IE

don't know bù zhīdao 不知道 VP

don't want to bú yào 不要 V/AV

downstairs lóuxià 樓下／楼下 PW

dragon (*Chinese zodiac*) lóng 龍／龙 N

dress chuān; chuān yīfu 穿；穿衣服 V/VO

drink hē 喝 V

drive a car kāichē 開車／开车 VO

driver sījī 司機／司机 N

dull méiyìsi 沒意思 SV

during . . . zài . . . de shíhou 在……的時候／在……的时候 VP

during the night yèli; wǎnshang 夜裏；晚上／夜里；晚上 TW

E

each měi (ge) 每(個)／每(个) SP

early zǎo 早 SV

earn money zhuànqián 賺錢／赚钱 VO

earth (*the radical*) tǔ 土 N

east (*side, direction*) dōngbian(r) 東邊(兒)／东边 (儿) PW

easy róngyì 容易 SV

eat chī 吃 V

eat a meal chī fàn 吃飯／吃饭 VO

eat to fullness chībǎo 吃飽／吃饱 V

eight bā 八 NU

eighth (one) dìbā (ge) 第八(個)／第八(个) N/NU

eighty bāshí 八十 NU

eldest (son, daughter, etc.) dà (érzi, nǚ'ér . . .) 大(兒子, 女兒……)／大(儿子, 女儿……) N

elementary school xiǎoxué 小學／小学 N

elevator diàntī 電梯／电梯 N

eleven shíyī 十一 NU

eleventh (one) dìshíyī (ge) 第十一(個)／第十一(个) N/NU

e-mail diànyóu 電郵／电邮 N

e-mail address diànyóu dìzhǐ 電郵地址／电邮地址 N

e-mail message diànxìn [fēng] 電信 [封]／电信 [封] N

engineer gōngchéngshī 工程師／工程师 N

England Yīngguó 英國／英国 PW

English (*language*) Yīngwén; Yīngyǔ 英文; 英語／英文; 英语 N

English (*person/people*) Yīngguórén 英國人／英国人 N

enter jìnqu 進去／进去 V

equal(s) děngyú 等於／等于 V

escalator fúshǒu diàntī 扶手電梯／扶手电梯 N

Euro (*currency*) Ōuyuán 歐元／欧元 N

Europe Ōuzhōu 歐洲／欧洲 PW

European (*person/people*) Ōuzhōurén 歐洲人／欧洲人 N

even more (*in comparisons*) gèng 更 A

evening (*6 P.M. until midnight*) wǎnshang 晚上 TW

eventually zuìhòu 最後／最后 A

ever (*"have you ever" [verbal suffix] . . .?*) guò 過／过 S

every (*day, week, year, etc.*) měi 每 SP

every day měitiān; tiāntiān 每天; 天天 TW

everyone měi ge rén; dàjiā 每個人; 大家／每个人; 大家 N

exam, take an kǎoshì 考試／考试 V

examination (*school*) kǎoshì 考試／考试 N

exceed (*the clock hour*) guò 過／过 V

exceedingly tài . . . (le) 太……(了) A

exchange huàn 換／换 V

exchange currency huànqián 換錢／换钱 VO

excuse me duìbuqǐ 對不起／对不起 IE

expensive guì 貴／贵 SV

extent, to what duō 多 A

extra large (*size in clothing, etc.*) jiādàhào 加大號／加大号 N

extra small (*size in clothing, etc.*) jiāxiǎohào 加小號／加小号 N

extremely (*good, fast, etc.*) jíle (hǎojíle, kuàijíle . . .) 極了(好極了, 快極了……)／极了(好极了, 快极了…… S

extremely fēicháng 非常 A

F

family jiā 家 N

family members jiālǐrén 家裏人／家里人 N

family jiā 家 N

far yuǎn 遠／远 SV

farmer nóngmín 農民／农民 N

fast kuài 快 SV

fat pàng 胖 SV

father fùqin; bàba 父親; 爸爸／父亲; 爸爸 N

February Èryuè 二月 N

feel juéde 覺得／觉得 V

feel (*like doing something*) xiǎng 想 AV

feel well shūfu 舒服 SV

fellow student tóngxué 同學／同学 N

fellow worker tóngshì 同事 N

few (*in number*) shǎo 少 SV

few yìxiē 一些 SP

fifteen minutes yí kèzhōng 一刻鐘／一刻钟 NP

fifth (one) dìwǔ (ge) 第五(個)／第五(个) N/NU

film (*movie*) diànyǐng [bù] 電影 [部]／电影 [部] N

finally zuìhòu 最後／最后 A

fine hǎo 好 SV

firefighter jiùhuǒyuán 救火員／救火员 N

first (*before, earlier*) xiān 先 A

first (one) dìyī (ge) 第一(個)／第一(个) N/NU

first floor yīlóu 一樓／一楼 N

first name míngzi 名字 N

fish yú [tiáo] 魚 [條]／鱼 [条] N

five wǔ 五 NU

floor (*in a building*) lóu 樓／楼 M

floss (*dental*) yáxiàn 牙線／牙线 N

for sure yídìng 一定 A

foreign country wàiguó 外國／外国 N

foreign language wàiyǔ; wàiguóhuà 外語; 外國話／外语; 外国话 N

foreigner wàiguórén 外國人／外国人 N

forgot wàng le 忘了 VP

four sì 四 NU

fourth (one) dìsì (ge) 第四(個)／第四(个) N/NU

France Fǎguó 法國／法国 PW

free, to be (*to have free time*) yǒukòng 有空 VO

free time kòng 空 N

French (*language*) Fǎguóhuà; Fǎyǔ; Fǎwén 法國話; 法語; 法文／法国话; 法语; 法文 N

French (*person/people*) Fǎguórén 法國人／法国人 N

frequently chángcháng 常常 A

Friday Xīngqīwǔ 星期五 TW

friend péngyou 朋友 N

from (*a place, a time, etc.*) cóng 從／从 CV

from (*distant from*) lí 離／离 CV
front qiánmian; qiánbian 前面;前邊／前面;前边 PW
full (*no longer hungry*) bǎo le 飽了／饱了 VP
fun yǒu yìsi 有意思 SV
furthermore háiyǒu 還有／还有 C
future jiānglái 將来／将来 TW/N

G

generally yìbān; píngcháng 一般;平常 A
generally speaking yìbān lái shuō 一般来说／一般来说 A
German (*language*) Déguóhuà; Déyǔ; Déwén 德國話;德語;德文／德国话;德语;德文 N
German (*person/people*) Déguórén 德國人／德国人 N
Germany Déguó 德國／德国 PW
get off (*bus, train, etc.*) xià(chē, huǒchē ...) 下(車,火車......)／下(车,火车......) VO
get off work xiàbān 下班 VO
get out of class xiàkè 下課／下课 VO
get out of school fàngxué 放學／放学 VO
get up (*from bed*) qǐchuáng 起床 VO
girl nǚháizi; nǚháir 女孩子;女孩兒／女孩子;女孩儿 N
girlfriend nǚpéngyou 女朋友 N
give gěi 給／给 V
give a discount dǎzhé 打折 VO
give birth shēng 生 V
give birth (*to a child*) shēng háizi 生孩子 VO
given name míngzi 名字 N
glass (*container*) bēizi [ge] 杯子 [個]／杯子 [个] N
glass of (*something*) yì bēi ... 一杯...... N/M
go qù 去 V
go abroad chūguó 出國／出国 VO
go back huíqu 回去 VO
go by bus zuò gōngchē qù 坐公車去／坐公车去 VP
go by car kāichē qù 開車去／开车去 VP
go have some fun qù wánr 去玩兒／去玩儿 VP
go home huíjiā 回家 V
go in jìnqu 進去／进去 V
go online shàngwǎng 上網／上网 VO
go out chūqu 出去 V
go out for some fun chūqu wánr 出去玩兒／出去玩儿 VP
go shopping qù mǎi dōngxi; guàngjiē 去買東西;逛街／去买东西;逛街 VP
go to (*a place*) dào ... qù; qù ... 到......去;去...... VP
go to class shàngkè 上課／上课 VO
go to school shàngxué 上學／上学 VO
go to sleep shuìjiào 睡覺／睡觉 VO
go to the mall guàng shāngchǎng 逛商場／逛商场 VO
go to work/the office shàngbān 上班 VO

going to yào; huì 要;會／要;会 AV
gold (*color*) jīnsè 金色 N
gone to (*a place*) qùguo 去過／去过 VP
good hǎo 好 SV
good-bye zàijiàn 再見／再见 IE
good grief tiān a 天啊 IE
good-looking hǎokàn 好看 SV
good morning nín/nǐ zǎo; zǎoshang hǎo 您/你早;早上好 IE
good-tasting hǎochī 好吃 SV
grade (*in school*) niánjí 年級／年级 N
grade school xiǎoxué 小學／小学 N
graduate school yánjiūshēngyuàn 研究生院 N
grandfather (*maternal*) lǎoye; wàigōng 姥爺;外公／姥爷;外公 N
grandfather (*paternal*) yéye 爺爺／爷爷 N
grandmother (*maternal*) lǎolao; wàipó 姥姥;外婆 N
grandmother (*paternal*) nǎinai 奶奶 N
Grandpa (*respectful form of address*) yéye 爺爺／爷爷 N
grass cǎo; cǎodì 草;草地 N
gray huīsè 灰色 N
green lǜsè 綠色／绿色 N
green light (*traffic*) lǜdēng 綠燈／绿灯 N
grow up zhǎngdà 長大／长大 V
guess, take a cāicai kàn 猜猜看 VP
Guilin (*city in southern China*) Guìlín 桂林 PW

H

haggle (*for a better price*) jiǎngjià 講價／讲价 VO
hair (*on human head*) tóufa 頭髮／头发 N
half an hour bàn ge zhōngtóu 半個鐘頭／半个钟头 N
half sibling (*same father*) (tóngfù) yìmǔ de xiōngdìjiěmèi (同父)異母的兄弟姐妹／(同父)异母的兄弟姐妹 N
half sibling (*same mother*) (tóngmǔ) yìfù de xiōngdìjiěmèi (同母)異父的兄弟姐妹／(同母)异父的兄弟姐妹 N
hamburger hànbǎobāo [ge] 漢堡包 [個]／汉堡包 [个] N
happy gāoxìng 高興／高兴 SV
happy to meet you hěn gāoxìng rènshi nǐ (nín) 很高興認識你(您)／很高兴认识你(您) IE
hat màozi [dǐng] 帽子 [頂]／帽子 [顶] N
have yǒu 有 V
have a desire to yào 要 V
have a fever fāshāo 發燒／发烧 VO
have a headache tóuténg 頭疼／头疼 VO
have a meal chīfàn 吃飯／吃饭 VO
have fun wánr 玩兒／玩儿 V
have something to do yǒushì; máng 有事;忙 VO/SV
have to děi 得 AV
he tā 他 PR
headache, have a tóuténg 頭疼／头疼 VO

hello nín/nǐ hǎo 您／你好 IE

help bāng; bāngzhù 幫；幫助／帮；帮助 V

here zhèr; zhèlǐ 這兒；這裏／这儿；这里 PW

hi hāi 嗨 I

high-heeled shoes [pair of] gāogēnxié [shuāng] 高跟鞋 [雙]／高跟鞋 [双] N

high school (*senior, grades 10–12*) gāozhōng 高中 N

Hindi (*language*) Yìndùhuà; Yìndùwén; Yìndùyǔ 印度話；印度文；印度語／印度话；印度文；印度语 N

hold class shàngkè 上課／上课 VO

holiday, be on a fàngjià 放假 VO

home jiā 家 N

homework gōngkè ‖ zuòyè 功課／功课 ‖ 作業／作业 N

Hong Kong Xiāng Gǎng 香港 PW

Hong Kong dollar Gǎngbì 港幣／港币 N

honorable surname, what's your Nín guìxìng? 您貴姓／您贵姓? IE

horse (*Chinese zodiac*) mǎ 馬／马 N

hot (*temperature*) rè 熱／热 SV

hot dog règǒu [ge] 熱狗 [個]／热狗 [个] N

hour zhōngtóu [ge] 鐘頭 [個]／钟头 [个] N

house fángzi [dòng] 房子 [棟／栋] N

household chores/duties jiāwù 家務／家务 N

how (*to what extent*) duō 多 QW

how (*what*) zěnme 怎麼／怎么 QW

how come zěnme 怎麼／怎么 QW

how many (*less than ten*) jǐ (ge) 幾(個)／几(个) QW

how many (*more than ten*) duōshao (*usually without measure word*) 多少 QW

How old are you? Nǐ duō dà?; Nǐ jǐ suì? 你多大；你幾歲／你几岁 PH

How's it going? zěnmeyàng 怎麼樣／怎么样 IE

however kěshì 可是 C

hundred (*one, two hundred, etc.*) (yì)bǎi, (èr)bǎi . . . (一)百,(二)百…… NU

hungry è 餓／饿 SV

husband lǎogōng; xiānsheng; zhàngfu 老公；先生；丈夫 N

I

I wǒ 我 PR

I'm OK hái hǎo 還好／还好 IE

I'm sorry duìbuqǐ 對不起／对不起 IE

identical yíyàng 一樣／一样 SV

if yàoshi 要是 A

ill/become ill bìng le 病了 VP

illness bìng 病 N

in lǐbianr 裏邊兒／里边儿 PW

in/at/on zài 在 V

in a little while guò yìhuǐr 過一會兒／过一会儿 PH

in addition háiyǒu 還有／还有 C

in advance of xiān 先 A

in all (*total*) yígòng 一共 A

in back of hòumian; hòubian(r) 後面；後邊(兒)／后面；后边(儿) PW

in comparison bǐ 比 CV

in front qiánmian; qiánbian 前面；前邊／前面；前边 PW

in that case nà; nàme 那；那麼／那么 C

in the future jiānglái 將來／将来 TW

in the position of, be dāng 當／当 V

in the same way zhàoyàng 照樣／照样 A

in total yígòng 一共 A

indeed zhēn 真 A

India Yìndù 印度 PW

Indian (*person/people*) Yìndùrén 印度人 N

inexpensive piányi 便宜 SV

inquire wèn; wènwen 問；問問／问；问问 V

inside lǐbianr 裏邊兒／里边儿 PW

intend xiǎng 想 AV

interesting yǒu yìsi 有意思 SV

Internet, go on the shàngwǎng 上網／上网 VO

introduce jièshào 介紹／介绍 V

introduction jièshào 介紹／介绍 N

invite qǐng 請／请 V

it (*most often not translated*) tā 它 P

Italian (*language*) Yìdàlìhuà; Yìdàlìwén; Yìdàlìyǔ 意大利話；意大利文；意大利語／意大利话；意大利文；意大利语 N

Italian (*person/people*) Yìdàlìrén 意大利人 N

Italy Yìdàlì 意大利 PW

J

jacket jiákè; wàitào [jiàn] 夾克／夹克；外套 [件] N

January Yīyuè 一月 N

Japan Rìběn 日本 PW

Japanese (*language*) Rìběnhuà; Rìyǔ; Rìwén 日本話；日語；日文／日本话；日语；日文 N

Japanese (*person/people*) Rìběnrén 日本人 N

Japanese yen Rìyuán 日元 N

jeans [pair of] niúzǎikù [tiáo] 牛仔褲 [條]／牛仔裤 [条] N

job gōngzuò 工作 V/N

jog pǎobù 跑步 VO

journey, go on a qù lǚxíng 去旅行 VP

July Qīyuè 七月 N

June Liùyuè 六月 N

junior high school chūzhōng 初中 N

just (*only a short time ago*) gāng 剛／刚 A

just now gāngcái 剛才／刚才 A

K

kid háizi 孩子 N

kind (*type; shape*) yàng 樣／样 M

know (*be acquainted with*) rènshi 認識／认识 V
know (*have knowledge of*) zhīdao 知道 V
know (*how to*) huì 會／会 AV
know Chinese characters rènshi zì 認識字／认识字 V

Korea Hánguó 韓國／韩国 PW
Korean (*language*) Hánwén; Hányǔ; Hánguóhuà 韓文；韓語；韓國話／韩文；韩语；韩国话 N
Korean (*person/people*) Hánguórén 韓國人／韩国人 N

L

laborer gōngrén 工人 N
large dà 大 SV
large (*size in clothing, etc.*) dàhào 大號／大号 N
last month shàng ge yuè 上個月／上个月 TW
last week shàng xīngqī 上星期 TW
last year qùnián 去年 TW
late wǎn 晚 SV
later yǐhòu 以後／以后 TW
lawn cǎo; cǎodì 草；草地 N
lawyer lǜshī 律師／律师 N
learn how to xué 學／学 V
leather shoes [pair of] píxié [shuāng] 皮鞋 [雙]／皮鞋 [双] N
leave (*depart from a place*) zǒu 走 V
leave (*go out*) chūmén 出門／出门 VO
left side zuǒbian(r) 左邊(兒)／左边(儿) PW
left turn wǎng zuǒ guǎi 往左拐 VP
less than (*followed by number expression*) búdào 不到 VP
lesson/class kè 課／课 N
library túshūguǎn [ge] 圖書館／图书馆 N
lifestyle shēnghuó fāngshì 生活方式 N
like/prefer xǐhuan 喜歡／喜欢 V
like this zhèyàng 這樣／这样 PR
likely to huì 會／会 AV
listen to tīng 聽／听 V
listen to music tīng yīnyuè 聽音樂／听音乐 VO
literate, be rènshi zì 認識字／认识字 V
little xiǎo 小 SV
little (*size in clothing, etc.*) xiǎohào 小號／小号 N
little while, in a yìhuǐr 一會兒／一会儿 TW
live (*at*) zhùzai 住在 VP
located at, be zài 在 V
location/address dìzhǐ 地址 N
long cháng 長／长 SV
look/watch kàn 看 V
look for zhǎo 找 V
look, take a kàn (yí) kàn 看(一)看 VP
Los Angeles Luòshānjī 洛杉磯／洛杉矶 PW
love ài 愛／爱 V
lunch wǔfàn; wǔcān; zhōngfàn 午飯；午餐；中飯／午饭；午餐；中饭 N

M

Macau Àomén 澳門／澳门 PW
Macau pataca (*currency*) Àoményuán 澳門元／澳门元 N
mad/angry shēngqì 生氣／生气 SV
mailing address dìzhǐ 地址 N
make (*cook*) zuò ‖ nòng 做 ‖ 弄 V
make a phone call dǎ diànhuà 打電話／打电话 VO
make change zhǎoqián 找錢／找钱 VO
make up (*with powder, rouge, etc.*) huàzhuāng 化妝／化妆 VO
makeup (*cosmetics*) huàzhuāngpǐn 化妆品／化妆品 N
mall shāngchǎng 商場／商场 N
mall, go to the guàng shāngchǎng 逛商場／逛商场 VO
manager (*of business, etc.*) jīnglǐ 經理／经理 N
Mandarin (*Standard*) pǔtōnghuà 普通話／普通话 N
many duō 多 SV
map dìtú [zhāng] 地圖 [張]／地图 [张] N
March Sānyuè 三月 N
market shāngchǎng 商場／商场 N
master craftsman shīfu 師傅／师傅 N
matter, what's the zěnme le 怎麼了／怎么了 VP
May Wǔyuè 五月 N
may (*permission to*) kěyǐ 可以 AV
May I ask . . . Qǐngwèn . . . 請問……／请问…… VP
maybe yěxǔ; kěnéng 也許／也许；可能 A
me wǒ 我 PR
meal (*cooked rice*) fàn 飯／饭 N
meal, eat a chīfàn 吃飯／吃饭 VO
medicine yào 藥／药 N
medium (*size in clothing, etc.*) zhōnghào 中號／中号 N
meet (*with someone*) jiàn 見／见 V
meet up with (*someone*) jiē 接 V
midday zhōngwǔ 中午 TW
middle zhōngjiānr 中間兒／中间儿 PW
middle school zhōngxué 中學／中学 N
midnight bànyè 半夜 TW
might (*maybe*) yěxǔ 也許／也许 A
mile (*Chinese mile*) lǐ 里 N/M
mine (*my own*) wǒ de 我的 PR
minute, (one) (*unit of time*) yì fēnzhōng 一分鐘／一分钟 N
Miss Xiǎojie 小姐 N
Mister Xiānsheng 先生 N
mom mā; māma 媽；媽媽／妈；妈妈 N
moment, at the (*now, at present*) xiànzài 現在／现在 TW
moment (*point in time; duration*) shíhou 時候／时候 N
Monday Xīngqīyī 星期一 TW
money qián 錢／钱 N
monkey (*Chinese zodiac*) hóu 猴 N

month yuè [ge] 月 [個]／月 [个] TW
mood (*state of mind*) xīnqíng 心情 N
more (*in number*) duō 多 SV
morning (*until about 9–10 A.M.*) zǎoshang 早上 TW
morning (*from about 10 A.M. to noon*) shàngwǔ 上午 TW
morning (*as a greeting*) zǎo 早 IE
morning calisthenics zǎocāo 早操 N
most (*superlative prefix*) zuì 最 A/PREF
mother mǔqin 母親／母亲 N
motorbike mótuōchē [liàng] 摩托車 [輛]／摩托车 [辆] N
motorcycle mótuōchē [liàng] 摩托車 [輛]／摩托车 [辆] N
mountain shān [zuò] 山 [座]／山 [座] N
mouse (*Chinese zodiac*) shǔ 鼠 N
mouth (*the radical*) kǒu 口 N
movie diànyǐng [bù] 電影 [部]／电影 [部] N
movie theater diànyǐngyuàn 電影院／电影院 N
mow the lawn gēcǎo 割草 VO
Mr. Xiānsheng 先生 N
much duō 多 SV
museum bówùguǎn 博物館／博物馆 N
music yīnyuè 音樂／音乐 N
musician yīnyuèjiā 音樂家／音乐家 N
must (*matter of obligation*) bìxū 必須／必须 AV
my wǒ de 我的 N
my heavens tiān a 天啊 IE
myself zìjǐ 自己 P

N

name míngzi [ge] 名字 [個]／名字 [个] N
named jiào 叫 EV
nap, take a (*afternoon*) wǔshuì 午睡 V
naturally dāngrán 當然／当然 A
near jìn 近 SV
need (*in time or effort*) yào 要 AV
need not búyòng; búbì 不用; 不必 AV
neighbor línjū 鄰居／邻居 N
nervous zháojí 著急／着急 SV
never cónglái bù; cónglái méi 從來不; 從來沒／从来不; 从来没 A
never mind/doesn't matter/nothing's wrong méi shì 没事 IE
New Taiwan dollar Táibì 台幣／台币 N
New York Niǔyuē 紐約／纽约 PW
newspaper bào [fèn] 報 [份]／报 [份] N
next (*in a series*) xià (ge) 下 (個)／下 (个) SP
next month xià ge yuè 下個月／下个月 TW
next time xiàcì 下次 TW
next week xià (ge) xīngqī 下(個)星期／下(个)星期 TW
next year míngnián 明年 TW

nice/good/fine hǎo 好 SV
nighttime yèli; wǎnshang 夜裏; 晚上／夜里; 晚上 TW
nine jiǔ 九 NU
ninth (*one*) dìjiǔ (ge) 第九(個)／第九(个) N/NU
no bù; bú shì 不; 不是 A
noon zhōngwǔ 中午 TW
no problem/it doesn't matter méi guānxi 没關係／没关系 IE
north (*side, direction*) běibian(r) 北邊(兒)／北边(儿) PW
North America Běi Měizhōu 北美洲 PW
northeast dōngběi 東北／东北 PW
northwest xīběi 西北 PW
not bù; bú shì 不; 不是 A
not able to bùnéng 不能 V
not bad búcuò 不錯／不错 SV
not have méiyǒu 没有 V
not often bù cháng 不常 SV
not until cái 才 A
notebook bǐjìběn [běn] 筆記本 [本]／笔记本 [本] N
nothing's wrong/never mind méi shì 没事 IE
November Shíyīyuè 十一月 N
now xiànzài 現在／现在 TW
number (*in a series*) hào 號／号 N
number (*telephone number, etc.*) hàomǎ 號碼／号码 N
numerous duō 多 SV
nurse hùshi 護士／护士 N

O

object dōngxi [ge] 東西 [個]／东西 [个] N
o'clock . . . diǎn (zhōng) ......點(鍾)／......点(钟) PH
occurrences/times cì 次 M
October Shíyuè 十月 N
of course dāngrán 當然／当然 A
office, go to the/go to work shàngbān 上班 VO
often chángcháng 常常 A
oh (*sudden understanding*) ō 噢 I
OK hǎo; xíng 好; 行 SV
old (*in age*) dà 大 SV
older brother gēge 哥哥 N
older sister jiějie 姐姐 N
oldest child lǎodà 老大 N
on zài . . . shang 在......上 VP
on a holiday, be fàngjià 放假 VO
on sale, be jiǎnjià 減價／减价 VO
once (*one time*) yícì 一次 NU/M
one (*the number*) yī 一 NU
oneself zìjǐ 自己 P
only (*just*) jiù 就 A
only (*merely*) zhǐ 只 A
only child (*boy*) dúshēngzǐ 獨生子／独生子 N
only child (*girl*) dúshēngnǚ [ge] 獨生女／独生女 N
or (*in statements*) huòzhě 或者 C
or (*when offering alternatives*) háishi 還是／还是 C

orange (*color*)   júhóngsè   橘红色   N
ordinary   yìbān; píngcháng   一般; 平常   SV
other people   biéren   别人   P
others (*the rest, what remains*)   qítā (de)   其他(的)   N
ought to   yīnggāi   應該／应该   A
our(s)   wǒmen de   我們的／我们的   PR
outside   zài wàibian   在外邊／在外边   VP/PW
overcoat   wàitào [jiàn]   外套 [件]   N
ox (*Chinese zodiac*)   niú   牛   N

P

painter   huàjiā   畫家／画家   N
pair of (*something*)   (yì) shuāng . . .   (一)雙……／(一)
双……   NU/M
pants [pair of]   kùzi; chángkù [tiáo]   褲子; 長褲 [條]／
裤子; 长裤 [条]   N
paper [sheet of]   zhǐ [zhāng]   紙 [張]／纸 [张]   N
parents   fùmǔ   父母   N
park (*public*)   gōngyuán(r)   公園兒／公园儿   N
part-time, work   dǎgōng   打工   VO
pass by (*on the way*)   guò   過／过   V
past (*the clock hour*)   guò   過／过   V
path   lù [tiáo]   路 [條]／路 [条]   N
pay in cash   fù xiànjīn   付現金／付现金   VO
pay money   fùqián   付錢／付钱   VO
pen   bǐ [zhī]   筆 [枝]／笔 [枝]   N
penny, a   yì fēn (qián)   一分(錢)／一分(钱)   N
people   rén [ge]   人 [個]／人 [个]   N
People's money (*PRC currency*)   Rénmínbì   人民幣／
人民币   N
perhaps   yěxǔ   也許／也许   A
person   rén [ge]   人 [個]／人 [个]   N
phone   diànhuà   電話／电话   N
phone, to   dǎ diànhuà   打電話／打电话   VO
physician   yīshēng   醫生／医生   N
pick up (*someone*)   jiē   接   V
pig (*Chinese zodiac*)   zhū   豬／猪   N
pink   fěnhóngsè   粉紅色／粉红色   N
place   dìfang [ge]   地方 [個]／地方 [个]   N
plan (*to do something*)   xiǎng   想   AV
play   wánr   玩兒／玩儿   V
play video games   wánr diànzǐ yóuxì   玩兒電子遊戲／
玩儿电子游戏   VP
please (*used in polite requests*)   qǐng   請／请   V
pleased/happy   gāoxìng   高興／高兴   SV
plus/add to   jiā   加   V
police officer   jǐngchá   警察／警察   N
polite   kèqi   客氣／客气   SV
possess   yǒu   有   V
postcard   míngxìnpiàn [zhāng]   明信片 [張]／明信片
[张]   N
prefer/like   xǐhuan   喜歡／喜欢   V
prepare a meal   zuòfàn   做飯／做饭   VO

present (*right now*)   xiànzài   現在／现在   TW
pretty   hǎokàn   好看   SV
pretty good   búcuò   不錯／不错   SV
previously   yǐqián   以前   TW
price   jiàqian   價錢／价钱   N
principal   xiàozhǎng [wèi]   校長 [位]／校长 [位]   N
probably   kěnéng   可能   A
problem   wèntí [ge]   問題 [個]／问题 [个]   N
professor   jiàoshòu [wèi]   教授 [位]／教授 [位]   N
public bus   gōng (gòngqì) chē [liàng]   公(共汽)車 [輛]／
公(共汽)车 [辆]   N
purchase   mǎi   買／买   V
purple   zǐsè   紫色／紫色   N
put on   chuān   穿   V
put on clothes   chuān yīfu   穿衣服   VO
put on makeup   huàzhuāng   化妝／化妆   VO

Q

quarter of an hour   yí kèzhōng   一刻鐘／一刻钟   N
question   wèntí [ge]   問題 [個]／问题 [个]   N
quick   kuài   快   SV
quite/rather   tǐng   挺   A

R

rabbit (*Chinese zodiac*)   tù   兔   N
rain   yǔ   雨   N
rain   xiàyǔ   下雨   VO
ram (*Chinese zodiac*)   yáng   羊   N
rarely   hěn shǎo   很少   A
rat (*Chinese zodiac*)   shǔ   鼠   N
rather   tǐng   挺   A
read   kàn   看   V
read a book   kànshū   看書／看书   VO
read a newspaper   kànbào   看報／看报   VO
really   zhēn   真   A
Really? (*Is that true?*)   zhēn de ma   真的嗎／真的吗   IE
recently   zuìjìn   最近   A
recognize   rènshi   認識／认识   V
recognize Chinese characters   rènshi zì   認識字／认识
字   V
red   hóngsè   紅色／红色   N
red light (*traffic*)   hóngdēng [ge]   紅燈／红灯   N
reduce price   jiǎnjià   減價／减价   VO
relative(s)   qīnqi   親戚／亲戚   N
remain at home   dāizài jiālǐ   呆在家裏／呆在家里   PH
repeat (*what was said*)   zài shuō yícì   再說一次／再说一
次   PH
require (*in time or effort*)   yào   要   AV
reside (*at*)   zhùzai   住在   VP
rest   xiūxi   休息   V
restaurant   fànguǎn(r)   飯館兒／饭馆儿   N

return (*to a place*) huí 回 V
return (*come back*) huílai 回來／回来 V
return home huíjiā 回家 VO
rice [bowl of] fàn [wǎn] 飯 [碗]／饭 [碗] N
ride (*a bike, horse, astride*) qí 騎／骑 V
ride a bicycle qí zìxíngchē 騎自行車／骑自行车 VO
ride on (*a bus, train, etc.*) zuò 坐 V
right (*correct*) duì 對／对 SV
right (*side*) yòubian(r) 右邊(兒)／右边(儿) PW
right after jiù 就 A
rise up qǐ 起 V
road lù [tiáo] 路 [條]／路 [条] N
room fángjiān [ge] 房間 [個]／房间 [个] N
room (*as in apartment unit*) shì 室 N
rooster (*Chinese zodiac*) jī 雞／鸡 N
run pǎo; pǎobù 跑／跑步 V/VO
rupee (*India and Pakistan*) Lúbǐ 盧比／卢比 N
Russia Éguó 俄國／俄国 PW
Russian (*language*) Éwén; Éyǔ; Éguóhuà 俄文; 俄語; 俄國話／俄文; 俄语; 俄国话 N
Russian (*person/people*) Éguórén 俄國人／俄国人 N

S

sad bù gāoxìng 不高興／不高兴 SV
sale, be on jiǎnjià 減價／减价 VO
sales clerk fúwùyuán; shòuhuòyuán 服務員; 售貨員／服务员; 售货员 N
same yíyàng 一樣／一样 SV
sandals [pair of] liángxié [shuāng] 涼鞋 [雙]／凉鞋 [双] N
Saturday Xīngqīliù 星期六 TW
say shuō; shuōhuà 說; 說話／说; 说话 V/VO
school xuéxiào [ge] 學校 [個]／学校 [个] N
schoolmate tóngxué 同學／同学 N
schoolwork gōngkè 功課／功课 N
second (one) dìèr (ge) 第二(個)／第二(个) N/NU
second child (*in a family*) lǎoèr 老二 N
secondary school zhōngxué 中學／中学 N
secretary mìshu 秘書／秘书 N
see (*catch sight of*) kànjian 看見／看见 V
see (*to watch, as a movie, etc.*) kàn 看 V
see (*meet with someone*) jiàn 見／见 V
see a movie kàn diànyǐng 看電影／看电影 VO
see you again/good-bye zàijiàn 再見／再见 IE
see you in a little while yìhuǐr jiàn 一會兒見／一会儿见 IE
seldom bù cháng 不常 SV
sell mài 賣／卖 V
senior high school gāozhōng 高中 N
September Jiǔyuè 九月 N
serve (*in a position*) dāng 當／当 V
service person fúwùyuán 服務員／服务员 N
seven qī 七 NU

seventeen shíqī 十七 NU
seventh (one) dìqī (ge) 第七(個)／第七(个) N/NU
seventy qīshí 七十 NU
several yìxiē 一些 NU/M
several times a week yì zhōu jǐ cì 一周幾次／一周几次 TW
shampoo [a bottle of] xǐfàshuǐ [píng] 洗髮水 [瓶]／洗发水 [瓶] N
Shanghai Shànghǎi 上海 PW
shape yàngzi 樣子／样子 N
shave (one's) beard guā húzi 刮鬍子／刮胡子 VO
she tā 她 PR
sheep (*Chinese zodiac*) yáng 羊 N
sheet (*of paper*) zhǐ [zhāng] 紙 [張]／纸 [张] N
ship chuán [tiáo] 船 [條]／船 [条] N
shirt chènshān [jiàn] 襯衫 [件]／衬衫 [件] N
shoes [pair of] xié [shuāng] 鞋 [雙]／鞋 [双] N
shop (*buy things*) mǎi dōngxi 買東西／买东西 VO
shop shāngdiàn 商店／商店 N
shop assistant fúwùyuán; shòuhuòyuán 服務員; 售貨員／服务员; 售货员 N
shopping center gòuwù zhōngxīn 購物中心／购物中心 N
shopping mall shāngchǎng 商場／商场 N
short (*in height or stature*) ǎi 矮 SV
short (*in length*) duǎn 短 SV
shorts [pair of] duǎnkù [tiáo] 短褲 [條]／短裤 [条] N
should yīnggāi 應該／应该 A
sick bìng le 病了 VP/SV
sick (*slightly*) bù shūfu 不舒服 SV
sickness bìng 病 N
side (*left, right, north, etc.*) bian(r) 邊(兒)／边(儿) PW
silver (*color*) yínsè 銀色／银色 N
simplified character jiǎntǐzì 簡體字／简体字 N
sing chàng 唱 V
sing a song chànggē(r) 唱歌(兒)／唱歌(儿) VO
singing star gēxīng 歌星／歌星 N
sister (*older*) jiějie [ge] 姐姐 [個]／姐姐 [个] N
sister (*younger*) mèimei [ge] 妹妹 [個]／妹妹 [个] N
sisters jiěmèi 姐妹 N
sit zuò 坐 V
six liù 六 NU
sixteen shíliù 十六 NU
sixth (one) dìliù (ge) 第六(個)／第六(个) N/NU
sixty liùshí 六十 NU
size (*small, medium, large, etc.*) hào 號／号 M
skilled worker shīfu 師傅／师傅 N
skirt qúnzi [tiáo] 裙子 [條]／裙子 [条] N
sleep shuì; shuìjiào 睡; 睡覺／睡; 睡觉 V/VO
sleep in shuì lǎnjiào 睡懶覺／睡懒觉 VP
sleepy kùn 睏／困 SV
slender shòu 瘦 SV
slippers [pair of] tuōxié [shuāng] 拖鞋 [雙]／拖鞋 [双] N
slow màn 慢 SV

small (*size in clothing, etc.*)   xiǎohào   小號／小号   N

small   xiǎo   小   SV

snake (*Chinese zodiac*)   shé   蛇   N

sneakers [pair of]   yùndòngxié [shuāng]   運動鞋 [雙]／运动鞋 [双]   N

so   zhème; zhèyàng   這麼; 這樣／这么; 这样   A/PR

so (*therefore*)   suǒyǐ   所以   A

soap [bar of]   féizào [kuài]   肥皂 [塊]／肥皂 [块]   N

socks [pair of]   wà zi [shuāng]   襪子 [雙]／袜子 [双]   N

soil   tǔ   土   N

soldier   jūnrén   軍人／军人   N

some   yìxiē   一些   NU/M

sometimes   yǒude shíhou   有的時候／有的时候   TW

son   érzi [ge]   兒子／儿子   N

sorry, I'm   duìbuqǐ   對不起／对不起   IE

so-so   mǎma-hūhū   馬馬虎虎／马马虎虎   IE

south (*side, direction*)   nánbian(r)   南邊(兒)／南边(儿)   PW

South America   Nán Měizhōu   南美洲   PW

southeast   dōngnán   東南／东南   PW

southwest   xīnán   西南   PW

souvenir   jìniànpǐn [ge]   紀念品 [個]／纪念品 [个]   N

Spain   Xībānyá   西班牙   PW

Spanish (*language*)   Xībānyáhuà; Xībānyáwén; Xībānyáyǔ   西班牙話; 西班牙文; 西班牙語／西班牙话; 西班牙文; 西班牙语   N

Spanish (*person/people*)   Xībānyárén   西班牙人   N

speak   shuō; shuōhuà   説; 説話／说; 说话   V/VO

speak Chinese   shuō Zhōngguóhuà   説中國話／说中国话   VP

speech/talk   huà   話／话   N

spend (*money*)   huā; huāqián   花; 花錢／花; 花钱   V/VO

spouse   àiren   愛人／爱人   N

start   kāishǐ   開始／开始   V

start/hold a class   shàngkè   上課／上课   VO

state of mind   xīnqíng   心情   N

station (*of bus, train, etc.*)   zhàn [ge]   站 [個]／站 [个]   N

stationery   wénjù [xiē]   文具 [些]   N

stay at   zhù; dāizai   住; 呆在   V/VP

stay at home   dāizài jiālǐ   呆在家裏／呆在家里   VP

stepfather   jìfù   繼父／继父   N

stepmother   jìmǔ   繼母／继母   N

still (*even more*)   gèng   更   A

still (*yet*)   hái; hái shi   還; 還是／还; 还是   A

stop (*of bus, train, etc.*)   zhàn   站   N

store/shop   shāngdiàn   商店／商店   N

story (*in a building*)   céng   層／层   M

straight, go   yìzhí zǒu; wǎng qián zǒu   一直走; 往前走   VP

street   jiē [tiáo]   街 [條]／街 [条]   N

student   xuésheng   學生／学生   N

study   niàn; xué   念; 學／念; 学   V

study   niànshū   念書／念书   VO

stuff   dōngxi   東西／东西   N

subtract   jiǎn   減／减   V

subway   dìtiě   地鐵／地铁   N

subway stop/station   dìtiězhàn [ge]   地鐵站 [個]／地铁站 [个]   N

such   zhème   這麼／这么   A

sun (*the radical*)   rì   日   N

Sunday   Xīngqīrì; Xīngqītiān; Zhōurì   星期日; 星期天; 週日／星期日; 星期天; 周日   TW

supper   wǎnfàn; wǎncān   晚飯; 晚餐／晚饭; 晚餐   N

sure to   huì   會／会   A

surname   xìng   姓   N

surname, what's your   guìxìng   貴姓／贵姓   IE

surnamed, be   xìng   姓   V

Suzhou (*a city in eastern China*)   Sūzhōu   蘇州／苏州   PW

sweater   máoyī [jiàn]   毛衣 [件]   N

swipe a credit card   shuākǎ   刷卡   VO

T

table   zhuōzi [zhāng]   桌子 [張]／桌子 [张]   N

Taipei   Táiběi   台北   PW

Taiwan   Táiwān   台灣／台湾   PW

take (*a bus, train, etc.*)   zuò; dā   坐; 搭   V

take a bath   xǐzǎo   洗澡   VO

take a cab   dǎdī   打的   VO

take a rest   xiūxi   休息   V

take a shower   xǐzǎo   洗澡   VO

take a walk/stroll   qù sànsanbù   去散散步   VP

take it easy/take a rest   xiūxi   休息   V

talk   shuō; shuōhuà   説; 説話／说; 说话   V/VO

talk/speech   huà   話／话   N

talk on the telephone   dǎ diànhuà   打電話／打电话   VO

tall   gāo   高   SV

taxi   chūzūqìchē [liàng]   出租汽車 [輛]／出租汽车 [辆]   N

tea [cup of]   chá [bēi]   茶 [杯]   N

teach   jiāo; jiāoshū   教; 教書／教; 教书   V/VO

teacher   lǎoshī [wèi]   老師 [位]／老师 [位]   N

telephone   diànhuà [ge]   電話 [個]／电话 [个]   N

telephone, to   dǎ diànhuà   打電話／打电话   VO

telephone number   diànhuà hàomǎ   電話號碼／电话号码   N

television   diànshì [tái]   電視 [台]／电视 [台]   N

tell (*inform*)   gàosu   告訴／告诉   V

tell (*someone to do something*)   jiào   叫   V

ten   shí   十   NU

tenth (one)   dìshí (ge)   第十(個)／第十(个)   N/NU

test   kǎoshì   考試／考试   N/V

Thai (*person/people*)   Tàiguórén   泰國人／泰国人   N

Thailand   Tàiguó   泰國／泰国   PW

than (*in comparisons*)   bǐ   比   CV

thank xièxie 謝謝／谢谢 V

thank you xièxie (nǐ/nín) 謝謝(你／您)／谢谢(你／您) IE

that nà/nèi 那 PR/SP

that one nàge/nèige 那個／那个 PR/SP

theirs tāmen de 他們的／他们的 PR

them tāmen 他們／他们 PR

then (afterward) ránhòu 然後／然后 C

then (in that case) nà; nàme 那；那麼／那；那么 C

there nàr; nàli 那兒；那裏／那儿；那里 PW

there is/are yǒu 有 V

thereafter ránhòu 然後／然后 C

therefore suǒyǐ 所以 C

these zhèxiē 這些／这些 PR

they tāmen 他們／他们 PR

thin shòu 瘦 SV

things dōngxi 東西／东西 N

think (feel) juéde 覺得／觉得 V

think (would like to, feel like) xiǎng 想 AV

third (one) dìsān (ge) 第三(個)／第三(个) N/NU

thirsty kě 渴 SV

thirteen shísān 十三 NU

thirty sānshí 三十 NU

this zhè; zhèi 這／这 PR/SP

this evening jīntiān wǎnshang 今天晚上 TW

this extent, to zhème 這麼／这么 A

this one zhège; zhèige 這個／这个 PR/SP

this way zhèyàng 這樣／这样 PR

this year jīnnián 今年 TW

three sān 三 NU

Thursday Xīngqīsì 星期四 TW

tiger (Chinese zodiac) hǔ 虎 N

time (period) shíjiān 時間／时间 N

time (point in time; duration) shíhou 時候／时候 N

time on the clock ...diǎn (zhōng) ......點(鐘)／......点(钟) PH

times/occurrences cì 次 M

tired lèi 累 SV

tissue (toilet paper) wèishēngzhǐ 衛生紙／卫生纸 N

to (a place or time) dào 到 CV

to what extent duō 多 A

today jīntiān 今天 TW

tofu dòufu 豆腐 N

together (in the company of) yíkuàir; yìqǐ 一塊兒；一起／一块儿；一起 A

together (in total) yígòng 一共 A

toilet cèsuǒ 廁所／厕所 N

toilet, use the shàng cèsuǒ 上廁所／上厕所 VO

toilet paper wèishēngzhǐ 衛生紙／卫生纸 N

tomorrow míngtiān 明天 TW

tonight jīntiān wǎnshang 今天晚上 TW

too (much) tài...(le) 太......(了) A

too (also) yě 也 A

toothbrush yáshuā [zhī] 牙刷 [枝] N

toothpaste [tube of] yágāo [guǎn] 牙膏 [管] N

top shàngmian; shàngbian 上面；上邊／上面；上边 PW

toward(s) (a certain direction) wǎng 往 CV

towel máojīn [tiáo] 毛巾 [條]／毛巾 [条] N

traditional character fántǐzì 繁體字／繁体字 N

traffic light hónglǜdēng 紅綠燈／红绿灯 N

train huǒchē 火車／火车 N

travel lǚxíng 旅行 V

travel by (train, bus, etc.) zuò; dā 坐；搭 CV

treat (somebody to a meal, etc.) qǐng 請／请 V

trousers [pair of] kùzi; chángkù [tiáo] 褲子；長褲 [條]／裤子；长裤 [条] N

truly zhēn 真 A

T-shirt T-xù shān [jiàn] T-恤衫 [件] N

Tuesday Xīngqī'èr 星期二 TW

turn (in direction of) wǎng...guǎi 往......拐 VP

TV diànshì [tái] 電視 [台]／电视 [台]

twelfth (one) dìshí'èr (ge) 第十二(個)／第十二(个) N/NU

twelve shí'èr 十二 NU

twelve animals of the zodiac shí'èr (ge) shēngxiào 十二(個)生肖／十二(个)生肖 N

twenty èrshí 二十 NU

twenty-one èrshíyī 二十一 NU

twice a day yì tiān liǎng cì 一天兩次／一天两次 TW

two èr 二 NU

two/a couple of liǎng (ge) 兩(個)／两(个) NU

type (kind) yàng; zhǒng 樣；種／样；种 M

U

uncle (father's older brother) bóbo 伯伯 N

uncle (father's younger brother) shūshu 叔叔 N

uncle (mother's older or younger brother) jiùjiu 舅舅 N

uncomfortable (physical feeling) bù shūfu 不舒服 SV

under xiàmian 下面 PW

underneath xiàmian 下面 PW

understand dǒng 懂 V

unhappy bù gāoxìng 不高興／不高兴 SV

uninteresting méi yìsi 沒意思／没意思 SV

United States Měiguó 美國／美国 PW

university dàxué 大學／大学 N

unless chúfēi 除非 C

unnecessary búyòng 不用 A

until cái 才 A

unusually fēicháng 非常 A

up shàngbian 上邊／上边 PW

upset shēngqì 生氣／生气 SV

upstairs lóushàng 樓上／楼上 PW

us wǒmen 我們／我们 PR

U.S. dollar/money Měijīn; Měiyuán 美金；美元 N

use yòng 用 V

useful yǒuyòng 有用 SV

usually tōngcháng 通常 A

V

vehicle chē [liàng] 車 [輛]／车[辆] N
very fēicháng 非常 A
very tǐng 挺 A
very (*usually light in sense*) hěn 很 A
video game diànzǐ yóuxì [ge] 電子遊戲 [個]／电子游戏 [个] N

W

wait (for) děng 等 V
waiter fúwùyuán 服務員／服务员 N
waitress fúwùyuán 服務員／服务员 N
walk zǒu; zǒulù 走; 走路 V/VO
want to yào; xiǎng 要; 想 AV
warm nuǎnhuo 暖和 SV
wash xǐ 洗 V
wash (one's) face xǐliǎn 洗臉／洗脸 VO
watch kàn 看 V
watch (*timepiece*) biǎo [kuài] 錶 [塊]／表 [块] N
watch TV kàn diànshì 看電視／看电视 VO
water [glass/bottle of] shuǐ [bēi/píng] 水 [杯／瓶] N
watermelon xīguā 西瓜 N
way (*direction*) fāngxiàng 方向 N
we wǒmen 我們／我们 PR
wear (*hat, glasses, etc.*) dài 戴 V
wear (*clothes*) chuān; chuān yīfu 穿; 穿衣服 V/VO
weary lèi 累 SV
weather tiānqi 天氣／天气 N
Wednesday Xīngqīsān 星期三 TW
week xīngqī 星期 N
weekend zhōumò 周末 N
welcome, you're bié kèqi; búyòng xiè 別客氣; 不用謝／别客气; 不用谢 IE
well/good/fine hǎo 好 SV
west (*side, direction*) xībian(r) 西邊(兒)／西边(儿) PW
what shénme 什麼／什么 QW
when (*at the time of*) ... de shíhou ......的時候／......的时候 TW
when (*at what time*) shénme shíhou 什麼時候／什么时候 QW
where nǎr; nǎli 哪兒; 哪裏／哪儿; 哪里 QW
which nǎ(ge); něi(ge) 哪(個)／哪(个) QW
while (*in the time that*) ... de shíhou ......的時候／......的时候 TW
white báisè 白色 N
who shéi 誰／谁 QW
why wèishénme 為什麼／为什么 QW
wife qīzi; lǎopo; tàitai 妻子; 老婆; 太太 N
will (*intend*) huì; yào 會; 要／会; 要 AV
willing to kěn 肯 A
wine jiǔ 酒 N
with (*in the company of*) hé; gēn 和; 跟 C

without méiyǒu 沒有 V
wood (*the radical*) mù 木 N
word zì 字／字 N
words (*speech*) huà 話／话 N
work gōngzuò 工作 N/V
work as dāng 當／当 V
work part time dǎgōng 打工 VO
worker gōngrén 工人 N
worried zháojí 著急／着急 SV
would like to xiǎng 想 AV
wow wā 哇 I
wristwatch shǒubiǎo [kuài] 手錶 [塊]／手表 [块] N
write xiě; xiězì 寫; 寫字／写; 写字 V/VO
writer zuòjiā 作家 N
writing brush máobǐ [zhī] 毛筆[枝]／毛笔[枝] N
wrong bú duì 不對／不对 SV

Y

Yangshuo (*city in southern China*) Yángshuò 陽朔／阳朔 PW
Yangtze River Cháng Jiāng 長江／长江 PW
year nián 年 N/M
year (*in school*) niánjí 年级 N
year after next hòunián 後年／后年 TW
year before last qiánnián 前年 TW
yellow huángsè 黄色 N
Yellow River Huáng Hé 黄河 PW
yes shì; shì de; duì 是; 是的; 對／是; 是的; 对 IE
yesterday zuótiān 昨天 TW
yet (*however*) kěshì 可是 C
yet (*still*) hái; hái shi 還; 還是／还; 还是 A
yet (*in a negative sentence*) hái méi 還沒／还没 A
yoga yújiā 瑜伽 N
yoga, do zuò yújiā 做瑜伽 VO
you (*informal*) nǐ 你 PR
you (*formal*) nín 您 PR
you (*plural*) nǐmen 你們／你们 PR
you're welcome bié kèqi; búyòng xiè 別客氣; 不用謝／别客气; 不用谢 IE
young lady xiǎojie 小姐 N
younger brother dìdi 弟弟 N
younger sister mèimei 妹妹 N
younger than bǐ ... xiǎo 比......小 PH
youngest child lǎoxiǎo; lǎoyāo 老小; 老幺／老幺 N
your(s) nǐ de 你的 PR
yourself nǐ zìjǐ 你自己 P
yourselves nǐmen zìjǐ 你们自己 P

Z

zero líng 零 NU

Index

This index includes grammatical terms and concepts, cultural information that appears in "FYI" boxes, and language functions, as well as occasional notes in the text.

Credits

Illustrations:

Illustrations by Huifeng Lü, unless otherwise noted.

Illustrations on pp. 70, 105, 128, 149 *(top)*, 151, 164, 191 *(bottom)*, 199, and 201 are taken from the animations on EncountersChinese.com.

Illustrations on pp. 89, 112, 159, and 254 by Anna Veltfort.

Map on inside back cover by Patti Isaacs/Parrot Graphics.

Photos:

Photos are taken from the video material for **Encounters,** unless otherwise noted.

p. v: Courtesy of Charles DeFrancis.

Photos on pp. 35, 36, 112, 159, 181, 182, 210, 211, 236, 237, 272, and 273 by Cynthia Ning.

Realia:

p. 7: "Waiting for Guests by Lamplight," reproduced by permission from the National Palace Museum, Taipei, Taiwan.

p. 36: *(bottom)* Courtesy of Cynthia Ning.

p. 11: Courtesy of Cynthia Ning.

p. 62: Courtesy of Ding Anqi, Beijing Foreign Studies University.

p. 63: Courtesy of Shih-Chang Hsin, Ph.D., Association of Teaching Chinese as a Second Language.

p. 64: *(top)* Copyright World Journal LLC. All rights reserved;
(bottom) Courtesy of Zhongwei Lu, Deputy Chief Editor of *The China Press,* 15 E 40th Street, New York, NY 10016.

p. 90: Courtesy of Cynthia Ning.

p. 113: *(top)* Courtesy of Kuang-tien Yao.

p. 137: *(left)* Courtesy of Robyn Xiuming Ning Yee;
(right) courtesy of Daniel Tschudi.

p. 183: Courtesy of Cynthia Ning

Chinese Place Names

(Starred cities are those visited by *Encounters*)

Ānhuī
Àomén (*Macau*)
*Běijīng
Chángchūn
Chángshā
Chéngdū
Chóngqìng
Dūnhuáng
Fújiàn
Fúzhōu
Gānsū
Guǎngdōng
Guǎngxī (*Guangxi Zhuang Autonomous Region*)
Guǎngzhōu (*Canton*)
Guìlín
Guìyáng
Guìzhōu
Hāěrbīn (*Harbin*)
Hǎikǒu
Hǎinán
Hángzhōu
Héběi
Héféi
Hēilóngjiāng
Hénán
Húběi
Hūhéhàotè (*Hohhot*)
Húnán
Jiāngsū
Jiāngxī
Jílín
Jǐnán
Kūnmíng
Lánzhōu

Lāsà (*Lhasa*)
Liáoníng
Nánchāng
Nánjīng
Nánníng
Nèiménggǔ (*Inner Mongolia Autonomous Region*)
Níngxià (*Ningxia Hui Autonomous Region*)
Qīnghǎi
Shāndōng
*Shànghǎi
Shānxī
Shǎnxī (*Shaanxi*)
Shěnyáng
Shēnzhèn
Shíjiāzhuāng
Sìchuān
*Sūzhōu
Táiběi (*Taipei*)
Táiwān
Tàiyuán
Tiānjīn
Wǔhàn
Wūlǔmùqí (*Urumqi*)
Xī'ān
Xiānggǎng (*Hong Kong*)
Xīníng
Xīnjiāng (*Xinjiang Uighur Autonomous Region*)
Xīzàng (*Tibet Autonomous Region*)
*Yángshuò
Yínchuān
Yúnnán
Zhèjiāng
Zhèngzhōu